History of Latino Cult
Readings from Spai
Latin America,
and the United States

Ed. Daniel S. Whitaker

California State University, San Bernardino

KENDALL/HUNT PUBLISHING COMPANY
4050 Westmark Drive   Dubuque, Iowa 52002

Contents

Introduction

History of Latino Culture

The Latino community continues to grow in numbers and in influence in the United States. Newly released figures from the U.S. Census Bureau indicate that the current Latino population in the United States has reached 45.5 million (2007), or 15.1% of the total population (of 306.6 million). This increase confirms the fact that Latinos are the largest and fastest growing minority group in the United States; additionally, California has the largest Latino population of any state, with 13.2 million, or 36%. Analyzing these statistics, a recent *Los Angeles Times* article contended that the continuing strength of Latinos is "a trend with far-reaching implications for American politics and immigration policies."

As in the case of many communities within the United States, Latinos have a rich and fascinating history, a story that includes Europe (Spain), North and South America, and the United States itself, as well as other regions of the world, especially Africa and Asia. This book, the *History of Latino Culture*, narrates the history of Latinos from ancient times to the present day. Readers should note that the *History of Latino Culture* is the companion text of the *Voices of Latino Culture*. In the *Voices of Latino Culture*, we listen to the words of famous Latinos from the past and the present; in the *History of Latino Culture*, we tell their story.

In the introduction of each section from the *History of Latino Culture*, the corresponding readings from the *Voices of Latino Culture* are given. It is recommended that you first read the selection from the *History of Latino Culture* to receive a general overview of the historical period you wish to study, and then read the accounts from the significant people who lived during that time from the *Voices of Latino Culture*.

The organization of the *History of Latino Culture* mirrors that of the *Voices of Latino Culture*, with readings from Spain, Latin America (or more precisely, Spanish America, or those countries where Spanish is spoken), and the United States. Thus, the *History of Latino Culture* begins with a survey of modern Spain, followed by readings that discuss ancient Iberia (focusing above all on the contributions of the Romans). The role of the Jews as well as the Islamic culture of medieval Spain are emphasized, and we end our focus on Spain by examining the Spanish Renaissance, the age of Columbus, and Spain's Golden Age of the seventeenth century.

Occurring at the same time as the development of ancient and medieval Spain, great indigenous cultures arose in the Americas, in a land then unknown to the Europeans. Thus we now turn to the civilization of the Maya, the Aztec, and the Inca, and explore their cultures before the contact with Spain. A special focus is given to 1492 and the invasion of the Americas by the Spanish conquistadores, including the exploits of Christopher Columbus, Hernán Cortés, and Francisco Pizarro. Another continental encounter—this time with Africa—occurs during the onslaught of black slavery in Spanish America shortly after the arrival of the Europeans. An additional important historical moment is the colonial period of the Americas, with a special emphasis on the great seventeenth-century Mexican writer Sor (Sister) Juana Inés de la Cruz. It was during this period that many of the famous California missions flourished. The Spanish colonial period abruptly comes to an end with the wars of independence led above all by Father Miguel Hidalgo (Mexico), Simón Bolívar (Venezuela), and José de San Martín (Argentina).

Two great revolutions occurred in Latino history in the twentieth century—the Mexican Revolution of 1910–1920 and the Cuban Revolution of 1959. Both these conflicts had significant influence on the history of their respective countries as well as families originally from Cuba and Mexico living in the United States. We then focus on the United States and discuss the history of Mexican-Americans, Puerto Ricans, and Cuban-Americans, along with other Latinos now living in the United States.

In all, the *History of Latino Culture* allots the reader a panoramic view of the past and present of Latinos, whose roots reflect an international and multicultural development throughout the ages.

Alexis de Tocqueville, a French essayist who traveled throughout the young United States early in the nineteenth century, wrote that "when the past no longer illuminates the future, the spirit walks in darkness." The Frenchman's view that a people must learn about their history in order to ensure a successful future mirrors the importance of our story of Latino culture throughout the ages, a narrative that strives to illuminate all those who desire to learn more about this significant American community.

Daniel S. Whitaker
California State University, San Bernardino

Part I
Readings
from Spain

A. Spain, Ancient and Modern

The history of Latinos comes above all from three general regions: Spain, Spanish America (those Spanish-speaking countries of North and South America), and the United States itself. Beginning with Spain, a brief history of contemporary Spain is followed here by a review of the ancient peoples that passed through the Iberian Peninsula.

Spain today continues an active cultural dialogue with the Spanish America in both business and the arts. For example, the Spanish telephone company *Telefónica* recently assisted in the complete restoration of the Cathedral of Cusco, Peru. In addition, many Latin Americans live and work in Spain (such as Peruvians, Ecuadorians, and immigrants from Central America and other parts of the Spanish-speaking world).

The defining event in Spain of the past century (twentieth century) was the Spanish Civil War, 1936–1939, in which the fascist-nationalist forces of General Francisco Franco defeated the legitimate (Republican) government of Spain, causing the death of more than five hundred thousand Spaniards. After Franco's death in 1975, democracy was restored under the control of elected leaders mentored by Spain's much-respected King, Juan Carlos I. Spain is now fully integrated into the European Union (EU) and the North Atlantic Treaty Organization (NATO).

The current head of state of the Spanish government is José Luis Rodríguez Zapatero, first elected in 2004 (replacing the conservative government of José María Aznar) and then reelected in 2008. Zapatero and his party, the PSOE (Spanish Social Workers Party), follow a reformist agenda that has included the withdrawal of Spanish soldiers from Iraq, contact with ETA (the Basque armed separatist organization), and the approval of same-sex marriages in Spain.

The roots of Spanish civilization date from ancient times and the arrival of many different peoples to the Iberian Peninsula (the peninsula that today contains Spain and Portugal). With the cultures of the Iberians, Celts, Phoenicians, Greeks, Carthaginians, and others, Spain indeed was a multicultural region many centuries before the Christian era. The most important ancient culture was that of the Romans, whose colonization of Spain lasted nearly five hundred years. The Roman name for Spain—*Hispania*—evolved into the modern English words of *Spain* and *Hispanic*.

Robert K. Spaulding reports in *How Spanish Grew* (citing the eighteenth-century Spanish Benedictine essayist Martín Sarmiento) that the modern Spanish language inherits most of its framework from Latin. In addition, Spaulding writes that a minimum of 60 percent of the vocabulary of modern Spanish evolves from the everyday language of the Roman soldiers, traders, and colonists. The Romans also left behind their law, art, and literature. During their watch, Christianity bloomed and established a firm base on Iberian soil (a new faith that would be tested in the year 711, when the Moors bring Islam to the Iberian Peninsula). Moreover, the layout of a typical Spanish and Spanish-American *plaza* or town square (zócalo in Mexico, or *plaza de armas* in Peru)—surrounded by the city hall, the governor's or mayor's residence, and a church—is directly descended from the Roman forum.

1. SPAIN TODAY

Spain at the end of the twentieth century is a nation of almost 40 million people. Its government is a constitutional monarchy with a democratically elected parliament called the Cortes that sits in Spain's capital, Madrid. Spain is a member nation of the European Community (EC). Today's democratic Spain is the product of a long and often troubled history. For much of the twentieth century Spain was governed by dictatorship, most recently during the years 1939 to 1975 under Generalísimo Francisco Franco. Franco died in 1975, and in 1978 Spain adopted its current democratic constitution.

Although Spanish is the language associated with Spain, what the world calls Spanish is more correctly called Castilian. Castilian or its regional dialects are spoken by almost three-fourths of Spain's people. But along much of Spain's east coast and in the Balearic Islands, Catalan, or variations of it, is spoken. In the northwest corner of Spain, Galician (*Galego*), akin to Portuguese, is the dominant language. These three languages are of the Romance language family, derived from Latin. In the Basque Country, people use the ancient Basque language, related to no other language on earth.

Spain's linguistic and historic regions form seventeen autonomous communities or regions, which are in ways similar to the states of the United States. From these regions Spain was forged, and even today some areas remain in a state of tension with greater Spain. Most other European nations were stitched together in similar ways from historic regions, and in most, regionalism has also rekindled in strength. Most of Spain's autonomous regions contain several provinces, long the administrative subdivision of the country; the remainder consist of one province only.

Geography and Regions

The kingdom of Spain measures 194,898 square miles (504,782 squre kilometers), which includes the Balearic Islands in the Mediterranean, the Canary Islands in the Atlantic, and the enclaves of Ceuta and Melilla on the North African coast. More than 190,000 square miles are on the Iberian Peninsula, of which Spain occupies 85 percent. Peninsular Spain is almost 20 percent larger than California, but in many ways it is comparable in climate and landscape. Except for the north coast and mountain regions, most of Spain is semiarid and receives less than twenty inches of rainfall a year, mainly between October and the end of April. Except along the northern coast, Spanish summers range from hot to very hot. Autumn and spring are pleasant. Winters on the mainland are cold, but only the mountains and highlands receive much snow. The southern coast and the Balearic and Canary Islands have agreeable year-round climates and are popular with tourists and retirees.

The Pyrenees Mountains, which crest at more than 11,000 feet, define Spain's northern land border and separate the Iberian Peninsula from the rest of Europe. Water bounds the remaining seven-eighths of the peninsula: the Atlantic Ocean on the north and west, the Strait of Gibraltar on the south, and the Mediterranean on the southeast and east. Most of the Iberian west coast is occupied by Portugal. Much of Spain is mountainous, and its vast center is a high tableland called the Meseta. Almost 70 percent of Spain stands above 1,640 feet (500 meters). In Europe, only Switzerland has a higher average elevation.

The far northwest corner of Spain comprises the autonomous region of Galicia, which consists of the maritime provinces of La Coruña and Pontevedra, the province of Lugo, and the landlocked province of Orense. Galicia is hilly, green, and very wet and possesses significant forest lands. Its people speak Galician. Its landholdings tend to be small, and it is one of Spain's poorer regions. Though Galicia's harbors, such as Vigo,

La Coruña, and the naval base at El Ferrol, are splendid and its fisheries excellent, they were long remote and difficult to access from the rest of Spain. Santiago de Compostela, site of a renowned shrine, is Galicia's regional capital and a university town.

Proceeding from Galicia eastward, the Cantabrian Mountains rise toward the jagged 8,000-foot summits of the Picos de Europa and divide the coastal region known as the Principality of Asturias, from the autonomous region of Castile and León to the south. Asturias, like Galicia, is wet, rugged, and green. Asturias was once rich in coal from which its capital, Oviedo, prospered, but the mines today are depleted, a serious problem for the region. Its slender coastal plain is better given to grazing than to crops, and the dairy industry dominates its agriculture. Its chief ports, Gijón and Avilés, fish, build vessels, and ship coal.

From the Picos de Europa the Cantabrian Mountains ramble east through the autonomous region that bears the name Cantabria. Its capital is the seaport Santander. With a more extensive coastal plain and easier access to the Spanish hinterland, Cantabria is more prosperous than Asturias or Galicia. The mountains continue into the autonomous region called the Basque Country (Euskadi, in its own unique language). Two Basque provinces, Vizcaya and Guipúzcoa, face the Bay of Biscay, and the third, Alava, straddles the mountains. By tradition Basques live from the sea, farm, or are mountain herdsmen. In modern times, the Basque Country has led the way in Spanish heavy industry. Its largest city, Vizcaya's capital Bilbao, bristles with smokestacks and factories. From the surrounding mountains come the iron ores, while the coal to fire the furnaces comes from Asturias. Guipúzcoa's capital, San Sebastián, is both an elegant summer resort and a busy shipping and fishing center. The regional capital of the Basque Country, Vitoria, long an agricultural backwater, is today a thriving industrial center. Basque agriculture rests on numerous small-holders with a tradition of mutual cooperation. Because the countryside is mostly hill and valley, dairying nowadays is most profitable. Autonomy and regional rights (*fueros*) within Spain are part of Basque history. These rights and autonomy were suppressed during the greater part of the period 1876-1975 but have been recovered since 1978 and include control over taxation and revenues. Most autonomous regions have only limited powers of taxation.

The Basque homeland laps into the mountainous region of Navarre, which straddles the western Pyrenees. Like the Basque Country, Navarre has a long history of autonomy and *fueros*, becoming part of Spain in 1513 through conquest. Like the Basque

Country, Navarre controls its taxes and revenues. Its capital, Pamplona, is the scene of the fiesta of San Fermín, famous for the running of the bulls through its streets. Today it is also a major manufacturing center. In the rugged countryside, herding and grazing are a traditional way of life. Tucked along the southern border of Navarre and the Basque Country is a tiny autonomous region called La Rioja, with its capital at Logroño, in the upper valley of the River Ebro. The Ebro's source lies high in the Cantabrian Mountains, and it is the only major Spanish river that flows to the Mediterranean. Spain's best-known red wines come from La Rioja.

East of Navarre, the autonomous region of Aragón rolls south from the Pyrenees. It begins in steep mountain valleys, then becomes a parched tableland, sliced through its center by the green swath of fertile soil watered by the Ebro. The valleys of the province of Huesca are sources of hydroelectric energy and grains. Aragón's capital, Zaragoza, is also capital of a province. Standing on the Ebro, it is a commercial and industrial center. South of the Ebro valley, Aragón rises again into rugged mountains, part of the Iberian system that runs north and south, and separates Mediterranean Spain from the interior. In the province of Teruel, mining is active. Aragonese speak Castilian Spanish, which in Aragón's rural dialect adds humor to Spanish comic movies.

As the Pyrenees roll eastward, its ridges descend to meet the Mediterranean and define the border between France and the autonomous region of Catalonia, where people speak Catalan and valleys become lush as they near the sea. On the Mediterranean shore in the province of Gerona, the Pyrenees and its southward extensions form a picturesque and wild stretch of coastline, some seventy miles long, called the Costa Brava, now dotted with tourist resorts. South of the Costa Brava, on the plain formed by the river Llobregat, stands the region's vigorous capital, Barcelona, the second largest city in Spain and capital of Catalonia and a province. Further south lies the province of Tarragona, while the province of Lérida forms Catalonia's rugged hinterland and abuts Aragón. With a history and language of their own, Catalans maintain a fierce sense of independence.

South of the delta formed by the Ebro where it reaches the sea, variations of Catalan continue to be spoken in the Valencian autonomous region, historically called the Levant. Its capital is Valencia, capital also of a province that encompasses a fertile plain abounding in citrus fruits and rice. To Valencia's north lies the province of Castellón, and to its south, round Cape Nao, the province of Alicante, famous for its beaches.

The Castilian language reemerges further south, in the autonomous region of Murcia, where history rather than any physical barrier defined the boundaries. Against a stark and arid landscape, irrigation and industry strive to lift Murcia from among Spain's poorest regions to a level of relative prosperity. Its seaport Cartagena has long been Spain's chief Mediterranean naval base.

Westward from Catalonia and Valencia, the land rises through the hills and mountains of the Iberian system, where Castilian reappears in the large autonomous regions of Castile and León and Castile-La Mancha. Near the highland city of Soria, the river Duero begins its course westward to the sea. Other rivers that rise in the Cantabrian Mountains or in the central cordillera that divides the Meseta join the Duero to form a broad valley, the heartland of historic Old Castile and León. The regional capital is Valladolid, also capital of a province, but the names of the region's other provincial capitals evoke equal or greater historic memories: Avila, Burgos, León, Palencia, Salamanca, Segovia, Soria, Zamora. Below Zamora, the Duero hits rough country, and for a brief span, its rapids separate Spain from Portugal until it turns and, now called the Duoro, courses through Portugal to the sea. Its pattern of descending from mountains, cutting across the Meseta, then tumbling via rapids into Portugal is repeated by the river Tagus further south and limits their usefulness for transport. Where they cut across the Castilian Meseta, steep banks hinder their use for irrigation.

South of the Duero the boundary that separates Spain and Portugal is determined mainly by rugged country with few inhabitants. The Spanish side gently rises toward the central cordillera that consists of the Sierra de Gata, the Sierra de Gredos, and the Sierra de Guadarrama. The westernmost, the Sierra de Gata, separates Castile and León from the rolling boulder-strewn autonomous region of Extremadura. The poorest region of Spain, Extremadura has its capital at Mérida, once a great Roman center, and includes the provinces of Badajoz and Cáceres. Livestock, cork, olives, tobacco, and some mining are its chief sources of income.

The Sierra de Gredos begins in Extremadura and connects with the Sierra de Guadarrama to separate historic Old Castile, now part of Castile and León, from historic New Castile, now the autonomous regions of Castile-La Mancha and Madrid. Madrid, Spain's capital and largest city, has a population of some 3 million and enjoys striking views of the Guadarrama. Its region is bordered by the provinces of Toledo and Guadalajara of Castile-La Mancha. From the sierras, scrub-covered tablelands roll southward toward the river Tagus, which rises in the Iberian Mountain system, in the province of Cuenca, and carves a valley across the tablelands to continue into Extremadura. Entering Portugal through a gorge, it meets the Atlantic at Lisbon. South of the Tagus low mountains punctuate the endless plains of La Mancha itself, the arid region made immortal by Don Quixote. In the sierras east of La Mancha rises the river Guadiana, to wend west through the provinces of Albacete and Ciudad Real, and turn south past Badajoz to mark the border between Spain and Portugal.

On the Spanish side of the lower Guadiana, the undulating Sierra Morena climbs to form the southern boundary of the Meseta and rolls eastward to separate the autonomous region of Andalusia from the rest of Spain. The Sierra Morena's eastern reaches join other mountains that separate Castile-La Mancha from the Levant and give birth to the river Guadalquivir, which seventeenth-century poet Luis de Góngora called "the great king of Andalusia." The Guadalquivir flows west through a rich broad valley of red earth and grasses that turn golden in summer. The valley begins in the province of Jaén and extends through the provinces of Córdoba and Seville, with their fabled capitals rising from its banks. Below Seville, Andalusia's regional capital, the river meanders through marshlands till it reaches the Atlantic in the province of Cádiz. The city of Cádiz is Spain's chief Atlantic seaport. North of Cádiz, between the Guadalquivir and Guadiana, stretches the province of Huelva, watered by the Rio Tinto from which Columbus sailed in 1492. Huelva is the site of important copper mines.

South of the valley of the Guadalquivir more sierras rise. Beginning in low hills above Cape Trafalgar on the Atlantic, they gain altitude as they stretch eastward to the Sierra Nevada, in the province of Granada, which boasts mainland Spain's tallest peak, Mulhacén (11,420 feet; 3,478 meters). From the Sierra Nevada more sierras spread toward the Mediterranean like craggy fingers to define the arid valleys of the Andalusian province of Almería and link with the mountains of Murcia and the Iberian system. Along the coast of the provinces of Málaga and Granada, sierras plunging to the sea allow little more than slender plains. Spain's southern tip is anchored by the British-held Rock of Gibraltar. From Spain's southernmost town, Tarifa, Africa is less than ten miles away.

Andalusia, the most populous of Spain's autonomous regions and second largest in extent, is second only to Extremadura in poverty. Its economy is mainly agricultural, though it also has mines, fisheries, and light industry. While climate, mountains, and heath put natural limits on Andalusian agriculture, Andalusia possesses fertile irrigated valleys and has made holders of vast estates very rich. Labor was long provided by a multitude of poor field hands, who under a warm sun lived in whitewashed barrios that looked charming from a distance but were without plumbing or most other ordinary amenities. Although emigration to industrial centers has lately alleviated the problem, and forced landowners to modernize, pockets of real poverty persist.

Across the Strait of Gibraltar from Andalusia, the whitewashed Spanish cities of Ceuta and Melilla cling to the Moroccan shore and enjoy a status similar to that of an autonomous region. They survive, with the forbearance of Morocco, as the last of the fortresses Spaniards and Portuguese planted over 500 years ago on the North African coast to combat Barbary pirates. In those same years, Spaniards sailed into the Atlantic and conquered the Canary Islands, which now form an autonomous region. Known to the ancients as the Fortunate Isles, they were inhabited by native people called Guanches. Their lifestyle was Stone Age, but their resistance proved tenacious. They have disappeared, either destroyed or assimilated. The seven large and six small islands are divided into two provinces, Las Palmas and Santa Cruz de Tenerife. While the islands have important fisheries and raise subtropical crops, tourism forms their chief industry. On Tenerife stands Spain's tallest peak, Teide, a dormant volcano. Long a free-trade area, the Canaries remain, unlike the rest of Spain, outside the European Community.

In the Mediterranean Sea, the Balearic Islands of Majorca, Minorca, Ibiza, and Formentera form another island autonomous region and a single province. They were joined to Spain in the thirteenth century, when the kings of Aragon conquered them from the Moors. Their inhabitants speak dialects of Catalan and enjoy Spain's highest per capita income. Tourism is the principal industry, and the islands are a favored place for Europeans from colder climes to retire.

Government and Politics

Spain's autonomous regions and fifty provinces exist within the framework of a unitary and indivisible Spanish state. Chief of state is King Juan Carlos I, who presides over Spain's constitutional government. The Constitution of 1978 places sovereignty with the Spanish people, who entrust it to the king. His powers are limited, and the actual conduct of government is the business of the prime minister, officially known as the president of the government. In Spain's peaceful transition from dictatorship to democracy, the role of King Juan Carlos has been crucial and at times heroic, which has given him significant moral authority both in Spain and in the wider world. Unlike some other European royal houses, Spain's royal family is not fabulously wealthy. The heir to the throne, Felipe, prince of Asturias, has become popular in his own right as an active military officer, aviator, and yachtsman who takes the ceremonial functions of his office seriously. His mother, Queen Sofía, and sisters have likewise become personally popular with most Spaniards.

The prime minister heads the executive branch of government and is elected by a majority of votes in the Congress of Deputies, the more important of the two chambers of Cortes. If none can muster a majority of votes in two month's time, the king dissolves the Cortes and calls for new elections. Ordinarily elections are held every four years. A prime minister can be removed only by a vote of censure. But as is often the case in parliamentary systems, a prime minister might resign when he or she cannot keep a majority of votes in Congress or sees a chance to increase that majority, which would mean new elections before the normal four-year term is up.

In the years since the restoration of democracy, Socialist Felipe González has held the post of prime minister longest (1982–1996) and has proved to be one of Europe's more remarkable political leaders of recent times. In 1996 José María Aznar, head of the center-right Popular Party, became prime minister. He is the protégé of Manuel Fraga Iribarne, whose long political career extends back to Franco's era, when he was among the regime's bright young men. In the 1980s, Fraga rallied the forces of the center and moderate right to form the Popular Alliance (AP [Alianza Popular]), now the Popular Party. The original democratic center-right coalition had come apart in 1981 following the resignation of Adolfo Suárez as prime minister. It was Suárez another who had served Franco, who astutely managed the early transition of Spain to democracy after Franco's death. Suárez is now semiretired; the king has made him a duke. Fraga remains an important figure in his position as president of Galicia.

It is the task of the prime minister to select a deputy prime minister (vice president of the government) and form a cabinet. The cabinet includes ministers for foreign affairs, justice, defense, economy and finance, education and science, interior, public administration, autonomous regions, agriculture and fisheries, industry and energy, labor and welfare, transportation tourism and communications, and culture. Most ministers are also members of the Cortes. While the cabinet meets periodically as a whole, most business is determined by five cabinet committees that consist of minister and secretaries of state. The five committees are Autonomous Regions; Economic Affairs; Education, Culture, and Science; Foreign Affairs; and State Security.

Spain's Cortes, the chief legislative body, consists of two chambers: the more important Congress of Deputies and the Senate. The Congress, like the U.S. House of Representatives, reflects population. Senate membership geographically based, although more populous regions receive additional senators. The Congress must pass all legislation and money bills and can override the Senate. The Constitution fixes the number of deputies at no less than 300 and no more than 400. In recent practice the number has been 35 or 1 deputy for each 114,000 Spaniards. Some 20 percent of the current deputies are women. Each of Spain's fifty provinces, established for administrative purposes in the last century, elects at least 1 deputy. The population of each province determines how many more it gets. In the election of deputies, party politics plays the decisive role, as citizens vote by straight-party tickets. Seats in the Cortes are distributed in proportion to the vote each party receives, in the order of priority set by the party. To assure themselves representation, in particular for their leaders, smaller parties often form coalitions with larger parties that share similar ideals. Although once elected, deputies are free to vote independently they tend to vote with the leaders of their party or coalition. In organization, both Congress and the Senate elect a president and a panel of vice presidents to direct debate and conduct business. Debate on the floor is tightly regulated. Both chambers use committees.

To the Senate each Spanish province elects four senators, except for the single-province Balearic Islands, which elect eight to match the number enjoyed by the two provinces of the Canary Islands; and tiny Ceuta and Melilla, which elect two. Each autonomous region also elects at least one senator, with an additional senator for each million inhabitants. Recently, membership has numbered around 250.

Like most continental European countries, Spain has a multiparty system, although two national parties have become dominant. Spaniards have long referred to parties by their initials, to the despair of non-Spanish students of Spain. The parties that dominate the Congress of Deputies in the 1990s are the Spanish Socialist Worker's Party (PSOE, [Partido Socialista de Obrero Español]) and the center-right Popular Party (PP [Partido Popular]), each with considerably over 100 seats. Another dozen national or regional parties hold seats, ranging in number from

1 to around 20. Among national parties, the largest has become the United Left (IU [Izquierda Unida]), a coalition of fragmented Communist parties and disaffected Socialists. The centrist Christian Democrats and traditional Liberals have lately joined forces with the Popular Party. The largest regional party is the Catalan Convergence and Union (CiU [Convergència i Unió]), a centrist party that averages close to 20 seats. An equally influential regional party, although it holds only 5 to 8 seats in the Congress, is the Basque Nationalist Party (PNV [Partido Nacionalista Vasco]). The middle-of-the-road PNV is the most important party in the troubled Basque Country and its local governments. For an effective voice and receipt of financial and administrative support in Congress, a party must hold at least 5 seats, which requires that members of parties with fewer than 5 seats must join with larger parties that hold similar views or form coalitions with others to reach at least 5. For those members who do not, a nondescript "mixed group" exists.

Historically the bureaucracy that carried out the aims of the government was bloated. Spanish governments bought support with government jobs in an economy that until recently did not create enough attractive jobs for the educated and energetic. Civil servants with a college diploma pushed papers; illiterates with the right connections became porters, opened doors, and carried papers back and forth. Government inefficiency became a national joke. The improved economy of the late twentieth century has at last provided adequate employment in the private sector, and the bureaucracy has been trimmed and become relatively efficient. At the top of the bureaucracy stands an elite corps of university-trained professionals. Many performed their jobs under Franco and, despite some complaints from the political left, continue to do their jobs under Spain's revived democracy. As this group retires, professionals who have entered civil service since 1975 and are more instinctively inclined toward democracy will replace them.

Spain's armed forces, like its bureaucracy, gradually became top-heavy. In the last century army officers became a crucial element in Spanish politics, and the army constituted the largest expenditure in the national budget. Since 1975, the officer corps has become more professional and amenable to democracy. Spain's army, navy, and air force currently number about 200,000, and Spain is a member of the North Atlantic Treaty Organization (NATO).

The Spanish judiciary, which is constitutionally independent, has taken shape over centuries and has a life of its own. Men—and since 1977, women—appointed to the bench have been characterized by probity and knowledge of the law and legal procedures. Instinctively conservative and adhering to the strict norms of legality, the judiciary has been little affected by changes in the form of government during the twentieth century. In the rhetoric of the left, the judicial system was long portrayed as a tool of the ruling classes. In 1988 the PSOE government extended civil rights in judicial proceedings, and in the 1994–1996 period it undertook major reforms of the court system, which included a provision for jury trials. In 1995 Spain's personal code, inherited from Franco's time, was thoroughly revised.

Economy

Many attribute the success of Spain's democratic government, after several historical failures, to the modernization of its economy. Spain is no longer a land of extreme wealth and poverty, with little in between. A prosperous middle class is evident everywhere. In the mid-1990s, the average annual income for a Spanish household, about $26,000, reached 75 percent of the average for French and Italian households and 70 percent of North American household income. The ratio of motor vehicles to persons, a popular measure of prosperity, is 1:2.5 in Spain, 1:1.9 in Italy, and 1:1.3 in the United States.

In Spain's modernization, improvements in transport and communication have been particularly important. Lacking navigable rivers, Spain had to wait on railroads to build a modern national economy. Historically the mountains that crisscross the country limited wheeled transport and defined a hodgepodge of local and regional economies. Apart from coastal areas that could be reached by ship, pack animals provided the chief means of getting goods from one place to another. The improvement of roads that began in the eighteenth century added lumbering carts and wagons drawn by bullocks and mules to the traffic. The Basque Country and Catalonia, both accessible to the sea, were the first areas of Spain to industrialize. Today, with modern rail and highway transportation, manufacturing industries have sprung up almost everywhere, taking advantage of a hardworking labor force. That labor force is also literate, thanks to the unsung work of generations of Spanish educators. At the beginning of the twentieth century, less than 50 percent of Spaniards were literate; now more than 90 percent are.

Well into the twentieth century, agriculture constituted the largest sector of Spain's economy. Today agriculture's share of the gross domestic product (GDP) hovers under 4 percent, and it employs at most 15 percent of the labor force. A historic problem for Spain is that scarcely half its land surface is arable, much of the soil is marginal, and only about 40 percent of the land is under permanent cultivation. Another 20 percent provides meadow and pasture. Of forest land, perhaps 15 percent is productive, the rest scrub. Some 10 percent of Spain is bare rock. Grains are the chief crop, although fruit production is important, with a large export market. Sheep and pigs account for some 80 percent of Spain's livestock.

Manufacture, construction, transport, utilities, and mining, in descending order, account for over 30 percent of GDP and 35 percent of employment. International competition has forced retrenchment in Spanish heavy industry. The service sector, including retail trade, hospitality, finance, information, education, and government, accounts for 60 percent of GDP and for almost half of employment. Tourism is particularly important to Spain's southern coast and islands, owing to the benign climate end the abundance of historic and artistic sites.

Society

Tourism also played a role in opening Spain's society to modernity, bringing together Spaniards with people from the rest of Europe, the Americas, and the world. Historically, Spanish society was ingrown, based firmly on family, urban barrio or rural village, and region. Great variety existed among the regions both in relative wealth and poverty and in personal demeanor. Today travelers describe the pride of Spaniards from every region, a pride better described as an innate sense of personal dignity and worth, rather than the tetchy *pundonor* (point of honor) of romantic drama. Most Spaniards display a certain reserve, what the Castilians call *sosiego* (composure), although they tend to be generous and warm in dealing with strangers and hearty with their friends. The volatility some attribute to Spaniards applies mainly to Andalusians, although Spaniards, when compared to most other Europeans, seem capable of extraordinary passion in love and war, which Spanish literature and history both tend to bear out.

As Spain lies between the rest of Europe and North Africa, in their physical appearance Spaniards tend to reflect both European and North African characteristics. Most have brown or black hair, and complexions range from fair to swarthy. Some 17 percent of Spaniards are under fifteen years of age; 20 percent are over sixty. Life expectancy at birth is seventy-two years for men and eighty for women, about the same as in France or Italy.

Spaniards follow the Mediterranean pattern of living in urban centers, towns, or substantial villages. Three-fourths of the population live in communities of 10,000 or more people. Except in the extreme north and northwest, the isolated farmhouse or even hamlet is rare. At the core of a typical Spanish town is the main plaza (*plaza mayor*), flanked by a church and public buildings. Large cities have many plazas: one for the cathedral and others for major public buildings. The largest have multiple barrios, each with its own civic center, parishes, businesses, and character. The populations of Spanish cities tend to be concentrated, with most families living in owned or rented flats in apartment blocks. A few old noble families live in urban palaces surrounded by gardens. Suburban sprawl, with freestanding homes called *chalets*, remains limited. Most who might afford a suburban chalet prefer to own a spacious condominium in an upscale apartment block and have a weekend house in the country or by the sea.

It is early to gauge the effect of contemporary culture on Spaniards, for whom it is still novel, and on that elusive mix of behavioral qualities known as the "Spanish character." Franco's dictatorship tried to keep much of modern culture at bay. Contemporary life in developed countries tends to homogenize personal behavior, while against it runs a small but noisy counterpoint of rebelliousness. Sensitivity to others is encouraged; egoism and idiosyncrasy are discouraged. Most Spaniards appear to retain their heartiness, dignity, and sense of propriety.

Modernity has touched and limited many of the traditional patterns of life, such as the large and late midday meal and the siesta. But come evening, men and women, old and young, still swarm to the streets to promenade in the daily *paseo*, to meet friends, to take a drink, and to savor tapas (appetizers and snack foods) in cafes and cafeterias before heading home. The *cafeteria* holds a special place in Spanish life. A popular hangout for friends, neighbors, and associates, it serves espresso coffee, wine, beer, liquor, tapas, and light meals.

Spanish life carries a sense of vitality, and despite increased crime, most Spaniards feel relatively secure. Children roam the streets freely and feel attuned to the life of their elders. Young Spaniards, better educated than ever, do look somewhat longingly toward the United States, northern Europe, and Italy and seem eager to "be with it," but they seem to appreciate what they and their parents have. Old and young may differ on the relative openness of "sexual freedom." Discretion rather than puritanism has characterized the Spanish attitude toward sex. A "double standard" is the traditional norm for men and women, and attitudes toward prostitution remain ambivalent. The notion of "machismo" exists but seldom with the same intensity it does in Spanish America. As everywhere, "gay" life has only lately become open, although only rarely has there been compulsive hostility against gays among Spaniards.

The crime rate has increased significantly in Spain since the end of the repressive dictatorship. Although the crime rate remains among the lowest in the European Community, and much lower than that of the United States, some wax nostalgic about the virtual lack of serious crime under Franco. Most regard the illegal drug problem as particularly ominous and blame the drug traffic on Spanish Americans and North Africans. In some neighborhoods, vigilante groups have farmed to combat drug dealers and users.

A group apart in Spain are the gypsies or Romani, who number perhaps 3 percent of the population. Although some have assimilated with the larger Spanish society, many have not. Gypsies first appeared in Spain in the sixteenth century, and most settled in Andalusia, replacing expelled Muslims. They did not provide agricultural labor, as was hoped, but engaged in ironwork, entertainment, and barter with what many believed were stolen goods. They remained a small but distinct population with their own folkways and mutual support system. In recent times they have been most conspicuous as flamenco dancers and musicians, which has made some rich. Gypsy women and children still appear to live by begging, to the despair of other Spaniards and the confusion of tourists. The Madrid government has tried to find housing, which the advocacy group Gypsy Presence likens to prisons, for families of gypsy "squatters."

Religion and Culture

Close to 95 percent of Spaniards are baptized Roman Catholics, but fewer than half are regular churchgoers. While the number of clergy pales compared to the number in the midnineteenth century, the presence of the Catholic Church still permeates Spanish life. Major rites of passage take place in church and with a priest—from baptism, first communion, confirmation, and marriage to last sacraments, funeral, and burial. So much of historic Spanish culture developed in the service of religion that in every city and town one sees splendid churches; Spanish museums are full of religious paintings and sculpture.

Cultural life in contemporary Spain, as elsewhere, is in flux. People watch television and wonder what became of the poets, novelists, and dramatists of yore. The years of Franco were not kind, and Spanish-American authors—not Spaniards—have recently won more world fame. However, two of the five Nobel Prizes in literature won by Spaniards have been awarded since Franco's death in 1975—in 1977, to poet Vicente Aleixandre; and in 1989, to novelist Camilo José Cela, who published mainly under Franco but bravely kept his critical independence. Spanish film has a large world market and has produced memorable works under directors such as Pedro Almodóvar.

While Spanish painting has of late produced no one to rival Pablo Picasso or Salvador Dalí, nowhere else are there artists of equal reputation. In the display of the heritage of art, Spain has added to its great museums like Madrid's Prado. New to Madrid are the Reina Sofía Art Center, which displays achievements of the twentieth century (including Picasso's famous *Guernica*), and the rich Thyssen-Bornemisza collection. Barcelona has a superb new Picasso museum, and in 1997 a spectacular Guggenheim Museum of Modern Art opened in Bilbao.

In music, Spanish symphony orchestras have come into their own and Barcelona and Madrid have world-class opera houses. The list of famous Spaniards on the opera stage is long and today includes Placido Domingo and Montserrat Caballé. In the popular music field Julio Iglesias is a superstar. Although young Spaniards have taken to rock music, Spain's own rock groups are little known outside the country. Flamenco, which had become mainly a tourist attraction outside Andalusia, is undergoing an international revival as an art form.

Sports occupy a big place in Spanish life. More a spectacle than a sport, the bull fight still has its aficionados, and most cities have an impressive *plaza de toros* (bull ring) despite opposition from animal rights activists and complaints from purists that things are not what they were. Among Basques, jai alai (also called pelota), a hard-ball indoor court sport, is popular. *Fútbol* (soccer in the United States), the great national attraction, packs huge stadiums and excites the wildest enthusiasm. When Madrid plays Barcelona or the Spanish national team vies for the World Cup, all of Spain is galvanized. Tennis, too, has become popular, as middle-class Spaniards flock to the courts, and Spanish tennis stars compete in international tournaments. Spaniards have also taken to golf. Bicycle clubs have sprung up all over, and on Sundays the back roads of Spain glow with cyclists clad in brilliant tights. Jogging, too, has gripped health-conscious Spanish yuppies.

Spain has come to resemble other modern Western and democratic nations. In spite of its transformation, its people have retained the warmth for which they have long been known, and the country's exotic differences make it special.

2. EARLY SPAIN: FROM THE CELTIBERIANS TO THE VISIGOTHS

Spain's geographical position has rendered her a natural focus for the attentions of a varied succession of migrants, traders, colonizers, and conquerors. Thrusting massively out of the southwestern corner of Europe and separated from the continent of Africa by a bare eight miles of readily crossed sea, she closes off the Mediterranean from the Atlantic and faces Asia across the inland sea whose shores saw the dawn of our civilization. From the north, from the south, and from the east came prehistoric tribes, Celts, Phoenicians, Greeks, Carthaginians, Romans, Barbarians, Arabs, and Africans, in obedience to their respective needs and compulsions, in search of *lebensraum*, empire, converts, booty, or trade.

About the earliest inhabitants of the Peninsula little is known with certainty. Upper Paleolithic man, whose origins are vague, bequeathed us some record of his hunter's life in the wall paintings in the caves of Altamira and Castillo. Neolithic man has rewarded archaeological research with artifacts of a different culture, pointing to agriculture and animal husbandry, rudimentary houses and metalworking. Toward the beginning of the second millennium B.C., a wave of megalith worshipers from the East initiated a period of agrarian prosperity and skilled craftsmanship in Andalusia in the south, while in the north another megalithic people settled in the Pyrenees to become the ancient precursors of the Basques, a race with a language whose roots still remain a mystery to philologists.

With the introduction of bronze metallurgy between 1900 and 1600 B.C. by a people who settled in Almería, Andalusia reached its peak of early civilization and entered the realm of legend as a land of fabulous riches and prosperity. Its capital was Tartessus—known in the Bible as Tarshish and conjecturally situated in the Guadalquivir Valley—and it was the silver of Tartessus that drew the eyes of the trading east and brought the Phoenicians to Spain. A short distance along the coast they founded the city of Gadir, the modern Cádiz, before 800 B.C. In time the Phoenicians established trading settlements along the south and east coasts of the Peninsula and in the Balearics. Although they were uninterested in colonization, their superior commercial and technical knowledge, and their cultural contacts, carved a deep impression upon the civilization of their adopted country. The Phoenicians also disclosed Spain to the civilized world, and with them the Peninsula emerged from its prehistoric penumbra and set foot upon the stage of Mediterranean history.

In the sixth century B.C. the example set by the Phoenicians was followed by their trading rivals the Greeks, lured westward by tales of the silver of Cartagena, the gold of the Sierra Morena, and the copper of Río Tinto. Their settlement at Emporion (Spanish Ampurias) in Catalonia succeeded Massilia (Marseilles) as Greece's principal port of trade in the western Mediterranean. Like the Phoenicians, the Greeks settled and traded along the southern and eastern coasts, adding another layer of civilization to these already comparatively cosmopolitan areas and bringing wealth to the inhabitants. Their superior culture enriched native art and, more practically, they introduced into the Peninsula two plants, the olive tree and the grapevine, which have played a crucial part in Spain's agriculture ever since.

By the time the Greeks reached Spain, the peoples living there on the east coast had come to be known as Iberians—a term now taken not as indicating a specific race of people, but as a generic label for the complex group of inhabitants of the Peninsula's Mediterranean coast from Catalonia to Andalusia. Little is known about these Iberians. What is clear is that they were quite distinct from the people of the interior. For while the Phoenicians and the Greeks were busy developing trade in the east, the interior was witnessing equally important events of a different order. Between 900 and 600 B.C. successive waves of Celts on their migrations through Europe from Asia penetrated the Pyrenees and, spreading over the central *meseta*, occupied much of Spain. All warrior peoples of Indo-European stock in search of new homes, they settled with ease amongst the natives of the north and west, and opened up hitherto unpopulated land in the center.

Naturally, Celts and Iberians did not remain entirely separate. On the great central plateau they mingled and interbred to form the hard core of the Peninsula's native substratum, the Celtiberians. Traditionally the Celts were regarded as a race of violent, rustic shepherds and the Iberians as pacific farmers and urban dwellers, but the reality, it is now felt, must have been more complex. The Celts have a clearer identity than the Iberians and we know that they brought to Spain the broad sword, the technique of iron metallurgy, and trousers. But even so, our knowledge of their way of life is severely limited because they also brought their custom of the ritual burning of the dead. And the dead are normally a major source of archaeological information.

After Nebuchadnezzar besieged Tyre in 586–573 B.C. and North African Carthage succeeded to Phoenicia's commercial empire, mineral attractions of the Iberian Peninsula once more exerted influence. Before long, Carthage was able to claim the western Mediterranean for her own, and although the Greeks continued to trade in sporadic fashion along the east coast of Spain, Carthage soon acquired a commercial hegemony in southern Spain which she managed to retain for the next two to three hundred years. Greek artifacts— bronze statues in the Sierra Morena and Corinthian helmets near Huelva—give way to evidence of Carthaginian sculpture, jewelry, and ceramics, while to the agricultural skills introduced by their predecessors the new traders added their expertise in fish curing and in the production of esparto grass. While the Carthaginians thus added to the ever deepening civilization of the south and east, their most significant bequest to Spain was on an order of magnitude out of all proportion to their direct influence. For they were responsible for bringing the Romans to the land in the far west, and making it the scene of Rome's greatest military struggle, the Second Punic War.

The First Punic War, in which Rome and Carthage had contested for Sicily, had ended indecisively in 241 B.C., but it had allowed the natives of the Iberian Peninsula to regain control of their land. However, the need for treasure and the strategic potential of Spain had led the Carthaginians under Hamilcar Barca to set about reasserting and extending Carthage's influence in the Peninsula. And what had formerly been commercial rule began to take on the suspicious look of an attempt at empire. When a Carthaginian capital was established at Carthago Nova (modern Cartagena) on the east coast, Rome decided that some limit ought to be imposed upon the Carthaginian Empire in Spain. Her envoys consequently elicited from Carthage a pledge not to advance northward beyond the Ebro River.

The situation was an explosive one and explode it inevitably did. The immediate cause of the explosion was the Iberian town of Saguntum which lay a hundred or so miles south of the Ebro but enjoyed Roman protection—an ideal departure point for a Roman take-over bid. Rome therefore intervened in Saguntum's affairs to promote interests hostile to Carthage. The outcome of this double dealing was that in 219 Hannibal, Hamilcar's young son, who had been Carthaginian commander in Spain since 221, laid siege to Saguntum. Eight months later, after a long and bitter struggle, the city fell. Hannibal had broken no treaty: Saguntum was well within Carthaginian

territory and was not among those allies of Rome which Carthage had pledged itself not to attack. Nevertheless Roman prestige was seen to be at issue. An ultimatum was given in the form of a demand for the surrender of Hannibal. It was refused and the two powers were at war. The struggle for Spain and for hegemony in the Mediterranean had begun.

Both sides simultaneously decided to carry the war straight to the nub of the opposition. In 218, as Hannibal and his elephants made their famous trek over the Alps to Italy, two Roman legions with sea support landed at Emporion in Spain. A few miles from Tarragona, the legions met and routed a force of 11,000 Carthaginians, and within two months the country north of the Ebro was securely in Roman hands. The following years, however, did not bring such easy successes for Rome, although the natives helped by snapping constantly at the Carthaginians' heels. Hannibal's brother, Hasdrubal, and Publius Scipio and his brother, Cornelius, snarled and attacked like rival wolves, without gaining much significant headway. The turning point came in 218 at the Battle of Dertosa on the north bank of the Ebro. The defeat suffered by the Carthaginians at the hands of the two Scipios was the first real threat to their empire in the Iberian Peninsula. Not until 210, however, as Hannibal's fortunes in Italy declined, was it possible for reinforcements to be sent to northern Spain to strengthen the Roman position. In the meantime the formidable Scipio had been killed and Rome's native recruits had deserted. A year later Carthago Nova itself fell before the daring onslaught of Scipio Africanus, son of the dead Publius, and the legions he had molded into a redoubtable army forced their way into southern Spain and the Guadalquivir Valley. In 206 Carthage's first, foremost, and last colony in Spain, Cádiz, made terms with Scipio Africanus. Roman rule in Spain had begun.

Carthage, however, was not all Rome had to contend with in Spain, as she soon learned. One of the earliest provinces to be acquired by the Romans under the Republic, the Iberian Peninsula was also one of the last to be truly pacified. The mountainous nature of the terrain and the fierce independence of the native tribes, particularly in the north, center, and west, made conquest a difficult and piecemeal affair: it took the legions of Rome the staggering period of two hundred years to bring the country to heel. One frustrated general after another discovered Spain to be the natural home of guerrilla warfare.

With the acquisition of Carthaginian Spain in 206 B.C., the Romans immediately set about the organization of the new province. The Peninsula, or rather the familiar and fruitful part of it that the enemy had occupied, was divided into two administrative areas, each with its own governor: Nearer Spain to the east and north and Farther Spain to the south. The founding of the first Roman town in Spain, Itálica, the splendid ruins of which can still be visited near Seville, celebrated the completion of the victory over Carthage. The inhabitants of the Peninsula, all indiscriminately labeled Iberians by the Romans and henceforth by posterity, automatically became subjects of Rome and only too soon began to feel the weight of the conqueror's boot. High tributes in minerals and in natural products such as corn and oil had to be paid, and compulsory levies of auxiliary troops had to be provided. But worse than these were the extortions of the governors, determined to wring all they could out of the land where, according to Strabo, even the horses were reputed to feed from silver mangers. This epoch in Spain's history was certainly not a happy one. As one historian has remarked: "What the pages of the history of Rome in Spain down to the year 133 have to tell us, whether explicitly or implicitly, takes its place among the most shameful records in the whole of that history."

The outcome of the repression was, not surprisingly, wholesale revolt. It broke out in 195 amongst the peaceable Turdetani in the south—a gauge of the severity and extent of the repression—spread to Nearer Spain, and eventually set the whole Peninsula aflame. It brought Cato to Spain with a full consular army, and its continuation eventually imposed upon Rome the necessity for a system of permanent military service. The sustained ferocity of two of the outbreaks has earned them the status of full-scale wars—the Lusitanian War and the Celtiberian. They raged more or less concurrently from 154 to 133 and at times the struggle acquired the semblance of a united national effort. On the Roman side the battle was characterized by some shameful examples of treachery and broken faith. The war with the heroically tenacious Lusitanians was in fact only brought to an end when the Roman leader engineered the murder, by two Lusitanian traitors, of their immensely gifted chieftain Viriathus—a shepherd turned bandit who eventually devoted himself to the higher cause of his country's freedom. Far more skilled in military strategy and tactics than his powerful adversaries, Viriathus had for eight years dealt the Romans one blow after another, revealing at the same time a capacity for clemency which they lacked. Equal in stature to the best of Spain's Roman opponents, he towers above most of them both as man and leader. He is Spain's first hero known to history.

Courage was not an attribute exclusive to the tribes of the far west. The warlike peoples of the interior resisted their oppressors with a dogged determination epitomized by the famous town of Numantia on the Duero River, which was immortalized by Cervantes in his play *The Siege of Numancia*. From 153 onward the settlement withstood repeated attacks by the Romans. Successive consuls came to grief on the reefs of Numantian energy and pride and had to buy peace with treaties which they soon broke. The crowning disgrace came in 137 when 20,000 Romans surrendered to a force of between 4,000 and 8,000 Numantians. The pressure exerted by a shocked Rome when this humiliation became known, resulted in the sending to Spain of Rome's greatest general Scipio Aemilianus. He prepared to reduce Numantia by starvation. With seven camps and 60,000 men he encircled the town of only 4,000 inhabitants with a cordon so tight that escape or relief was impossible. Sixteen months later, after the Numantians' attempt to obtain honorable terms had been turned down, and after they had been driven in their desperation to suicide, Scipio burned the valiant town to the ground. In the following year Scipio gave it a supreme accolade; he chose to be known thereafter as Scipio Numantinus.

The fall of Numantia which marked the end of the Celtiberian War, was a major event in the colonization of the Peninsula. Except for Asturias and Cantabria, native resistance had effectively spent itself. The subjugation of the northwest, not fully accomplished for another hundred years, has been described as "more a large-scale police action than a war." The wars brought about certain reforms, but in general Roman rule in Spain under the Republic continued to be characterized by its brutality. The resulting sporadic outbursts of insurrection drew to Spain some of Rome's greatest names. In 80 B.C. Quintus Sertorius, a former praetor of Nearer Spain and the son of a Roman father and Iberian mother, set up an independent government in Spain and flouted Rome as the hero of an oppressed people. Against him Rome sent Pompey, who marched through the interior, founding the city of Pamplona on the way; but Pompey's progressively successful campaigns were rendered no longer necessary in 72 by the murder of Sertorius at a banquet at Huesca. Some twenty-three years later the Peninsula became the scene of the struggle for power between Pompey and Caesar himself. That Roman dominance in one form or another was by now accepted in Spain is witnessed by the fact that Spaniards rallied to Pompey's cause. The cause was lost, however, and Caesar triumphed.

The end finally came in 19 B.C. Seven years earlier Emperor Augustus in person had initiated the reduction of Cantabria. A war-weary soldiery and a desperate enemy made the death struggle a prolonged one and Augustus was forced through illness to retire. But in 19 Agrippa was called to Spain and he succeeded in breaking the last centers of native resistance. The two-hundred-year battle was over and Roman Spain was a fact.

With pacification came the unhampered development of Hispania, as the Romans had christened the Iberian Peninsula, and its integration into the newly founded Roman Empire. After some reshuffling of territory, the Peninsula at the beginning of the Christian era consisted of three distinct zones: Tarraconensis, by which Nearer Spain was extended to include most of central Spain, Cantabria, Asturias, and Galicia; Baetica (Andalusia) with its boundary pushed back from the Tagus River to the Guadiana; and Lusitania, a newly created province that laid the geographic foundations of modern Portugal. Later on, the Balearic Islands and Morocco were incorporated into the government of the Peninsula, establishing thus early on Spain's claim to them.

This full-scale administrative effort was accompanied by all the civilizing benefits of rule by imperial Rome. A program of urbanization was initiated. Towns were built to lure the recalcitrant into stability and acquiescence with privileges that ranged from minor liberties to the ultimate prize of Roman citizenship; and the survivors of the insurrection in the north were encouraged or compelled to settle in them. The towns were eventually linked by a 12,000-mile network of roads, including the mammoth Via Augusta which stretched from Cádiz along the coast to the Pyrenees. Although originally intended as military routes these naturally contributed enormously to the economic development of the Peninsula and to the spread of the Roman way of life. With the towns, the aqueducts, and the amphitheaters, many remains of which still survive today, they were the visible symbol of a new advanced era of civilization.

After Italy Spain became one of the most productive parts of the Roman Empire. Wines, olives, oil, and grain were exported to all parts of the Mediterranean, and Spanish gold, silver, lead, copper, iron, and tin poured onto the world market, with tin and lead reaching even India. According to Pliny the annual gold output of the mines of Asturias, Galicia, and Lusitania amounted to twenty thousand pounds in weight. As for agriculture, under the Romans the agrarian pattern of the country, especially in the south, became one of large landed estates (latifundia) in the hands of native leaders—now transformed into powerful landowners—and of rich immigrants from Rome. It is a pattern that has survived in the south until this day and that has proved one of the major obstacles to Spain's agricultural well-being.

In spite of the inadequacies of Roman rule and in spite of the fact that in the north numerous tribes re-mained aloof until the last to the seductive benefits of the Roman machine, the truth remains that under the first period of empire Spain enjoyed a prolonged period of political stability and commercial prosperity such as she has rarely, if ever, achieved since. Peace and civilization bring their own freedoms. And inevitably, progressive Romanization and integration brought improvements. Augustus initiated the process by making the provincial governors salaried officials and by introducing reforms, such as the levying of a new general tax that distributed the burden of taxation more evenly. So great was the impact of this tax that the year in which it was introduced, 38 B.C., was taken as the dawn of a new era: until the late Middle Ages it was the point of departure for reckoning dates in Spain instead of the year of Christ's birth. The Roman legions in the Peninsula were gradually reduced, and increasing numbers of townships achieved civic emancipation. The ranks of the enslaved and the semi-free decreased with the passage of time and more men achieved the status of tenant farmer. And of course intermarriage did its work. The population of Hispania soon became a mixture of natives and part-natives, of Romans born in Rome and Romans born in Spain, a mixture so varied that the people the Visigoths would find in fifth-century Spain have to be called, for want of any more accurate term, Hispano-Romans. And this mongrel population contributed its great men to Roman history. A century after final pacification, a Spanish Roman, Trajan, became emperor, to be followed by his nephew Hadrian. Both were born in the Andalusian capital of Itálica. The two Senecas and Lucan were all three Spanish Romans from Córdoba, while the rhetorician Quintilian and the satirist Martial were not only born in Spain but were partially of native Spanish stock. The stage on which these famous men exercised their respective talents was not of course the Peninsula, but Rome itself. All roads led to Rome and all eyes were on it. There, to the very heart of the civilized world, flocked the gilded youth of its far-flung empire. Hispania remained what it had been since the conquest, a satellite of Rome.

One of the lasting bequests of Rome to the Peninsula, and one of the most powerful factors in its Romanization, was Latin itself. No subsequent occupation, however protracted, managed to usurp it in the way Anglo-Saxon usurped the Roman tongue in England. Its eventual adoption by the people as a whole is easy to understand. The pre-Roman population spoke a vast range of languages and dialects which could in no way withstand the convenience and effectiveness of a sophisticated language spoken by conquerors and settlers, by educators, administrators, and magistrates alike. Naturally, the Latin spoken in Spain was not for long Latin in its pristine state. The Latin of officialdom remained comparatively unadulterated, but the Latin of everyday life was vulgar, not classical, Latin. It was a Latin conditioned by the peculiarities of speech of uneducated soldiers and of settlers and traders from different parts of the Roman world, and not least by the natural wayward development of a language deprived of direct contact with its life source. It was a Latin, moreover, colored by the vocabulary and habits of pronunciation of the languages it overlaid. It was a Latin which centuries of evolution were to turn into the romance tongues of the Peninsula in the way that the Latin of Italy became Italian and the Latin of Gaul French.

The empire's other permanent gift to Spain was Christianity, which reached the Mediterranean coasts in the middle of the first century. As had happened before in the case of new ideas and new cultures, it was initially in the cities of the south and east that the Gospel prospered. In the interior the new religion had to fight a hard battle with pagan superstition and religiosity. But gradually the influence of "Old Spain" imposed itself. The repressions suffered by Christians in the second and third centuries struck a sympathetic chord among a people who, like Roman subjects everywhere, were feeling the effects of the increasing authoritarianism of an empire in decline. Christianity was the religion of the poor and the downtrodden, and as extortion and rapacity once more became the characteristics of Roman rule, increasing numbers of the Peninsula's inhabitants were thrust into destitution and found themselves forced to sell themselves into slavery. Spain, therefore, contributed its share of martyrs to the Christian-thirsty State. Indeed it was a Spaniard, Emperor Theodosius, who in 380 made Christianity the empire's official religion and denounced adherents of other faiths as heretics to be punished; and it was in Spain that three of the Church's most important early councils establishing dogma and discipline took place. These facts are strangely prophetic of the unique nature of Spain's subsequent relationship with Christianity and the Church.

Ironically, as the threatening rumble of the barbarian world outside grew louder—between the years 264 and 276 the Peninsula was devastated by Franks and Suevi—and the very foundations of the edifice of Rome began to crumble, the Church succeeded its former enemy the State as the source and symbol of stability in a hostile and chaotic world. With the growth of Christianity, Spain began to develop a certain consciousness of itself as a thing apart from the Roman Empire, a certain sense of separate identity, and as the empire disintegrated the Church played an increasingly larger role in secular as well as religious life. When the end came, Roman Spain, disillusioned with, and impervious to, a decayed and weakened Rome, succumbed with hardly a struggle. But in one lasting sense the empire survived. As a state-oriented hierarchical and authoritarian organization patterned on Rome, the Church outlived and at the same time perpetuated the organism that helped produce it. It imposed itself upon the heresies of the invaders and provided the Peninsula with its strongest source of continuity throughout the upheavals of the long centuries to come.

In A.D. 409 the Germanic hordes poured across the Pyrenees into a terrified and defeated Spain. Ironically, the peoples from the north were to all intents and purposes Rome's guests. The Alans, the Suevi, and the Vandals were invited into Spain by a general of the empire making his own personal bid for power. In order to oust these tribes, the Romans in 418 signed a pact with the Visigoths, another Germanic people who, during the fifth century operated in the south of France, ostensibly as an army of Roman auxiliaries. The Visigoths were to be granted lands in Aquitaine in exchange for restoring the three Hispanic provinces to Rome. They did indeed drive the Suevi into far Galicia, defeat the Alans, and oust the Vandals from Andalusia, to which they gave their name. But the Visigoths also, in the absence of effective control from Rome, established themselves as Spain's new governors.

In the midst of the Peninsula's estimated six million inhabitants the 200,000 Visigoths with their long hair and massive jewelry were a mere handful. They established their capital at Toledo, for the first time making the center, rather than the older periphery, the focus of the Peninsula. And there in the center they remained, a caste apart from the mass of the population, an aristocratic and military elite hardly affected even by the eventual removal of the ban on mixed marriages. As a direct consequence of this social and geographical isolation, the language of the Peninsula remained Vulgar Latin, and the invaders, far from imposing their own tongue on the inhabitants they found there, themselves became the victims of a linguistic imposition. They had to content themselves with contributing a mere few hundred words to the language of their adoption.

It is now realized that the Visigothic era in Spain, rather than significantly changing the development of the Peninsula in any way, must be regarded for the most part as an "appendix" to the six-hundred-year rule of Rome. The economic and social tendencies of Spain under the late empire continued, becoming simply more marked. The Visigoths being first a military and then a land-oriented people, the process of deurbanization was accelerated. The bourgeoisie that Roman rule had brought into being in Spain, and then proceeded to undermine, was virtually extinguished. Industry continued to decline and Mediterranean trade was severely affected. Roman coinage remained the only currency until the reign of King Leovigild (569–586). The sole major contribution made to the pattern of peninsular economy by the Visigoths seems to have been their predilection for herding animals. They appear to have been initially responsible for the development of the transmigratory flock as the very core of Spain's agrarian policy, at the cost—the enormous cost as it was to transpire centuries later—of a prosperous agriculture. The Visigothic era, in fact, marks a period of transition between the flourishing mercantile economy of Roman rule in its heyday and the rural domestic economy of the early Middle Ages.

The Visigothic takeover was by any standards a speedy and painless affair, but they did not continue to have things entirely their own way. Pressure from encroaching Franks in the north, from resurgent Suevi in the northwest, and from Byzantium in the south and east, for years kept the Visigothic armies on the march, until the great Leovigild succeeded in establishing Visigothic supremacy after A.D. 569.

The greatest source of disruption, however, was not an outside, hostile world, but the Visigothic elite itself. The monarchical system that they introduced into Spain and which for the first time, in theory at least, made the Peninsula a nation in its own right instead of a collection of tribes or a mere Roman province, was elective, not hereditary. This system, forged by the conditions of a military, nomadic life, proved totally inadequate for the requirements of a stable government and society. Every noble was his king's peer and therefore capable and desirous of succeeding him. The result was constant upheaval at the very summit of society. Sensitive to the full charisma of monarchy, Leovigild was the first Spanish king to wear a crown, to sit on a throne, and to have coins minted in his image, and he obtained a token acceptance of the idea of a hereditary monarchy from his nobles. But within the space of a few reigns, the innovation collapsed.

If the monarchy was a continuous source of instability and unrest, the Christian Church increasingly became a source of power and strength. The Church's career can indeed be seen as the victory of Hispano-Roman Spain over the Visigothic intrusion.

The Visigoths, of course, had been already converted to Christianity before their arrival in Spain and had possessed the Bible in their own Germanic tongue. They were, however, adherents of the Eastern heresy of Arianism, which denied the Trinity, while the Hispano-Romans were staunchly Catholic and solidly remained so. Catholicism eventually triumphed. But it was a triumph achieved only through the bitter expediency of civil war. Leovigild's son, Hermenegild, married a Catholic, was converted by her, and then rose in rebellion against his father. His five-year struggle ended in failure. Hermenegild was murdered by his jailer when he refused to abjure and became the first Visigothic martyr. However, his elder brother, Reccared—a more subtle man—had learned much from the protracted battle put up by the Hispano-Romans of the south. Realizing that only a Catholic would ever command the loyalty of the mass of the people, he announced his own conversion a year after his succession to the throne. Two years later in 589 Catholicism was made the official faith of the Peninsula.

Catholic Christianity had become the state religion of Spain, and out of the ensuing alliance between Church and Crown the Church as a secular power was born. Bishops were incorporated into the royal council and soon played their part in elections to the Crown. The Church's contribution, however, was not merely a political one. As well as providing Visigothic Spain with its two intellectual giants— Saint Leander and his more famous brother Saint Isidore, both, archbishops of Seville—the clergy gave definitive form to the State as a legislative entity. Visigoths and Hispano-Romans were for the first two hundred years subject to their own laws, Germanic or Roman. Then in the middle of the seventh century the task of legislative unification was undertaken under King Chindaswinth. The result, the *Liber Judiciorum*— or *Fuero Juzgo* as it was later called in Castilian—was promulgated by his son Recceswinth in 654. Whether the code's primary debt is to Germanic customary law or to Roman law is still a subject for debate, but the traces of Visigothic attitudes—their concept of honor and personal vengeance, the personal relationship of overlord-serf, the anti-Semitism—are undeniably and predictably apparent. The code, which has left its mark on Spanish life and literature, is in fact the lasting monument to the Visigothic state. Some of its provisions remained law for centuries.

In spite of the achievements of the Church, Visigothic Spain failed ultimately to become a working reality. Like oil and water the Visigothic aristocracy and the Hispanic population stubbornly refused to mix, and the social and ethnic contradictions on which the ship of state gingerly floated rendered it a fragile vessel indeed. It foundered finally in the turbulent waters of that aristocratic anarchy which the monarchy had proved unable to quell. King Witiza, who like former sovereigns had tried to control the succession, had shared the throne with his son Achila. But upon Witiza's death in 710, the nobles elected a king of their own choice, Roderick, and provoked Achila into rebellion. Civil strife of this sort was a familiar accompaniment to the death of kings, but this time events followed a course which led to one of the major milestones in the Peninsula's history.

Count Julian, the governor of the Spanish outpost of Ceuta on the Moroccan coast, joined the battle against Roderick and enlisted Arab aid from North Africa. In 711 an African Berber army of 7,000 under their leader Tarik landed on the prominence called thenceforth the Rock of Tarik (Gebel Tarik, or Gibraltar). In the ensuing Battle of Guadalete, near Jerez de la Frontera, the invaders brought Visigothic rule in Spain crashing down. Roderick disappeared in the battle, leaving behind his white horse with its saddle of gilded buckskin adorned with rubies and emeralds, his gold mantle embroidered with pearls and rubies, and one silver shoe. The Church appears to have played an ignominious part in the Visigoths' defeat. One of the wings of Roderick's army which went over to the enemy was commanded by the archbishop of Seville, a brother of the late Witiza. His motives were obviously purely political, but unwittingly he betrayed his country and his religion to Islam. For, hardly surprisingly, the Moslems summoned in the name of political expediency would not be so readily conjured back across the Strait of Gibraltar once their job was done.

In less than a century Islam had steam-rollered its way from Arabia to Africa's Atlantic shores. The legendarily rich land eight miles across the Mediterranean to the north was an obvious outlet for its religious and expansionist zeal, and almost certainly in its relentless spread it would have arrived there in any case. As it was, once invited over, the Moslems had no intention of returning. With ease they overran the greater part of a country which had withstood the might of Rome for two centuries but which now felt no political allegiance to its former masters. Nearly eight hundred years were to pass before the whole of the Peninsula was wrested from their grasp.

The legend that surrounds the doom of the Visigothic Spain is far more romantic than the reality. King Roderick, it goes, one day took by force the beautiful daughter of Count Julian as she bathed in the Tagus in Toledo. Her father, answering her messages for help, arrived to take her home to Africa. As they left, the king, unaware that his crime was known, asked Julian to send him a certain breed of hawk from Africa. The count agreed, promising to send hawks such as the king never dreamed of. Shortly afterward the "hawks" landed in Spain—Count Julian had opened the floodgates to Islam in vengeance for his dishonor.

Romance or reality, the implication is the same—Visigothic Spain carried within itself the seeds of its defeat. There could have been no more apt relic of Spain's Visigothic period—outwardly splendid but inwardly soft and insecure—than Roderick's mislaid silver slipper.

B. Islamic Spain

After the Romans, the culture that left the greatest mark on early Spanish civilization was that of Islam, whose followers in medieval Spain were called the Moors. In the article that follows, a survey of this great culture and its eight centuries of presence on the Iberian Peninsula are outlined, beginning with their invasion of Visigothic Spain in the year 711 of the modern era. In addition to contributions in literature, science, and the arts, Spanish Muslims brought new products to Al Andalus (the name the Moors gave to Spain, from which is derived the modern *Andalucía*), including cotton, rice, sugarcane, palm trees, fine Arabian horses, paper, algebra, Arabic numbers, and the mathematical concept of zero. Mexican essayist and novelist Carlos Fuentes maintains that fully a quarter of all Spanish words are of Arabic origin. In the tenth century, the greatest city of Europe was the Muslim city of Córdoba, in southern Spain.

Today, Muslims have returned to southern Spain (Andalucía), after nearly five hundred years of absence. In 1492 the Catholic monarchs Isabella and Fernando defeated the Moors at Granada, and from that time through the regimen of the twentieth-century Spanish dictator Francisco Franco (1939–1975), the construction of mosques was discouraged or even prohibited in the country. However, with the rebirth of democracy and freedom of religion in contemporary Spain, mosques and the adherents of Islam can be again found in their historical homeland. For example, a new mosque now overlooks the historic Alhambra Palace in Granada. Once again, the calls to prayer can be heard echoing through the streets of this city, which once flourished under the culture of the Moors.

1. AL-ANDALUS

It is difficult to determine in detail exactly what happened in Hispania during the crucial years after 700, for little direct source material has survived. Though the Visigothic aristocracy had achieved a degree of fusion with Hispanic society and had secured its dominance as a warrior caste, much of it was corrupted by wealth and power and it had at best a very feeble sense of political legitimacy. The Visigothic monarchy had failed to build stable institutions, successful means for transmitting power, or a stable and loyal elite behind the throne. Strife between rival pretend-ers and their supporters persisted throughout the history of Visigothic Hispania. Leovigild, the strongest of its rulers, had himself to face a five-year revolt by his son. Ratification of the elective, as opposed to the hereditary, right by the councils of Toledo in the seventh century sustained Visigothic law but guaranteed endemic civil war. It was not uncommon for factions to accept and encourage foreign intervention on their behalf. In part because of this, Byzantium had been able to control much of southern Hispania for approximately seventy years, from the mid-sixth century down to the third decade of the seventh century, and the Frankish monarchy intervened actively on several occasions in the seventh century. The quick and easy Muslim takeover is understandable only in terms of this persistent failure of political institutions, the accepted custom of foreign intervention, and the apathy or submissiveness of most of the Hispanic lower classes, accustomed to nearly a millennium of rule by outsiders, first by the Romans, then by the Visigoths.

During the latter part of the seventh century the main antagonism was between the descendents of Chindaswinth (642–653) and those of a subsequent ruler. Witiza (702–710). Supporters of Witiza's clan refused to accept the election of a rival candidate. Roderic, in 710, and sought assistance from the newly established Muslim overlords of North Africa. The Visigothic dissidents obviously failed to appreciate the dynamism and integrative potential of the Islamic culture that had swept out of Arabia only a few generations earlier. Their miscalculation was probably due in part to the considerable difficulty encountered by the Muslims in subduing the Berber Kabyles of the Maghreb during the preceding half-century. The latter, like the Hispanic tribes confronting the Romans, had put up a more determined resistance than had most of the more civilized regions farther east. The conquest of the Maghreb had taken nearly forty years, and was nominally completed only in 705–710.

After a small exploratory raid, the Muslim commander of Tangier, Tariq, led a force of perhaps no more than 12,000 men, mostly Berbers from northern Morocco, across the straits in 711. Their goals were apparently ambiguous at first. The intervention was organized at the behest of the Witizan clan; the invaders probably hoped at the least to win booty and to exert some degree of Muslim influence in Hispania, possibly to make it a client state of the Arab caliphate. However, discovery of the hollowness of Visigothic power, both crown and oligarchy, coupled with a swift and decisive victory, expanded Muslim ambition. At that moment Roderic was engaged in trying to subdue Basque and Visigothic rebels in the northeast. He hurriedly marched south, where the invaders awaited him in July 711 at the Guadalete, a small stream in the extreme southern tip of Spain. There the Witizans arranged the withdrawal of the bulk of Roderic's forces; the outnumbered remainder resisted stubbornly but were destroyed. Roderic was killed, and the remnants of his army were shattered near Ecija, where they made a desperate attempt to bar the road to the north. Córdoba, demoralized and almost undefended, was quickly taken. Roderic's supporters in the Visigothic capital, Toledo, were then overthrown by the Witizans, who opened the gates to Tariq.

Civil war was at first even more debilitating to the Visigothic kingdom than the foreign invasion. By 712 the kingdom lay divided and virtually leaderless, its central military elite destroyed. Consequently the Arab governor of northwest Africa, Musa ibn Nusair, personally led a force larger than the first, some 18,000—a high proportion of them the best Arab warriors—in the second wave of invasion. Muslim armies had perfected a swift, flexible, hard-hitting style of battle that proved extremely difficult for Visigothic levies to cope with. Seville, the largest city in the peninsula and center of Hispano-Roman culture, fell easily after a short siege. The remaining elements of the Roderician faction withdrew to Mérida, which withstood a long siege but finally fell on June 30, 713. Much of the Visigothic aristocracy resisted little or not at all. Theodemir, duke of the Cartagena district in the southeast, made a treaty allowing him to retain control of his territory so long as the inhabitants paid regular taxes to the Muslim command. The spring and summer of 714 were then devoted to subduing the heavily populated northeast. Zaragoza was conquered and many of its aristocrats put to the sword. Nearly all the territory northeast of Zaragoza was rendered tributary, after which the main Muslim column apparently marched westward across north-central Hispania before returning southward.

The Muslim "conquest" took only three years, but the Muslims in fact made no effort to conquer and occupy the entire peninsula. That would have been impossible for an army of no more than 30,000 to 40,000 men. They occupied directly only the main strongholds of south-central and northeastern Hispania, the old centers of Roman civilization. The old Suevic district in Portucale to the west and Galicia to the northwest were rendered tributary but not occupied.

The Witizan clan served as clients of the Muslims, who could in a sense present themselves as the protagonists of a legitimist cause. During the first generation of occupation, three thousand estates from the royal domain were bestowed on the Witizans.

The Muslims were concerned first with booty and secondly with the prosecution of the jihad—the holy war to extend Islamic dominion ever farther afield. By 720 an expedition had crossed the Pyrenees and seized Narbonne, and this was followed for the next twenty years by intermittent onslaughts into France. Conquest beyond the Pyrenees was the major new concern of the overlords of "Al-Andalus" (literally "land of the Vandals"), as the Muslims called their new peninsular domain. Between 721 and 732 three governors of Al-Andalus were killed leading expeditions into France, the last expedition culminating in a major defeat by the Frankish army at Poitiers in 732. This did not put an end to the Muslim offensives, however, for the Muslims were further encouraged by internal strife in southern France. The Gallo-Roman inhabitants of Provence stubbornly resisted domination by the Frankish monarchy to the north and summoned Muslim forces to their aid in 735. Two expeditions were dispatched into Provence during the next three years, but the expansion of Frankish military power threw the Muslims on the defensive, and they were barely able to retain a foothold in Septimania immediately northeast of the Pyrenees.

The relative ease with which Muslim domination was established over most of the peninsula can be explained by the fact that only some of the Visigoths resisted, and almost none of the rest of the population. Religious antagonism caused surprisingly little difficulty. Early Islam, despite its emphasis on the jihad, was comparatively tolerant of Christians and Jews as "peoples of the book." Moreover, there was little sense of racial antipathy; the majority of the first wave of invaders were not even Arabs, but Berbers who differed little in appearance from the Hispanic people. Some of these Berbers were themselves not yet fully assimilated into Islam. (For that matter, the Berbers of northwest Africa were not effectively converted until after the adoption of the local Kharijite doctrines in the eighth century.)

The Muslim invaders were greedy for land and booty, but the main targets of their rapaciousness were the Visigothic aristocrats who resisted them. To most of the population the conquest was represented as a liberation. Christians were promised free practice of their religion and in some cases greater social and economic justice as well. The rights of the minority of Hispanic smallholders were apparently respected. Though Christians were required to pay a special tribute, it was at first modest. In all, exactions were perhaps no greater than under the Visigoths. For more than a century, the Christians in the towns were permitted to live a semi-autonomous local existence, and in some cases shared their churches with Islamic worshippers.

People began to accept conversion to Islam almost immediately, in large numbers. The process went forward most rapidly in the population centers of the south and east, and in the meantime practically all the collaborationists among the Visigothic aristocracy embraced the Muslim religion. It is sometimes alleged that the rapid and comparatively facile Islamization of most of the peninsula was the result of the corruption and inattentiveness of the Hispanic church and the lack of piety and orthodoxy among the Visigothic aristocracy. In fact, it is difficult to demonstrate that the Hispanic church was significantly weaker than others of Latin Christendom or that the Visigothic nobles were appreciably less religious than their Frankish counterparts. Rather, Islamization probably stemmed primarily from the complete military and political defeat of the Catholic Visigothic state and from the prestige of the dynamic Muslim empire and its all-conquering armies. At first Islamic overlords did not encourage mass conversion, because it reduced the number of non-Muslims who paid heavier taxes, but once the Muslim authorities were firmly established in power many Christians converted simply to be on the dominant side, escape special taxes, and gain greater economic opportunity. It has also been suggested that a portion of the enserfed sector of the peasantry accepted Islam to be freed of their servitude. Moreover, it is doubtful that many ordinary people perceived the great religious gulf between Christianity and Islam that has subsequently been taken for granted. Rather than as the antithesis to Christianity, many probably saw it as a mere variant of simplification. Finally, according to a later claim of Muslim chroniclers, some Visigothic aristocrats were attracted by the opportunity under Islamic law for polygamy and legal concubinage.

The third religious group in the peninsula, the Jews, who may have numbered 2 or 3 percent of the population, eagerly collaborated with the Muslims. Hispanic Jews had achieved considerable wealth under the Visigoths but were subjected to intermittent persecution. Muslim rule promised greater freedom and security. Jews sometimes assisted the Muslims, and a detachment of Jewish soldiers (perhaps related to Hispano-Jews exiled to the Maghreb) accompanied the invaders. Several important cities were given to Jewish leaders to govern temporarily after the Muslims took over. During the next three centuries Jewish financial and cultural influence expanded in southern and south-central Hispania. Because of their unique position, and also because of their linguistic skills, Jews served for generations as mediators between sectors of the Muslim and Christian populations.

The Arabs, who formed a minority among the mostly Berber invaders, assumed the place of privilege from the beginning and began to set themselves up as a landed Muslim neo-aristocracy. Urban life in the peninsula, too, attracted many. Entering at a higher cultural level than had the Visigoths three centuries earlier, they formed an urban elite, and though at first only a small minority in the Hispano-Christian cities, sank deeper cultural and economic roots and helped expand the influence of Islam in the cities rapidly. The Berber warriors, the rank and file of the invaders, tended to be shunted toward the less productive highlands. Many were settled on territory seized from or abandoned by the Visigoths in the northwest-central region.

The destruction of the Visigothic system of state and society was one thing, and the building of a Muslim Hispania something else that was much more difficult and took more time—indeed, nearly two centuries. After the Visigothic collapse there was a tendency for the inhabitants of various parts of the peninsula to revert to the regionalism and localism characteristic of an earlier era. Muslim power advanced too far too fast to combine all these territories into a well-ordered system. The Arab clan leaders who formed the core of the new oligarchy quickly fell out with each other, and the heads of the caliphate in faraway Damascus revealed concern about maintaining control of their most distant dominion. The first official governor of Muslim Hispania, Abdul Aziz (who incidentally married Roderic's widow), was murdered by rivals in 716. During the four decades 715–755 there were approximately twenty different governors, many of them assassinated and only three retaining office as long as five years.

In addition to feuds between Arab clans and factions, a broad ethnic split emerged between the Arab aristocrats and the Berber population. By 740 a major rebellion was underway across the straits in the Maghreb, where the Berbers were adopting Kharijism, a new, heretical form of Islam that accompanied protest against Arab domination of the Muslim empire. The revolt spread to the Berbers settled in the northwest-central part of the peninsula. They marched against the urban-associated Arab aristocracy in south-central and southern Hispania, outnumbering them, for the Arabs could not depend upon their new Christian subjects to fight for them. It may be that only the arrival of some 7,000 Syrian cavalry saved the aristocracy. During the 740s, the new polity in the peninsula virtually dissolved. The spectacle of general Muslim civil war did not encourage Hispanic loyalty, and small elements of the Christian population took advantage of this opportunity to migrate to the unoccupied northern mountains, whence border warfare had been waged since 718. After 750, crop failures and raiding brought widespread famine to the Berber-inhabited Duero valley of the northwest, forcing the remainder of the invaders to withdraw farther south. When political order was finally restored and the Berbers brought under control, the Duero valley south of the Asturian and Cantabrian hills had been evacuated, leaving a no-man's-land fought over by northern Christians and Muslims for the next two centuries.

Rulers of Al-Andalus	
Abd-al-Rahman I	756–788
Hisham I	788–796
al-Hakam I	796–822
Abd-al-Rahman II	822–852
Muhammad I	852–886
al-Mundhir	886–888
Abdallah	888–912
Abd-al-Rahman III	912–961
al-Hakam II	961–976
Hisham II	976–1009
Amirid dictators:	
al-Mansur	c.976–1002
Abdul-Malik	1002–1008
Taifa kings	1009–1090
Almoravid empire	1090–1147
Almohad empire	1147–1212

Unified government in Muslim Hispania was finally achieved after 755 by its first independent ruler, Abd-al-Rahman I (756–788), last surviving heir of the traditional Muslim Umayyad dynasty in Damascus after it had been deposed by the rival Abbasid dynasty. In flight from the Near East, Abd-al-Rahman, whose mother was a Berber, sought to regain an independent kingdom at the far western end of the Muslim world. Arriving in the peninsula in 755, he won the support not only of the Berbers but also of the strongest Arab faction, enabling him to overthrow the forces of the erstwhile governor outside Córdoba,

the Hispano-Muslim capital since 719. There Abd-al-Rahman announced the establishment of an independent Umayyad emirate based on "true justice" and toleration for all religions and ethnic groups. This stand greatly strengthened his position among the heterogeneous population of the peninsula. He was eventually recognized as heir of the legitimate dynasty by nearly all regions save the independent Christian hill country of the far north, but years of intermittent campaigning were required to subdue dissident Muslim regional overlords.

Little effort was made to conquer and occupy the northern mountain areas, because of difficult geographic obstacles, the poverty of those regions, and the resistance of their inhabitants. Instead, three frontier districts or marches were established to hold the border, and the emirate adopted or accepted a variant of west European feudalism in dealing with the frontier areas. The key spots were mountains, castles, or fortified towns difficult to incorporate into a central system. Loose personal relations akin to vassalage were worked out with Muslim and at times with Christian overlords in the frontier area. This meant an uneven border and an incomplete political system on the Christian fringe, but the offensive military strength and the economic resources of the northern Christian hill people did not seem great enough to warrant the expenditure of means that would have been required to subdue those harsh, backward regions.

It is impossible to calculate the number of immigrants who entered the peninsula during the three centuries of the emirate. All told they may have accounted for the ancestry of 20 percent of the peninsula's population by the end of the tenth century, yet the influx in most years was quite small. Moreover, the bulk of the immigrants were not oriental Arabs but Maghrebian Berbers. The prosperous, increasingly cultured Al-Andalus must have looked very attractive to the rude tribesmen across the straits. But the more cultured Arabs tended to monopolize the most important lands, posts, and perquisites, and relations with the Berbers and other elements were never very good. Muslim Hispania never achieved a fully homogeneous society. Descendents of Arabs jealously preserved their family and tribal identities, together with a distinct sense of superiority to the rest of the Muslim population. Many of the Berber immigrants did not at first speak Arabic and for some time retained their separate community identity. The majority of the Muslims were of course descendants of Hispanic converts and never managed to absorb fully the aristocratic Arab elements; rather, upper-class Hispano-Muslim *muwalladun* (or *muladíes*, as converts to Islam were later known in Castilian) later came to affect Arab ancestry or names for themselves. Interethnic tensions persisted throughout the history of Al-Andalus. They probably lay at the root of continuing internal political conflicts that were only temporarily assuaged, never eliminated.

The emirate was nevertheless free of such strong anti-Arab outbursts as occurred among the native Muslim populace of Iraq and Iran during those centuries. Abd-al-Rahman I encouraged the settling of Arab aristocrats directly on the land, overseeing the cultivation of estates, and by the tenth century the gap between the Muslim aristocrats and the *muladí* peasants was apparently not as great as that which had existed in much of the former Hispano-Visigothic society.

An Islamic culture in the peninsula developed with surprising rapidity. Though the first generation of Muslims had been relatively uncultured and had a rather weak grasp of Islamic theology, religious teachers arrived from the Near East soon after the conquest, and their numbers increased during the course of the eighth century. The roots of a genuine Muslim orthodoxy were established, in response to the problem of cultural heterogeneity and the challenge to the identity of the convert. Within three or four generations, Hispanic Islam was strongly identified with the Malikite rite. The religious teacher Malik (who died in Medina ca. 795) had propounded a rather simple and traditionalistic understanding of Islam, based on the formula of "the Koran, the words of the Prophet, and admitting that otherwise I do not know." The antirationalist conservatism of the Malikite rite was adopted as the semi-official observance of Muslims in the emirate during the reign of al-Hakam I (796–822). Malikite traditionalism, as propounded by local *faqihs* (jurists) throughout Al-Andalus, provided a degree of cultural unity for most of the Muslim population. Ultra-orthodoxy was characteristic of Islam in the peninsula throughout almost the entire Muslim period, and contrasted notably with the greater tendency toward heterodoxy in other parts of the Muslim world. This may perhaps be explained by the peripheral location of Al-Andalus at the outer limit of Islamic lands, adjacent to Latin Christendom, containing a Christian minority (at first a Christian majority), and usually in a state of tension with its religious and cultural rival. It is interesting, too, that during the Middle Ages western Christianity also emphasized pragmatic legalism, ethics, and orthodoxy in contrast with the more speculative metaphysics of the Christian east.

A wave of major "orientalization" began during the reign of Abd-al-Rahman II (822–852), who imported numerous oriental Muslim artists and educators. The high culture of the Middle East elicited a strongly eastward-looking orientation; though a few individual Hispano-Muslim art forms were developed by the tenth century (the *muwashaha* and *zéjel* songs and poems), the art and literature of Al-Andalus was established almost completely on oriental Arabic forms.

Christian society in the south and east was completely unable to hold its own. The independent Christians of the north came to call their counterparts in the south *Mozarabs*, derived from the Arabic *musta'rib*, meaning Arabized or Arabic-speaking. Mozarab culture became fossilized, its postconquest literature for example rhetorical and usually mediocre, deficient in dialectic and analysis. Of course it must be recognized that Mozarab culture was placed under increasing pressure and not able to develop in full freedom. Limited tolerance never meant equality, and Christians were never permitted to dispute publicly the teachings of Islam. Religious practice and cultural opportunity were increasingly circumscribed. It is true that some towns had Christian majorities for a century or more, that most Mozarab dioceses were able to continue an uninterrupted line of episcopal succession for nearly three hundred years, that all-Mozarab church councils were occasionally called, and that some religious and cultural contacts were maintained with other parts of western Christendom. Nonetheless, the strength and influence of Islam was increasingly felt. From about the beginning of the ninth century pressure mounted; taxes were raised and new restrictions were introduced, while the Muslim proportion of society steadily increased. One response to latent and then mounting persecution was the Christian "martyrs of Córdoba" movement of 850–859 in the course of which several score Christian spokesmen, confronting Islam directly, were put to death. A more common response was Mozarab emigration to the Christian principalities in the northern mountains. The Muslim state did not embark on a policy of extreme persecution until late in the tenth century, however, and the Mozarab minority persisted, in ever-dwindling numbers, until almost the end of Al-Andalus.

The growing strength and sophistication of Hispano-Muslim society was not reflected by political unity, for the ninth century was a time of political troubles for the emirate. Resentment among both Christians and Hispano-Muslims increased: against the overlordship of Córdoba by Muslims in other regions, against exclusivist Arab clans on the part of non-Arab Muslims, and against supposedly heterodox emirs by fanatical Malikite faqihs. A major revolt occurred among the lower classes of Córdoba in 814, when popular discontent took the form of an uprising against the emir himself. This reflected the uncertainty about political legitimacy that had existed in Muslim Hispania since the emirate broke away from the central caliphate in the Near East. After the revolt was quelled, one-fourth of the population of the Andalusi capital was expelled.

Muslim revolts grew serious during the second half of the ninth century. At times the emir controlled only the greater Córdoba region. Major rebellions occurred in the districts of Toledo in the center, Seville and Bobastro in the south, Mérida in the southwest, and Zaragoza and Lérida in the northeast. The partly Christian city of Toledo was more or less autonomous from 873 to 930, required only to pay a nominal tribute to the emirate. A more fully autonomous principality was carved out in the upper Ebro valley of the northeast by the Banu Qasi dynasty, descendants of the Visigothic overlord Casio (Cassius) of Tudela, who had accepted Islam in 714 at the start of the conquest. The Banu Qasi ruled the upper Ebro region for two hundred years, waxing at times rich and powerful. At their height in the late ninth century they were sometimes called "third kings of Hispania" (following the emirs of Al-Andalus and the kings of Christian Asturias-León). The most serious of the new revolts, however, was that begun by Umar ibn Hafsun at Bobastro in the hills above Málaga in 883. The descendant of muladíes, ben-Hafsun rallied Muslims and Christians alike and soon made most of the eastern Andalusian hill country independent of the emirate. In 894 he returned to Christianity, the religion of his ancestors. That cost the support of most of his Muslim following, but even so he held out in the Bobastro district until his death in 917. This domain was defended by his sons for another twelve years until it was finally rein-corporated by the emirate in 929.

An effectively unified state was finally achieved during the long reign of Abd-al-Rahman III (912–961). The son of a Navarrese princess, this greatest of Cordoban rulers was a short, blue-eyed Muslim who dyed his red hair black to match that of most of his subjects. In 929 he took the step of raising his dominion from an emirate, or kingdom, to a caliphate, or empire. Originally the Islamic world had been unified under a single caliphate as the political successor to the prophet's authority. The Umayyad emirate of Al-Andalus had been nominally subordinate to the Abbasid caliphate in Baghdad, but establishment of a new caliphate under the aggressive Fatimids in Egypt threatened military and political pressures through North Africa. Abd-al-Rahman III countered the claims and ambitions of the Fatimids by taking advantage of new Muslim theories to assert the imperial independence of Al-Andalus. This nominal authority also strengthened the claims of the Cordoban state over the local regions of the peninsula.

The caliph restored central control over all the Muslim population and carried on major border campaigns against the small Christian principalities of the north, receiving token submission from most of them. During the latter part of his reign he extended military dominion over part of the northwest Maghreb, briefly expanding Al-Andalus into an imperial domain.

The strength of the tenth-century caliphate was due as much to the efficiency of the state system as to the size and prosperity of its population, for the caliphate developed the best organized administration found anywhere in western Europe during that era. This had begun nearly a century earlier under Abd-al-Rahman II, who had commenced to refashion what had begun as a fairly simple despotism into a well-articulated structure patterned after the Abbasid caliphate in Damascus. Executive authority was nominally autocratic, administered by an *hajib* or chief minister through batteries of *visirs* or departmental ministers for varied aspects of administration, with complements of subsecretaries, scribes, and clerks. A fairly efficient treasury with some degree of central accounting was eventually developed. Theoretically, each district of the emirate was administered by a regional wali, or governor, responsible to the central government for the affairs of his province. The legal system was headed by a *cadi aljamaa* (chief justice), though his authority was restricted to the Córdoba district. The court structure was divided by region and municipality, with separate jurisdictions for different kinds of grievances according to civil need and Muslim custom.

Muslim military organization in the peninsula had long been rather rudimentary, resting upon the militia of the local Arab clans and other regional elites. Though originally made up mostly of infantry, Muslim armies came to rely especially on light cavalry, patterned in part on the Arabic model and armed with lances, darts, and small shields. Early in the emirate a permanent standing army had been begun with the formation of an elite corps of several thousand slaves from eastern Europe and Africa. Abd-al-Rahman III did not solve the problem of central military organization, but his forces were the most numerous yet employed by Muslim power in the peninsula and in their time were without peer in western Europe. The ports of the eastern, southern, and western coasts of the peninsula had long had large commercial fleets, but an armed navy of significance took form lacking in Al-Andalus. Abd-al-Rahman III's successor, al-Hakam II, ruled for fifteen years, but when he died in 976 he left as heir a twelve-year-old son who was recognized as Hisham II. The government was soon dominated by its vigorous and efficient hajib, an Hispano-Arab known to history as al-Mansur ("The Victorious"). In 981 young Hisham was forced to officially ratify the complete authority of the hajib over all aspects of government.

Al-Mansur relied on two factors to cement his dictatorship: religion and a strong centralized army. He allied himself with the influential Malikite faqihs in suppressing the few scattered expressions of Islamic heterodoxy that had appeared at Córdoba and won a reputation among the superstitious lower classes as a defender of the faith. He also expanded the standing army. Large numbers of Berber mercenaries were brought in from the Maghreb, and Christian mercenaries were accepted as well. The ordinary militia levies of Al-Andalus were reorganized by special regiment rather than by local district in an effort to counteract the centrifugal effect of regional loyalties. Al-Mansur built the most powerful military machine yet seen in the peninsula, but it broke the traditional service patterns of Al-Andalus and severed bonds between local leaders and the Cordoban government. It became to some extent an instrument of control over the rest of Al-Andalus and a resented agent of centralization.

The historic title al-Mansur was won in a long series of summer campaigns against the Christian principalities of the north. The motives were more political and economic than religious, but al-Mansur found it useful to strengthen his position by preaching the jihad against the northern Christians, little troubled by the fact that Christian mercenaries sometimes served in his forces. At one time or another he ravaged every major part of Christian territory save Navarre, with whose ruling dynasty he was allied by marriage. No ruler since the original conquest had inflicted such heavy damage on Christian Hispania. Moreover, at the very end of the century his son, Abdul-Malik, restored Cordoban authority over the northwest corner of the Maghreb, of which the city of Fez was the center. Al-Mansur died in 1002 at the height of power, exhausted by his triumphant exertions. He was succeeded by Abdul-Malik, who quickly obtained from the impotent Hisham the same plenary authority held by his invincible father. Abdul-Malik survived his father by only six years, however, dying in 1008, possibly assassinated.

The Amirid dictatorship* wielded by al-Mansur and Abdul-Malik from 976/981 to 1008 had raised the caliphate to the pinnacle of its military power, yet sowed within it the seeds of its political destruction. For one thing, the dictatorship fatally weakened the principle of political legitimacy. Al-Andalus had always been difficult to rule, relying on both forceful leadership and administration and the legitimate authority of the Ummayad dynasty. In the long run, the dictatorship supplied force alone; it replaced the dynasty, yet could not develop a new principle of legitimate descent from Mohammed. By the tenth century Shiite doctrines in the Muslim orient had tried to establish a new principle of legitimacy on the basis of divinely appointed leaders, imams, who were nominal descendants of the Prophet and were held to enjoy divinely delegated charismatic authority. But the Amirids could claim no such descent from Mohammed. Appeals to the jihad proved insufficient to bolster what was eventually revealed as a purely opportunistic military regime. Traditional relations between the regions were disrupted, and replaced with purely military bonds.

Breakup of the Caliphate 1008–1031

Soon after the death of the second Amirid, the political unity and authority of the caliphate collapsed altogether. Once the legitimate succession had been interrupted it was never successfully restored. Many regions of Al-Andalus were resentful of their treatment under the dictatorship and refused to heed new leaders in Córdoba. The feckless Hisham was deposed in 1009, briefly restored the following year, then deposed again. Altogether, over a period of twenty-three years, six relatives of the Ummayads and three members of a rival, half-Berber family disrupted the throne. The slave pretorians functioned as a powerful independent faction and the bands of Berber mercenaries who had become more numerous during the preceding half-century usurped power in local districts. Regional Arab oligarchs and clans withdrew into local exclusivism, and the state system soon dissolved. Córdoba was wracked by demagogy, riots, and pillaging, while the educated and wealthy fled. In 1010 the city was sacked by a Catalan expedition brought in by Muslim dissidents at Toledo.

Had a leader as resolute and resourceful as Abd-al-Rahman III or al-Mansur emerged, he might have been able to restore caliphal authority. As it was, the caliphate had been unable to institutionalize political unity in the face of geographic obstacles, ethnic diversity, class divisions, and a persistent spirit of localism. The idea of Muslim unity had little currency,

---

*The title was derived from Al-Mansur's family name.

for Cordoban power in the tenth century had been based largely on political, not religious, standards and values. Nor did the small Christian states of the north seem very threatening in the early eleventh century; united defense of the faith was not an issue. Rather than undergo the Amirid experience again, the regions almost unanimously preferred to pull apart. The localism and factionalism that had proved an almost insuperable obstacle for the Visigothic monarchy also undermined the caliphate, and its official end was finally declared by a group of local leaders meeting in Córdoba in 1031. In the former capital it was replaced by a local government of notables ruling only the greater Córdoba district.

The Taifa Kingdoms

After the collapse of the caliphate, political power coalesced around local leaders, oligarchies, or ethnic groups and coalitions in the principal urban economic centers of Al-Andalus. Nearly all the first overlords were local commanders and notables who had achieved power through the political and military network created by al-Mansur. The result was a series of about thirty regional *taifa* (local faction) kingdoms that divided up approximately the southern 75 percent of the peninsula. Some of the taifas, chiefly Seville, Granada, Badajoz, Valencia, Toledo, and Zaragoza, quickly developed into fairly strong regional emirates or principalities, dominating large areas of the surrounding countryside and devouring their weaker neighbors. The taifas were typically governed by local dynasties of Arab aristocrats or local Berber military factions, but power was sometimes disputed by a variety of heterogeneous claimants: Arab oligarchs, Berber mercenaries or immigrants, the "Andalusian" or ordinary Hispano-Muslim majority, and other mercenaries or forces of slave pretorians. Political transition went most smoothly in border districts dominated by military leaders. In the Andalusian interior quarreling was more protracted.

The taifas managed to preserve most of the economic achievements of Al-Andalus and often to develop them further. Some of their capitals reached a greater level of prosperity and sophistication in the eleventh century than any towns under the caliphate save Córdoba. Hence the collapse of the Hispano-Muslim state did not bring the collapse of Hispano-Muslim culture.

Indeed, the famous "high culture" of Muslim Hispania, while building on the achievements of the tenth-century caliphate, was mainly a product of the new scholarship and writing of the eleventh and twelfth centuries. The same was true of the most enduring creations of Hispano-Muslim art and architecture. It was during the taifa and the subsequent Almoravid period that the popular Hispanic song and verse forms—the muwashahas and zéjels—were formally incorporated into written literature and subsequently gained a vogue in Islamic art.

A striking and dominant characteristic of Hispano-Muslim literature was its essential materialism and hedonism. Love lyrics and erotic poetry in Al-Andalus often surpassed those of the middle East, religious literature and mystical verse were rather poorly developed. The society's religion remained hyperorthodox, but it did not lead to a high religious culture in literature or theology. There were few new religious ideas in Al-Andalus.

The taifa kingdoms and their successors were the late blooming of Muslim Hispania's Indian Summer. Wracked by incessant factionalism, they divided and dissipated their civic and military energies. When the military balance in the peninsula began to change in the middle of the eleventh century, the taifas could not defend themselves in regional isolation and were destroyed one by one. The dissolution of the caliphate had been the political prelude to the political and military decline of all of Al-Andalus.

Parallel between the Caliphate and the Later Spanish Empire

There are certain intriguing parallels between the circumstances and historical patterns of tenth-century Al-Andalus and sixteenth-century Spain. Both empires were launched, as is customarily the case with expansionist systems, before their respective societies had reached their fullest cultural development. Both emphasized imperial expansion and foreign issues to the detriment of internal problems. Neither achieved a fully integrated civic entity: the Umayyad caliphate was not effectively integrated, and the Habsburg monarchy was pluralistic, revealing centrifugal tendencies. Both strongly emphasized religious issues in mobilizing for expansion; religious orthodoxy was later stressed by both in their periods of political decline. The renewed assertion of reorganized military power marked the last generation of strong government and the prelude to civic decline (compare al-Mansur and Olivares). The full flowering of Andalusi culture came after the collapse of the caliphate; that of Habsburg Spain, at least in esthetics, after the apogee of politico-military power under Felipe II. A major difference between the two was that the economic prosperity of Al-Andalus survived the passing of the caliphate. Seventeenth-century Spain exhausted its economy in war; the Muslim taifas never organized the military strength that their economies could have supported.

C. The Jews of Spain

During Roman times, one of the greatest concentrations of Jews outside their traditional homeland of the Middle East was Roman Spain (Hispania). Many Jewish families arrived to Hispania after the destruction of Jerusalem and the temple in year 70 of the modern era, and especially during the reign of the Emperor Hadrian in the second century. In Spain, Jews were allowed to worship and continue their culture under the watchful and more tolerant provincial Roman government. Hispania itself—an arid land at the shores of the Mediterranean Sea—reminded Jews of their cherished homeland to the east. The Jews with the Moors (Islam) and the Christians formed the three great cultures of medieval Spain.

Jewish families and their descendants became as "Spanish" as any of the great cultures of the Iberian Peninsula. They called Spain *Sepharad* in Hebrew and from ancient times to 1492—the year of their expulsion—the Jews were central to the civilization of Spain. The relation of the Jews with other cultures in Spain varied: they flourished under the Romans, and were persecuted by the Visigoths; they generally welcomed the arrival of Islam in the year 711 (a culture that had lived side by-side Jews since the times of the Prophet Mohammed). The Jews' contact with Christian Spain was problematic: Christian kings admitted them to their courts as bankers and physicians, but the common people and especially the Catholic Church often persecuted them. In 1492 Isabella and Ferdinand expelled all Jews who refused to convert to Christianity, and the descendents of these families—the *Sephardic* Jews of today—continue to mourn the loss of their beloved *Sepharad*.

At the present time, some traditional Sephardic families speak a version of the fifteenth-century Spanish, called Ladino (Judeo-Spanish). If you want to hear some of this Spanish, a good film to watch is *Every Time We Say Goodbye*, starring Tom Hanks (released in DVD in 2006). Tom portrays an American pilot who falls in love with a Sephardic young woman in Palestine during World War II. Throughout the film, you hear an occasional Ladino spoken by her and her family members. Most Spanish speakers will be able to understand this version of Spanish preserved by the Sephardic Jews.

1. HISPANO-JEWISH SOCIETY

The history of the Jews in Spain until their expulsion in 1492 is the history of a people settled in one place for a very long time—at least as long as Christian dating.[1] To this land of the Diaspora the Jews brought their own way of life and their own institutions. Here they evolved, both influencing and being influenced by their surroundings, and adopting what they needed for their own customs and forms of life. Historically, this long period begins in the days of Roman rule over *Provincia Hispania*. Afterwards, when Byzantines and Visigoths held sway in the Iberian Peninsula, the people underwent harsh decrees and persecution, for their rulers sought to force Christianity upon them and to eliminate them as Jews. The Visigothic regime, relying on Conciliar decrees to which it had been a party, sought to destroy their public and social framework, without suggesting any solution to the bewildering problem of how people who had accepted Christianity under duress were to exist. It was not only that Christian Visigothic society and government were incapable of offering any such solution; they were a sort of upper stratum in the state—a ruling caste. Obviously, this ruling caste had no interest in the problem of relations other than taking the steps necessary to keep itself in power in the Peninsula. The existence of a separate and distinct Jewish people and society did not suit its purposes at all. In the hundred years of Visigothic rule, the government failed to create values that might serve as a foundation for public and social evolution in the state. Its efforts at different times to mould a Christian society amounted to little more than paper decisions.[2]

In 711 the Arabs burst into the Iberian Peninsula and this government fell. The Jewish public, some of whom lived in areas where Visigothic rule had been weak, and

---

1. H. BEINART, "¿Cuando llegaron los Judíos a España?", *Estudios*, 3 (1961), pp. 1–32.

2. J. PARKES, *The Conflict of Church and Synagogue* (2nd printing, Cleveland-New York, 1961), pp. 345 ff. (See bibliography there); J. VICENS VIVES, *Historia Economica de España* (Barcelona, 1959), pp. 81–89; J. VIVES, *Concilios Visigoticos e Hispano-Romanos* (Barcelona-Madrid, 1963), *passim*.

---

some of whom had arrived to settle in the wake of the conquest, were faced with many public and social problems, connected with their organization as a community living as wards in "protected" congregations. Of course, the problems of existence and organisation in Moslem al-Andalus were no different from those to be found in any other territory ruled by Islam. But the independent Ommayad rulers of al-Andalus soon had need of the Jews, for internal and external reasons. The appearance of Jewish leaders like Hasdai Ibn Shaprut, who was appointed head of the Jews of al-Andalus in the tenth century, or Jacob Ben-Jo, appointed tax-collector and Head of the Jews of al-Andalus and the Maghreb, the fact that they both resided in Cordoba, the subsequent rise of R. Shmuel ha-Nagid in Granada—all these attest the close links between the government and the Jews and are a clear sign of Jewish organization. And although social relations were still rather limited between the Jews and the government and the surrounding Moslem world, it seems that as the government ramified, so did the network of relations grew more complex. As a general rule, however, the Jewish public in the communities of Moslem Spain—and here and there in the ever-advancing, ever-conquering Christian Spain—never went outside the religious-national framework. They kept to themselves, whether in matters of organization and social structure or in those outward forms of life that they had adopted in Spanish lands. This general rule goes far to explain the social and public characteristics of Spanish Jewry, despite the fact that Jewish communal organization in Christian Spain was influenced by the forms of organization of the Christian public. Another important fact is that Christian rule was divided among kingdoms and principalities and the fiefs of churchmen and nobles. This was a unique phenomenon, of whose total extent under Christian sway we shall speak in greater detail. We shall try to build up a picture of the Jewish society that existed for centuries, through many vicissitudes, in the kingdoms of Castile and Aragon.

At the outset we may fairly ask: is it in fact possible to ascribe a particular social personality to the Jewish public in Spain? The characteristics of Spanish Jewry were, after all, shared by Jews in other countries. There were city-dwellers, smalltown dwellers, villagers. All social relations, public and social tension, existed in streams both above and below the surface. Spanish Jewish society contained rich men, middling men and poor men—the latter supported by the public—, scholars, students, religious dignitaries renowned for their learning, physicians, merchants, artisans in the widest variety of crafts, and peasants leaseholders and freeholders. Thus, socially, they were no more exempt from the stress of relations than any society and any community.

And this, it seems, describes the network of relations in the Jewish public in Spain throughout the centuries of its existence. Yet, the social situation of the congregations of Israel in Spain was not the same at all times and places. Changing political conditions affected them. We should remember that Christian Spain existed for hundreds of years in the political stress of Reconquista and in the problems of resettlement of the frontier, on which there was room for the Jews as a community. These conditions of stress affected the Jewish public, laying it open to the challenge of settlement, the challenge of creating centres and new congregations. These were especially demanding tasks, since in conquered cities, townships and villages there were old communities which had now to fit into the conquering Christian state. This is not to say that the communities, wherever they were, had to undergo changes in their organization, or that the social structure of the Jewish public in the conquered areas underwent an immediate change. The Jews of the conquered places met (sometimes as ransomed captives)[3] Jewish settlers who had come from the Christian zones. The new Jewish settlers from Spanish-Christian ruled areas enjoyed settlers' privileges and were given lands, estates, vineyards, houses and workshops in the conquered areas.[4] Both sides built up the Jewish communities anew, without more friction than is normal in any community.

The condition of settlement in new places and the demand for Jewish settlement continued among the Jewish public until the last Reconquista campaign to conquer Granada, in the eighties of the fifteenth century. Yet in this final campaign of conquest, whose aim was to cast out the last stronghold of Islam in Europe, in arrangements for resettlement of the area about to be conquered, the victorious Ferdinand and Isabella had not the slightest intention of calling on the Jewish element in settlement or its power of initiative. As is well known, the Catholic kings intented to found a purely Christian state. And it must be said that this idea contained as a prior assumption, the expulsion of the Jews from Spain. It was an idea that had grown out of the religious and social evolutionary process that had been going on since 1391, through the wave of forced conversions

---

3. The government sometimes demanded that the Jewish public should ransom its Jewish brothers in the conquered Moslem territories.

4. On this question see, e.g., R. CARANDE, "Sevilla, Fortaleza y Mercado," *Anuario de la Historia del Derecho Español*, 2 (1925), *passim*; J. GONZALEZ Y GONZALEZ, *Repartimiento de Sevilla*, 1–2 (Madrid, 1951); J. TORRES FONTES, *Repartimiento de Murcia* (Madrid, 1960).

and abandonment of the Jewish faith. This process continued throughout the fifteenth century.

In every Jewish community in Christian Spain, whether in the kingdoms of Castile-Leon, Navarre or Aragon, the style of public life was set by members of the best families, those, that is to say, whose pedigree was good, who also possessed property in the city or its surroundings.[5] Some of these pedigrees were imaginary, amounting to no more than the fact that the family in question had been among the first settlers in the place. Such families were Abu-Alafia, Ibn-Ezra, Alfakar, Ibn Shushan and Ibn Zadok in Toledo; the families of Caballeria, Alconstantini and Golluf in Saragossa; the families of Abravalia and Berfet in Barcelona; the Portela family in Tarragona and so on. Not all had an ancient pedigree on which to base their claim to place for themselves and their descendants. Not a few families owed the success of their claims within (and sometimes without) the community to contacts with the government and connections with kings, bishops, princes and dukes.[6] But it would be utterly baseless to say that only persons whose origins are insufficiently clear to us, or persons having government connections, were the social and moral arbiters of the Jewish public. Within these very families we find rabbis and scholars. We also find great rabbis from other families who exercised much greater influence than these families on the Jewish way of life and on the leadership of the Jewish public. It is enough to recall a few of their names: Ramban (R. Moshe b. Nachman, Nachmanides), R. Shelomo ben Adret (Rashba), R. Aaron ha-Levi na Clara, R. Hasdai Crescas in Aragon, R. Joseph Orabuena in Navarre, or Rabbi Joseph ha-Nasi ben Pruziel, known as Cidellus, R. Abraham Ibn-Shushan, R. Judah Ibn Wakar, R. Meir Alguades, R. Abraham Benvenisti of Soria, R. Isaac Abrabanel in Castile. It was such personalities and many others like them, who set the pattern for public and moral life in Spanish Jewry for generations. Needless to say, there were also Jewish leaders from "good" families who were pushing and unlearned. And there were others too among the men of "lineage" who cared and worked for the Jewish community. Whether in their own native place or in the state where they lived. Only against rioters, violent men, rough attackers did the sages of Israel in Spain in every generation see it as their duty to fight—sometimes even with government aid—for the sake of the welfare of Jewry. And if, on the other hand, the sages of Israel saw danger of an outburst from within that might harm the Jewish community, they did not hesitate to take measures against those who had lost control of themselves, and would even employ local strong men in order to impose discipline on the Jewish community.[7] Throughout Spain, we may justly see in the sages of Israel the wardens of the Jewish community, the guardians of its path towards a decent way of life based on public and social morality, as all true Jewish life must be.

Jewish communal leaders and sages were, however, only a thin stratum of Jewish society. If we turn to the more go-ahead members of the community, we find that their chief business was large-scale credit for state and private needs, tax-farming and tax-collecting—activities that spread throughout Castile and Aragon. They were the first to receive lands in border areas; they had shops and commercial enterprises in many parts of Spain. Alongside these dwelt persons of middle and lower rank: grocers and craftsmen, who did not differ much from each other. A valuable criterion for assessing social differences in Spain is the amount of the annual tax paid by individuals to the chest that existed in every congregation to meet the tax that Jewish communities were required to pay every year to the king's treasury.[8] In this respect we find that a line can be drawn between the great ones or 'great taxpayers', as they were called, and the 'medium' and 'small' men; we shall revert to this topic later. We find concentrations of small craftsmen in almost every community in Spain; the 'great ones', the rich are scarcer.

It is certainly possible to find a "rich man" in every community—be he merchant, money-lender, owner of vineyard or olive-grove—compared with whom the other members of the community live on a very modest level. But we must remember that the criterion of wealth is purely relative. Among the merchants, the cloth dealers of Saragossa enjoyed special status and filled important positions in the communal leadership.[9] There were also perfume

---

5. See H. H. BEN-SASSON, "The Generation of Spanish Exiles on Itself," *Zion*, 25 (1961), pp. 23–64 (Hebrew).

6. H. H. BEN-SASSON, *Chapters in the History of the Jews in the Middle Ages* (Tel Aviv, 1958), pp. 144 ff. (Hebrew). See H. BEINART, *The Character of the 'Court Jews' in Christian Spain: Elite Groups and Leadership Strata* (Jerusalem, 1966), pp. 55–71 (see bibliography there).

7. Rashba's way, for example, is known. See F. BAER, *History of the Jews in Christian Spain* (Philadelphia, 1960), I, pp. 257 ff.

8. See BAER, *History*, I, pp. 198 ff.

9. Jews worked in every stage of this profession, from the spinning of the woolen thread, the weaving of the cloth and the dyeing to the selling of the cloth and the making of the garment.

dealers, apothecaries, goldsmiths, etc. In a community of 50 families like that of Segovia or Avila in Castile, Teruel in Aragon or Tudela in Navarre, we find a full array of skilled workers, a wide variety of crafts and services to supply every private and public need.[10] Weavers, shoemakers, tailors, butchers, furriers, smiths, saddlers, tanners, leatherworkers, potters, cloth dyers and so on very often sold their products themselves. Some of these skilled craftsmen had a plot of land next to their homes on which they grew vegetables for their own table. Some families had a few head of sheep or cattle grazing on the common pasture of the village, township or town. Only a minority actually owned land on the waste outside the town or township. This land, which grew unirrigated field crops, vines or olives, was cultivated by the owner aided in some cases by his Jewish or Christian serfs or non-Jewish labourers. Such was the general arrangement throughout the centuries of Jewish settlement in Spain, and lists of property sold about the time of the 1492 expulsion confirm it.[11] However, the Jews of those days cannot be called farmers in any accepted contemporary or modern sense of the word. There was a Jewish doctor in almost every settlement, who served not only the Jews but the community at large—whoever needed his help, whether in ordinary times or in time of plague. Towns expressed their thanks more than once to the Jewish physician.[12] His services were given despite the fact that the Church and civil authorities alike forbade Christians to be treated by Jewish physicians and forbade Jews to practise medicine.[13] Kings had their Jewish physicians, as did bishops, abbots and nobles in their degrees. Indeed to employ a Jewish physician was felt to lend tone by many nobles and great men of the realm. Clearly, money lending at interest was by no means the only Jewish profession,[14] though Jews engaged in it. It was a service needed by a society unable to find any other source of financial credit; it is unnecessary to repeat the reasons that drove Jews to support themselves by moneylending. Jewish society included, along with all these, widows and orphans, poor people, religious functionaries, teachers and cantors, all of whom were supported at the public charge. They were exempt from taxes: the Jewish community paid their taxes for them. Small and medium-sized communities not frequently depended in this respect on their rich and 'great' brethren, or on the one individual in the place who was rich enough to help the whole community in its need. This kind of communal support was given throughout the period of Jewish settlement in Spain, middling and large communities alike.

The majority of Jews were of the middling sort: they had little capital, and what they had was sunk in their trade or craft. When they were forced to abandon Judaism in the troubles of 1391 and during the fifteenth century, they brought with them into the Christian fold all the traditional Jewish crafts and callings handed down for generations. Thus we can sometimes tell a man's origin by his occupation, and say: that is a Jew by origin. Christian society in Spain in the fifteenth century was unable to absorb this special world, this Jewish public forced from its faith and its framework. It was not only that the Christians lacked the necessary public and social means to absorb the Jews: they lacked the socio-psychological conditions as well. The public debate that went on in Castile in the middle of the fifteenth century shows how much the problem of the Conversos and their absorption into Christian society was a social problem. It had various aspects: there was the question of sheer subsistence for the Conversos and there was the question of the need for a partial change of heart by the society that was supposed to absorb them. The difficulties were particularly prominent in professions which had never admitted Jews, like those of public notary and judge, and other positions of decisive weight in the Christian society of genuine, original Christians. The educated Conversos could find no place for themselves in this Christian community and were pushed firmly back by legislation aiming to forbid people who 'are of the Jews' (i.e. of Jewish origin) from taking posts involving jurisdiction over Christians.[15] But for the majority, the mass of skilled workers, the question of sheer subsistence was the crucial one. For hundreds of years, Christian Spain was forced to grapple with the problem of absorbing a whole society that had been cut off by force from the faith of its fathers. Without entering into a

10. See BAER, History, I, p. 197. It is impossible here to enumerate every trade in which Jews engaged. See F. CANTERA and A. GARCÍA ABAD, Sefarad, 27 (1967), pp. 39–63.

11. See, e.g., F. BAER, Die Juden im christlichen Spanien, 2 (Berlin, 1936), pp. 429–435 (JchS). R. del ARCO and F. BALAGUER, Sefarad, 9 (1949), pp. 390 ff.

12. BAER, History, passim.

13. See, e.g. the Decrees of Valladolid of 1412; BAER, JchS, 2, pp. 263 ff.

14. H. BEINART, "Judíos y Conversos en España después de la Expulsión de 1492," Hispania, 24 (1964), pp. 293 ff.

15 See H. BEINART, Conversos on Trial before the Inquisition (Tel Aviv, 1965), pp. 14 ff. (Hebrew).

discussion of the religious aspects of forced conversion, or the deep desire of Conversos to return to their ancestral faith, or their efforts to practise Judaism in secret, We shall see that the social problem of their existence remained unsolved. It is still unsolved in a way in some localities at the present day.

There is another aspect of public life on which we would dwell, and this too draws sustenance from the Jewish voluntary tradition. We have already noted how realistic the Jews were in adapting a Jewish way of life to surrounding conditions. Yet within this framework they could not always find satisfaction for all the needs of an organized community and of individuals. The need was filled by welfare and mutual help, the efforts of individuals or groups who combined to give charity and do works of mercy. When we contemplate the few records that have come down to us of these activities, we realize on what deep foundations they rested. Withal we must emphasize that nearly all the associations sprang from the lower classes of society, who felt the need for mutual aid and went on to fulfil the sacred duty of humanity reciprocally and together. It is impossible to be sure when these organizations began. First, perhaps, were the craft fellowships that joined together in charitable work. When such fellowships desired to pray together, they founded their own synagogues, thus giving added expression to the bonds that united them in the jointed fulfilment of the duty of charity. Thus we find in Saragossa[16] a fellowship of 'Doers of Mercy', another of 'Pursuers of Righteousness', a third of 'Nights of Vigil' for prayer, intercession and moral reform of the world. The 'Grave diggers' of Huesca left statutes which have survived[17] and teach something of this group devoted to works of mercy, mutual help and reciprocal duty. This combination into groups to do works of genuine mercy is also found in Christian society in Spain and sometimes among the Conversos too.[18] The Conversos of Spain drew from the source this Jewish tradition of mercy and charity.

It remains to mention among voluntary work the steps the public took to organise Torah study. There was a special tax system for this purpose,[19]

and there was a method of individual dedication for *Talmud* Torah, by which people devoted a part of their property, their capital and their income for the support of scholars and sages. They would similarly support the poor and contribute to other public needs.[20] Of special interest are the public ransoming of captives and 'bringing in the bride'. Until the Expulsion from Spain we do not find among Spanish Jewry any organization whose specific aim is the ransoming of Jewish captives or bringing brides to the marriage canopy by helping to provide their dowries.[21] Every individual in Israel helped according to his means to fulfil these sacred duties, these mitzvoth. The needs of Spanish Jewry were answered from within.

The story of the Jews in Spain, how they organized their society and how they lived together within it, is embroidered on a background of Jewish life—the rich and full life that maintained them. Their endurance of political vicissitudes, culminating in the expulsion from Spain in 1492, is a story in itself. Their inner strength, the close-woven web of their public life, the organization and social relations of their public life, the organization and social relations that prevailed among them—all these were the heritage of Spanish Jewry, which sustained and upheld them in their wanderings after the Expulsion and stood them in good stead in their exile.

THE MAKING OF MEDIEVAL SPAIN

The governments of both kingdoms lacked the information and the skilled personnel to rule their heterogeneous dominions. They each suffered from repeated internal dynastic struggles. Aragon was deeply involved in French and Mediterranean affairs. Castile dreamt of conquering North Africa and of absorbing Portugal. Once the military reconquest of the peninsula had been completed, with the deliberate exception of Granada, the wealthy families and the military orders turned their bellicose energies on one another. The nobility, on grounds of their military functions, claimed exemption from taxation, and demanded that the responsible government jobs be given to them, rather than to the small and despised

16. See BAER, *JchS*, 1, pp. 855 ff.; et Reg. s.v. Confratria. And see F. BAER, "Ur-sprung der Chewra", *Zeitschrift für jüdische Wohlwartspflege*, 1 (1929), pp. 241–247.

17. *JchS*, 1, pp. 229 ff., pp. 641 ff.

18. 55 See H. BEINART, *Conversos on Trial before the Inquisition* (Tel-Aviv, 1965), pp. 49 ff., and the bibliography there (Hebrew).

19. See, for example, the statutes of Valladolid of 1432, n. 21 *supra*.

20. See BAER, JchS, 2, pp. 156 ff.

21. See H. BEINART, "A Hebrew Formularium from Fifteenth Century Spain," *Sefunot*, 5 (1961), pp. 80 ff. (Hebrew).

bourgeoisie. Someone had to manage the sale of wool, the upkeep of forests and dry farmed estates, the care of large flocks, the supply of arms, the organization of trade fairs, the import and payment for luxuries. Someone had to have an approximate idea of the forms and extent of wealth available in different parts of the country, someone had to collect taxes, someone had to negotiate with nations which did not speak Castilian.

For the performance of these functions, exception made for the city-state of Barcelona, both kingdoms depended heavily upon the Jews. It is by no means easy to estimate the size of the medieval Jewish community. Professors Jaime Vicens Vives and Jorge Nadal, the most careful demographic historians of Spain up to the present, use a figure of 200,000 for the year 1391 (at which time the great persecutions and forced conversions began), and they speak of the reconquest of Andalusia as possibly adding 100,000 Jews to the crown of Castile. But the great Jewish historian Yitzhak Baer tells us that the tax rolls of Castile in 1290 show only 3,600 tax-paying Jewish families in the whole kingdom, which would suggest an upper limit of perhaps 20,000 Jews for Castile; since Castile was about six times as populous as Aragon-Catalonia, the total for all of Spain could hardly, extrapolating from this information, have reached 22,000. Besides which, according to Baer, there were practically no Jews in the cities of Andalusia at the time of their occupation in the 1240s. Vicens and Nadal also believe that, from the late twelfth to the early fifteenth century, the population of Spain approximately doubled, from three to six millions in the case of Castile, from 500,000 to 1,000,000 in the case of Aragon. If we make the reasonable assumption that the Jewish population also doubled in this period, such an assumption could in no way account for a jump from 20,000 to 200,000. In addition, it is as well to remember that both the Vicens-Nadal and the Baer estimates are open to challenge. Thus it would be more misleading than helpful to offer any numerical estimate. The significant point is that the Jews played a role in medieval Spain far out of proportion to their numbers, a role which can be described, and partially explained.

Jewish communities had existed in the Levant and Andalusia at least from early Roman times. They had been persecuted by the Visigoths, and on the whole had preferred to live under Muslim rule from 711 to about 1100. The emirs and caliphs of Cordoba, and the *taifa* kings, had almost all followed the enlightened Muslim policy of toleration for the 'Peoples of the Book', i.e. the Jews and the Christians, whose religions were thought of as stages on the road to the final revelation which had been given to Muhammad. Muslim law treated the Jews and Christians as separate communities with considerable internal autonomy in the administration of taxes, justice, sanitation, commercial regulations, etc. The sovereigns of the small Christian states in the early Middle Ages imitated this Islamic practice, and so, from the beginning, the *aljamas* of Leon, Castile, Navarre, Aragon and Catalonia controlled the internal administration of their villages and were collectively responsible for taxes levied by the crown.

As long as Muslim rule remained tolerant, the great majority of Spanish Jews lived in al-Andalus. But after about 1100 Almoravid and Almohad intolerance, together with the significant economic growth of the Christian kingdoms, had made northern Spain more attractive than al-Andalus. In the occupation of Toledo (1085) Alfonso VI had confirmed the existing rights of self-government enjoyed by the Muslim, Mozarabic and Jewish communities of that city. In the Ebro valley and the Levant, the new Christian rulers during the twelfth century valued and protected the middle-class functions performed by both Jews and Muslims. In Old Castile and the north the Jews faced a degree of prejudice as 'outsiders' and 'city slickers' among a sober farming population, but there were no restrictions on their right to hold land or to engage in any occupations they chose.

In relation to the Christian community the Jews were proportionately more urban in their occupations; but in view of widespread prejudice even today, the emphasis belongs on the word proportionately. They appear typically in the *aljama* records as weavers, tanners, shoemakers, dyers, carpenters, blacksmiths, saddlers, furriers, potters. Local *fueros* also specified lands which were either owned or farmed on a rental basis by Jews. Relatively few Jews were full-time soldiers, but Jewish communities living on monastic lands or those of the military orders often held frontier fortresses and had their taxes reduced for military service, just as did Christians performing similar services. Class gradations within the Jewish community were less marked than among the Christians, however, since they had no hereditary nobility and no military caste.

Jewish community life, like that of its Castilian neighbours, was marked by sober, austere standards. Marriages were usually arranged early, and without romantic courtship. Divorce policies were less liberal than those of Talmudic Palestine. There were severe penalties for adultery, and bastardy was rare. Masters were made to marry their concubines, and polygamy was tolerated, but rare. As in Christian Spain generally, there was plenty of private violence despite severe laws and punishments. In distinction from Christian Spain there was strong community support for education, and the literacy rate was much higher among Jews than among Christians. In the twelfth and early thirteenth century severe social tensions accompanied the northward migration of the Andalusian Jews, whose sophisticated urban culture made them look upon their northern coreligionists as yokels. Wealthy Andalusian Jews, whose services were doubly valuable to the kings because of their knowledge of Arabic and of Islamic politics, were frequently exempted from the legal jurisdiction and the collective tax responsibilities of the local *aljamas*. Needless to say, such privileges caused bitter jealousy. The rabbis of northern Spain also objected vehemently to the intellectual influence of Maimonides, claiming that the rationalism of his *Guide to the Perplexed* was undermining the faith of the orthodox.

Alfonso X, who was the first sovereign to rule a Castile which stretched from the Cantabrican ports to the tip of Andalusia, liked to style himself the 'King of the Three Religions'.

His father-in-law, James I of Aragon, was also equally solicitous for the welfare of his subjects of all three religions, and their successors in the fourteenth century generally affirmed similar intentions. This was a matter of both personal enlightenment and political necessity. European as well as Muslim legal conceptions treated the religious communities as separate bodies owing allegiance to a common king, but not held together by any 'national' bond. The Jews, a very small minority never amounting, by the highest estimates, to more than 4 per cent of the population, were literally the property of the crown. It was in the interest of the king to protect that property as he would any other valuables; conversely, at times of revolt against the king, armed rebels would attack the Jews as a way of attacking the king.

Quite aside from their availability as crown property, the Jews were the natural intermediaries between Muslim and Christian Spain. The educated among them often spoke both Arabic and Castilian, and many Jews had family connections in both parts of Spain. Perhaps more important: at the intuitive, non-verbal, level Jewish culture occupied an intermediate position between that of the Muslim south and the Christian north. The Jews resembled the Christians in their emphasis on monogamy, their communal anxiety about intermarriage, their stress on the virtues of work and sobriety and the greater dignity they accorded women in their laws and social customs. They resembled the Muslims in their urban culture, their artisan skills, their philosophical

speculations, their scientific and scholarly pursuits. Certain elements in the church, and the fervour generated by the crusades, always constituted a latent threat of persecution. But in the eleventh and twelfth century the Jews were not subjected to legal disabilities in Christian Spain.

During the thirteenth century contradictory currents prevailed. On the one hand the majority of ordinary Jews continued the artisan and agricultural functions which had long been characteristic of them. They also participated in the reconquest of Andalusia, and were rewarded with land and houses, just as were the Christian participants. But the Albigensian crusade in France, and the rise of the mendicant orders, produced a new wave of intolerance within the church itself. Pope Innocent III and his successors multiplied their warnings to the kings of Aragon and Castile not to trust the Jews, and the Dominican friars called insistently for mass conversions. But toleration was both traditional and necessary for the Spanish sovereigns, and so, while they made verbal, and even legal, concessions to the pressure of the church militant, they continued on the whole to employ Jewish officials and to protect the established Jewish communities.

Perhaps the most valued field of Jewish service to Christian sovereigns and lords was finance. Here too, because of deeply rooted anti-Semitic traditions based upon ignorance and false emphasis, it is essential to understand the entire context. The church forbade Christians to lend money to one another for interest. The Talmud laid a similar prohibition upon Jews with regard to their co-religionists. But Jews and Christians were free to lend money to each other. It was customary for Jews, Christians and Muslims as well to form partnerships in order to be able to invest in, and share the profits of, each other's business ventures without engaging in 'usury'. It was equally customary, in cases where businessmen found it absolutely necessary to lend money to their co-religionists, for a Christian to act as broker for a loan between Jews and for a Jew to act as broker for a loan between Christians.

The need for loans at interest was well recognized. The rates were indeed usurious by modern standards. The Cortes of Barcelona in the thirteenth century fixed the maximum at 20 per cent, and under Alfonso X the Castilian rate stood at 33 per cent. The relatively lower Catalan rate reflects the greater commercial development of Catalonia in comparison with Castile, but the lack of stable currency, of safe roads or shipping lanes and of sure legal recourse in case of theft, accounts for the steep percentages in comparison with modern bank rates. Christians, including clerics, lent money at interest. There was nothing about either the practice or the rates which was distinctively Jewish.

The military orders and the great landed magnates frequently employed Jews to supervise both the general economy and the financial needs of their estates. The kings, having nothing resembling a bureau of internal revenue, depended upon tax-farming—the practice of contracting with an individual who would collect taxes on behalf of the king, and receive an agreed commission payment for such service. A high proportion of the tax-farmers was Jewish, not because the kings so desired, but because, as they frequently complained, Christians did not offer themselves as candidates for this dangerous and unpopular occupation. It seems also to be true, on the basis of scattered records (which are nevertheless consistent with each other), that the Jewish communities paid a very high proportion of the total taxes collected by the kings of Castile and Aragon. Thus the tax registers of the crown of Aragon for the year 1294 indicate that the Jews paid 22 per cent of all the taxes collected. The Jews could not have constituted more than 3 to 4 per cent of the population, nor does the register include special levies such as those for diplomatic missions, royal journeys and marriages, etc.

Financial transactions led naturally to other forms of social contact between Christians and Jews. Jews were often godfathers and baptismal witnesses for Christian associates, and Christians frequently witnessed circumcisions and marriages. In small towns as well as among wealthy families, business contracts and wills were often notarized by both a Jewish and a Christian official. Among the wealthiest families of both communities intermarriage became increasingly frequent from the thirteenth century onwards, a practice frowned on by the religious authorities and by the common man in both communities.

The Jews in Spain might prosper, and might enjoy close business and personal relations with Christians, but they could never feel truly secure. In the late twelfth century Almohad raids along the frontier were often attributed to Jewish intrigues, and resulted in violence against the *aljamas*. When Alfonso IX of Leon died in 1230, resistance to the re-unification of Leon and Castile included attacks on the Jews, in this case accused of supporting Castilian centralism. The thirteenth-century kings vacillated in their policies. James I of Aragon considered himself a friend of the Jews, a tolerant and enlightened sovereign. When he occupied the kingdom of Valencia he granted important trading concessions in grain, oil and cattle to the Jews, and allowed them to retain their own quarter in the capital city. Jewish farmers in the Levant, like their Christian counterparts, depended on the labour of Muslim serfs. One of the ways that such serfs could become free men was to become Christians. The king heeded the request of the Jewish landlords to curb the proselytizing efforts of the church and to make manumission more difficult. But in 1254 (the same year in which Louis IX of France, newly returned from the crusade, expelled the Jews and cancelled all debts to them) James confiscated for the crown all debts owed to the Jews of Aragon, 'for the salvation of our soul', and to punish alleged violations of royal edicts.

Alfonso X of Castile also considered himself a friend of the Jews, awarding land, houses and mills to Toledo Jews in the resettlement of Seville, and treating the local Andalusian Jews as if they were Christians. But his policies were inconsistent, to say the least. In Murcia, where the Muslim population was large and restive, and where he could surely have used the cooperation of a satisfied Jewish community, he did not permit Jews to reside in the Christian quarter of the city. Legislation written under his direction included restrictions on business dealings between Jews and Christians, though no serious attempt was made to enforce such restrictions. One of the great Jewish civil servants of the time, Solomon Ibn Zadok of Toledo, had collected the tribute of Granada for Ferdinand III and been the chief tax-collector for Alfonso X. When he died in 1273 all his real estate and accumulated goods in Seville warehouses were confiscated for the benefit of the cathedral of Seville.

No permanent dishonour may have been intended. Solomon's son Isaac, known in Castilian as D. Zag de la Maleha, also served as chief tax-farmer. But when royal funds were lost during the civil war between Alfonso X and his son, the future Sancho IV, the king was quick to see Jewish treason. Thus, in 1278, he ordered D. Zag to deliver a large sum of money to the Alfonsine forces besieged in Algeciras. When the partisans of prince Sancho got hold of the money, Alfonso imprisoned all the Jewish tax-farmers of Castile. D. Zag himself was hanged, and a group of wealthy Sevillian Jews were held hostage in their synagogue until they could raise a ransom of some 4,380,000 *maravedis* (twice the total annual contributions normally collected from the *aljamas* of Castile). Doubtless both James I and Alfonso X saw no inconsistency in their behaviour. They felt nothing but admiration and friendship for Jews who were their faithful servants, and who contributed signally to the prosperity of their domains. But as the church ceaselessly emphasized, Jews could never be completely trusted, and their transgressions must be sternly punished by a king responsible for the material and spiritual welfare of three religious communities.

Besides their important economic functions the Jews at the court of Alfonso X played an essential role in the development of Spanish literary and intellectual life. The Jews of Christian Spain did not produce great creative figures of their own in the thirteenth century. Rather, they offered to Castile and Aragon the entire heritage of Islamic and Hebrew culture, as it had flourished steadily in al-Andalus from the ninth to the twelfth century. King Alfonso was much interested in astronomy and applied science, and in history, in so far as it might contribute to the glory of Castile and to his hopes of becoming Holy Roman Emperor. He was interested also in Roman law, especially since it might be used in the codification of the disparate *fueros*, and might enhance the prestige and authority of the monarchy rather than the local nobility. The Jews had already translated the Old Testament into Castilian, making it in some ways the language of their spiritual life, whereas the Christians were still using only Latin for such purposes.

The Jewish development of Castilian as an intellectual vehicle, together with their knowledge of Arabic and Hebrew, made them eager collaborators of a sovereign enthusiastic to make learned works available to his people in their own language. Jewish scholars, compilers and editors played a role comparable with that of the *philosophes* of eighteenth-century France. They translated into Castilian the major astronomical, mathematical, botanical, medical and philosophical works of the Arab world. The famous *Alphonsine Tables* were the work of two Jewish astronomers, who dedicated their book to the king, and who told him that his reign should be considered the start of a new era, just as the Greeks had based their chronology on the reign of Alexander, and the Romans theirs on the rule of Caesar. French and Italian scholars were imported to translate major Latin works, and to collaborate on the *Grande e General Estoria* which was the first national history published in a European vernacular language. As the great twentieth-century Spanish scholar Americo Castro has pointed out, Castilian became, through the collaboration of Alfonso X and the Jews of his court, the natural vehicle for a high intellectual culture combining the heritages of Islam, Judaism and Romano-Germanic Europe.

D. From the Reconquest to the Spain of Empire—From the Middle Ages to the Seventeenth Century

The Moors indeed quickly overran most of Spain after their arrival in the year 711, only to have their European conquest halted across the Pyrenees in France by Charles Martel in the battle of Poitiers (also called the battle of Tours) in the year 732. The Islamic forces retreated to their Spanish base, not bothering to subdue the few small bands of the Visigothic Christians hiding in the mountainous regions of northern Spain. This decision—not to conquer the remaining Christian strongholds—turned out to be a grave tactical error, for these last Visigothic holdouts soon reorganized and charged south into Muslim Spain.

The *Reconquista* or period of the Spanish *Reconquest* was born, a war that would last eight centuries, leading up to the final surrender of the Moors at Granada in 1492. The alleged discovery in Galicia of the remains of St. James (Santiago), the apostle of Christ, who, according to the faithful, brought Christianity to Spain during Roman times, increased the religious fervor of the fighting Christian forces. (The Moors, for their religious inspiration, claimed to have a bone from the arm of the Prophet Mohammed in the great mosque of Córdoba). As the Spanish moved south, the kingdom of Castile grew to be the most powerful Christian state, a new nation of three cultures—Christians, Moors, and the Jews. Two central figures of the Reconquest are the eleventh-century Castilian knight El Cid (Rodrigo Díaz de Vivar) and the thirteenth-century King of Castile Alfonso X, El Sabio (the Wise, or Learned).

With the fall of Granada and final victory over the Moors by the Catholic monarchs Isabella and Ferdinand in 1492, Spain became the first great European power. As the royal couple took up residence in the Alhambra Palace, Christopher Columbus arrived to propose exploration to the west; the future "Admiral of the Ocean Sea" recommended a new trading route to Japan and China. Thus, the encounter with the Americas and the exploitation of this new land's wealth and peoples gave Spain a new glory that would last through the seventeenth century, when its decline from the world stage was apparent as other nations—especially France and England—claimed European hegemony.

Spain fought numerous foreign wars and wasted the New World's gold and silver on extravagances at home, throughout the reigns of Charles V, Phillip II, and the weak monarchs of the Spanish Baroque (seventeenth century). Carlos Fuentes sums up Spain's fortune during this time by saying that "Spain was poor because Spain was rich"—she squandered all the resources that came into the treasury. Spanish culture, however, flourished in a period we now call the Golden Age of Spain. During this time lived some of the greatest Spanish writers such as Cervantes, Lope de Vega, María de Zayas, Santa Teresa, and Tirso de Molina, as well as the painters El Greco and Velázquez. In all, using the metaphor employed by John A. Crow in *Spain: The Root and the Flower*, the waning Spanish Empire was like a garden full of weeds, but here and there arose brilliant flowers—Spain's magnificent cultural attributes during an age of decline.

1. RECONQUEST

The regions of Spain that successfully resisted the Muslim invaders were in the far north of the peninsula, mountainous, and poor. The earliest success noted by chroniclers occurred in Asturias, where a refugee Visigothic nobleman, Pelayo, rallied local tribesmen. In 718, at the caves of Covadonga in the Picos de Europa, he defeated Moors sent to pursue him. The Asturians acclaimed him king. Before he died in 737, he made his capital at Cangas de Onís. His heirs consolidated their rule over Asturias, and Alfonso I (739–757) extended it into Galicia after its Berber garrison mutinied and withdrew. Alfonso led raids into the Duero Valley and turned its northern reaches into a no-man's land. In 810, King Alfonso II "the Chaste" moved his capital to Oviedo, a stronghold that covered the passes south. Outside Oviedo stands the tiny but remarkable Romanesque church of Santa María de Naranca, built around 840 as a royal hall and consecrated in 905 as a church.

For the Asturian kings, literate churchmen claimed legitimate rule over Christian Visigothic Hispania, however far-fetched that claim seemed in the ninth century. Around 813 a patron saint was found, with the location of the reputed tomb of Santiago (St. James the Greater), in Galicia. The shrine built over it, known as Santiago de Compostela, became the goal of a renowned medieval pilgrimage. Along the road to Santiago, which began in central France, crossed the Pyrenees, and proceeded west through Burgos and León, sprang churches, monasteries, and cathedrals. The surviving shrine is one of Europe's finest twelfth-century Romanesque churches, with an eighteenth-century Baroque facade.

Christian principalities also emerged in the Pyrenees, while from the Frankish kingdom Charlemagne led several incursions into Spain and established a Spanish March based on Barcelona. His expedition of 778 is famous for the ambush in the Pass of Roncesvalles of his rearguard, commanded by Count Roland and immortalized in Old French by the epic *La Chanson de Roland*. Basques from Pamplona, rather than Muslim warriors, were the likely culprits. Although it was not mentioned in the epic, Charlemagne had destroyed the walls of Pamplona before he withdrew into France. The Pamplonans destroyed Roland and his rearguard in retaliation.

In the same years, Christianity revived among the region's population, which gave a new dimension to the border conflicts. Powerful Christian Basque families, supported by Frankish Aquitaine, wrested Navarre from local Muslim strongmen. In the Pyrenean valley of the river Aragón the town of Jaca many have been occupied by Christians as early as 760, but not until after 800 is the county of Aragón heard of. Other Pyrenean counties, some originally dependent on Frankish Toulouse and Aquitaine, included Ribagorza, Sobrarbe, Pallars, and Urgell.

Against these petty Christian principalities, Muslim Spain arrayed a chain of strongholds along the Duero and Ebro Rivers. Their governors did not always obey the emirs of Córdoba but often pursued their own interests in the vicissitudes of border warfare. Emir Abd-al-Rahman II led or sent forces north almost annually to harass the Christian north. When Vikings sacked Seville in 844, he defeated them and drove them from the country. He apparently fell victim to a harem intrigue, and his heir Muhammad I (852–886) was distracted by rebellions.

Christian rulers took advantage of the situation to gain territory through stubborn persistence. Asturian kings began to repopulate the area around León, not only with northerners but with Mozarabs from Andalusia, who drifted north to escape persecu-

tions they sometimes courted. Alfonso III the Great (866–910) pushed Galicia's frontier into today's Portugal and tightened his grip over the northern half of the valley of the Duero. Around 882 he founded Burgos.

Aid from France fell off when Charlemagne's empire broke up. A band of Moorish raiders, supported by Córdoba, established a base on the French coast, not far from Marseilles. The counts of Barcelona, in theory vassals of France, were on their own. Vifredo the Hairy (d. 898), the semilegendary founder of independent Catalonia, combined his own inheritance of Urgell with the counties of Barcelona, Vich, Gerona, Ripoll, and Cerdanya. He pushed the frontier south to the sawtooth massif of Montserrat, where in the next century the historic Benedictine monastery of the Black Madonna appeared. Few areas in Europe are so rich in Romanesque monasteries and churches as the slopes of the Pyrenees in Catalonia.

In al-Andalus unrest persisted but mainly affected the elites, and Andalusia prospered in spite of them. When Abd-al-Rahman III became emir of Córdoba in 912, he spent his first twenty years quelling rebellions. He also battled the rulers of León and Navarre, who raided deep into Muslim Spain in search of plunder. In 920 he defeated the Leonese and in 924 sacked Pamplona. As he reasserted his authority in Spain, the unity of the world of Islam shredded. In 909 the Fatimid ruler of Tunis broke with the Abbasid caliph of Baghdad and claimed caliphal authority for himself. In 929, Abd-al-Rahman took the same step, invoking his Umayyad descent, and established the caliphate of Córdoba. Vested with the authority of caliph, he eliminated the last rebellions in al-Andalus.

In 932 King Ramiro II of León (931–951) crossed the Sierra de Guadarrama to sack Madrid, then a Muslim fortress. In 939, Abd-al-Rahman marched with a vast host to destroy León in what he called his "campaign of omnipotence." King Ramiro, Fernán González, count of Castile, and Toda, queen-mother of Navarre, rallied their people and on August 1, 939, at Simancas on the Duero defeated the caliph's "omnipotent" host.

Castile formed a new element in the struggle. As rulers of León extended their sway eastward along the north bank of the Duero and headwaters of the Ebro, they were checked by Moorish strongholds at Zaragoza and Medinaceli. Holding the land they had occupied and providing protection for the people who worked its soil required castles—and lots of them. Castles soon dotted the countryside and gave the region its name, Castile. Around 930 the king of León appointed Fernán González count of Castile. An ambitious border lord, Fernán González added to the region's population and took advantage of the fluid situation to make himself virtually independent.

Because of the dangers of frontier life, fighting men given lands by grateful princes had to offer generous terms to peasants who worked the soil and herded the animals. Castilian peasants remained free people; serfdom was not for them. When unhappy with their lord, peasants easily found another lord who would protect them. In some cases princes let the peasant settlers choose their lord. Landholding arrangements were many. A few owned land from time immemorial. Because much of the frontier had been a no-man's land, many acquired land by squatter's rights, secured by money payment to some higher authority. Lords usually ended up with a domain that included some land of their own, for which they usually made sharecropping arrangements with peasants, and lands owned by others, over which lords enjoyed seigneurial jurisdiction. They provided justice, collected fines, and charged dues for administration and defense. Payments were often in kind, and much business was done through barter, though money did circulate in Spain. Some of what lords collected they might have to pass on to the count or king, whose treasuries were still hoards. The moving frontier also affected lord and peasant relations in regions where serfdom had survived from Roman and Visigothic times, since lords often needed to offer their peasants freer conditions to prevent them from running off in search of something better.

Town life, which had been limited in Christian Spain, also quickened. Towns had been few and small in the north and west, although centers for commerce and markets did exist, and new towns appeared alongside those rebuilt on Roman foundations. Defense was the prime motive, since a concentration of people could build fortifications and provide centers of resistance to raids and shelter for peasants who worked the fields. *Burgos* basically means "fort." Valladolid seems to have begun as a Moorish stronghold. Rulers offered extensive privileges to the men and women who revived or established towns.

Both Burgos and Valladolid claim to speak the purest Castilian, which employs the *theta* sound for *c* before *e* and *i*, and the letter *z*; and often turns the Latin *f* into *h*, unique phenomena among Romance languages. Linguistic scholars believe it related to a local pre-Roman language, or perhaps Basque. Not until later did the Castilian dialect become the language of the court.

Abd-al-Rahman III maintained pressure on the Christian north, but his claim to be caliph embroiled him in North Africa, as it would his successor Hakam II (961–976). Against Christian rulers, Hakam alternated diplomacy and force. When he died, his heir, eleven-year-old Hisham II (976–1013), succeeded to the caliphate after his mother and his tutor conspired to strangle his uncle. By 981 the tutor, best known to history as al-Mansur ("the Victorious," 940–1002), eliminated all rivals and gained dictatorial power. He let Hisham reign as a figurehead and indulged him with pleasures. Once he had the upper hand in North Africa, al-Mansur turned on the Christian principalities of the north. Each summer he sent expeditions to keep them at bay, while exercising diplomacy to break up their leagues and force tribute from them. His most famous expedition sacked Santiago de Compostela in 997. Christians taken captive were paraded through Córdoba carrying the cathedral bells, to the delight of the Muslim mob.

When he died in 1002, the sheer power of the caliphate of Córdoba had reached its apogee, but its foundations were fragile. Al-Mansur controlled the bureaucracy through loyal slaves, and he used Slavic slaves and Berbers to man his large and costly armies. None of this was popular with the local elites or larger population. His eldest son held things together but died suddenly in 1008. His younger son, nicknamed Sanchuelo, lost the support of the army and was murdered. Hisham was dethroned and restored. Muslim dissidents, Catalan Christians, and mutinous Berbers sacked Córdoba and destroyed the caliph's summer palace. Over the next twenty years, more than a half-dozen Umayyad kinsmen claimed to be caliph, supported by this or that faction, till the last, Hisham III, was deposed in 1031 and hustled off to obscurity.

In the power vacuum created by the collapse of the caliphate, ambitious commanders and ever-restless local oligarchs took over the urban centers of al-Andalus. Muslim Spain splintered into some thirty *taifas* or faction-states, each with its own ruler. In Spanish history, they customarily appear as petty kings. Among the more important *taifa* kingdoms were Seville, Badajoz (which held much of Portugal), Córdoba, Granada, Málaga, Almería, Murcia, Denia (which included the Balearic Islands), Valencia, and Zaragoza. Despite the fragmentation of political authority, the economic prosperity of al-Andalus continued, and the cultural momentum acquired under the caliphs attained new heights in poetry, architecture, philosophy, and science. The initiative, however, was about to shift to the backward Christian north.

Most of the Christian principalities of the north had come, through inheritance or conquest, under the sway of Sancho III the Great, king of Navarre (1004–1035), save for Galicia and the county of Barcelona. Both Navarre and Barcelona benefited from developments north of the Pyrenees, which included the revival of the Church by the monks of

Cluny in France and the use of mailed knights on big horses to overpower enemies on the battlefield. By means of shrewd diplomacy, Navarre suffered least from the annual campaigns of al-Mansur.

Sancho's eldest son, García, inherited Navarre. Another son, Fernando, count of Castile (1029–1065), married the heiress of León and in 1038 combined Castile with León. Another, Ramiro, was given Aragón with the title king, to which he added Ribagorza and Sobrarbe on the death of his brother Gonzalo. Medieval proprietary monarchy was taking form. A region and its people, with the obligations to provide government, justice, and defense, became a form of property to be passed from parents to children. It was not the republic—*res publica*, "public thing"—of the Romans, although the word was still used. Nor was the office of ruler elective, as it had been for the Visigoths, although powerful lords, with some legal support, reserved the right to make or unmake a ruler if a family line died out or a ruler failed to rule effectively. Most churchmen, given the circumstances of the times, agreed that hereditary monarchy provided more stability than elective monarchy, and they blessed rulers with the concept that he or she ruled "by the Grace of God."

By now, we have already seen enough names of kings and dates of reigns, and we shall see more. Do not despair. The destinies of their countless subjects were intertwined with theirs, with their successes and their failures. Their names and dates are convenient devices for historians to summarize in few words situations and developments that involved infinitely more than the printed page can sustain.

Although once more fragmented, the Christian north had become tougher through the new military techniques and religious revival and confronted an even more fragmented al-Andalus, weakened by faction and lulled by prolonged economic prosperity. We have reached that fluid moment in Spain's history when a personality like El Cid could flourish. Not long after his death in 1099, El Cid (sidi, "lord," from Arabic sayyid) became the subject of epic poetry and historical chronicle. The greatest, *The Poem of My Cid (El poema del mio Cid)*, appeared in Castilian no later than 1207, although it lay till 1779 in a remote monastery near Burgos. The historic Cid was born Rodrigo Díaz in the town of Vivar, near Burgos, according to tradition, not long after 1040, with 1043 most likely. His father was connected to the court of Castile and placed Rodrigo in the household of Prince Sancho, where he learned letters as well as military skills. By 1063 he was in battle alongside Sancho, who aided the emir of Zaragoza against King Ramiro of Aragón. Ramiro, founder of the

kingdom of Aragón, was fatally wounded. Sancho's father, King Fernando I, died in 1065 and once more divided his kingdoms. Sancho became king of Castile. The second son, Alfonso, became king of León, and the youngest, García, king of Galicia. An unedifying family saga follows. In 1071, Sancho and Alfonso despoiled García of Galicia. Sancho next forced Alfonso into exile at Toledo. Then partisans of Alfonso and their sister Urraca, who took Alfonso's side, murdered Sancho. Opinion blamed Urraca and Alfonso, who hurried from Toledo to claim both Castile and León. The legend grew that Rodrigo Díaz, before pledging fealty to Alfonso, made him swear that he had no part in Sancho's murder. Alfonso VI (1072–1109) would prove a successful king, but in tales of El Cid, he comes off as a scoundrel.

At first Rodrigo served Alfonso, but according to the poem, Rodrigo's enemies at court persuaded Alfonso to exile him. A case can be made that Rodrigo exceeded his authority. In the epic, he leaves his family behind and with his followers heads for the borderlands. The epic is rich in the names of places that still exist. In it, Rodrigo plundered Moorish strongholds and sent gifts to King Alfonso. Fact suggests that he served the emir of Zaragoza for pay against the count of Barcelona and the king of Aragón. His successes earned him acclaim as a war leader, "El Cid."

In 1085 King Alfonso VI occupied Toledo. The fall of a leading *taifa* capital alarmed other *taifa* rulers, who summoned help from the Almoravids of North Africa. Recent converts to Islam, the Almoravids formed a zealous and puritanical sect and had conquered the western Sahara and Morocco. Yusuf, Almoravid chief and founder of Marrakech, crossed to Spain in 1086 with a disciplined host of Senegalese, Berber, and desert warriors. At Sagrajas, near Badajoz, he defeated Alfonso, who escaped and clung to Toledo. Yusuf became distracted by developments in Morocco and did not return to Spain until 1090. Muslim zealots formed Almoravid parties in the *taifa* kingdoms, denounced the laxity of their rulers, and favored Yusuf's empire.

Alfonso reconciled with El Cid and sent him to assist the *taifa* kinglet of Valencia, a foe of Yusuf's. When Yusuf's partisans threatened to seize Valencia in 1094, El Cid took it for himself. His defense of Valencia features prominently in the poem. After his death in 1099, his wife Jimena had to abandon it. But El Cid did well: Jimena retired comfortably and his daughters married into the princely houses of Navarre and Barcelona. Tales of their marriages to the Infantes (princes) of Carrión, their humiliation, and El Cid's revenge are fiction.

Attitudes and religious feelings in the Spain of El Cid were changing rapidly. In the year of his death, crusaders stormed Jerusalem. In Spain, the Almoravids revived the jihad, holy war, and the Christians responded. In 1086 Alfonso went back on his generous terms to the Muslims of Toledo. He allowed the destruction of Toledo's Great Mosque and its replacement with a Christian cathedral. The Almoravids were tolerant of neither Mozarab Christians nor Jews. The days of ambitious border lords fighting on both sides were largely past. The southward advance of the Christian states became the *Reconquista*, the Reconquest, under the banner of the Cross. "*¡Cierra, Santiago y España!*"—"Close for Santiago and Spain!"—became their battle cry.

The disintegration of the Almoravid empire over the next generation, coupled with succession squabbles among the Christian kingdoms, allowed the taifa kingdoms to revive. Their legendary luxury continued, and the intellectual life of al-Andalus reached new peaks. The most influential thinker was Averroës, born in Córdoba in 1126. A distinguished physician he served the Almohad rulers of al-Andalus and died in 1198 at their court in Marrakech. He is most famous for his commentaries on Aristotle, which had a profound impact on medieval Christian philosophy. Another renowned thinker and physician was Moses Maimonides (1135–1204), the best-known Jewish philosopher of the Middle Ages and author of *Guide for the Perplexed*. His family hailed from Córdoba, but Almoravid intolerance caused them to relocate, first in Spain and later to Morocco. He spent most of his career in Cairo. The twelfth would be the last century of cultural greatness for al-Andalus, to which Granada would provide but an afterglow. When the Almohads, who supplanted the Almoravids in Morocco, began to intervene in the defense of al-Andalus from the Christians, they drew their chief support from Muslim zealots who shared the intolerance of the Almoravids.

Alfonso VI outlived El Cid by ten years. Although he held on to Toledo, he suffered a series of defeats on the battlefield, and at the disaster at Uclés in 1109, he lost his only son. His daughter, Queen Urraca (1109–1126), succeeded him. Widow of a knight-adventurer, Raymond of Burgundy, Urraca was succeeded by her son Alfonso VII (1126–1157), aged twenty-one. Determined to restore the glory and preeminence of the kingdom of León, Alfonso had himself crowned emperor in 1135 at the cathedral of León. His imperial pretensions had little effect. In 1139 his cousin Afonso Enriques, prince of Portugal (1128–1185), proclaimed himself king of Portugal and in time won papal confirmation. Their grandfather Alfonso VI had given the frontier region of Portugal to his illegitimate daughter Teresa and her husband Henry of Burgundy (Raymond's cousin). Teresa inspired their son's desire for an independent kingdom, which he achieved.

While Portugal became independent, Aragón became bigger. King Alfonso the Battler (1104–1134) conquered Zaragoza in 1118 and pushed his frontier ever southward. In a daring raid on Granada, he liberated a large number of Mozarabs, whom he resettled in his own kingdom. When he died, Navarre chose a French dynasty, while the Aragonese persuaded Alfonso's brother Ramiro, a monk, to leave the monastic life and become their king. Ramiro II the Monk (1135–1137) reigned long enough to marry and sire a daughter, Petronilla. She was betrothed to Ramón Berenguer IV, count of Barcelona (1131–1162), with Aragón as her dowry. Ramiro retired to his monastery, and Ramón Berenguer became the effective ruler of the potent federation of Aragón and Catalonia. Because Aragón was a kingdom, it gave the federation its name. Historians refer to the federation as the Crown of Aragon to keep the inland kingdom, with its Castilian dialect, apart from the Catalan-speaking county. The kingdom, its capital at Zaragoza, and the county, its capital at Barcelona, each kept its separate laws and institutions and were held together by their ruler only in personal union.

This established a precedent for Spain's future growth. The kings of greater Aragon usually reigned from Barcelona, the booming seaport that made Catalonia wealthy. By contrast, the economy of old Aragón was rural based on the agriculture of the valleys of the Ebro and its tributaries and herding in the mountains. In the Ebro valley many Muslims, under Christian rule called *mudéjares* (Mudejars), remained to work the soil. Catalonia also had an agricultural base, which was marginally richer than old Aragón's. Both had an active warrior nobility whose feudal relationships among themselves, a pyramid of lords and vassals, approximated the feudal system of France and differed from the seigneurial system of Castile and León, with its direct tie between the king and every lord. The nobles of Aragón and Catalonia also enjoyed a firm legal grip over their peasants whose status was closer to that of the serfs of France than to that of the relatively free villagers of Castile. The roots of Aragonese feudalism and serfdom are Frankish.

Ramón Berenguer added Lérida and Tortosa to his dominions but also became involved in the politics of Provence, where his nephew was count and with Italy, through the maritime ambitions of Barcelona. His son, Alfonso II, continued to pursue dynastic interests in Provence which embroiled Aragon in the conflicts of southern France.

The would-be emperor, Alfonso VII of León, divided his own inheritance and bestowed Castile upon his eldest son, Sancho III (1157–1158), and León on his youngest, Fernando II (1157–1188). Sancho's early death and his succession by Alfonso VIII (1158–1214), aged three, left the field to Fernando. Fernando backed Alfonso in Castile but compensated himself with territory. He repopulated his kingdom south of the Duero and revived Salamanca. He pushed his frontiers southward beyond Badajoz, and has encouraged the establishment of Spanish crusading orders. Already Knights Templar and Knights of St. John served in Spain. The Spanish orders began with the Knights of Calatrava, followed by the Knights of Santiago. The Knights of Alcántara appeared soon after. The orders were given strongholds that still rise stark on the Spanish landscape and were endowed with lands and peasants, *encomiendas* (commanderies), to support their crusading activities. *Encomiendas* made the orders rich and careers in them desirable for younger sons of nobles, who did not fancy becoming monks and whose older brothers inherited the family estates. Knights took the monastic vows of poverty, chastity, and obedience but changed St. Benedict's injunction from "work and pray" to "fight and pray."

Fernando II had trouble with Portugal, which feared his pretensions, as well as with Castile and Aragon. In a series of meetings, he and the other rulers came to agreements regarding the conquest of Moorish Spain, temporarily shored up by the Almohads. Each Christian kingdom was basically allotted the territory south of its current border to conquer. When Alfonso IX (1188–1230) succeeded Fernando to the Leonese throne, he was only eighteen. To win support against rival factions and foreign threats, he summoned to León an assembly that included clergy, nobles, and townsmen and was called the *Cortes*, the name still used for Spain's parliament. It was arguably the first parliament in Europe. The Cortes came to meet frequently in medieval Spain and gave urban interests a voice against the powerful landed nobility.

Alfonso IX had territorial differences with his cousin Alfonso VIII of Castile, but under papal pressure, the two cousins renewed the crusade against the Almohads. In 1195 the Castilians suffered a crushing defeat at Alarcos, when the Leonese failed to appear. Infuriated, Alfonso of Castile allied with Portugal against Alfonso of León, who in turn allied with the Almohads. When the pope intervened in 1197, Alfonso of León yielded. He married Alfonso of Castile's eldest daughter, Berenguela, and undertook a pilgrimage to Santiago as penance. But when the Church preached a crusade in 1212, León did not heed the call. Alfonso of Castile, joined by Pedro II of Aragon and Afonso II of Portugal, did and led Spain's crusaders to victory at Las Navas de Tolosa, shattering the power of the Almohads. The Christian allies had developed a devastating combination of heavy and light cavalry, backed by infantry, that routed the Almohad light horsemen and opened al-Andalus to conquest.

After Alfonso of Castile died, followed by his only son, Castile passed to Fernando III (1217–1252), son of Berenguela and Alfonso of León. In 1230, on Alfonso IX's death, Fernando permanently united the two kingdoms of Castile and León. Fernando III the Saint, after whom California's San Fernando mission and valley are named, conquered Córdoba (1236), Murcia (1243), Jaén (1246), and Seville (1248). When he captured Seville, he mocked his Muslim enemies by riding his horse up the massive Giralda tower, the minaret for Seville's Great Mosque.

The vanquished Moors retained only the mountainous kingdom of Granada, where most Andalusian Muslims eventually relocated. For Fernando, his triumphant warriors, and their successors, the big task was to repopulate and make the lands they had won productive. In the time it took, much of the long and arduous work of the Moors to irrigate the valley of the Guadalquivir and make it rich came undone. It was several centuries before western Andalusia again approached the population and prosperity of its Moorish days, and even then, its production focused on a few cash crops, such as olives, wine, and to a lesser extent, grains. The number of livestock using the land for grazing increased greatly.

From the opening of the Duero valley to the conquest of western Andalusia, the repopulation of Christian Spain had centered on cities, towns, and villages. This was both in the Mediterranean tradition and necessary for security on a shifting frontier. Isolated homesteads and hamlets were rare, save in the more secure far north. In the earlier years of the reconquest, people who migrated to newly conquered frontier regions insisted on their liberties and privileges (*fueros*). Towns and villages in Castile had became relatively self-governing under their councils, mostly elected by householders (*vecinos*), although the kings or *señores* retained ultimate jurisdiction over them. Spanish women, too, enjoyed specific rights in a land where female succession to the crown or lordships was possible in the absence of brothers. Women did, in a rough and tumble world, need strong husbands. Marriage was the norm, and the only other option was the religious life. Widows succeeded husbands as heads of households while their children were minors, and women's dowries gave them rights. Fathers, whether from love, family pride, or both, remained concerned for their daughters even after they had married. El Cid's legendary pursuit of the Infantes who abused his daughters, their wives, is a case in point.

In newly conquered Andalusia, however, privileged towns and villages were less numerous and the rights of their inhabitants less secure. The Castilian and Leonese nobles who participated in its conquest acquired vast estates, and *latifundios* prevailed. The Spanish peasants who replaced the Moors in the south became in general more dependent on their *señores*, for whom they usually labored by the day, rather than tend plots of their own.

After the spectacular surge of reconquest under Fernando III, his son Alfonso X (1252–1284), known as "the Learned," presided over the flowering of medieval Castilian culture from the lovely alcázar (citadel) of Seville. Alfonso wrote and collected poetry, although Galician rather than Castilian was the favored poetic language. He had histories written and, in his most significant achievement, had the laws of the kingdom codified in the *Siete Partidas* (Seven Sections). Although the Cortes did not ratify the *Siete Partidas* until later, they became the foundation for legal training and affected judicial decisions. In Toledo a school of translators flourished who transmitted Arab philosophy and science to Christian Europe, including Averroës's commentaries on Aristotle. Spain's first universities appeared at Salamanca and Valladolid.

Alfonso wasted his energies seeking election as Holy Roman Emperor by appeals to the pope and German princes. His sons began to jostle for power after his eldest died, leaving behind two boys, the Infantes de la Cerda. Alfonso's last years were troubled by conflict with his oldest surviving son, Sancho el Bravo, who was determined to displace his nephews. On Alfonso's death, Sancho IV donned the crown. Civil war with his nephews and other brothers, and their ambitious supporters, erupted at once. Aragon, Portugal, and France became involved. Sancho held his own but died in 1295, leaving the crown to his son Fernando IV, aged ten. Fernando's mother, María de Molina, proved herself one of the more remarkable women in Spanish history, as she manipulated noble and urban factions in the Cortes and parried the ambitions of foreign princes till Fernando came of age. He did not last long. Marching to conquer Granada, he took sick and died. From retirement María de Molina emerged to defend the rights of her one-year-old grandson, Alfonso XI (1312–1350), against untrustworthy kinsmen, among them Infante Don Juan Manuel (1282–1348), political theorist, poet, and warrior. After she died in 1321, the kingdom nearly came apart. Alfonso came of age in 1325, and with the cooperation of the Cortes, he restored effective government. In 1340 at the Rio Salado, he smashed the last major Moorish invasion of Spain from North Africa. In 1350 he died of the Great Plague that swept Europe.

The Great Plague hit Barcelona, the heart of Aragonese power, hard and plunged it and Catalonia into a long depression. In the years after Las Navas de Tolosa Aragon had undertaken its own reconquest, lost most of its holdings in southern France, and gained dominions in Italy. King Pedro II of Aragon (1196–1213), after Las Navas de Tolosa, fell in France the next year at the Battle of Muret in another kind of crusade, called by Pope Innocent III to uproot the so-called Albigensian heresy. King Philip II Augustus of France used it to crush the powerful nobles of southern France, where Pedro held the counties of Beziers and Provence.

Pedro's son Jaime I (1213–1276), aged five when his father died, lost Beziers and Provence, but his uncle kept Aragon intact. When Jaime came of age he proved an energetic warrior and is known to history as "the Conqueror." In 1229, at age twenty-one, he used the maritime might of Barcelona to conquer Majorca in the Balearic Islands. Its Muslim population was expelled and replaced by poor Catalan peasants, lured to work domains distributed to the nobles and knights who participated in the conquest. The remaining Balearics were conquered from Majorca; and while more of the Muslim population was expelled, others were made serfs or even slaves by the conquerors.

Jaime next conquered the Moorish kingdom of Valencia. Here, unlike Majorca, most of the Muslim rural population was kept to work the irrigated plains under Aragonese and Catalan overlords. Urban Muslims were expelled, and in 1263 many Muslim peasants rebelled and suffered expulsion. Yet Valencia remained a sort of colony, in which Muslims outnumbered the Christian population of 30,000 by over 3:1. Not until the late 1400s did Christians equal the subject Muslims, in number.

Barcelona was the great commercial and maritime center of the Crown of Aragon, though both the city of Valencia and Palma de Majorca also enjoyed vigorous economies and prospered from shipping. When the opportunity arose for King Pedro III (1276–1285) to claim the Crown of Sicily, he could muster the naval might he needed. In 1282 the Sicilians rebelled against their French-born ruler, Charles of Anjou, in the uprising called the Sicilian Vespers, because it began at vespers time on Easter Monday. The rebels turned to Pedro because he was the husband of Constance of Sicily, daughter of popular King Manfred, from whom Charles had conquered both Naples and Sicily. Although Charles had the backing of the papacy and France, Pedro won Sicily, which he bestowed on his younger son, Jaime, Jaime hung on to it, with aid of the formidable Catalan admiral Roger de Lluria, who defeated all of Charles's fleets. In Catalonia, Catalans and Aragonese repelled an invasion from France. In return for their vote of money for the war, the Catalan and Aragonese nobles and urban rich exacted extensive privileges from Pedro's successor, Alfonso III. In time the Crown of Aragon settled its differences with France and the papacy and secured Sicily for the junior branch of the dynasty.

Aragon's expansion into the Mediterranean embroiled it with the rivalry of Genoa and Pisa and led to the arduous conquest of the island kingdom of Sardinia. Perhaps the most dazzling story of these years deals with a Grand Company of some 6,500 Catalan mercenaries, who hired themselves in 1303 to the Byzantine Empire in its struggle with the emerging Ottoman Turks When the suspicious Byzantines murdered the company's leaders, the Catalans mutinied and marched into fragmented Greece. In 1311 they seized the duchy of Athens, presented it as a fief to the faraway Crown of Aragon, and held it for two generations before it fell in 1381 to the rulers of Corinth.

When the Great Plague stuck the Aragonese kingdoms, King Pedro IV (1336–1387), called "the Ceremonious" for a treatise he wrote on courtly life survived. Medieval Catalan poetry flourished, Aragon had its university a Lérida, and the kingdom produced a philosopher of unique genius in Ramón Llull. King Pedro, as best he could, maintained Aragonese influence in the western Mediterranean. In the next generation, a Castilian dynasty would succeed to the Crown of Aragon.

2. FOUNDERS OF EMPIRE

Isabel la Catolica

King John II of Castile, of the House of Trastámara, married twice. From the first union sprang, or rather shuffled, the strange figure of Enrique the Impotent; from the second an Alfonso who died in his teens and his sister Isabel, known in Spain (for Isabel—

Elizabeth—is a common enough name) as la Catolica. Among the decayed remnants of once prosperous towns in Old Castile is one of the most remarkable—Madrigalde las Altas Torres, the birthplace of Isabel. Apart from the beauty of its name (which has nothing to do with singing) the circle of its ruined *mudéjar* walls with their high towers still encloses the whole town, an indication that no expansion has taken place for six hundred years. In places the towers have kept their original height; elsewhere a shapeless stump rises from a heap of rubble or a line of humble cottages marks an original curtain wall.

When Isabel was three her father died and the kingdom devolved on her half-brother Enrique. Like his father, he was governed by his favourite and of course unpleasant stories were told to account for their affection. The favourite was Juan Pacheco, later Marquis of Villena, and though authors often repeat the story that he was of noble birth, the truth is that he and his uncle, the Archbishop of Toledo, were New Christians descended from the *converso* Jew Ruy Capón. On Enrique's accession to the throne his stepmother (the queen who had accomplished the downfall of Alvaro de Luna) retired with her children Alfonso and Isabel to her castle at Arévolo. Here Isabel passed her formative years, learning the skills expected of a gentlewoman—all her life she was to occupy her rare moments of rest with exquisite needlework—and absorbing from her mother that almost fanatical devotion to the Faith which either prompted or cloaked the important decisions of her reign. Her mother was meanwhile lapsing into a state of melancholic insanity, not, as is often said, because of frustration and solitude, but rather through that hereditary taint which produced madness in Isabel's daughter Juana and eccentric behaviour, to say the least, in some of her descendants.

After six years of marriage the second wife of Enrique "the Impotent" produced a daughter. The court favourite at the time was called Beltrán de la Cueva and the baby, though christened Juana, was and still is known as La Beltraneja. Many believe that the smear was thought up and spread by the previous favourite Juan Pacheco. After the passage of centuries it is even more difficult to ascribe paternity; but one should remember first that Enrique was allegedly potent with mistresses, and secondly that the earliest recorded attempt at artificial insemination concerned the Queen as recipient and Enrique as donor. We shall never know whether the experiment was a success, but the story raises the intriguing question

From *The Spanish: The Intrepid Nation* by Alfonso Low, London: Gordon Cremonesi Publishers, 1975, pp. 117-138.

whether Enrique's disability may have been sterility due to anatomical causes, rather than impotence.

We have seen how Isabel's extreme youth was spent; even as a child her main concern was to thwart attempts at using her as a pawn in power politics. It is unnecessary for us to follow these in detail or to guess why Enrique is said to have alternately acknowledged and repudiated the legitimacy of La Beltraneja. Once Isabel was promised in marriage to Pedro Girón, brother of Juan Girón and Master of Calatrava; it is told that she spent a day and a night on her knees praying for divine help and that the aspiring groom was smitten with a fatal quinsy on his way to claim his fifteen-year-old bride. Did this deliverance from marriage to a New Christian, the answer to prayer, play its part in Isabel's later policy?

Two years after this episode her brother Alfonso died suddenly and she withdrew to a convent at Avila. Here she was sought out by Pacheco's uncle, the Archbishop of Toledo, proposing that she should take her late brother's place as a figurehead for a revolt of the nobles. With commendable prudence she refused, demonstrating that submission to established regal authority which she was to exact from others after her accession. Of course her correct behaviour to her half-brother Enrique did not extend to the unfortunate Beltraneja, whose faction she and her husband (to anticipate) finally defeated in 1479. Meanwhile she kept away from the crowd of degenerates who swarmed round the throne and, when ordered to live at the court, remained unsullied by the general licence that prevailed there. It is difficult for us to imagine her feelings after leaving the quiet of Arévalo and Avila, when transplanted to a court whose principal characters were the unsavoury king, the unscrupulous Pacheco and the unspeakable Beltrán de la Cueva, vain as a peacock and revelling in the dubious notoriety of Her Majesty's bed.

In 1469, before succeeding to the throne, indeed before her succession was assured, Isabel of Castile married her second cousin Ferdinand, heir apparent to the throne of Aragón. In this way, and at long last, the unity and grandeur of the greater part of Spain was achieved. Isabel and Ferdinand built a mighty edifice through the exercise of courage, constancy and cruelty; devotion and duplicity; heroism and hypocrisy. It is customary to attribute the nobler qualities to the Queen, and chivalrous historians write as though Ferdinand was responsible for every reprehensible deed; but many of them must have had at least the tacit approval of Isabel for we are told that she never allowed Ferdinand to dictate matters of policy. On the contrary, von Popielow, a visitor from Silesia, who met the royal family in Seville in 1484, wrote: "I saw then that the King is servant to the Queen,

because he has her on his right hand . . . so marked is this that the nobility fears the Queen more than the King."[1] He goes on to describe the King's subservience and to emphasise that he can do nothing without her permission. She reads all his letters, and we cannot blame her if it was to ascertain that Ferdinand regarded his marriage vows as lightly as other solemn promises. It is noteworthy that, even in her will, Isabel excluded her husband from inheriting the crown of Castile.

In accordance with custom, each sovereign chose as an emblem an object that began with the partner's initial. Thus Ysabel (as she spelled her name) chose *flechas* (arrows) for "Fernando" and he the *yugo* or yoke.[2] Their joint motto was a jingle that we see displayed on many a building:

Tanto monta, monta tanto
Ysabel y Don Fernando

signifying that the eminence of each was *tantamount* to that of the other.

The young pair was faced immediately with three major problems. The first was that of the succession of Castile, for the King of Portugal supported the claim of La Beltraneja. The ensuing war ended in a victory for Isabel and Ferdinand. The second problem was posed by the Castilian nobles, who had never resumed obedience since the death of Alvaro de Luna, sixteen years before. Thanks to Isabel's inflexible will, the prestige of the crown was again established, principally by rigorous application of the law; in this the *Hermandad*, whose headquarters we saw in Toledo, played a large part. The high towers of proud nobles were lopped off leaving them defenceless before retribution. In England the Wars of the Roses achieved the same result at the same time, but more by suicidal strife than by royal authority.

The third threat was poverty. Enrique the Impotent, ably supported by his courtiers, had emptied the royal treasury; over a hundred mints had been set up, most of them in private hands, and inevitably the coinage was debased. My own opinion, which you need not share, is that the great achievements of the remainder of the reign of Isabel and Ferdinand were prompted by the perpetual threat of insolvency. It certainly seems likely that it played a part in the three dramatic events of the wonderful year 1492: the conquest of Granada, the expulsion of the Jews and the discovery of America.

In the fight against financial collapse one institution was of supreme importance. The Inquisition, though well established in the Western world, was new to Castile and was different in some respects. It was approved, reluctantly and after much hesitation, by Pope Sixtus IV in 1478; the reluctance was due to the demand that the Spanish Inquisition should be under royal and not papal control. This was in keeping with the aim of the Catholic Sovereigns—unified command over a unified country. The results of their policy amply justified the means they used. That the Spanish Inquisition was run as a lucrative business is usually played down, if mentioned at all, and Durant,[3] for instance, states that Ferdinand refused bribes from rich victims begging him to overrule the inquisitors; but why should he accept a bribe of part of the victim's wealth when the latter's condemnation would ensure that all of it became the property of the state? However sympathetically we try to view the stamping out of heresy and the saving of souls, the profit motive keeps intruding. It is easily discerned in the war against Granada. Apart from the ostensible cause, the witholding of tribute by the Moslems, there were cities to be won, rich plains— the *vegas*—to support the loyal nobles and ransoms to swell the treasury. But artillery was essential and the latest and best weapons had to be bought from the Venetians; the lombards, designed to throw marble cannon balls but also used in this campaign with iron ones, were bought through Barcelona and Valencia brokers, and it was for this and not for Columbus' voyage that Isabel is said to have pawned her jewels or promised to pawn them, if needed.

After the execution of Alvaro de Luna physicians were called in to prescribe for King John, sick with remorse; in desperation a soothsayer was eventually summoned. He advised the King to get rid of the sinister Girdle of Zobeida. The jewels were removed from their settings and given to nobles or sold to merchants. Only the two giant emeralds remained, for their value was beyond the means of the usual buyer. Now, when Isabel needed money so desperately, they were sold to a Genoese Jew who knew that a bankrupt country is the place to find bargains. The emeralds went to Italy. From thereto Portugal was a fairly obvious move, for Henry the Navigator's captains were slaking Europe's thirst for gold and Portugal was the great market for precious stones, spices and other products of the East.

The war as a whole was fought by both sides with horrifying ruthlessness, occasionally punctuated by an act of chivalry. After the capture of Málaga Ferdinand worthily sustained his reputation for perfidy. True, the Malagueños had resisted with deplorable obstinacy and could hardly expect terms; many Christians urged that the whole population be put to the sword, but, as Irving tells us "the human heart of Isabella revolted at such sanguinary counsels: she insisted that their triumph should not be disgraced by cruelty"[4]

and she persuaded Ferdinand to permit the ransom of *those citizens who could afford it*. How this was done makes interesting reading: being told that the citizens of Málaga might hide their valuables, Ferdinand sentenced them all to slavery but allowed them to ransom themselves for an exorbitant sum, admitting their valuables in part payment. When the agreed time had expired and the full ransom had not been produced the Catholic Sovereigns found themselves in possession of all the movable property, half the ransom and all the persons of the citizens of Málaga. Thus, in a crusade, you *can* have your cake and eat it, and win esteem at the same time.

With their supplies of men and materials cut off by the fall of Málaga, the destruction of their fertile fields and a perpetual civil war raging at home, the fall of Granada was a foregone conclusion. The history of the ten years' war is marked, as you might expect, by the vigour and resolution of its female participants. On the Christian side Isabel performed miracles of organisation, herself supervising the well-being of her troops in difficult mountain territories and amid appalling climatic contrasts. Of the Moslems, the most indomitable was Boabdil's mother Aixa, whose well-known reproof to the men who wept on leaving their earthly paradise of Granada is typical of Spanish womanhood.

The treaty of capitulation gave most generous terms, including a cash payment to the Moorish king and the guarantee of freedom of worship in their own mosques. What, then, of the high ideals of the crusade, of the eradication of the Mohammedan heresy? Have patience. Boabdil, the deposed King of Granada, soon tired of his token kingdom in the Alpujarras and was tricked into withdrawing to North Africa, he sold his estate, as allowed in the treaty, to the conquerors, who cheated him of part of the price. Isabel's saintly confessor, the *converso* Hernando de Talavera, was made Archbishop of Granada and began the task of conversion with tact and sympathy. After eight years the results were so meagre that Cardinal Ximemez de Cisneros was sent to help. Strangely, for one who founded the important University of Alcalá, he began by copying Almanzor and burning thousands of Arabic books. His methods were effective: among his stratagems was the ringing of church bells loudly enough to drown the muezzins' call to prayer. By this and other means the Moors were goaded into revolt, defeated and then faced with the choice of exile or conversion. Most chose the latter and by 1502 there were no overt Moslems, only Christian *moriscos*, ripe for the big squeeze — the Spanish Inquisition.

This institution had to pay its own salaries and expenses from fines and confiscations, and its share was only a small one. I take it the reader has a fair idea of its methods—the secret accusation, the withholding from the prisoner of the very nature of the charge, the anonymity of the witnesses—and of the years that could be spent in solitary confinement with repeated examinations by the inquisitors who had records of the answers at every previous questioning. Finally of the torture, applied to both sexes and at all ages, the records giving the limits of ten and ninety-seven years. My object in touching on this revolting subject is to point out that confession, by whatever means obtained, meant condemnation and confiscation of all property. This had already been sequestered at the moment of arrest and from it the expenses of keeping the victim in prison had also been deducted. It may be true, and has often been maintained, that the Spanish Inquisition, judged by the standards of the times, was neither cruel nor unjust in its procedures and its penalties. But most of us find it impossible to judge by those standards.

The jurisdiction of the Spanish Inquisition, it must be remembered, extended only to Christians suspected of heresy. Those most suspect, often with reason, were Moslems and Jews who had embraced Christianity to save themselves and their families from death during the waves of persecution that every now and then swept through Spain. Professing Jews and Moslems, whatever disabilities they might suffer in other respects, were immune from the attentions of the Holy Office. It was the *conversos*, therefore, who attracted the interest of the Inquisition and who, being a comparatively wealthy class, could be expected to keep the home fires burning. For a condemned heretic—a Catholic who had relapsed into his former religion—could be burned alive or after a merciful strangulation, or in effigy if he had escaped the country; his remains could be produced for the *auto de fé* if he had died under torture and pushed in a wheelbarrow to the *quemadero*, or place of burning, like the still living survivors who could no longer walk. In all cases he, or his effigy or his bones, had been condemned and his property now belonged to the state.

The trouble, of course, was to pick out the *conversos* who could profitably be investigated without risk of protest from influential quarters. There had been so much intermarriage between money and blue blood that a borderline was difficult to establish. Sir Charles Petrie declares not only that the financial profits from the Inquisition were considerable, but that it was a useful threat to hold over the nobles, whose Christian blood was seldom pure. At this late date it is difficult to decide on the truth of statements that are repeated by one writer after an-

other. Archbishop Talavera, the Queen's confessor, was the son of converted Jewish parents; Tomás de Torquemada, a notorious leader in the fight against heresy, was also alleged to be of Jewish descent, and the same taint is said to have affected the Enriquez family, from which Ferdinand the Catholic was descended on his mother's side. To illustrate the complexities of the problem I must mention that Isabel's best friend, Beatriz de Bobadilla, married into a *converso* family and that the war against Granada was largely financed by Jewish loans, the actual management of finances being in the hands of two Jewish members of the council, Abraham Senior and Isaac Abarbanel. It is interesting to note that the *marrano*, or secret Jew, whom Borrow met in the 1830s was called Abarbenel, which is similar enough to suggest identity, and that he referred to the long dead Catholic Sovereigns as "Fernando the Accursed and Jezebel".

Historians have exercised much ingenuity in explaining the edict of 1492, decreeing the expulsion by 30th July of all Jews who had not in the meantime embraced Christianity. The usual explanation is that the Catholic Sovereigns, flushed with the victorious outcome of their crusade, now wanted to unite the whole country in religion as well as government. Had they forgotten the treaty they had just signed with the Moors, pledging themselves to respect all their religious institutions and buildings? Surely they were not already contemplating breaking their royal word? However that may be, the edict went forth and within four months the Jews of Spain had to leave, forbidden to carry money, precious metal or stones. They were forced to pay all taxes due before the end of the year but had to leave the collection of money owed them in the hands of Christians. Among these debts were some of the loans the Catholic Sovereigns had raised for the prosecution of the war against Granada. One can sense the strain on the shaky economy of the conquerors when they had paid King Boabdil the first instalment of the 30,000 gold castellanos agreed on in the treaty and the arrears of pay of the mercenaries they were now dismissing; among these were 2,000 Swiss pikemen who gave and expected the full value of their services. A final reason for the edict of expulsion was the hope that numbers of Jews would elect to remain as New Christians—actually only about 50,000 did so—thus providing the Inquisition with more souls to save and property to confiscate. In order to make quite sure of their prey the *conversos* were not allowed to leave Spain, while the unconverted were forbidden to remain.

The financial results of their efforts were meagre but in 1494 the Spanish Borgia Pope Alexander VI conferred on Isabel and Ferdinand the proud title of "Catholic Sovereigns". That of "Most Christian" was first suggested but passed over because it had already been bestowed on the kings of France (who were soon to ally themselves with the Turks against the Spanish); when it became Henry VIII of England's turn, as a reward for his opposition to Luther, "Defender of the Faith" was the best that could be contrived.

But before all this Isabel helped to mould history by a decision far more important than the conquest of Granada or the exile of defenceless citizens; she was instrumental, albeit with hesitation and parsimony, in the discovery of America. The importance of the voyages of Columbus cannot be overestimated and it is only right that the New World should have a country, several provinces and numerous towns named after the hero. To the foreigner the Spanish version of his name may at first seem strange and thousands have passed through the Panama Canal without recognising the explorer's names in the twin towns of Cristóbal and Colón.

It is almost a miracle that Spain was the sponsor of the Genoese sailor who had been rejected, first by Portugal and then by Spain herself. Columbus brought forward his proposal at the worst possible time, when Isabel and Ferdinand had won a civil war, repelled a French threat, broken the power of the nobles, restored order in a united Spain and embarked on a long and costly war against Granada, all in ten years. Furthermore, ideas of expansion were apt to be fixed on the French border, in the disputed provinces of Cerdagne and Roussillon, Sicily and Southern Italy, to which the crown of Aragón was intimately tied, and North Africa, whence any new Moorish or Turkish invasion must come.

But just as lack of money was a stumbling block to Columbus' enterprise, so its need was an incentive. At this time more and more gold was coming into circulation and the demand in Europe increasing; countries such as Spain and England were suffering from its lack, while Portugal was steadily increasing her reserves from the Guinea coast. Columbus shared the now common knowledge that the earth was a sphere and, hoping to find a new route to the Indies, crossed the Atlantic eight times and died fourteen years later without an inkling that he had discovered a new continent. His obsession, for that is what it amounted to, may have begun on a voyage to Iceland in 1477; here he learned of the colonies established in Greenland by the Norsemen and heard traditions of Norse expeditions to the New World, called Vinland in the sagas, and which he would believe formed part of Asia.

It is unnecessary to repeat the story of his protracted dealings with the court of Spain. Of one thing we are sure: Columbus did not underestimate his own value and was determined to wager his life for nothing less than social standing and the means to maintain it. At Santa Fé, the city built to house the besiegers of Granada, Columbus witnessed the final surrender and was then interviewed by the court. He apparently succeeded, as Prescott terms it, in stimulating the cupidity of his audience and, himself almost as devout as Isabel, held out the prospect of extending the empire of the Cross.

All would have been settled had Columbus been prepared to bargain. As it was, negotiations were broken off and he left with the intention of approaching France or England. He had gone only four miles when a message of recall overtook him at Pinos Puente, some say on the very bridge where a chapel stands to this day. Much ink has flowed in attempting to explain this hasty change of mind, the favourite explanation being an offer to finance the expedition on the part of the *converso* treasurer Luis de Santángel. The solution I offer is that someone remembered that the port of Palos, because of an act of piracy, had been condemned to maintain two caravels for a year for the public service. Negotiations were resumed and, as an example of the poverty or parsimony of the Sovereigns, Columbus was promised an extra eighth of the profits in return for contributing a proportionate part of the expenses. From then on the expedition was energetically and economically organised; stores were bought duty-free and reluctant sailors were tempted by immunity from criminal prosecution. The total cost of the expedition is said to have been only 17,000 florins, a sum so trifling that the Queen had no need to pawn her jewels.

Palos de la Frontera, the port from which the 100-ton *Santa María* and the two felucca-rigged caravels sailed, has been abandoned by the receding waters of the Río Tinto but you may still visit the Franciscan monastery of La Rábida, where Columbus was so hospitably entertained and supported. Columbus sailed from Palos on 3rd August, 1492 and returned on 15th March, 1493; in a meadow are rusty iron rings which are shown to the credulous as having secured the three ships, though in fact they rode at anchor in the river.

For the site of his triumphal reception you must go to Barcelona where, on the steps of the Chapel of St Agatha, near the Cathedral, the Catholic Sovereigns did him the unprecedented honour of rising as he came forward to bring them the momentous news. At the harbour end of the great thoroughfare, the Ramblas, is the towering monument to Columbus, and not far away, made fast to the quay, is a replica of his flagship, the *Santa María*. Strolling round the tiny vessel you must try to imagine the late afternoon of 11th October, when floating vegetation and a stick or two persuaded even the near-mutinous crew that land was near. We can only guess at his emotions when it was sighted and again when he, the unknown visionary, sat at the right hand of kings.

But his glory diminished, even during his lifetime. Isabel was loyal to her admiral when the inevitable reaction occurred and word went about that there was little profit in the new lands. Even when he was found to be enslaving the natives, she was his champion and is said to have wept when she saw him sent back in chains, though another account states that she ordered him to be set free long before they met again. Her character was, in fact, remarkable and she shines above her contemporaries for devotion to duty, resolution and loyalty, Where she fell short of our ideals we should blame her mother and her religious advisers, who had infused in her the belief that Moslem and Jewish heretics were a distinct species, for whom no pity need be felt and to whom no promises were binding. It is incorrect to say, as some have, that she had no vindictiveness in her character, for what else prompted her to reprove the Pope for his humane reception of the unfortunate citizens whom she had driven out penniless? Let us regard her bigotry as an acquired quality, an obedience to her advisers comparable to her resignation to God's will, when her children and grandchildren died and she saw the inheritance of all she had built up passing to a demented daughter. There are many who retain the belief that Spain is still a bigoted and backward country. I would remind them that modern Spanish as well as foreign authors stress the two great mistakes of Isabel's reign: the institution of the Spanish Inquisition and the expulsion of the Jews. Educated Spaniards usually agree.

Seville Cathedral, the largest Gothic building in the world, is the setting for the last act, for here is the sumptuous tomb that holds the remains of Columbus, expressing all the triumph and homage that he enjoyed for so short a time. A few steps away, in the floor of the nave, is the grave of his son Fernando; of him Baron de Bourgoing, plagiarised by Richard Ford, wrote, "He would have been considered a great man had he had a less famous father." [5] The gift of a new world, in return for a modest outlay, is acknowledged by an inscription on both tombs:

A CASTILLA Y A LEON
MUNDO NUEBO DIO COLON

3. THE GOLDEN CENTURY AND AFTER

While Castile was securing her hold on the New World Aragón was pursuing her old Mediterranean aims. Thanks to the genius and loyalty of Gonzalo Fernández de Córdoba, "The Great Captain", Spain added the kingdom of Naples to that of Sicily, thus extending her rule to include the southern half of Italy. Isabel died in 1504, her husband in 1516, allegedly from too earnest an attempt to ensure the succession by his second marriage (to Germaine de Foix). It thus passed to Juana, married to Philip the Fair of Burgundy. In her the eccentricities of her grandmother and elder sister declared themselves as frank insanity and as *Juana la Loca* ("Crazy Jane") she is still known.

CHARLES V, Juana's elder son, was born in 1500. He inherited not only Spain, where (at Villaviciosa) he set foot for the first time in 1517, and the Spanish possessions of Sicily and southern Italy, but also Burgundy, the Low Countries and Austria or, in other words, the Hapsburg slice of the European cake. In 1521 he wisely handed Austria over to his brother Ferdinand but he more than compensated for this lost portion by the vast territories his explorers carved out in the New World and by further conquests in Italy and North Africa.

That he ruled the first empire on which the sun never set [1] is of little importance. He learned how not to rule by the revolt of the *comuneros*. Interestingly, the uprising was centred on Castile, the heart of Spain, and was the protest of squirearchy against foreign influence. Had it succeeded, the eventual decline of Spain might have been postponed. Though negligible in battle the leaders, Juan Bravo, Juan de Padilla and Francisco Maldonado, behaved like heroes on the scaffold and are so regarded by Spaniards today, witness the statue to the first-named in his native town of Segovia and the imaginative painting of Gisbert, illustrating Padilla's last words, "Señor Juan Bravo, yesterday was the day for fighting like knights; today for dying like Christians." From them Charles learned his lesson: the revolt was not against him but against his absence and his reliance on Flemish favourites. He decided to be a Spaniard, learned the Castilian language and appointed Spanish officials. The *comunero* revolt gives us an example, not only of Spanish bravery, but of Spanish discord. Brother fought, literally, against brother. Padilla's was an officer in the loyalist army; in another family, Pedro Laso de Vega, an elder brother, was a *comunero* while a younger, Garci, fought and was wounded in the service of Charles, the King-Emperor. We met him briefly in Toledo as Garcilaso, the poet of rare and delicate sensibility.

Charles' other mistake was more serious. Like Alfonso el Sabio he wanted the crown of the Holy Roman Empire and he bought it. Thus, though he was the first Charles to rule Spain, he is generally known as Carlos V, the fifth emperor of that name. For the title, which served only to embroil him in religious wars and may have contributed to the grievances of the *comuneros*, he squandered the wealth of Spain. To ensure peace at home while he pursued fame abroad he entrusted much of the government of Spain to the lesser nobility; the *hidalgos* (more correctly *hijosdalgo*) then ensured their own prosperity by sheep farming. Arable became pasture and consequently wheat had to be imported; in an attempt to remedy this the vital wool industry was crippled by well-meaning legislation. Thus the *hijosdalgo*, as feeble-minded a class as their supreme example, Don Quixote, gnawed at Spain's roots while her branches were spreading over and beyond the known world.

Charles' happiest days were those which followed his marriage in 1526 to Princess Elizabeth of Portugal. Accounts of the sumptuous wedding, which took place in the splendid Hall of the Ambassadors of Seville's Alcázar, mention two great emeralds that the bride brought in a pendant. They were the emeralds of Zobeida's Girdle. A year later we find him unable to restrain his own army, of which at least half consisted of German Protestants; Rome was sacked and the Pope taught a lesson, for Spanish kings were apt to be ultra-catholic and anti-papal at the same time.

We can hardly blame Charles for his greatest mistake: while the country was impoverished by war and the bribing of German electors, gold and silver began to pour in from America; he was not to know that, far from solving his difficulties, it would increase them. The effect was comparable to the results of printing more paper money to stave off bankruptcy, or giving sugar to a diabetic. And so his son and successor, Philip II, inherited a virtually bankrupt state with the obligation to wage expensive war in the defence of his religion.

Charles was one of the few powerful rulers who retired voluntarily; you may still see his suite at the Monastery of Yuste, set among the scenic mountains of Extremadura. Two episodes mark his passing: he audibly regretted that he had not broken his word when he gave Luther a safe-conduct; perhaps he remembered how Harpsburg agents had caught John Huss by this despicable trick and had him burned alive. And the emeralds of Zobeida's Girdle were sent to his son Philip by a trusty messenger. On his tomb were carved the words, "Between Villaviciosa and Yuste he conquered an empire for Spain." Its financial state is not mentioned.

PHILIP II is seen by Spanish historians as the leader under whom their country reached its highest peak of glory; but the facts show that his ambitions were thwarted in every field. More devout than his father, he met with opposition from the German nobles when Charles V wanted to nominate him King of Rome, a preliminary to the title of Holy Roman Emperor. More dedicated to the mechanics of ruling, it was in his reign that Spanish influence in the Low Countries began to decline. More enterprising in the task of stemming the Turkish menace in the Mediterranean, his fleet and that of Venice triumphed at Lepanto in 1571, only for the Turks to seize Tunis a year later. In fact the only result of the "decisive" battle to arouse our interest was Philip's present to the victor, his half-brother Don Juan of Austria—the emeralds from Zobeida's Girdle.

The truth is that "El Prudente", as he is called, took on too much for one man to manage, however dedicated. Wherever he turned he was faced with impossible tasks. After the death of his second wife, Queen Mary of England, he needed her successor Elizabeth on the throne as a counter to the powerful Guises of France; Elizabeth used his support, helped the Protestants in the Low Countries and did nothing to check her captains in their careers of piracy and of smuggling negro slaves into the Spanish colonies. After he eventually accepted the Guise faction as allies in the great task of sustaining Catholicism, he was soon to see the Protestant Henry of Navarre change his liturgy, but not his beliefs, in order to inherit the throne of France. Sitting in his office in the Escorial he tried to exercise control over the whole known world; now he would be writing to the King of Poland about the menace of Lutheranism, now discussing the projected assassination of Queen Elizabeth with his London ambassador; and he would spend hours reading and annotating the minutes of the Councils of State. With him bureaucracy and centralisation and their inevitable train of delays and mistakes, entered Spain. They have survived as the only bequest of Philip the Prudent.

Poor Philip. Bankruptcies were not his only problem. As champion of the Catholic faith he had to fight, not only revolt in the Netherlands and the Turkish menace, but a serious uprising of the *moriscos* (Moslem *conversos*) in Andalucía. He felt that he had some sort of claim on England by being the widower of "Bloody Mary". Queen Elizabeth rejected him as a suitor and not only openly helped the rebellious Dutch but finally executed Mary, Queen of Scots, who was pledged to support Spanish interests. All the prestige won by the gallant Spaniards at Lepanto was lost when the equally brave crews of the Armada were defeated by the captains of England and their own ship-chandlers. The dreadful return voyage round the north of Scotland through storms and against head winds is an epic in itself. Taking into account the shortage of water, the number of sick and wounded and the battered state of their vessels, it is a tribute to Spanish seamanship that all forty-four ships clearing the coast of Ireland eventually got home.

The following year England thought to take advantage of the Armada's defeat. On 4th May 1589 Drake appeared before Corunna and landed an assault party. The breach was made, the attackers reached the summit of the wall and there was talk of capitulation when María Pita, who had just seen her husband killed, snatched the sword from the hand of an exhausted countryman and with it killed the English standard-bearer, whose banner then formed a rallying point for the garrison. Her actions and her words which, we are led to believe, were appropriate to a Galician fishwife, shamed the defenders; the breach was cleared and the English fleet sailed off on their main assignment, to restore a pretender to the Portuguese throne that now belonged to Philip. This too was a failure.

Philip has always been cast as the villain. When his eldest son died under restraint Philip was considered the murderer and the boy's stepmother the cause. The natural death of the deformed, perverted young lunatic was greedily seized upon, altered and adapted as part of the Black Legend of Spain, in the form that it takes, for instance in Schiller's play and Verdi's opera *Don Carlos*. We are too apt to forget the Philip whose smiling portrait in miniature adorns a manuscript in the town hall of Alora, the Philip who was vexed if the gardener forgot his morning bunch of roses, the Philip who loved to listen to the nightingales in the patios of the Escorial. Did you know that nightingales used to nest in the courtyards of that great grey, grim palace-monastery that Herrera finished in 1684? Think of it next time you walk through the granite corridors. But when you come to the marble Christ that Benvenuto Cellini made, remember also that the enigmatic Philip tied his own handkerchief round the loins for modesty's sake; and that he ordered a painting of St Maurice from El Greco for the chapel of the Escorial and then refused it for being "futuristic". After his death in 1598 the decline of Spain became apparent. As I have remarked, it set

in over half a century earlier, when bad housekeeping led to bankruptcy. His successors entrusted the affairs of the nation to a series of incompetent and self-seeking favourites, until at the end of the seventeenth century the House of Hapsburg perished from inanition and inbreeding. That it lasted so long is remarkable; Philip III, for instance, was a seventh child and succeeded only through the premature death of four brothers. Luckily for Spain, her common people were of tougher fibre.

But enough of emperors and kings. We get an idea of the harm they can do by Philip III's edict of 1609, decreeing the expulsion of the *moriscos*—Christians in name and largely Spanish by descent—Spain thus ridding herself of her most skilled and industrious artisans. The Spain you should see was largely the work of an astonishing Renaissance, if I may use the term loosely. Late but brilliant, it flowered more luxuriantly as kings became more incompetent, reflecting and in many cases outshining that of Italy. In representational art alone, sixteenth- and seventeenth-century Spain numbers its giants by the score: El Greco, the Berruguetes, Martínez Montañés, Ribera, Zurbarán, Alonso Cano, Murillo and Velázquez are but a handful that have been raised to the pinnacle of popular esteem from among the mass of their peers. In literature, contemporary Spain can be challenged only by Shakespeare, for Garcilaso de la Vega, Góngora, Lope de Vega and the matchless Cervantes were all before Milton's time. As the ponderous, rusty machinery of absolute, centralised rule was creaking to a halt, the arts despairingly tried to save its face. Calderón de la Barca was still writing about honour and duty when the words had become meaningless in the Spanish court, long after Cervantes had "smiled Spain's chivalry away." And while the rottenness was percolating through the ranks, until the invincible Spanish infantry were annihilated at Rocroi in 1643, mediaeval formality survived with a thousand useless vanities. So-and-so was addressed as "cousin" by the king while such-and-such were allowed to remain covered in the royal presence. A horse once ridden by the king might never again be mounted by another and, *mutatis mutandis*, no one might marry the king's discarded mistress.

The Catholic faith, destined to spread the light of knowledge in countries still undiscovered, was facing its greatest threat. Happily, a blend of mysticism and common sense arose in Spain, first with Loyola, then with St Teresa and her pupil St John of the Cross. Through them and many others Catholicism became more than a formula; by providing what humanity needed, the practical, disciplined mystics made Spain the spearhead of the Counter-Reformation.

Brother Luis de León proved that religion need not be divorced from rational thinking. He differed from Maimonides, Averroes and St Thomas Aquinas, who strove to reconcile religion with the world; instead, he saw the world as the unworthy step by which, with the help of music and understanding, his heaven could be reached.

No account of Spain's rise to supremacy would be complete without a mention of her explorers and colonisers. With a handful of men she acquired extensive footholds in the Americas; if you feel that fighting men are unproductive and unworthy to be classed with the builders of civilisation; remember Garcilaso de la Vega, the beloved poet, whose sonnets were read avidly throughout Europe; he died aged thirty-three leading the assault on Le Muy. Alonso Cano killed his man in a duel. Cervantes was maimed at the Battle of Lepanto, having left his bunk of sickness to fight on deck, and Calderón fought in more than one campaign. Lope de Vega, the most prolific poet and playwright the world has seen, was a member of the Armada.

And some who have no claim to immortality in the arts may also live in our memory for their heroism. Cortés, who conquered Mexico and Guatemala—the former alone is four times the size of Spain—found time to serve under the Great Captain in Italy and Charles V before Algiers. Leading his tiny army into the unknown interior, he first burned their ships at Vera Cruz, in case any were faint-hearted enough to think of returning home. Pizarro, who conquered Peru with a handful of men, was one of the bravest villains who ever lived. Balboa was the first to look on the Pacific and De Soto not only colonised Florida but explored as far as the Mississippi. All these were men of Extremadura, a harsh land, fit mother of heroes. In 1544 Orellana crossed the Andes, as the Incas had done before him, and led his party down the Amazon over an uncharted 2000 miles, through lands of fever and poisoned arrows, now exposed to scorching heat, now in the perpetual twilight of vast forests, where even their direction could no longer be determined; he knew only that somewhere, some time, they ought to come out in the Atlantic. De Elcano accompanied Magellan as far as the Philippines, where the latter was killed, then sailed on westward. The first to circumnavigate the earth, he survived storms, hunger, thirst and scurvy, arriving in Spain with seventeen men of the original 280. He accomplished the feat about sixty years before Francis Drake in the *Golden Hind*.

The list could be endless, but may fittingly close with mention of two priests, of whom the first was Bartholomew de las Casas. His father had accompanied Columbus in his second voyage in 1493. He himself sailed in 1502 as a simple colonist. In 1511 he took Holy Orders and from then on declared himself champion of the ill-treated Indian. Like many another, he painted a colourful, rather than a realistic, picture, but thanks to his persistence and the support of Cardinal Cisneros, he was declared "Universal Protector of the Indians". To prove that the Indian could be made a useful citizen by pacific means, he founded a monastery and colony at Cumaná, where he lavished gifts and friendship on the noble savage. The Indians responded by attacking and destroying it. Nevertheless Bartholomew de las Casas persisted; he crossed the Atlantic fourteen times—no mean feat for those days—and spent the rest of his ninety-two years largely in composing polemics defending his theory. His memory has survived the fierce attacks of his opponents and he is known today as "The Apostle of the Indians". History is the supreme humorist. It was Brother Bartholomew who introduced Negro slaves into America, so that creatures of a supposedly different species could release the Indian from the degradation of slavery. Apparently he had not met Juan de Valladolid, a contemporary Negro administrator of Seville. A century later our second priest appears, the Catalan Jesuit St Peter Claver, who eased the hardships of the Negro slaves in this life and ensured their salvation in the next. The Apostle of the Negroes.

Bartholomew outlived contemporary Indians and Spaniards with only the pen for a weapon and the breviary for a shield. Though he captured no native emperor and brought home neither gold nor silver he deserves to rank with the *conquistadores* who never refused to fight against odds of a hundred to one.

With thinkers and doers like these one would imagine that the Spanish Empire would have time to enjoy her supremacy. But her kings made sure that it would be brief, by systematic inbreeding and thorough neglect of their duties. Their favourites had none of Alvaro de Luna's efficiency, only his greed and ambition. In 1643 the catastrophic Battle of Rocroi saw the end of the Spanish infantry's supremacy, which had lasted nearly a century and a half. They and their allies were out-generalled by the Great Condé but none could deprive them of their glory. They died to a man, rank by rank, their leader Enriquez Acevedo de Toledo in the chair from which he commanded in the forefront. He was aged eighty-three.

4. SPAIN'S GOLDEN AGE IN THE ARTS

Architecture, Sculpture and Handicrafts

The splendid inspiration of the Renaissance could not fail to exert itself in Spain in realms other than literary. In architecture a new style developed which many would not think for the better, for the full splendor of the Middle Ages reached a glorious culmination in their cathedrals. The style characteristic of the fifteenth and early sixteenth centuries is called plateresque, and like the art of a *platero*, or silversmith, it emphasizes ornamentation rather than line and structure. The style was imported from Italy, and the basis was supposed to be the Roman column, but the distinction between the classic orders of architecture was not observed and various mixed styles can be noted. Moorish and Gothic influences were still in evidence. Within the sixteenth century there is a tendency toward a purer Roman style, a greater symmetry, a greater influence of the classic architectural ideals of Italy. A good example is the palace built (1526) for Charles V in the Alhambra. Its massive lines could hardly be less in keeping with the delicate lightness of the Moorish buildings adjacent to it. The severest example of classic architecture in Spain is the group of buildings begun by Philip II in 1559 at El Escorial: massive, stark, somber, impressive. The architects were Juan de Toledo and Juan de Herrera. The latter was also responsible for the Lonja (Stock Exchange) at Seville and the Cathedral of Valladolid, which was completed with numerous alterations after Herrera's death.

Spain has never been a land devoted to rigid classic ideals in anything and a greater exuberance began to reassert itself in the baroque in all forms of art. The emphasis is on the curved and broken, rather than the straight line, on crowded and swirling decoration, on ornamentation rather than on plane surfaces. At its worst such art is tortured, over-rich, excessively complicated, indigestible, but at its best it is vivid, splendid, gorgeous. It is mainly this style which was transplanted to Latin America, naturally, since it lasted until it was replaced by neo-classicism in the eighteenth century. The exaggerated baroque is also called *churrigueresco*, after the Spanish architect José de Churriguera (died 1725).

Some of the sculptors who flourished in Spain during the Renaissance were foreigners, like the Frenchmen Felipe Vigarni and Juan de Juni, and the Italians Francesco Pisani and Pietro Torrigiano. Many of Spanish origin, like Alonso Berruguete (c. 1480–1561), had studied in Italy. He and Gil and Diego de Siloé are among the best known, even if no one in Spain created statues to rival in fame those of a Donatello or a Michelangelo. Sculpture continued to flourish in the seventeenth century, as in the work of Martínez Montañés, Jerónimo Hernández, and Alonso Cano.

Some of the best work in Spanish sculpture was done in wood, not only in choir stalls, doors and altarpieces, but in statues. Many of the statues were painted and embossed with gold (*estofado*).

The sixteenth century was the great age of the Spanish goldsmiths, whose delicate crosses and monstrances can still be seen in cathedrals in many parts of Spain. Two families of goldsmiths were particularly distinguished, the Arfes and the Becerrils.

Spain had constantly been distinguished for fine ironwork, and the tradition continued through the Renaissance, producing admirable grilles for churches and convents as well as decorative stairrails, balconies and gratings for private houses.

Furniture reflected Italian influences. Many examples of chairs, chests, wardrobes and desks survive from the sixteenth and seventeenth centuries, beautifully carved, often encrusted with gold, silver, ivory, or mother of pearl. Glazed tiles (*azulejos*), for which Spain has always been noted, now tended to show classic forms instead of the older *mudéjar* geometrical patterns. The best-known center for the production of pottery was Talavera, near Toledo, where some four hundred workmen were employed in the seventeenth century. The products were noted for their brilliant glaze and for their characteristic blue and white designs.

The raised embroidery on silk ecclesiastical vestments can still be admired, as in the Cathedral of Toledo, which has preserved many beautiful examples of the fifteenth and sixteenth centuries. One specimen is a mantle for the Virgin, embroidered in the early seventeenth century, which contains some eighty thousand pearls and other jewels. Tapestries and carpets were mainly imported from Italy and Flanders.

Painting

The period of greatest splendor in Spanish painting came in the time of the first four Philips. The influences were mainly Italian, of the schools of Florence (Raphael), Venice (Titian), and to a lesser extent, of Bologna. Italian painters came to Spain, and Spanish artists studied and worked in Italy. Influence by no means implies Spanish imitation, and the greatest Spanish painters exhibit marked originality.

It is too bad to neglect the numerous Spanish painters who are only near-great, but even if the visitor to the Prado and other Spanish museums saw only El

Greco and Velázquez he could store enough esthetic joy for a long time. Doménico Theotocópuli, better known as El Greco, was born in Crete slightly before mid-sixteenth century. Perhaps he was influenced by Byzantine art surviving there. He early went to Venice, and is mentioned as a pupil in Titian's studios. There is no record that he studied with Tintoretto, but he appears to have learned more from the latter than from the former. He did not imitate Michelangelo, whose canvases he must have known in Rome around 1570. He came to Toledo in 1577 and painted almost exclusively there until he died in 1614, two years before Cervantes and Shakespeare. Instead of aping the three great Italian masters, he was intensely Spanish, one of the world's most original and individualistic painters, worthy to stand with the best who ever put paint on canvas. A modern American critic (Sheldon Cheney, *A World History of Art*, New York, 1937, pp. 603, 612) has said of him, "No one else has so overlaid his subject matter and inner design with so rich a play of moving rhythmic forms, with so fiery an orchestration of visual elements. Yet underneath is the soundest plastic structure, the most nearly infallible handling of abstract elements known to Western painting.... Where painting touches upon the ecstatic and the supernal, he is master above all others." Externally he can be recognized not by his use of color, in which he was less lavish than the Venetians, but by his matchless use of light and shade, his contrasts of gleaming white darting and swirling into somber backgrounds, as one can see in his Crucifixions, his Resurrections, his Annunciations, even some of his portraits. The faces of contemporaries (self-portraits, the two Covarrubias, his son Jorge Manuel, Cardinal Tavera) are no doubt literal enough, but they look beyond the flesh into the spirit. The portrait of the Grand Inquisitor Don Fernando Niño de Guevara (Metropolitan Museum, New York) helps one to understand the Spanish Inquisition. The face is intelligent, intense, fanatical. Most of El Greco's work, however, was on religious subjects, and done for the Church in some way. The striking elongation of figure which upsets the literal-minded, responds to El Greco's inner vision, his longing to express something that transcends the merely terrestrial. That spiritual quality appears even in his landscapes, which he was one of the first Spanish painters to develop.

One of the most admired of all El Greco's numerous canvases and one of the world's great pictures is *The Burial of the Count of Orgaz*, painted for the Church of Santo Tomé in Toledo. An extraordinary group of spiritualized portraits appears in the lower half; an ecstatic vision of Christ, the Virgin and Heavenly hosts in the upper half. In it, perhaps better than in any of his other works, El Greco realized an aspiration of the Spain of his age, to spiritualize earth, and to lift it to heaven.

El Greco did not found a school. His technique could be imitated, but not his burning inner vision. His successors are realists, especially the Valencian José de Ribera (1588-1656), often called by his Italian nickname, Spagnoletto. He starved and studied in Italy until his canvases became fashionable at the Spanish court of Naples and in Madrid. Although he was a disciple of Michelangelo and Correggio, he seems to have learned most from the ardent realist Caravaggio, and he presented his figures, dwarfs, buffoons or saints with startling fidelity and with even a melodramatic note. His best-known canvas is the *Martyrdom of St. Bartholomew*. He painted many lean ascetic saints, and produced twenty-six fine etchings. His art was far better than his personal character.

Francisco de Zurbarán (1598–1663) was likewise a realist, possessed of a profound religious spirit. His *Monk in Meditation*, his various friars, painted with faithful detail and in deep reds and blacks, give a simultaneous impression of richness and somberness. He was a better man than Ribera, but not quite so good a painter.

Diego Velázquez de Silva (1599–1660) of Seville was one of the most prolific of painters. Some have thought him the world's greatest realist. He became rich, admired, successful, for kings and royal favorites smiled on him, and the Goddess of Fortune took him to her arms.

Francisco Pacheco of Seville, his teacher as well as his father-in-law, sent him to Madrid, where he won the favor of the Count-Duke of Olivares, and so of Philip IV, whose painter he was for nearly forty years. Forty of his canvases are portraits of that ugly long-jawed sovereign.

In his first period Velázquez painted religious pictures and crowded interiors (*bodegones*) with great fidelity of detail, but without realizing that the human eye cannot see very much at once. The most famous of his early pictures is *The Topers* (*Los Borrachos*), a fine group of attractive drunkards, with a half-nude village youth posing as Bacchus, cup in hand, vine leaves in his hair, receiving adoration. The portraits are individually splendid, the parts of the picture superior to the whole. The picture was painted in 1629, and in that same year Rubens, visiting the Spanish court, advised Velázquez to go to Italy.

The young artist spent two years there, and was influenced more by Titian and Tintoretto than by Michelangelo and Raphael. He learned greater concentration, greater balance in composition, greater depth. Back in Madrid after two years, he produced a long series of portraits of the King and court personages, even including court dwarfs. He did not then or ever completely forget the influence of El Greco. About 1647 he painted one of his great pictures, *The Surrender of Breda*, often called *The Lances*, a masterpiece of realistic and historic presentation.

In 1648 Velázquez paid his second visit to Italy. He was immediately commanded to paint Pope Innocent X, and the portrait, which Sir Joshua Reynolds considered the best picture in Rome, is an extraordinary canvas. It is reported that when His Holiness saw the artist's sketch, revealing the shrewd, hard face, he winced and said, "Too true."

It was after this second visit to Italy that Velázquez painted the only female nude known to have been put on canvas in Spain up to this time, the "Rokeby Venus." It is beautiful, but does not come up to the fleshly loveliness of the Venetian school. The Spanish Church forbade painting nudes.

It was in this last period that Velázquez painted some of his best pictures, when he had mastered the presentation of space and the effects of color, light, and shade. His radiant pearl-grey and rose are particularly remarkable in the picture of little Princess Margarita Teresa. *Las Hilanderas* (The Spinners) and *Las Meninas* (The Maids of Honor) show external naturalness, great selectivity, true harmony. His amazing craftsmanship makes up for a certain lack of imagination and fullness.

Bartolomé Esteban Murillo (1617–1682), also a Sevillian, was during the eighteenth and nineteenth centuries regarded as one of the world's great masters. Today his fame has suffered greatly. He painted popular types, which would make fine illustrations for picaresque novels, such as *The Melon Eaters, The Boy Drinking, The Flower Girl*, and many others. He also painted religious pictures, especially the twenty *Immaculate Conceptions*, with sweet blues predominating. To put it mildly, they are extremely sentimental. Murillo possessed zest and laughter and tenderness, plus craftsmanship, but he was never profound. After him Spanish painting showed little inspiration up to the time of the titanic Goya.

Music

Music, like the other arts, developed splendidly in Spain during the Renaissance and Golden Age, in both theory and practise. From the fifteenth to the seventeenth century, about a hundred books were written in Spain or by Spaniards on musical theory, and there were many world-famous performers.

Spanish folk music is generally considered the richest in the world (see, for example, Gilbert Chase, *The Music of Spain*, New York, Norton, 1941, Chap. XV) and we fortunately still possess many tunes used in Spain in the period mentioned for ballads and popular songs. Some are slow and solemn, evidently developed from church music, others sprightly and highly dramatic. The *Cancionero de Palacio* (*Palace Song Book*) contains some five hundred compositions of the fifteenth and sixteenth centuries, most of them for three and four voices. Juan del Encina, the dramatist, was a fertile composer and was represented in the collection by seventy-five songs.

One of the most famous musicians of the sixteenth century was the Valencian courtier, wit, poet and gallant, Luis Milán, born about 1500. In 1561 he published a book called *El Cortesano*, based, naturally, on Castiglione, in which he proclaims music to be one of the indispensable accomplishments of a gentleman. In his *El Maestro*, a theoretical and practical manual for the six-stringed *vihuela de mano* (guitar), Milán includes nearly seventy compositions, among them six lovely pavanes. There were other noted theorists who wrote for the *vihuela*, such as Luis de Narváez, *maestro de vihuela* to King Philip II, and Alonso de Mudarra, a canon of the Cathedral of Seville.

Everyone knows that the guitar, for which these gentlemen wrote, became the characteristic musical instrument of Spain. How did that come about? A primitive sort of guitar was known in Egypt nearly four thousand years B.C., and it was probably introduced into Spain by the Romans. At least the *guitarra latina*, of four, five, six or seven gut strings, was more like the modern instrument than the *guitarra morisca*, which bears closer resemblance to the lute. Luis Milán's tuning was g-c-f-a-d'-g', and the neck was always fretted for semitones. The composers were inspired by a combination of polyphonic music and dance and folk tunes. This style of playing, occasionally revived by contemporary guitarists like Andrés Segovia, remained in vogue until a Spaniard of Italian birth, Federico Moretti, published his *Principles for Playing the Six-stringed Guitar* in 1799 (see Gilbert Chase, op. cit., Chap. III).

The University of Salamanca had as professors of music several remarkable men. Ramos de Pareja, for example, who flourished in the later fifteenth century, wrote a noteworthy treatise on music, in Latin, and published it at Bologna in 1482. He abandoned the old theories, based on the Greek, of Boethius and Cassiodorus, and those of Guido d'Arezzo (eleventh century), and substituted a system based on the octave, as at present, divided into twelve semitones. He also used the consonant triad, the basis of the modern harmonic system.

A great organist and composer, called "The Spanish Bach," was the blind Antonio de Cabezón (died 1566). He was clavichordist and organist to Charles V and Philip II, and his fame spread over all Europe. His liturgical pieces, contrapuntal preludes and themes with variations were among the most remarkable composed in the sixteenth century.

Another blind musician, Professor of Music at Salamanca, was Francisco de Salinas (1513–1590), to whom the poet Luis de Léon dedicated one of the loveliest odes ever written to music (*El aire se serena...*). Salinas was performer, theorist and collector, and he preserved numerous folk tunes, to be found in his *Seven Books on Music* (1577, in Latin).

Salinas was for a while organist at the Spanish court of Naples, and many other Spaniards also contributed to European music in Italy, especially at Rome. One was Diego Ortiz, who published a treatise (Rome, 1553) on the improvisation of accompaniments over a given bass, which had great influence on the development of instrumental music.

The greatest of all Spanish religious composers was Tomás Luis de Victoria, of Avila (c. 1548–1611), usually mentioned with Palestrina, whose pupil he probably was. He wrote about 180 compositions, all connected with church worship, grave, grandiose, deeply spiritual. The greatest is probably the last he wrote, a Requiem Mass (*Officium Defunctorum*). Of the two great liturgists it has been said: "Palestrina is the Raphael of music, Victoria the El Greco. Each is great and unique in his own way" (Chase, op. cit., p. 85).

The full-fledged opera did not flourish in Spain in the seventeenth century, but a combination of spoken lines, dance, and music did, a sort of musical comedy or *opéra bouffe*, called a *zarzuela*. Philip IV enlarged a palace, originally a hunting lodge, which he had in the Pardo (a few miles from Madrid), and supplied it with gardens, fountains, and a theater. The place was called La Zarzuela. (The word means "bramble"; it must have been a bramble thicket once.) At this royal retreat the pleasure-loving king liked to hear short pieces, with music and singing, and they were called *fiestas de zarzuela*. The text of such a *divertissement* by Calderón survives: *El golfo de las sirenas*, performed January 17, 1657, in only one act. The zarzuela regularly has two acts, as did Calderón's *El jardín de Falerina*, performed earlier at the palace in Madrid. The sets for the *zarzuelas* were likely to be elaborate. In the eighteenth century *zarzuelas* came to be lighter in tone, for all the people and not just for court exquisites. They were extremely popular in the eighteenth and nineteenth centuries. The step to the full opera, entirely sung, was a short one. Calderón wrote two, *La púrpura de la rosa* and *Celos aun del aire matan*, the latter with music by Juan Hidalgo.

5. CERVANTES AND *DON QUIXOTE*

Biography

Holy oil was put on the head of an infant christened Miguel de Cervantes Saavedra in Alcalá de Henares on Sunday, October 9, 1547. There was probably not much excitement over the matter, because the parents already had three children, and the father, Rodrigo de Cervantes, was a doctor anyway.

Really nothing is known of Miguel's childhood, but he must have seen various Spanish cities as his father wandered around, presumably in search of better fortune. The boy studied in Madrid, in the *Estudio* of Juan López de Hoyos, but was he also educated in Seville and Salamanca? Some have thought so. A legal warrant has been found dated September 15, 1569, for the arrest of some Miguel de Cervantes "for having wounded a man," but was the man wanted by the police the future novelist? Did he flee the country on that account? There is no proof.

He was indeed in Rome in December 1569, and in 1570 he was a soldier in a Spanish regiment in Italy, which was mainly a Spanish possession at the time. On October 7, 1571, he fought gallantly in the great battle of Lepanto, and received gunshot wounds in the chest and the left hand. He spent the following winter recovering, but his left hand remained useless, and he gloried in the title "The Cripple of Lepanto."

He went back in the army, and remained there until 1575. He was returning to Spain in September of that year, to sue for promotion, when his galley, *El Sol*, was attacked and taken by Barbary pirates. Since he carried letters of recommendation from Don Juan of Austria, half-brother of Philip II and victor of Lepanto, and from the Duke of Sessa, viceroy of Sicily, his captors thought him a man of importance and set his ransom high. It had been an Albanian renegade who captured him, and a Greek renegade owned him as a slave. Cervantes' doings in captivity read like an adventure novel. He organized five attempts to escape, one of which (1578) brought him two thousand lashes. He survived, however, and next year almost succeeded in getting away, but a fellow conspirator betrayed him. By September, 1580, his family and friends had got together two hundred and eighty escudos for his ransom, but Hassan Pasha, King of Algiers, who now owned him, demanded five hundred. So Cervantes, in chains, was put on board a galley to be taken to Constantinople. At the last moment the Trinitarian Friars, who took charge of ransoming Christian prisoners, collected the remaining two hundred and twenty escudos and Cervantes was rescued, as his brother Rodrigo had been before him.

Having returned to Spain, Cervantes made unsuccessful efforts to secure lucrative employment. He engaged in an amorous intrigue with a certain Ana Franca de Rojas, and a daughter, Isabel de Saavedra, was born to them about 1584. In that same year, he wrote a pastoral novel, *La Galatea*, and sold the printing rights, and on December 12, 1584, he married Catalina de Salazar y Palacios, who was nineteen years younger than he, and had a fair dowry. He was also writing plays, most of which are lost, but apparently he found the pen even feebler than the sword as far as material support was concerned.

In 1585 Cervantes was in Seville, engaging in financial business. Finally he secured a government position as a commissary collecting supplies for the Spanish Armada. Even after the defeat of that expedition (1588) he continued in the government service, but he was paid slowly and irregularly. In 1590 he had to buy on credit enough cloth for a suit of clothes. His total experience as a government employee was quite unhappy. He must have been a very poor bookkeeper, and his luck was certainly bad, though there is no reason to consider him dishonest. A subordinate of his was untrustworthy, and a banker with whom he had deposited official funds went bankrupt, so Cervantes landed in jail (Seville, 1597). He came out after three months, on bond. The Treasury kept bedeviling him about his shortage and he was in jail again in 1602 for a short while.

During all this time he may not have been enjoying life, but he was learning an extraordinary amount about it. He evidently was doing a bit of writing too, in spite of his difficulties. In 1603–4 he was in Valladolid, where the court was, negotiating for the publication of the *Quijote*. He secured the privilege to print September 26, 1604, and the book was published in Madrid in January 1605. It was popular and five more editions appeared the same year, but Cervantes was still a poor and struggling author.

On June 27, 1605, a nobleman was murdered outside the house in Valladolid in which Cervantes, his two sisters, his natural daughter Isabel, and a niece were living. They were haled into court, and though they readily proved that they had nothing to do with the murder, it turned out that Isabel's mode of life was at least open to suspicion. She later married twice, and brought her father much trouble, mainly over her dowry. The family was living in poor, even sordid surroundings, and Cervantes' advance royalties helped only temporarily.

Cervantes' later life was devoted more closely to literature. Just before his death he announced the names of four works upon which he was engaged. He died April 23, 1616, and was buried at the Convent of the Discalced Trinitarian nuns in Madrid. No stone marks his grave. Of the works that he had in hand, his widow published only one after his death.

The *Quijote*

If Cervantes had written nothing but his Novelas ejemplares and his entremeses, he would be an important author of the seventeenth century, but it happens that he wrote in addition to them the world's greatest novel. The first part of *Don Quixote* appeared in 1605, the second part in 1615. The oftener one reads it, the more one realizes its extraordinary depth and breadth, the author's penetration into human motives and actions, his profound sympathy, his gift of seeing life whole, his artistry in portraying it.

From an external point of view, one may consider *Don Quixote* as a sort of literary pot-pourri, like Alonso Quijano's own *olla*, containing all the ingredients of the preceding novel. Obviously the pattern of Cervantes' masterpiece is that of the Novel of Chivalry, with a knight and his squire running from one adventure to another. At the same time it is a parody. It contains pastoral elements, as in the episode of Cardenio. The picaresque is there too, as in the innkeepers, the galley slaves, Ginés de Pasamonte. The episode of Marcela and Grisóstomo is an Italianate short story, the *History of the Captive* an example of the Moorish. There are disquisitions on literary criticism, as in the famous examination of the books in Chapter VI of Part I, and in the discussion with the Canon in Part II. There are reminiscences of Ariosto's *Orlando Furioso* it the madness of the hero himself, though the author's technique is different. Many a conversation suggests a Lucianesque dialogue. Folk literature sprouts freely from Sancho's sly mouth, particularly in the form of proverbs. It is scarcely to be imagined that Cervantes put in all these elements unconsciously. He hardly needed so many ingredients if he intended to write merely an amusing satire of the exaggerations of the deluded followers of Amadís de Gaula.

How much planning Cervantes did before writing his great novel no one can know. There are suggestions, at least, that he changed the form of his hero's madness. At first Don Quixote thinks he is someone else, such as the Moor Abindarráez or the Marquis of Mantua. A commonplace sort of delusion. After his first sally, Don Quixote is himself, always, no matter how much he may try to emulate his favorite heroes.

His actions therefore have more integrity and more significance for the reader. It seems more than likely that Cervantes added episode after episode, as they occurred to him, and not according to some prearranged schedule. Hence the novel seems loosely constructed. It is very different in form from Madame Bovary, for example—even though Flaubert claimed that his own origins were in *Don Quixote*, that he knew the book by heart even before he learned to read for himself. This relative formlessness has repelled a few readers, such as the pseudo-exquisite Barbey d'Aurevilly, but it does not seem to bother very many people. Next to the Bible, Don Quixote has been the world's most frequently published book.

How is that to be accounted for? There have been many books which won great popularity at the moment of publication but this one has been popular for more than three hundred years.

Cervantes did not have modern psychiatric training, but he managed to portray in his semi-mad literary creature an incarnation of many of humanity's dearest ideals, a synthesis of human traits. He is very foolish indeed, this anachronistic knight, tilting at windmills, mistaking women of the town for high born ladies, transforming a stable-smelly country wench into the Princess Dulcinea del Toboso, promising islands to his squire and pronouncing flowery discourses on the Golden Age to a hungry group of goatherds. Through it all he remains both dignified and noble, and we almost feel that reality itself is at fault rather than Don Quixote.

Those who are young actually or in mental age can enjoy *Don Quixote* merely for the adventure, the humor, the merry quips, the story. The middle-aged can find inspiration for constant endeavor, new light on their own problems, a penetrating commentary on life around them. The old may find consolation for dreams unrealized, communion with a spirit treated unkindly by life but never beaten.

It is trite enough to say that *Don Quixote* is an epic of humanity, not just of the realist and of the idealist separately, but of the two together, reacting upon each other. It is equally trite to say that Don Quixote and Sancho are one, for Cervantes said it before us. A consoling thought, that the earthy, over-practical and selfish Sancho within us is counterbalanced by a Don Quixote who will confront any danger, endure any hardship and suffer any pain in the steadfast pursuit of an unblemished ideal. Of course idealists fare badly in this world and are more than likely to be thought mad. And yet, do they fare badly within themselves? Don Quixote won his own victory. Perhaps the only salvation for humanity, at this mo-

ment in one of its least lovely moods, lies exclusively within the individual.

Sancho began by being about as free from idealism as anyone ever born, but association with his master changed him. He had no desire whatever to make the world over. His ideal was to get his stomach well filled with food and drink. He was crafty, shrewd in all matters covered by his limited experience, well supplied with popular wisdom, but faithful, devoted, capable of real affection, susceptible to influences which he had never even suspected. When his master lies dying, Sancho tells him movingly that it is very silly to die, that there are still many wrongs left for them to right, that they must go forth to new deeds of derring-do. Sancho had become infected with his master's idealism, as *Don Quixote* in Part II had under Sancho's influence made a closer approach to practical reality.

Although Cervantes was keenly aware of the cultural problems of the Renaissance, *Don Quixote* is by no means a manual of systematic philosophy. Yet every episode has a strangely stimulating quality, touching upon the deepest and most vital preoccupations of humanity. Every reader can make his own interpretation of the whole book and of its details, and each rereading suggests something new and fresh. It is quite possible to regard *Don Quixote* as a symbol of Spain: a country which in the time of Charles V and Philip II went forth to deeds of high emprise, trying to bring the world to what those sovereigns regarded as the true faith. Spain failed, as *Don Quixote* failed, and the signs must have been evident to Cervantes. Nevertheless he thought the struggle for the ideal worth while. He himself never lost his sense of reality, but at the very end of his life he wrote one of his most idealistic works. He penned the touching dedication to *Los trabajos de Persiles y Sigismunda* just five days before he died.

Don Quixote received some unwelcome tributes in Cervantes' own lifetime. Two pirated editions of the First Part were swiftly published in Lisbon, and when in 1614 the author had reached Chapter 59 of his Second Part, a gentleman calling himself Alonso Fernández de Avellaneda published a spurious continuation in Tarragona. No one knows who this author was, though much learned ink has been spilled about the matter. Avellaneda possessed considerable skill in construction and narration, though his characters lack depth and subtlety. Cervantes told him off in his own Second Part, rather more mildly than we would expect. Perhaps Avellaneda made Cervantes hasten his work to completion. If so, posterity is deeply in his debt, for Cervantes might have died without finishing his great masterpiece.

Part II
Readings from
Latin America

A. Latin America

At this point in our survey of Latino History it is necessary to shift from Spain to the Americas, the "New World," a land in which the Spanish attempted unsuccessfully to replace the cultures there with its own. In fact, after the death of millions of indigenous peoples and the destruction and exploitation of their region during the Spanish conquest, a new culture was born of a synthesis of European (Spanish) and indigenous cultures, nourished later with the addition of the cultures of Western Africa. The birth of this new culture—which Carlos Fuentes calls *Indoiberoamerican*, and others, *mestizo*—is an important milestone of Latino history.

Regarding some common terms of the area we now study, *Spanish America* (in Spanish, *hispanoamérica*) refers to all the Spanish-speaking countries of North and South America; while *Ibero-America* labels all Spanish-speaking countries as well as Brazil (whose ancestry in part comes from Portugal, the other country located on the Iberian Peninsula with Spain). Today, *Latin America* generally refers to all the countries in the region, outside of Canada and the United States, including all the Spanish-speaking countries and Brazil, as well as lands where many cultures (with their languages) have left their mark (such as Haiti–French, or Suriname–Dutch).

The Spanish speaking countries (Spanish America) are as follows. **North America**: Mexico, Guatemala, El Salvador, Honduras, Nicaragua, Costa Rica, and Panama (the last 6 countries are also located in a region called Central America); Cuba, Dominican Republic, and Puerto Rico (a commonwealth of the United States); **South America**: Venezuela, Colombia, Ecuador, Peru, Bolivia, Paraguay, Chile, Argentina, and Uruguay.

For a visual survey of a contemporary Spanish-speaking country, view *Peru: Magic and Mystery*, a DVD attached to the text *Voices of Latino Culture*. The DVD will give you a virtual tour of contemporary Peru along with typical foods and music of the Andean region of South America.

1. LATIN AMERICA: ITS LAND AND PEOPLE

The 375 million people of Latin America live in twenty-five countries. They make up ten percent of the world's population and possess about fifteen percent of its land. They do not occupy this land in equally distributed numbers. Few areas of the world are so unevenly settled and developed. Vast stretches, especially the Amazon basin in the center of South America, remain virtually uninhabited. The people of Latin America have always preferred to gather in clusters rather than to spread out. Much land remains open today for frontier settlement.

VARIED LANDSCAPE

The region's geography is one explanation for this remarkable pattern of settlement. The Latin American landscape is dramatic and varied. A satellite passing over the area from Mexico in the north to Argentina and Chile in the south would transmit a picture of mountains, plains, rivers, islands, and mainland. A closer view would reveal such important details as tropical rain forests; dry, inhospitable deserts; green, fertile mountain valleys; gently rolling upland regions; and well-watered plains.

Scanning northern Mexico, the satellite would show a wide, dry plateau bracketed with mountain ranges. These ranges seem to merge into a single, rugged mountainous area as the land itself narrows further south. The bulk of the Mexican people live in this narrowing, rugged land in central and southern Mexico. Mexico City is the core of this densely populated zone.

Moving toward the Isthmus of Panama, a narrow strip of land that connects North and South America, our imaginary satellite would show that the mountain ranges of Mexico continue underwater in an easterly direction toward the Caribbean, where they emerge as the Greater Antilles, a chain of islands. Included in this island chain are such nations as Cuba, Jamaica, Haiti, and the Dominican Republic. Puerto Rico, a possession of the United States, is also part of the Greater Antilles.

While spinning south, the satellite passes over Central America. The viewer will notice that all of the Central American republics have mountains or highlands and that Mexico has become a wet zone, generously supplied with rainfall. Reaching the continent of South America, the satellite sends back a kaleidoscopic view. Perhaps the most dramatic feature is the high, jagged mountain range that spreads along the entire west coast of South America.

Beginning as a "Y" formation around oil-rich Lake Maracaibo in Venezuela, the Andes march south over four thousand miles in three parallel chains. The combined average width of these mountains ranges from two hundred to four hundred miles. They are at their highest and widest in Bolivia. Bolivia's most important city, La Paz, lies nestled in a valley that is 12,500 feet above sea level. The majority of the people of all the west coast countries of South America, with the exception of Chile, live clustered in the high valleys of the Andes.

East of the Andes a variety of features appear. In the north and east are the Guiana highlands and the flat *llanos*. These llanos, found mostly in Venezuela, are two hundred miles wide and six hundred miles long and are one of Latin America's two spacious plains. They have been used for cattle ranching rather than for farming. The reasons are easy to understand. Six months a year, the llanos are hot and wet. The other six months, they are hot and dry. The soil is often poor quality clay. Flood control projects, irrigation works, and an attack on the great variety of mosquitoes, flies, and other insects that thrive in the llanos are necessary to turn these plains into a large-scale supplier of meat and grains. The Venezuelan government has been slowly introducing these changes.

To the south of the llanos is a geographic complex that dwarfs any other in Latin America, except the Andes. It is the huge Amazon basin, which occupies nearly one-half of South America and includes the world's largest tropical rain forest. For the most part, the Amazon basin is in Brazil, but thousands of square miles of it extend into Venezuela, eastern Colombia, Ecuador, Peru, and Bolivia. Flowing through it is the Amazon River and its tributaries. Together, they constitute the world's mightiest river system. This system drains forty percent of the land area of South America.

During its course, the Amazon sometimes attains a width of three miles. It carries at least five times more water to the ocean than its nearest competitor, the Mississippi. The water of the Amazon flows into the Atlantic with such force that one can find fresh water for two hundred miles into the ocean. The Amazon basin, however, has only begun to be penetrated. Most of its resources must still be discovered and inventoried.

Our hypothetical satellite is now speeding over the southern half of South America. Here, the continent narrows. Three outstanding land features are evident. In Brazil, south of the Amazon, there is a great mass of highlands. For nearly two thousand miles along the coast, these highlands practically rise out of the Atlantic Ocean like a wall. Little or no coastal plain exists over this lengthy stretch. This abrupt wall is called the *Great Escarpment*.

The remarkable feature about the Brazilian highlands is that they reach their greatest height at their coastal beginnings. Thereafter, they slowly descend and move into the interior, falling away and down from the Great Escarpment. This fact explains why many rivers that begin in the seven thousand to eight thousand feet heights only a few miles from the coast wind their way hundreds of miles inland. Much of the Brazilian highlands remains a frontier area. Generations of Brazilian leaders have hoped that the interior would be settled; but full settlement is still just a hope.

Moving farther south over the rapidly narrowing continent, a sparsely settled lowland interior plain in Paraguay and northern Argentina called the *Gran Chaco* comes into view. An area of tall grass, interrupted by scrub forest, the Gran Chaco was the scene of a gruesome war between Paraguay and Bolivia from 1932 to 1938. The war was fought for possession of lands that, according to rumor, were rich in oil. History has partially confirmed these suspicions. Eventually, oil was discovered—but in the adjacent Argentine *Chaco*, and not the land over which Paraguay and Bolivia fought.

To the east and south of the Gran Chaco, around the mouth of the Río de la Plata system, lies the *Pampa*, one of the most generously endowed of the world's plains. The rich soil of the pampa has made Argentines and Uruguayans among the world's best-fed people.

Flowing from Paraguay and Brazil through northern Argentina and into a muddy estuary is the Río de la Plata river system. This system can accommodate ocean-going vessels one thousand miles upstream to Asunción, the capital of Paraguay. The main branch of the Río de la Plata system, the Paraná-Paraguay River, is the most heavily used natural artery of commerce in all of Latin America.

This rapid view of Latin America's physical geography should confirm that the area is anything but uniform and that it is often uninviting to settlement. However, the barriers posed by Latin America's often unfavorable geography must not be overrated. Shallow, silt-laden harbors can be dredged and made suitable for the deepest ocean-going vessels, as it has at Buenos Aires, Argentina, one of the world's great port cities. Highways can and have been constructed through the earthquake-ridden Andes, even though they are twisting, narrow, two-lane roads that follow an unending series of hairpin curves, and force cars and trucks to creep along in second gear. During the 1970s, the Brazilian government constructed a road through the Amazon rain forest because the government wanted to connect Brazil's poverty-ridden, drought-stricken northeast with the unpopulated Amazon wilderness. This highway cuts through hundreds of miles of dense rain forest, crosses periodically flooded grasslands, and fords mile-wide rivers. It stretches all the way to the border with Peru.

The more than 800 thousand miles of roads (only ninety thousand of which are all-weather) and the eighty-five thousand miles of railroads attest to the fact that the rugged geography of Latin America is not an insurmountable obstacle. Furthermore, the airplane has linked places and areas that roads, railways, and rivers have not been able to bring together. Cargo-carrying planes have been especially important. The small, level clearing needed for takeoff and landing can be built for a small fraction of the cost and time required by the railroad and highway. Many areas of Latin America would remain isolated today and deprived of larger regional and national markets were it not for the arrival and departure of freight-carrying airplanes.

As important as geography has been, it is not the element that best explains what is now happening or has happened in Latin America. For example, whatever potential wealth was known to exist, geography has rarely been a barrier to getting at it. Nothing in Latin American history has been more certain than the mining of valuable natural resources by cheap labor, no matter how inaccessible or forbidding the location. The towering Andes mountains, rich in silver, the bone dry Atacama Desert of northern Chile with its copper mines, and, presently, the Amazon rain forest with its reserves of different metal and minerals have not posed, nor will they in the future pose, barriers to human settlement or to large scale industrial production.

Developing wealth by means of cheap or forced labor has probably been the most important continuing process in Latin American history. This process, in turn, is responsible for the riches and poverty seen everywhere in the region.

THE PEOPLE

The Latin American people have come principally from three areas of the world. The American Indian, native to the region, may have originally numbered anywhere from thirteen to fifty million. These peoples were densely settled in the islands of the Caribbean; in the highlands, mountains, and Yucatán peninsula of Central America; and in the Andes Mountains of South America. In other areas, the Indian population was more sparse. There were probably no more than a million and a half Indians in all of Brazil. By comparison, some of the islands of the Caribbean may have had as many people as all of Brazil.

From Africa came fifteen million human beings destined for a life of slavery. Slaves were most highly concentrated in Brazil and the Caribbean Islands. However, at least a few black slaves—and sometimes quite a few—were worked in nearly all parts of Latin America.

From Europe came nearly fifteen million people. Their migration has continued from 1492 to the present time. Indeed, the majority of them have arrived since 1870.

In addition to these three main groups, a few hundred thousand Asians migrated to Latin America. Settlers from India have come to the former British colonies of Jamaica and Guyana. Nearly 250 thousand Japanese settled in Brazil. Small groups of Chinese emigrated to Peru and Brazil.

The Indian, the African, the European, and combinations of these three groups of people make up the overwhelming majority of today's Latin American population. Over the centuries, they have intermingled culturally and biologically in a "melting pot" that dwarfs anything known in the United States.

In the beginning, great gaps separated the three groups. Race and personal status were interlinked. The European came as a conqueror, ruler, and master. The African came as a slave, who labored for the European master class. The Indian occupied a dual status. He was exploited by the European, who demanded free labor, food, and commodities as a tribute. The Indian was also a ward to be protected, Christianized, and re-made into a European peasant.

As soon as the European arrived, the process of miscegenation, or race mixture, began. Out of this process came new individuals who were neither European nor Indian. They were soon joined by the children of African slaves and their European masters. A bewildering variety of unions eventually occurred, and the offspring they produced were given a host of names. The child of an Indian and a European was called a *mestizo*. The union of African and European produced a *mulatto*, and that of the Indian and the African, a *zambo*. Many other names were later added in the effort to distinguish different racial combinations. Given the extent of race mixture in Latin America, such distinctions were impossible to maintain.

Yet, color remains a way of classifying people today. In Brazil's multi-racial society, for example, census takers label people black, brown, yellow, or white. But one Brazilian's definition of "brown" will be "white" or "black" to another Brazilian. Color is a highly subjective idea in Latin America. It lies, quite inconsistently and unpredictably, in the eyes of the beholder.

One fact stands out. The individual whose genes contain different combinations from America, Europe, and Africa has become the characteristic Latin American type. The only exceptions among the Spanish-speaking republics are Costa Rica, Uruguay, and Argentina, whose populations are almost exclusively of European origin. Haiti, on the other hand, is an almost exclusively black republic.

Race mixture itself cannot be thought of scientifically as either a good or bad process. Some Latin Americans have argued that it was necessary for their nation's past success. They also imply that it will strengthen them in the future. In some places, then—most notably in Brazil and Mexico—race mixture is thought of as being positive.

Race mixture is one of the long-term processes of Latin American history. It is necessary to examine this history, which may be conveniently broken into three periods: the colonial period, lasting about three hundred years (1492–1790); the independence period, lasting approximately thirty-five years (1790–1825); and the period since independence (1825 to the present), especially the years since 1930.

B. The Indigenous Cultures of the Americas

When the Spanish came across the great lands of the Americas, they soon realized that these territories were not part of western Asia (called the "Indies" at the time), but a whole "new" world. However, the Europeans called the inhabitants *indios*, still confused about their geography.

In fact, the Spaniards had arrived at region that had great civilizations, cultures that had been nourished for thousands of years, isolated from Europe and other parts of the world. It is estimated that over 1,500 different languages were spoken in the Americas when the Europeans arrived. The Peruvian city of Caral was being built at the same time as the Egyptian Great Pyramid at Giza, from about 3000 years before the modern era. The classic Maya culture of southern Mexico, Guatemala, Honduras, and Belize flourished during the Visigothic and Islamic period of medieval Spain. The great Aztec Empire in Mexico and the Inca Empire in Peru grew during the height of the Renaissance in Spain; their national destiny was cut short by the swords of the Spanish conquistadores.

When the Europeans arrived in Maya country in the 16th century, the great cities—such as Tikal and Copán—were overgrown with the jungle. The Maya people were still there, as they are now, living in small villages and continuing a rich oral tradition. One of the great mysteries of the Americas is *why* this brilliant culture suffered such a rapid decline, some 500 years before the appearance of the conquistadores. In the article that follows by the Pulitzer-prize winning author Jared Diamond, some reasons for the fall of the classic Maya culture are given. His comments are followed by a general review of the Aztec culture of Mexico and the Inca culture of Peru, two empires that were at zenith of their power when the Spanish arrived.

You might now want to view the CD *Sacred Sites* attached to the *Voices of Latino Culture*. This CD will give a detailed tour of Tikal (classic Maya), Machu Picchu (imperial Inca culture), and the Aztec Great Temple (in modern-day Mexico City). The CD also includes music reproduced on original instruments from each of these cultures.

1. THE MAYA COLLAPSES

Mysteries of lost cities • The Maya environment • Maya agriculture • Maya history • Copán • Complexities of collapses • Wars and droughts • Collapse in the southern lowlands • The Maya message •

By now, millions of modern tourists have visited ruins of the ancient Maya civilization that collapsed over a thousand years ago in Mexico's Yucatán Peninsula and adjacent parts of Central America. All of us love a romantic mystery, and the Maya offer us one at our doorstep, almost as close for Americans as the Anasazi ruins. To visit a former Maya city, we need only board a direct flight from the U.S. to the modern Mexican state capital city of Mérida, jump into a rental car or minibus, and drive an hour on a paved highway.

Today, many Maya ruins, with their great temples and monuments, still lie surrounded by jungle, far from current human settlement. Yet they were once the sites of the New World's most advanced Native American civilization before European arrival, and the only one with extensive deciphered written texts. How could ancient peoples have supported urban societies in areas where few farmers eke out a living today? The Maya cities impress us not only with that mystery and with their beauty, but also because they are "pure" archaeological sites. That is, their locations became depopulated, so they were not covered up by later buildings as were so many other ancient cities, like the Aztec capital of Tenochtitlán (now buried under modern Mexico City) and Rome.

Maya cities remained deserted, hidden by trees, and virtually unknown to the outside world until rediscovered in 1839 by a rich American lawyer named John Stephens, together with the English draftsman Frederick Catherwood. Having heard rumors of ruins in the jungle, Stephens got President Martin Van Buren to appoint him ambassador to the Confederation of Central American Republics, an amorphous political entity then extending from modern Guatemala to Nicaragua, as a front for his archaeological explorations. Stephens and Catherwood ended up exploring 44 sites and cities. From the extraordinary quality of the buildings and the art, they realized that these were not the work of savages (in their words) but of a vanished high civilization. They recognized that some of the carvings on the stone monuments constituted writing, and they correctly guessed that it related historical events and the names of people. On his return, Stephens wrote two travel books, illustrated by Catherwood and describing the ruins, that became best sellers.

A few quotes from Stephens's writings will give a sense of the romantic appeal of the Maya: "The city was desolate. No remnant of this race hangs round the ruins, with traditions handed down from father to son and from generation to generation. It lay before us like a shattered bark in the midst of the ocean, her mast gone, her name effaced, her crew perished, and none to tell whence she came, to whom she belonged, how long on her journey, or what caused her destruction.... Architecture, sculpture, and painting, all the arts which embellish life, had flourished in this overgrown forest; orators, warriors, and statesmen, beauty, ambition, and glory had lived and passed away, and none knew that such things had been, or could tell of their past existence.... Here were the remains of a cultivated, polished, and peculiar people, who had passed through all the stages incident to the rise and fall of nations; reached their golden age, and perished.... We went up to their desolate temples and fallen altars; and wherever we moved we saw the evidence of their taste, their skill in arts.... We called back into life the strange people who gazed in sadness from the wall; pictured them, in fanciful costumes and adorned with plumes of feather, ascending the terraces of the palace and the steps leading to the temples.... In the romance of the world's history nothing ever impressed me more forcibly than the spectacle of this once great and lovely city, overturned, desolate, and lost,... overgrown with trees for miles around, and without even a name to distinguish it." Those sensations are what tourists drawn to Maya ruins still feel today, and why we find the Maya collapse so fascinating.

The Maya story has several advantages for all of us interested in prehistoric collapses. First, the Maya written records that have survived, although frustratingly incomplete, are still useful for reconstructing Maya history in much greater detail than we can reconstruct Easter Island, or even Anasazi history with its tree rings and packrat middens. The great art and architecture of Maya cities have resulted in far more archaeologists studying the Maya than would have been the case if they had just been illiterate hunter-gatherers living in archaeologically invisible hovels.

Climatologists and paleoecologists have recently been able to recognize several signals of ancient climate and environmental changes that contributed to the Maya collapse. Finally, today there are still Maya people living in their ancient homeland and speaking Maya languages. Because much ancient Maya culture survived the collapse, early European visitors to the homeland recorded information about contemporary Maya society that played a vital role in our understanding ancient Maya society. The first Maya contact with Europeans came already in 1502, just 10 years after Christopher Columbus's "discovery" of the New World, when Columbus on the last of his four voyages captured a trading canoe that may have been Maya. In 1527 the Spanish began in earnest to conquer the Maya, but it was not until 1697 that they subdued the last principality. Thus, the Spanish had opportunities to observe independent Maya societies for a period of nearly two centuries. Especially important, both for bad and for good, was the bishop Diego de Landa, who resided in the Yucatan Peninsula for most of the years from 1549 to 1578. On the one hand, in one of history's worst acts of cultural vandalism, he burned all Maya manuscripts that he could locate in his effort to eliminate "paganism," so that only four survive today. On the other hand, he wrote a detailed account of Maya society, and he obtained from an informant a garbled explanation of Maya writing that eventually, nearly four centuries later, turned out to offer clues to its decipherment.

A further reason for our devoting a chapter to the Maya is to provide an antidote to our other chapters on past societies, which consist disproportionately of small societies in somewhat fragile and geographically isolated environments, and behind the cutting edge of contemporary technology and culture. The Maya were none of those things. Instead, they were culturally the most advanced society (or among the most advanced ones) in the pre-Columbian New World, the only one with extensive preserved writing, and located within one of the two heartlands of New World civilization (Mesoamerica). While their environment did present some problems associated with its karst terrain and unpredictably fluctuating rainfall, it does not rank as notably fragile by world standards, and it was certainly less fragile than the environments of ancient Easter Island, the Anasazi area, Greenland, or modern Australia. Lest one be misled into thinking that crashes are a risk only for small peripheral societies in fragile areas, the Maya warn us that crashes can also befall the most advanced and creative societies.

From the perspective of our five-point framework for understanding societal collapses, the Maya illustrate four of our points. They did damage their environment, especially by deforestation and erosion. Climate changes (droughts) did contribute to the Maya collapse, probably repeatedly. Hostilities among the Maya themselves did play a large role. Finally, political/cultural factors, especially the competition among kings and nobles that led to a chronic emphasis on war and erecting monuments rather than on solving underlying problems, also contributed. The remaining item on our five-point list, trade or cessation of trade with external friendly societies, does not appear to have been essential in sustaining the Maya or in causing their downfall. While obsidian (their preferred raw material for making into stone tools), jade, gold, and shells were imported into the Maya area, the latter three items were non-essential luxuries. Obsidian tools remained widely distributed in the Maya area long after the political collapse, so obsidian was evidently never in short supply.

To understand the Maya, let's begin by considering their environment, which we think of as "jungle" or "tropical rainforest." That's not true, and the reason why not proves to be important. Properly speaking, tropical rainforests grow in high-rainfall equatorial areas that remain wet or humid all year round. But the Maya homeland lies more than a thousand miles from the equator, at latitudes 17° to 22°N, in a habitat termed a "seasonal tropical forest." That is, while there does tend to be a rainy season from May to October, there is also a dry season from January through April. If one focuses on the wet months, one calls the Maya homeland a "seasonal tropical forest"; if one focuses on the dry months, one could instead describe it as a "seasonal desert."

From north to south in the Yucatán Peninsula, rainfall increases from 18 to 100 inches per year, and the soils become thicker, so that the southern peninsula was agriculturally more productive and supported denser populations. But rainfall in the Maya homeland is unpredictably variable between years; some recent years have had three or four times more rain than other years. Also, the timing of rainfall within the year is somewhat unpredictable, so it can easily happen that farmers plant their crops in anticipation of rain and then the rains do not come when expected. As a result, modern farmers attempting to grow corn in the ancient Maya homelands have faced frequent crop failures, especially in the north. The ancient Maya were presumably more experienced and did better, but nevertheless they too must have faced risks of crop failures from droughts and hurricanes.

Although southern Maya areas received more rainfall than northern areas, problems of water were paradoxically more severe in the wet south. While that made things hard for ancient Maya living in the south, it has also made things hard for modern archaeologists who have difficulty understanding why ancient droughts would have caused bigger problems in the wet south than in the dry north. The likely explanation is that a lens of freshwater underlies the Yucatán Peninsula, but surface elevation increases from north to south, so that as one moves south the land surface lies increasingly higher above the water table. In the northern peninsula the elevation is sufficiently low that the ancient Maya were able to reach the water table at deep sinkholes called cenotes, or at deep caves; all tourists who have visited the Maya city of Chichén Itzá will remember the great cenotes there. In low-elevation north coastal areas without sinkholes, the Maya may have been able to get down to the water table by digging wells up to 75 feet deep. Water is readily available in many parts of Belize that have rivers, along the Usumacinta River in the west, and around a few lakes in the Petén area of the south. But much of the south lies too high above the water table for cenotes or wells to reach down to it. Making matters worse, most of the Yucatán Peninsula consists of karst, a porous sponge-like limestone terrain where rain runs straight into the ground and where little or no surface water remains available.

How did those dense southern Maya populations deal with their resulting water problem? It initially surprises us that many of their cities were not built next to the few rivers but instead on promontories in rolling uplands. The explanation is that the Maya excavated depressions, modified natural depressions, and then plugged up leaks in the karst by plastering the bottoms of the depressions in order to create cisterns and reservoirs, which collected rain from large plastered catchment basins and stored it for use in the dry season. For example, reservoirs at the Maya city of Tikal held enough water to meet the drinking water needs of about 10,000 people for a period of 18 months. At the city of Coba the Maya built dikes around a lake in order to raise its level and make their water supply more reliable. But the inhabitants of Tikal and other cities dependent on reservoirs for drinking water would still have been in deep trouble if 18 months passed without rain in a prolonged drought. A shorter drought in which they exhausted their stored food supplies might already have gotten them in deep trouble through starvation, because growing crops required rain rather than reservoirs.

Of particular importance for our purposes are the details of Maya agriculture, which was based on crops domesticated in Mexico—especially corn, with beans being second in importance. For the elite as well as commoners, corn constituted at least 70% of the Maya diet, as deduced from isotope analyses of ancient Maya skeletons. Their sole domestic animals were the dog, turkey, Muscovy duck, and a stingless bee yielding honey, while their most important wild meat source was deer that they hunted, plus fish at some sites. However, the few animal bones at Maya archaeological sites suggest that the quantity of meat available to the Maya was low. Venison was mainly a luxury food for the elite.

It was formerly believed that Maya farming was based on slash-and-burn agriculture (so-called swidden agriculture) in which forest is cleared and burned, crops are grown in the resulting field for a year or a few years until the soil is exhausted, and then the field is abandoned for a long fallow period of 15 or 20 years until regrowth of wild vegetation restores fertility to the soil. Because most of the landscape under a swidden agricultural system is fallow at any given time, it can support only modest population densities. Thus, it was a surprise for archaeologists to discover that ancient Maya population densities, estimated from numbers of stone foundations of farmhouses, were often far higher than what swidden agriculture could support. The actual values are the subject of much dispute and evidently varied among areas, but frequently cited estimates reach 250 to 750, possibly even 1,500, people per square mile. (For comparison, even today the two most densely populated countries in Africa, Rwanda and Burundi, have population densities of only about 750 and 540 people per square mile, respectively.) Hence the ancient Maya must have had some means of increasing agricultural production beyond what was possible through swidden alone.

Many Maya areas do show remains of agricultural structures designed to increase production, such as terracing of hill slopes to retain soil and moisture, irrigation systems, and arrays of canals and drained or raised fields. The latter systems, which are well attested elsewhere in the world and which require a lot of labor to construct, but which reward the labor with increased food production, involve digging canals to drain a waterlogged area, fertilizing and raising the level of the fields between the canals by dumping muck and water hyacinths dredged out of canals onto the fields, and thereby keeping the fields themselves from being inundated. Besides harvesting crops grown over the fields, farmers with raised fields also "grow" wild fish and turtles in the canals (actually, let them grow themselves) as an additional food source. However, other Maya areas, such as the well-studied cities of Copán and Tikal, show little archaeological evidence of terracing, irrigation, or raised- or drained-field systems. Instead, their inhabitants must have used archaeologically invisible means to increase food production, by mulching, floodwater farming, shortening the time that a field is left fallow, and tilling the soil to restore soil fertility, or in the extreme omitting the fallow period entirely and growing crops every year, or in especially moist areas growing two crops per year.

Socially stratified societies, including modern American and European society, consist of farmers who produce food, plus non-farmers such as bureaucrats and soldiers who do not produce food but merely consume the food grown by the farmers and are in effect parasites on farmers. Hence in any stratified society the farmers must grow enough surplus food to meet not only their own needs but also those of the other consumers. The number of non-producing consumers that can be supported depends on the society's agricultural productivity. In the United States today, with its highly efficient agriculture, farmers make up only 2% of our population, and each farmer can feed on the average 125 other people (American non-farmers plus people in export markets overseas). Ancient Egyptian agriculture, although much less efficient than modern mechanized agriculture, was still efficient enough for an" Egyptian peasant to produce five times the food required for himself and his family. But a Maya peasant could produce only twice the needs of himself and his family. At least 70% of Maya society consisted of peasants. That's because Maya agriculture suffered from several limitations.

First, it yielded little protein. Corn, by far the dominant crop, has a lower protein content than the Old World staples of wheat and barley. The few edible domestic animals already mentioned included no large ones and yielded much less meat than did Old World cows, sheep, pigs, and goats. The Maya depended on a narrower range of crops than did Andean farmers (who in addition to corn also had potatoes, high-protein quinoa, and many other plants, plus llamas for meat), and much narrower again than the variety of crops in China and in western Eurasia.

Another limitation was that Maya corn agriculture was less intensive and productive than the Aztecs' *chinampas* (a very productive type of raised-field agriculture), the raised fields of the Tiwanaku civilization of the Andes, Moche irrigation on the coast of Peru, or fields tilled by animal-drawn plows over much of Eurasia.

Still a further limitation arose from the humid climate of the Maya area, which made it difficult to store corn beyond a year, whereas the Anasazi living in the dry climate of the U.S. Southwest could store it for three years.

Finally, unlike Andean Indians with their llamas, and unlike Old World peoples with their horses, oxen, donkeys, and camels, the Maya had no animal-powered transport or plows. All overland transport for the Maya went on the backs of human porters. But if you send out a porter carrying a load of corn to accompany an army into the field, some of that load of corn is required to feed the porter himself on the trip out, and some more to feed him on the trip back, leaving only a fraction of the load available to feed the army. The longer the trip, the less of the load is left over from the porter's own requirements. Beyond a march of a few days to a week, it becomes uneconomical to send porters carrying corn to provision armies or markets. Thus, the modest productivity of Maya agriculture, and their lack of draft animals, severely limited the duration and distance possible for their military campaigns.

We are accustomed to thinking of military success as determined by quality of weaponry, rather than by food supply. But a clear example of how improvements in food supply may decisively increase military success comes from the history of Maori New Zealand. The Maori are the Polynesian people who were the first to settle New Zealand. Traditionally, they fought frequent fierce wars against each other, but only against closely neighboring tribes. Those wars were limited by the modest productivity of their agriculture, whose staple crop was sweet potatoes. It was not possible to grow enough sweet potatoes to feed an army in the field for a long time or on distant marches. When Europeans arrived in New Zealand, they brought potatoes, which beginning around 1815 considerably increased Maori crop yields. Maori could now grow enough food to supply armies in the field for many weeks. The result was a 15-year period in Maori history, from 1818 until 1833, when Maori tribes that had acquired potatoes and guns from the English sent armies out on raids to attack tribes hundreds of miles away that had not yet acquired potatoes and guns. Thus, the potato's productivity relieved previous limitations on Maori warfare, similar to the limitations that low-productivity corn agriculture imposed on Maya warfare.

Those food supply considerations may contribute to explaining why Maya society remained politically divided among small kingdoms that were perpetually at war with each other, and that never became unified into large empires like the Aztec Empire of the Valley of Mexico (fed with the help of their *chinampa* agriculture and other forms of intensification) or the Inca Empire of the Andes (fed by more diverse crops carried by llamas over well-built roads). Maya armies and bureaucracies remained small and unable to mount lengthy campaigns over long distances. (Even much later, in 1848, when the Maya revolted against their Mexican overlords and

a Maya army seemed to be on the verge of victory, the army had to break off fighting and go home to harvest another crop of corn.) Many Maya kingdoms held populations of only up to 25,000 to 50,000 people, none over half a million, within a radius of two or three days' walk from the king's palace. (The actual numbers are again highly controversial among archaeologists.) From the tops of the temples of some Maya kingdoms, it was possible to see the temples of the nearest kingdom. Maya cities remained small (mostly less than one square mile in area), without the large populations and big markets of Teotihuacán and Tenochtitlán in the Valley of Mexico, or of Chan-Chan and Cuzco in Peru, and without archaeological evidence of the royally managed food storage and trade that characterized ancient Greece and Mesopotamia.

Now for a quick crash-course in Maya history. The Maya area is part of the larger ancient Native American cultural region known as Mesoamerica, which extended approximately from Central Mexico to Honduras and constituted (along with the Andes of South America) one of the two New World centers of innovation before European arrival. The Maya shared much in common with other Mesoamerican societies not only in what they possessed, but also in what they lacked. For example, surprisingly to modern Westerners with expectations based on Old World civilizations, Mesoamerican societies lacked metal tools, pulleys and other machines, wheels (except locally as toys), boats with sails, and domestic animals large enough to carry loads or pull a plow. All of those great Maya temples were constructed by stone and wooden tools and by human muscle power alone.

Of the ingredients of Maya civilization, many were acquired by the Maya from elsewhere in Mesoamerica. For instance, Mesoamerican agriculture, cities, and writing first arose outside the Maya area itself, in valleys and coastal lowlands to the west and southwest, where corn and beans and squash were domesticated and became important dietary components by 3000 B.C., pottery arose around 2500 B.C., villages by 1500 B.C., cities among the Olmecs by 1200 B.C., writing appeared among the Zapotecs in Oaxaca around or after 600 B.C., and the first states arose around 300 B.C. Two complementary calendars, a solar calendar of 365 days and a ritual calendar of 260 days, also arose outside the Maya area. Other elements of Maya civilization were either invented, perfected, or modified by the Maya themselves.

Within the Maya area, villages and pottery appeared around or after 1000 B.C., substantial buildings around 500 B.C., and writing around 400 B.C. All preserved ancient Maya writing, constituting a total of about 15,000 inscriptions, is on stone and pottery and deals only with kings, nobles, and their conquests. There is not a single mention of commoners. When Spaniards arrived, the Maya were still using bark paper coated with plaster to write books, of which the sole four that escaped Bishop Landa's fires turned out to be treatises on astronomy and the calendar. The ancient Maya also had had such bark-paper books, often depicted on their pottery, but only decayed remains of them have survived in tombs. The famous Maya Long Count calendar begins on August 11, 3114 b.c.—just as our own calendar begins on January 1 of the first year of the Christian era. We know the significance to us of that day-zero of our calendar: it's the supposed beginning of the year in which Christ was born. Presumably the Maya also attached some significance to their own day zero, but we don't know what it was. The first preserved Long Count date is only a.d. 197 for a monument in the Maya area and 36 b.c. outside the Maya area, indicating that the Long Count calendar's day-zero was backdated to August 11, 3114 b.c. long after the facts; there was no writing anywhere in the New World then, nor would there be for 2,500 years after that date.

Our calendar is divided into units of days, weeks, months, years, decades, centuries, and millennia: for example, the date of February 19, 2003, on which I wrote the first draft of this paragraph, means the 19th day of the second month in the third year of the first decade of the first century of the third millennium beginning with the birth of Christ. Similarly, the Maya Long Count calendar named dates in units of days (*kin*), 20 days (*uinal*), 360 days (*tun*), 7,200 days or approximately 20 years (katunn), and 144,000 days or approximately 400 years (*baktun*). All of Maya history falls into baktuns 8, 9, and 10.

The so-called Classic period of Maya civilization begins in baktun 8, around a.d. 250, when evidence for the first kings and dynasties appears. Among the glyphs (written signs) on Maya monuments, students of Maya writing recognized a few dozen, each of which was concentrated in its own geographic area, and which are now considered to have had the approximate meaning of dynasties or kingdoms. In addition to Maya kings having their own name glyphs and palaces, many nobles also had their own inscriptions and palaces. In Maya society the king also functioned as high priest carrying the responsibility to attend to astronomical and calendrical rituals, and thereby to bring rain and prosperity, which the king claimed to nave the supernatural power to deliver because of his asserted family relationship to the gods. That is, there was a tacitly understood quid pro quo: the reason why the peasants

supported the luxurious lifestyle of the king and his court, fed him corn and venison, and built his palaces was because he had made implicit big promises to the peasants. As we shall see, kings got into trouble with their peasants if a drought came, because that was tantamount to the breaking of a royal promise.

From a.d. 250 onwards, the Maya population (as judged from the number of archaeologically attested house sites), the number of monuments and buildings, and the number of Long Count dates on monuments and pottery increased almost exponentially, to reach peak numbers in the 8th century a.d. The largest monuments were erected towards the end of that Classic period. Numbers of all three of those indicators of a complex society declined throughout the 9th century, until the last known Long Count date on any monument fell in baktun 10, in the year a.d. 909. That decline of Maya population, architecture, and the Long Count calendar constitutes what is known as the Classic Maya collapse.

To summarize the Classic Maya collapse, we can tentatively identify five strands. I acknowledge, however, that Maya archaeologists still disagree vigorously among themselves—in part, because the different strands evidently varied in importance among different parts of the Maya realm; because detailed archaeological studies are available for only some Maya sites; and because it remains puzzling why most of the Maya heartland remained nearly empty of population and failed to recover after the collapse and after re-growth of forests.

With those caveats, it appears to me that one strand consisted of population growth outstripping available resources: a dilemma similar to the one foreseen by Thomas Malthus in 1798 and being played out today in Rwanda, Haiti, and elsewhere. As the archaeologist David Webster succinctly puts it, "Too many farmers grew too many crops on too much of the landscape." Compounding that mismatch between population and resources was the second strand: the effects of deforestation and hillside erosion, which caused a decrease in the amount of useable farmland at a time when more rather than less farmland was needed, and possibly exacerbated by an anthropogenic drought resulting from deforestation, by soil nutrient depletion and other soil problems, and by the struggle to prevent bracken ferns from overrunning the fields.

The third strand consisted of increased fighting, as more and more people fought over fewer resources. Maya warfare, already endemic, peaked just before the collapse. That is not surprising when one reflects that at least 5,000,000 people, perhaps many more, were crammed into an area smaller than the state of Colorado (104,000 square miles). That warfare would have decreased further the amount of land available for agriculture, by creating no-man's lands between principalities where it was now unsafe to farm. Bringing matters to a head was the strand of climate change. The drought at the time of the Classic collapse was not the first drought that the Maya had lived through, but it was the most severe. At the time of previous droughts, there were still uninhabited parts of the Maya landscape, and people at a site affected by drought could save themselves by moving to another site. However, by the time of the Classic collapse the landscape was now full, there no useful unoccupied land in the vicinity on which to begin anew, and the whole population could not be accommodated in the few areas that continued to have reliable water supplies.

As our fifth strand, we have to wonder why the kings and nobles failed to recognize and solve these seemingly obvious problems undermining their society. Their attention was evidently focused on their short-term concerns of enriching themselves, waging wars, erecting monuments, competing with each other, and extracting enough food from the peasants to support all those activities. Like most leaders throughout human history, the Maya kings and nobles did not heed long-term problems, insofar as they perceived them. We shall return to this theme in Chapter 14.

As on Easter Island, Mangareva, and among the Anasazi, Maya environmental and population problems led to increasing warfare and civil strife. As on Easter Island and at Chaco Canyon, Maya peak population numbers were followed swiftly by political and social collapse. Paralleling the eventual extension of agriculture from Easter Island's coastal lowlands to its uplands, and from the Mimbres floodplain to the hills, Copan's inhabitants also expanded from the floodplain to the more is fragile hill slopes, leaving them with a larger population to feed when the agricultural boom in the hills went bust. Like Easter Island chiefs erecting ever larger statues, eventually crowned by pukao, and like Anasazi elite treating themselves to necklaces of 2,000 turquoise beads, Maya kings sought to outdo each other with more and more impressive temples, covered with thicker and thicker plaster—reminiscent in turn of the extravagant conspicuous consumption by modern American CEOs. The passivity of Easter chiefs and Maya kings in the face of the real big threats to their societies completes our list of disquieting parallels.

2. MEXICO AND THE MEXICA

The people of this province are well proportioned, tending to be tall rather than short; they are swarthy or brownish, of good features and mien. For the most part they are very skillful, stalwart and tireless, yet they sustain themselves with less food than any other people. They are very warlike and fearless of death. (Anonymous Conqueror, 1520s; in de Fuentes 1963:168)

Their understanding is keen, modest, and quiet, not proud or showy as in other nations. (Motolinía, 1536–1543; 1950:238)

Many of [the warriors] carried standards and gold shields, and other insignia which they wore strapped to their backs, giving them an appearance of great ferocity, since they also had their faces stained, and grimaced horribly, giving great leaps and shouts and cries. These put such fear into us that many of the Spaniards asked for confession. (Francisco de Aguilar, 1560; in de Fuentes 1963:139)

[T]he men or women who were to be sacrificed to their gods were thrown on their backs and of their own accord remained perfectly still. A priest then came out with a stone knife... and with this knife he opened the part where the heart is and took out the heart, without the person who was being sacrificed uttering a word... [The priests] went about very dirty and blackened, and wasted and haggard of face. They wore their hair hanging down very long and matted, so that it covered them, and went about infested with lice.... At night they walked like a procession of phantoms to the hills where they had their temples and idols and houses of worship. (Francisco de Aguilar, 1560; in de Fuentes 1963:163–164)

[W]hen we saw so many cities and villages built on the water and other great towns on dry land and that straight and level Causeway going towards Mexico [Tenochtitlán], we were amazed and said that it was like the enchantments they tell of in the legend of Amadis, on account of the great towers and cues [temples] and buildings rising from the water, and all built of masonry. And some of our soldiers even asked

whether the things that we saw were not a dream.
(Bernal Díaz del Castillo, 1560s; 1956:190–191)

> Like line burnished turquoise thou givest thy heart.
> It cometh to the sun.
> Thou wilt yet germinate—
> Wilt once again blossom.
> On earth.
> Thou wilt live among Uexotzinco's drums—
> Wilt gladden the nobles.
> Thy friends will behold thee.
> (*Aztec song*; in Sahagún 1950–1982. book 6:115)

Skillful and tireless, keen and modest. Ferocious in battle and stoic in sacrifice. Builders of magnificent cities and composers of sensitive songs and poems. Who were these people—so clever in both war and poetry?

They called themselves Mexica (me-SHEE-ka), although it has become popular today to refer to them as Aztecs. They arrived in central Mexico in the thirteenth century as a despised nomadic tribe. Through clever alliances and relentless warfare, they rapidly emerged as the leading military and political power in central Mexico. By the time of the Spanish arrival in 1519, the Mexica, with their capital at Tenochtitlán, had formed a strong alliance with their neighbors to the east and west: the Acolhuacans of Texcoco and the Tepanecas of Tlacopan. Together, these three groups forged a vast empire in Mesoamerica,[1] which may be called the Triple Alliance empire, or the Aztec empire.

The Basin of Mexico was the center of Aztec activity. Here they built their grandest marketplaces and greatest temples. Here they celebrated the most extravagant rituals, with gala processions and solemn priestly rites. Here was the empire's greatest concentration of wealth—nobles living in exquisite palaces and wearing fancy clothes; wealthy merchants fond of giving lavish feasts. Here elderly sages examined the wisdom of the ages, while inspired poets reflected on the virtues of beauty, honor, and death. And from this valley marched the great armies of conquest, often returning in glory with riches and slaves.

---

1. The culture area anthropologists designate as Mesoamerica encompasses a large area extending from central Mexico, south through Belize and Guatemala, and into Honduras and El Salvador. It is particularly set apart from the rest of Mexico and Central America by the presence of a settled agricultural life leading to the growth of a succession of great civilizations in pre-Spanish times. In addition, this culture area embraced a great variety of ethnic groups living in an atmospher of shifting alliances and open conflicts.

Covering some 2,500 square miles, the Basin of Mexico lies at an elevation of over 7,000 feet. Low-lying hills circumscribe it to the north, and impressive mountains to the west, south, and east, with some perpetually snow-capped peaks reaching elevations of more than 17,000 feet. Rimming the valley, this mountainous and hilly terrain presented a variety of microecological zones, each offering slightly different potential for human use.

Also adding to variety in ecological potential was a series of connected lakes. Water from mountainside runoff and numerous springs collected in them, yet they had no natural outlet. As a result, flooding and water quality were persistent problems for human habitation, and severe floods damaged parts of the city in 1382–1385, 1450, and 1499. Major feats of hydraulic engineering would be undertaken in the fifteenth century to control this powerful resource. Some of these massive hydraulic projects, which included dikes, aqueducts, canals, and causeways, were also designed to alleviate a second problem: the highly saline nature of the central lake, Lake Texcoco. Lying at a slightly lower elevation than the lakes to the north and south, it tended to collect salts deposited from those lakes and from the eastern drainage area. Securing access to fresh water became an important motivation for some instances of early Aztec imperial expansion.

Although they sometimes posed a severe threat to life, property, and urban expansion, these lakes also favored the human populations residing along their shores and on their islands. The lakes provided an effective means of transportation. At least by the time of the Spanish arrival, they were laden with canoe traffic, inviting commerce and other forms of interaction throughout the valley. The lakes also supplied varied and abundant aquatic resources: fish and fowl, reptile and amphibian. *Chinampa* cultivation, a highly productive form of agriculture, was practiced in several lacustrine districts by claiming lands from the lakes.

Origin of the Mexica and Arrival in Central Mexico

Like many earlier groups, the Mexica migrated into the Basin of Mexico. As related in myths and histories collected by indigenous and Spanish chroniclers of the sixteenth century, this migration extended over some 200 years (AD 1111–1325). Although numerous pictographic manuscripts and texts recorded the migration, it is now difficult to separate fact from myth, and to establish many details.

The migration began from a place called Aztlan (Place of the Herons). The exact location of Aztlan is in hot dispute: Some claim it was as distant as the southwestern United States; others, as close as 60 miles northwest of the final destination of the Mexica. There is general agreement, however, that Aztlan was probably located in a northwesterly direction from the Basin of Mexico.

From the elusive lake site of Aztlan the Mexica traveled to Chicomoztoc (Seven Caves), another unidentified locale. Chicomoztoc reputedly served as a jumping-off spot for a large number of nomadic groups. From here had departed the Tlaxcalans, settling to the east of the Basin of Mexico and later becoming bitter enemies of the Mexica. The Xochimilca, Chalca, Tepaneca, Culhua, Tlahuica, and others apparently congregated at Chicomoztoc; and each in turn subsequently traveled southeast, settling in the Basin of Mexico. The Mexica were reputedly the last to leave. By the time the Mexica arrived in central Mexico, the area was densely populated by sedentary populations of great antiquity and by recently arrived nomads from the north. Collectively, these groups lent an air of lively ethnic diversity to the basin setting.

The Mexica, like other migrants before them, called themselves and were called by others Chichimeca. The Chichimeca included a large number of ethnic groups (such as the Mexica), and may be broadly defined as nomadic hunting and gathering tribes of the northern desert regions. The sixteenth-century ethno-historical accounts actually identify more than one type of Chichimeca. The classic type was called the Teochichimeca, or "true Chichimecs." Groups so labeled were nomadic hunters and gatherers; they relied heavily on the bow and arrow, wore clothing made from animal skins, produced fine objects of stone and feathers, and used peyote (Sahagún 1950–1982, book 10:171–175).

The Mexica, both during their long journey and at the time of their arrival in the Basin of Mexico, more closely resembled a second type of Chichimeca, the Tamime: peoples who were neither truly nomadic and "barbaric," nor truly settled and "civilized." A sixteenth-century Franciscan friar, Bernardino de Sahagún, provides the following description of the Tamime as they were at the time of the Spanish conquest:

This name Tamin means "shooter of arrows." And these Tamime were only an off-shoot, a branch, of the Teochichimeca, although they were somewhat settled. They made their homes in caves, in gorges; in some places they established small grass huts and small corn fields. And they went mingling with the Mexica, or the Nahua, or the Otomí. There they heard the Nahuatl language, they spoke a little Nahuatl or Otomí, and in a measure they there learned a civilized way of life from them. Also they put on a few rags-tattered capes. Also in places they laid out small maize plots; they sowed them, they harvested them. (Sahagún 1950–1982, book 10:171)

In this statement, Sahagún mentions Tamime of the early sixteenth century coming into contact with settled groups such as the Mexica; in the twelfth century, the Mexica themselves would have been much like these Tamime, associating with earlier settled peoples.

This picture of the early Mexica as Tamime is supported by pictographic and textual accounts produced in the sixteenth century. During their extended journey into the Basin of Mexico, the Mexica are reported to have cultivated maize, chile, and other crops. They constructed "great and curious buildings." including temples, and were aware of luxury goods such as jade, cacao, and rich capes (Durán 1994:12, 19, 22).

They appear to have been a heterogeneous lot: they had a social hierarchy with priests as well as followers, and they developed internal factions. One sixteenth-century pictorial manuscript, the Codex Boturini, illustrates three priests and a priestess leading various nomadic groups; one of the priests carried the god Huitzilopochtli, patron deity of the Mexica, and was responsible for transmitting the will of that deity to the followers. The priests apparently were in a position of significant authority, as attested by the sixteenth-century chronicler Durán:

The people held this idol [Huitzilopochtli] in such reverence and awe that no one but his keepers [priests] dared approach or touch him.... The priests made the people adore the idol as a god, preaching to them the conduct they were to follow, and the ceremonies and rites to be observed in honor of their divinity (1994:19).

Whenever they stopped, even for short periods, the people were commanded to build a temple for their patron deity, Huitzilopochtli, and even occasionally to construct a ball court for the already widespread Mesoamerican ritual ball game (Alvarado Tezozomoc 1949:32). Ceremonies at times included human sacrifice. These sacrifices were used to honor Huitzilopochtli, but they may also have served a social control function. Durán (1994:26-28) speaks of certain Mexica who opposed the will of Huitzilopochtli. These people were content to stay in an inviting place near Tula, even though their god, through the priests, commanded them to continue on their journey. Under cover of night, the hearts of the upstarts were torn out: The wrath of Huitzilopochtli was expressed, and the rebellious faction was eliminated.

The journey from Aztlan to nearby Chicomoztoc and eventually to the Basin of Mexico was long and arduous. The wandering tribe not only encountered unfriendly peoples along the route but also was plagued with rivalries and tensions within its own group. The example cited above suggests that consensus was not necessarily the rule; disagreements were present, and some dissenters were simply eliminated through sacrifice. Apparently, parts of the nomadic population also were intentionally left behind along the route. The events at Malinalco offer an example:

> The god of the Aztecs had a sister who was called Malinalxochitl [Wild Grass Flower], who had accompanied the group on its migration. She was beautiful and of spirited disposition and was so clever and cunning that she became skillful in the use of magic and sorcery. Her craftiness was so great that she caused much harm among the people and made herself feared in order to be adored later as a goddess. The people had endured her because she was the sister of Huitzilopochtli, but finally they asked the god to get rid of her. Huitzilopochtli advised the priests through dreams, as was his custom, to abandon her in the place he would indicate, together with her attendants and certain elders of her group. (Durán 1994:24)

Whether or not true in detail, accounts such as this suggest that dissension and factions were present in this wandering population.

Other aspects of Mexica culture at this rime suggest ties with the settled Mesoamerican way of life. During their more than 200 years' journey the Mexica celebrated, at 52-year intervals, the "new fire" ceremony. This ritual commemorated the passage of a calendrical cycle, and indicates knowledge of the sophisticated Mesoamerican calendrical systems. Even their patron deity. Huitzilopochtli, was born of a goddess (Coatlicue) with deep Mesoamerican roots.

Although the Mexica, like earlier nomadic migrants, had many traditional Mesoamerican cultural traits, they were Chichimeca. They were nomadic and skilled in hunting. Their specialists were apparently limited lo the religious realm. They wore clothing made from maguey fiber. They were viewed by the sedentary peoples they encountered as vile and barbaric in their customs. However, by the time they arrived in the Basin of Mexico in the thirteenth century, their culture had become an intricate blend of nomadic and sedentary, "barbaric" and "civilized."

Also by this time, the classic features of civilizational states were already well entrenched in the Basin of Mexico. Cities, characterized by monumental public constructions and conscious urban planning, surrounded Lake Texcoco. Sophisticated irrigation agriculture, based on knowledge of a complex and specialized technology, produced abundant harvests of a variety of crops. Occupational specialization was common, complemented by a variety of exchange mechanisms including markets, foreign trade, and state-administered tax and tribute systems. A number of political city-states, composed of bureaucratic machineries and built on complex social stratification, exercised some control over the production and allocation of critical resources. Polytheistic religions reflected both cultural heterogeneity (through numerous specialized and patron deities) and hierarchical principles of organization (through the ranking of both deities and their public servants, the priests).

Primarily through warfare and conquest, these principles of heterogeneity and hierarchy were woven into concrete social realities. The structure of social classes and means for attaining rewards and social mobility were closely tied to military activities; imperial territorial structures were established on a foundation of domination through conquest. A companion of warfare is alliance, and alliances were established through marriage and through purely political arrangements between rulers. As the Mexica became integrated into these patterns, they would enlarge on these already existing themes, creating in some cases new and unique content.

The entrance of the Mexica into this complex urban situation (around AD 1250) was neither spectacular nor welcomed. Traveling through the basin and guided by their patron deity, they searched for some unoccupied place to settle. By the end of the thirteenth century, they had occupied Chapultepec, a strategic hilltop site beside Lake Texcoco. Twice forcefully expelled from Chapultepec, feared and despised by more powerful groups, the Mexica retreated to Culhuacan for asylum. The rulers there sent the Mexica to Tizapan, a dismal, volcanic, snake-infested place a few miles east of Culhuacan. Surprised at the ability of the Mexica to thrive in such an unpleasant environment, the Culhua finally accepted the new arrivals. Conforming to an apparently traditional pattern, the Mexica then served the Culhua as mercenaries, exhibiting exceptional abilities in the martial arts.

These capabilities, as well as certain of their customs, generated some fear and a great deal of hatred for the Mexica. The most notable example of the latter involves the deterioration of the previously amiable relations with the Culhua. Duran describes the following series of events:

> The Aztecs... went to the ruler of Colhuacan and asked for his daughter to be mistress of the Aztecs and bride of their god.... When the princess had been given the finest quarters there... Huitzilopochtli spoke to his priests... "You must kill her and sacrifice her in my name.... After she is dead, flay her and with her skin dress one of the principal youths...." (1994:37)

The Culhua ruler was then asked by the Mexica to attend a ceremony dedicating his daughter as a goddess:

> The king, with great confidence, arose and went to the temple... He entered the chamber of the idol and began to perform many ceremonies. He cut off the heads of the quail and the other birds and offered sacrifice by scattering the birds' blood and placing the food before the idols. Then he offered incense and (lowers and everything he had brought for that purpose.
>
> Taking in his hand a brazier with fire, he threw incense into it fervently and drew close to the figures. Suddenly the room was filled with light from the fire and fresh incense, and the king perceived the priest who was seated next to the idol, dressed in his daughter's skin. This was such a frightful sight that the king was overcome with horror. (ibid.:38)

The wrath of the Culhua ruler forced the Mexica to retreat. Fleeing into the marshes of Lake Texcoco, they were informed by their patron god that nearby they would soon see an eagle perched on a prickly pear cactus. This sign was to indicate the location of their final destination, the goal of an extended and difficult journey. Seeing this sight on a nearby island, they immediately occupied the island and set to erecting a small temple to Huitzilopochtli. They named their settlement Tenochtitlán (Place of the Fruit of the Prickly Pear Cactus), commemorating perhaps the symbolism of the founding event or perhaps the priest-ruler named Tenoch who had led them there or both. In the European calendar, the year was probably AD 1325.[2]

Both symbolism and practicality played a part in the choice of this site. For the Mexica, the eagle symbolized the sun, as also did their patron deity. In addition, the fruit of the prickly pear cactus (*nochtli*)

represented the human hearts, which were the sustenance of Huitzilopochtli. Symbolically, then, this was truly a place destined for occupation by the Mexica, Huitzilopochtli's servants.

On a practical level, the island site presented both advantages and problems. Fish and aquatic birds and animals were abundant. The surrounding lake was amenable to intensive chinampa cultivation. The little island location was also advantageous in terms of transportation and communication: in Mesoamerica transport was by foot or canoe, with the canoe having obvious advantages of ease of effort and size of load.

But this struggling settlement was also beset by problems: the total lack of certain essential raw materials (particularly wood and stone for construction), the periodic threat of flooding, and (later on) limited access to potable water.

Historical Background of the Aztec Empire

From the founding of Tenochtitlán in 1325 to the time of the Spanish arrival in 1519, the Mexica strove to carve a niche for themselves in this physical and sociopolitical environment. Their history may be viewed as a dynamic process of adaptation to an environment in some respects hospitable, in others, hostile. In the first phase of this history, 1325–1428, the Mexica were subject to forces already at play in the Basin of Mexico, and they primarily adapted to existing patterns. From 1428 to 1519, they took an aggressive, imperial position, actively shaping and directing the course of history of much of Mesoamerica.

For the first century after the founding of Tenochtitlán, the Mexica successfully tackled numerous problems. They had settled on land that formed the boundary among three powerful political entities. Unsure of their political status in this situation (although assuredly it was a weak position), they faced the problem of becoming tributaries of one of these states or of striving to maintain political independence. Although the latter alternative was most desirable to them, and in fact attempted, they quickly became subjects of the Tepanec city of Azcapotzalco. By the mid-fourteenth century, Azcapotzalco had taken aggressive military action in central Mexico, conquering one by one the numerous cities dotting the basin. In some cases, conquest involved actual military engagements; in others, agreements were made recognizing Azcapotzalco as the dominant power. The Mexica took the latter course. In a subordinate position to the growing Tepanec empire, they rendered tribute in lake products and in military service.

---

2. AD 1325 is the date traditionally assigned to the founding of Tenochtitlan. However, a few modern writers, using a different year count. place the event in Ad 1345.

To strengthen their political position, the Mexica sought allies. Marriage provided an effective means of establishing alliances, and the Mexica rulers made a series of clever marriages into long-established dynasties. Their first ruler, Acamapichtli, was reputedly the son of a Mexica nobleman and a Culhua princess. He married a woman from the royal line of Culhuacan, thus cementing a close alliance with the Culhua. This choice of ruler and his strategic marriage also provided future generations of Mexica rulers with a claim to Toltec heritage. In the Basin of Mexico, descent from the ancient Toltec nobility was translated into legitimacy to rule.

Acamapichtli's son and successor. Huitzilihuitl, used the same means to create firm ties with the famed Tepanec ruler of Azcapotzalco, Tezozomoc. Huitzilihuitl's second wife was a granddaughter of the old Tepanec ruler himself. Following this marriage, and particularly after the birth of a son, relations between Tenochtitlán and Azcapotzalco became quite amiable. The Tepanec ruler seemed to favor the Mexica, lightening their tribute burdens and involving them in numerous conquests from which they gained some territory for themselves. This favored position was also reflected in a gradual shift in power relations:

> In proportion to the rate at which the [Tepanec] conquests grew, the importance of the Aztecs also increased. They were treated less and less as ordinary vassals and mercenaries and more and more as allies. A number of regions which they had conquered for Atzcapotzalco were made over to them and from there they obtained the timber which they lacked and a constantly increasing supply of food. As their strength increased their influence in the making of political decisions seems also to have risen. (Katz 1972:138).

Although not well documented until 1428, when the Mexica defied Azcapotzalco, a definite system of social differentiation characterized Mexica society in this earlier time. A growing nobility class, headed by rulers descended from Acamapichtli, claimed special rights and privileges. Such privileges included private ownership of land and rights to serve in major public offices. The bulk of the Mexica population were commoners (*macehualtin*), who served as tillers of the soil and wielders of arms on the battlefield. Between these two distinct classes developed groups of occupational specialists: professional merchants and artisans of luxury wares, many of whom may have been later immigrants into the new city.

Military strategies and political machinations must have occupied much of the energy of the nobility, but the slow, everyday drudgery of building a city fell primarily to the commoner population. A major problem was the lack of building materials on the little island. Initially, the Mexica took advantage of a well-established market system to obtain stone and wood, trading available lacustrine products such as fish and frogs, mosquitoes and worms, ducks and other waterfowl. Later the Mexica supplemented the market system with a tribute system, obtaining many necessary goods from conquered peoples. Although little detailed information remains, the construction of dwellings, temples, palaces, and administrative buildings must have occupied a considerable portion of the time of the early settlers.

Another tremendously time-consuming task was the construction of chinampas. The claiming of lands from the lake for cultivation was a complicated yet vital activity. If the Mexica were to retain some degree of political autonomy, they would have to provide for the bulk of their own needs. With very little land available for cultivation, chinampas not only provided this land but also afforded a means for urban expansion.

The Mexica population seems to have quickly outgrown the tiny island. This rapid growth stemmed from both natural increases and a substantial amount of immigration. The expanding population was divided, territorially, into four large quarters. Each quarter was then divided into smaller territorial units usually called *calpulli*. Some elders and their followers were apparently displeased with their position in this new arrangement. They left to settle at Tlatelolco, a small island to the north and nearly adjacent to Tenochtitlán. Tlatelolco rapidly assumed considerable status as a commercial center, developing the largest and most active marketplace in the Basin of Mexico.[3]

The Mexica accomplished much in their first century at Tenochtitlán. They established alliances with the major Basin of Mexico cities. Strategic marriages cemented these alliances, and also allowed the Mexica rulers to claim Toltec ancestry, the key to political legitimacy. The city of Tenochtitlán grew in size and splendor, its population augmented by a variety of immigrant groups. Chinampa production provided the population with a reliable and intensive resource base. This resource base broadened as the Mexica succeeded in conquering others, from whom they demanded tribute.

---

3. Tlateloleo was conquered by the Mexica of neighboring Tenochtitlan in 1473.

The time spent under Tepanec domination allowed the Mexica to develop a strong and effective military force. This force, allied with neighboring and embittered Texcoco, turned against Azcapotzalco in 1428. The success of these allied forces in crushing the Tepanec empire of Azcapotzalco in 1430 ushered in another chapter in Mesoamerican history, a chapter dominated by the Mexica and their two allies: the Acolhuacans of Texcoco and the Tepanecas of Tlacopan. For the next 90 years this Triple Alliance embarked on a course of military expansion unparalleled in the history of Mesoamerica.

Urban Settlement and Organization

By 1519, the dual city of Tenochtitlán-Tlatelolco was connected to the mainland by three large manmade causeways—one stretching south, another north, and another west. From the southern causeway the Spanish conquistadors gained their first awed impressions of the Mexica capital and surrounding cities.

The causeways extended from the shores of the lake to the central ceremonial district of Tenochtitlán. There, in a sacred area enclosed by a wall, rose the major ceremonial buildings of the capital. Beyond this sacred district were the palaces of rulers, the houses of nobility, and the numerous buildings necessary for the administration of the empire. The vast remainder of the city was composed of urban dwelling sites, many with accompanying chinampas.

The central ceremonial area of Tenochtitlán measured approximately 360 meters square. Its immensity greatly impressed Cortés, who remarked that it could have contained "a town of fifteen thousand inhabitants'" (1928:90). Friar Diego Durán, speaking of a preconquest festival, states that the ceremonial area "must have been immense, for it accommodated eight thousand six hundred men, dancing in a circle" (1971:78). The district was the scene of the major public ceremonies of the Mexica. Most of these ceremonies involved human sacrifice, which was a particularly common activity here.

To date, over 30 structures have been archaeologically identified in this sacred precinct, although Sahagún enumerates 78 different structures within the district. Cortés mentions that there must have been at least 40 "towers" within the confines of the wall. Durán drawing on the memory of another conquistador, adds elaborate detail:

The eight or nine temples in the city were all close to one another within a large enclosure. Within this compound they all stood together, though each had its own staircase, its special courtyard, its chambers,

and its sleeping quarters for the priests of the temples.... How marvelous it was to gaze upon them.... All stuccoed, carved, and crowned with different types of merlons, painted with animals, (covered) with stone figures.... (1971:75–76)

The central district was restricted to religious edifices and activities, including godly temples and shrines, a priests' school and residence, a ritual chamber for eagle warriors, skull rack, and ball court. This ceremonial center, encompassing nearly 13 hectares, also covered 136 buried offerings containing thousands of artifacts, and was ornamented with many sculptures and murals (Lopez Lujan 2001:174). All of this was set on a raised platform and surrounded by a "wall" that more closely resembled another raised platform that was 30 meters wide (Serrato-Combe 2001:128).

The premier temple in this sacred precinct was the monumental Templo Mayor, or Great Temple. This dual temple faced west and was dedicated to two of the most important Mexica gods: on the south side was Huitzilopochtli (Hummingbird on the Left), a god of war and their patron deity, and on the north was Tlaloc, god of rain and fertility with deep roots in Mesoamerican cultural history.

Within its walled precinct, the temple sat at the very center of the Mexica world, both horizontally and vertically: "the place from which you could ascend to the sky or descend to the underworld, the point from which the four directions of the universe began" (Matos Moctezuma 2003:48). This was dedicated sacred space, and it occupied much of the energy and attention of a succession of Mexica rulers. It was, indeed, frequently in one or another stage of construction as it was completely enlarged seven times and expanded only on its front (western) façade five times during Tenochtitlán's nearly 200-year existence. The first small and rather humble temple was built in 1325 upon the arrival of the Mexica on the island, and it was then fully or partially enlarged in approximately 1390, 1431, 1454, 1469, 1482, 1486, and 1502 (Matos Moctezuma 2003). The final temple reached an estimated height of 45 meters and required 100 to 130 steps to reach the godly sanctuaries at the top.

While we can see only the stone foundations of these building periods today, in its heyday the temple would have been covered with a white plaster, and its surrounding patios were elegantly laid with slate flagstones or blocks of pink andesite (López Luján 1994:62). In overall effect, the precinct and its most monumental temple were designed to impress and inspire awe in the local urbanites as well as the occasional visitor or political guest.

Just beyond this sacred space were found the palaces of rulers and nobles, and the various buildings necessary for the administration of a great empire. Apparently Motecuhzoma Xocoyotzin constructed a new palace on his accession to the throne in 1502. When the Spaniards first arrived, they were housed in the palace of Axayacatl, a building also called by the names of earlier rulers who may have also occupied it. Motecuhzoma Xocoyotzin's palace consisted of numerous rooms arranged around courtyards; these apparently served not only as a residence but also as administrative space dedicated to the complex management of state and empire. These latter included a "courthouse." where the most important judges presided; a council chamber for the leading warriors; rooms for storing the extensive imperial tributes, along with a dwelling for the caretakers of these stores; housing for other rulers, both allies and enemies; rooms for dancers and singers of the palace; and even a room where those in charge of the activities of young men received their daily instructions. In addition, the conquistador Bernal Díaz del Castillo (1956:211–214) observed that Motecuhzoma had two armories filled with lances, bows and arrows, slings, *macquauitl* (wooden clubs inset with many sharp obsidian blades), shields, and quilted cotton armor. He also described an extensive aviary, as well as a zoo, the inhabitants of which gave off an "infernal noise." Díaz del Castillo also mentioned a library, gardens, and ponds.

Motecuhzoma's palace measured approximately 200 x 200 meters and was finished with stucco and painted adobe or stone (Evans 2000:207). It housed artisans and servants, nobles and government officials. Cortés speaks of 300 men to look after the royal aviary and zoo, and over 600 nobles present at Motecuhzoma's palace every day (the servants of these nobles overflowed two or three palace courtyards). Diaz del Castillo (1956:211) estimates that over 1,000 dishes of food and 2,000 containers of cacao were served to the ruler's palace guard. Add to these people the vast numbers of artisans, laborers (such as masons and carpenters), dancers, and royal wives and children, and the palace must have been an awe-inspiring, animated, and colorful scene.

The dwellings of the nobility were concentrated in the central part of the city, although many were also found in the outer quarters. In contrast to the humbler dwellings of the macehualtin, the residences of nobles were frequently stuccoed and had two stories.

Outside this central ceremonial and administrative area, the city was divided into four large quarters: Cuepopan, Teopan, Moyotlan, and Aztacalco. These quarters were further divided into numerous other territorial divisions, or calpulli. There is little agreement as to the exact number of calpulli in Tenochtitlán at the time of the Spanish conquest; a good estimate is 80.

As each quarter possessed a ceremonial district, so also did each calpulli. The public areas of the calpulli contained a temple for the calpulli god, a school for the young men (*telpochcalli*), and an administrative building. Life at the local level was carried on primarily within the confines of an inward-looking house site with an all-important patio and, in some cases, an adjacent chinampa. Based on extensive archival research, Edward Calnek concludes:

> The basic residential unit in each [documented] case was a walled or fenced compound.... This enclosed a number of separately entered dwelling units which faced inward on an open patio space. Access to the compound... was frequently indirect, so that the living area was visually isolated from the outside world. (1972:111)

These residential units were occupied primarily by joint families; Calnek reports populations ranging from as few as 2 to 3 per unit up to 25 to 30 per unit, the average being around 10 to 15 persons per unit (see Chapter 3).

Traffic was facilitated and regulated by numerous waterways, footpaths, and combinations of the two:

> The principal streets are very broad and straight, the majority of them being of beaten earth, but a few and at least half the smaller thoroughfares are waterways along which they pass in their canoes. (Cortés 1928:86)

Most canals and streets were apparently arranged alternating with one another: house sites faced the streets, while adjacent chinampas faced the canals. Where chinampas (ranging in size from 100 to 805 square meters) had been built, this pattern resulted in a mirror image effect (see Calnek 1972).

Some calpulli were home to certain occupational specialists who operated in a manner similar to medieval European guilds. These specialists included featherworkers, lapidaries, goldsmiths and professional merchants, all of whom maintained a degree of exclusiveness and control.

The adjacent city of Tlatelolco was similarly organized, with a central ceremonial square and several calpulli, but apparently without the four larger divisions. In addition, Tlatelolco boasted the largest marketplace in central Mexico, located beside its ceremonial center. The total urban area of Tenochtitlán-Tlatelolco encompassed at least 13.5 square kilometers.

The dual city of Tenochtitlán-Tlatelolco contained a diversified population. It would be a mistake to assume that this city was exclusively Mexica. Urban areas characteristically have the ability to incorporate a wide array of groups. And not only did Tenochtitlán grow through immigration, for Mexica peoples were found inhabiting sections of neighboring cities. Groups specializing in particular crafts (e.g., lapidaries and manuscript painters) may have originated elsewhere and migrated to Tenochtitlán, becoming concentrated in special calpulli. Nezahualcoyotl, ruler of Texcoco from 1418 to 1472, encouraged such immigration of specialists into that lakeshore city. In addition, Calnek (1976:289) suggests that some immigrants were war refugees seeking asylum after military defeats they had suffered elsewhere. Through immigration and natural growth, the island city of Tenochtitlán had reached a population of approximately 200,000–250,000 persons by 1519.

3. THE INCA EMPIRE

Although archaeological research over the last decades has unearthed a wealth of information on the Pre-Columbian Andean world, the origins of the Inca civilization still remains shrouded in mystery. What is known is that one of the small kingdoms formed during the Late Intermediate Period in the region of Cuzco managed to establish itself through force and then by a cultural dominance. We know a great deal about the so-called Inca 'imperial age' because of the detailed information of the Spanish chroniclers of the 16th century, but evidence of the formation of the Inca ethnic group is scarce.

Inca history is permeated with legends that have been handed down orally. The most frequently told legends at the court of Cuzco at the time of the conquest concerned the ancestor couple of the Inca line. Their names were Manco Capac, the hero-civilizer, and his sister and wife, Mama Ocllo. These mythical figures were sent from the waters of Lake Titicaca by their father, the sun god Inti-Viracocha, and traveled to Cuzco to bring a new culture there. Another version relates that the founders of the line were four semidivine brothers called the Ayar who tried to colonize the region of Cuzco with their sister-wives. Following a series of adversities, only one of the brothers, Ayar Manco, survived with his wife, Mama Ocllo, who together founded the capital of the future empire. Many other stories were told to the Spaniards and though we can be sure that historical fact is hidden in these myths, it is very difficult to separate one from the other.

There is a similar problem concerning the dynastic succession of the Inca emperors. The list as it existed in the centuries following the Spanish Conquest contained thirteen names, of which the first was that of Manco Capac and the last Atahualpa. Yet it is only from the ninth emperor, Inca Yupanqui (Pachacuti or Pachacutec), who came to power around AD 1438, that dates and events can be related to historical facts.

It seems that, until the middle of the 13th century, the Incas were just one of the many ethnic groups that lived in the valleys around the site of the future Cuzco. It was only during the following decades that they organized a form of rule based on their military successes over the peoples in the neighboring valleys. Around 1400 they succeeded in creating a true 'state.' The determining factor in their rapid development was the ever-growing threat from the war-like Chanca people settled in the valley of the river Pampas who had formed a powerful confederacy some time earlier. Some scholars think that the Chanca were descended from the ancient Huari civilization. Intimidated by the rise and expansion of the new power in the southern valleys and having expelled the Quechua tribes from their own lands, the Chanca tried to put pressure on the Incas in an attempt to slow their military and economic rise, but it was they who were defeated in a bloody battle sometime between 1430 and 1440. Pachacuti ascended to the throne around this period who put an end to the disputes with the bellicose Chanca. After his victory he was awarded the honorary title of 'Inca.'

Little archaeological evidence exists relating to the legends of the birth and consolidation of the Inca kingdom following their defeat of the Chanca and other hostile peoples such as the Colla and the Lupaca. Several interesting theories have been put forward, however. As a result of research carried out during the 1960s, some archaeologists, including the American J.H. Rowe, claimed that the origins of the Inca civilization should be looked for not in the cultural and geographic area of the highlands of Cuzco but in the region that was once dominated by the Huari and, probably, in the region of Tiahuanaco. In spite of strong criticism by opponents of this theory, it has recently received some support from investigations of finds dating from the Middle Horizon, the age in which the Huari civilization dominated and unified the Andean world. Huari domination strongly influenced an ethnic group today called the Quotakalli that was settled in the northern part of

Cuzco valley and known from its pottery. During the centuries following the fall of the Huari civilization, the Quotakalli did not lose their links and affinities with their overlords but maintained their fundamental traits. These eventually found their way into the Killke culture whose pottery production is classified as belonging to the 'early Inca' period that preceded the 'imperial early Inca' age. Indeed, finds relating to the Killke culture seem to belong to a precise moment in history, corresponding to the ascent to the throne of Pachactiti.

In addition to elements that were peculiar to the region of Cuzco, the Killke culture therefore seems to have been strongly influenced by the Huari civilization. This influence was not limited to material culture and pottery design, but was later also to emerge more clearly in the imperialist and militarist ideology of the Inca world and in its model of political and social organization. No other example of a similar political system has been documented in this region. Given the current state of our knowledge, therefore, it can be stated that the emergence of the last Andean empire - the Inca - was closely associated with strong Huari influence and that unarguable similarities existed between the two. Furthermore, considering the close relationship between the Huari and Tiahuanaco civilizations, it is possible to connect the legends that speak of the origins of the Incas in Lake Titicaca and the archaeological evidence.

Due to the many question marks that still over the origin of the Incas, it is difficult to suggest precise dates for the main historical events. In the chronology formulated by J.H. Rowe, which is considered the most reliable, the beginning of the Inca dynasty is put at around AD 1200.

From that moment on, the kingdom continued to grow in strength until the ascent of Pachacuti, supposedly the ninth Inca, to the throne in 1483. This prince's original name was Cusi Yupanqui but, following the crushing defeat of the Chanca, he changed it to Pachacutec Inca Yupanqui.

The king settled in the city of Cuzco and initiated a policy of expansion that took his kingdom to a position of supremacy over the many other groups in the region. As head of the army with his brother Capac Yupanqui and his son Tupac Inca, Pachacuti embarked on a series of conquests to strengthen his power and to expand the borders of the Inca state. These military adventures were the first move in the creation of the empire.

Around 1450, the Inca army conquered the territory of the Colla people who lived on the shores of Lake Titicaca; shortly after, they overran the region of Arequipa, reaching the southern coast. To the north

they captured territory as far as the city of Cajamarca, almost 620 miles (1000 km) from Cuzco in an area inhabited by hostile and warlike tribes and, in the meantime putting down a revolt by the Chanca. Along the northern coast, the Chimú king, warned of the advance of the Incas, and sent an army against them, but his capital, Chan Chan, fell into Inca hands around 1463 and the last prince, Minchançaman, was forced to capitulate. The advance of the Inca army continued unchecked along the northern coast as far as the area of Quito, which was annexed together with the lands of several Ecuadorian tribes.

Around 1471, when the Inca troops had returned to Cuzco, Tupac Inca succeeded his father as ruler and continued the policy of conquest. At the end of his reign, which lasted at least 22 years, the Inca empire ruled the greater part of the southern Andes, and lands which today part of Chile, Bolivia and Argentina were included in its borders. Following the assassination of Tupac Inca, his son Huayna Capac ascended the throne. He undertook numerous expeditions to the northern territories of the empire to put down revolts by subjected peoples, many of whom were openly opposed to the conquerors. The ruler was made clearly aware of the difficulties involved in running a large empire that included different ethnic groups speaking various languages and practicing local customs. His political and military problems were exacerbated by the arrival of an unknown and incurable epidemic which began to decimate his people. It is thought today that the sickness was smallpox, transmitted to the indigenous population by traders with the Spaniards who were settled in Darien, now Panama. Huayna Capac, already alarmed by the difficult situation and by the rumors of the approach of bearded white men with strange animals, was himself struck down by the illness and died in 1527.

After its brief but glorious peak, the Inca kingdom began its decline caused more than anything by the struggle between the two sons of the dead ruler: Huascar, who as the designated successor to the throne, and his ambitious brother, Atahualpa. The foolish greed and jealousy that caused the war contributed to the weakening of Inca power and opened the way for the European Conquistadors, who overran the great Andean empire in just a short time.

But what was the rapid development of Inca power founded upon, and what was it that allowed a small state to transform itself into a gigantic empire of during the reign of Tupac Inca? It was probably a series of interlinked elements: the absolute power of the rulers, the exceptional organization of the army; and a state and society structured according to a rigid hierarchy. Today we wrongly call empire 'Inca,' but its correct name is Tahuantinsuyu. This is a Quechua word, the language spoken by the Inca people which literally means 'The Four Quarters United.' 'Inca' was simply the title given to the rulers, who might inherit it at birth or be awarded it for their qualities–it was analogous to the title Caesar given to Roman leaders. It is usual to call people Inca too–their original name is still unknown–as well as the civilization as a whole.

The empire was divided into four parts, each of which was called a *suyu*. Each *suyu* was further divided into provinces with an urban center from which a local governor ruled. Cuzco was considered the 'center of the world' by its inhabitants as it was the ideal geographical center of Tahuantinsuyu, as well as the center of power. Yet, despite its organization and extent, the empire was not unified but rather a vast confederation of ethnic groups with their own cultural and linguistic characteristics, only tied to Cuzco by treaties and alliances. Contrary perhaps to popular imagination, these alliances were often not the result of Inca conquest. One of the methods the Inca rulers adopted to promote their imperialistic policies was that of 'reciprocity.' The Inca in person, or an army representative, met with the ruler of another kingdom or tribe and presented him with gifts, including women exchanged as wives. He then proposed the annexation of the lands to the Inca state. If the ruler of the lesser power accepted, the enticing promises were kept and sealed with banquets. If the offer was refused, battle ensued which nearly always ended with an Inca victory and the capture of the leader who had dared oppose the will of his powerful adversary. It is therefore not surprising that the foundations of the political balance of the Tahuantinsuyu were weak and that the Inca leader was forced to put down continual rebellions and to devise strategies to maintain the cohesion of his immense territory.

One of these was the imposition of a common language, Quechua, on the political and administrative elite, although the use of the various local dialects was not prohibited. Quechua was probably spoken by the oldest tribes in the Cuzco region; it was adopted by the Incas and spread throughout all the empire during the 15th and 16th centuries. Today it is still spoken by three million people in the Peruvian Andes. Imperial officials were sent to the different regions to teach Quechua and the sons of the nobles who governed the annexed provinces were required to go to school in Cuzco to assimilate the Inca culture. Another political strategy was that of the *mitmac*. These were forced migrations in which groups of people, sometimes entire populations, were transferred from their homeland to other regions, often distant and already colonized, so that they could quickly adapt to Inca customs.

The officials of the empire were charged with administering the provinces and taxing the inhabitants. A *quipu* - a recording device perhaps inherited from the Huari - was used for this purpose. It consisted of wool or cotton strings tied at one end to a cross cord; simple or compound knots tied in the strings represented information. Studies of the *quipu* have discovered that each was different from the others (for example, the color and length of the strings) but had a meaning that all versed in *quipu* could understand.

In 1910, the archaeologist Locke discovered an element that was common to all *quipu*: the groups of strings represented numbers and each knot was a number in the decimal system. The *quipu* was therefore a tool for recording quantities and was above all used for assessing the economic assets of the empire.

The cities and provinces were connected to Cuzco and each other by an immense network of roads, many originating in the Huari period, which extended along the coast and into the mountains. The *chasqui*, message carriers used by the Inca, ran dozens of miles each day along paths, across rope bridges over rivers, and up and down steep flights of mountain steps, stopping only at rest places called *tambo*. It is important to remember that the Inca people had no animals for transportation or traction, such as mules or horses, which is why they never built carts or similar vehicles, nor did they develop practical uses for the wheel. Goods were carried on people's backs or llamas.

The different ethnic groups were obliged to convert to the official religion of the empire, the worship of the sun, although local cults were permitted and that of the ancient Creator-Deity, Viracocha. A new temple dedicated to Inti, the sun, was built beside that of the ancient Creating Divinity at the enormous sanctuary of Pachacamac on the coast, which had been a place of pilgrimage for centuries. Besides the gods, the Inca himself was also worshipped as the incarnation and son of the sun - this was in addition to his absolute power as single political and religious leader, comparable with authority of the Egyptian pharaohs. He reigned assisted by his wife-sister, called Coya, and supported by a swarm of dignitaries and officials whose responsibilities were assigned according to a strict pyramidal hierarchy. According to the chroniclers, land was divided between religion, state and community.

C. The Conquest of the Americas

The first Spaniards that arrived in the Americas were from the most powerful country of Europe—Spain—and all were nurtured by the culture of the Spanish Renaissance. Their fathers and grandfathers had fought the Moors, and now they were continuing a history of combat against the indigenous peoples of the Americas. In fact, Spanish ideology was modified for these new world challenges: in the small church at Chincheros, Peru, for example, one finds in the sanctuary a magnificent mounted statue of Santiago, the "Moor killer," who inspired Spaniards for centuries in their battle against Islam. However, instead of a Moor under the hooves of Santiago's horse, one sees a prostrate and hapless *indio*.

Of all the Europeans who first came to the Americas, Christopher Columbus is perhaps the most enigmatic. The fact that no known picture of him exists—despite many attempts of artists to imagine how he looked—is symbolic of the difficulty in sorting out the fact and myth of his life. He was Italian—that much is known (born in Genoa), but many details about his life either are stated by Columbus himself or his son, Fernando, without outside collaboration. For example, there is no documented independent evidence that Columbus ever was captain of any ship prior to his expeditions to the Americas. Even after the Admiral's four voyages to the new world, experts are not sure what Columbus thought he had "discovered."

Much more is know about two of the most famous *Conquistadores*, or conquerors: Hernán Cortés and Francisco Pizarro. Detailed records outline their advancement against the Aztecs (Cortés) and Incas (Pizarro). While Cortés was aided by his lover and translator Doña Marina (*La malinche*) in the conquest of Mexico in 1521, Pizarro's sudden victory over the supreme Inca leader Atahualpa in 1532 was in part successful because Pizarro and his brothers imitated some of the bold (and cruel) techniques of Cortés. Both conquistadores were able to enlist indigenous allies who believed that the Spaniards would conquer the Aztec and the Inca and then leave, allowing them freedom from these oppressive imperial regimes. In the end, the European diseases that accompanied the Spaniards, above all small pox (of which there was no immunity in the Americas), killed millions of Spain's newest subjects.

The Chilean poet Pablo Neruda (1904-1973) acknowledges the richness of the Spanish language at the very end of his life in his famous prose poem, "La palabra," found in his memoirs, *Confieso que he vivido: Memorias* (1973). The sounds of Spanish are "like brilliantly colored stones, they leap like tiny silver fish, they are foam, thread, metal, dew...:" He recognizes too that in spite of all the pillage of the conquistadores, and all the gold and silver they looted from the Americas, the unwelcome newcomers left behind something even more valuable—their Spanish language. Since the Encounter, Spanish has become in Spanish America the fuel for its culture, in language, law, government, and literature, producing many Nobel laureates (like Neruda). Neruda concludes "La palabra" in this manner:

> What a wonderful language, mine, a good language we inherited from those grim conquistadores... Those men who took long swift strides through the great Cordilleras, through the rugged Americas, searching for potatoes, sausages, beans, black tobacco, gold, corn, fried eggs, all with a voracious appetite that has never been seen again in all the world... They swallowed up everything, religions, tribes, pyramids, idolatries equal to what they brought in their enormous sacks... Everywhere they went, they demolished the land...
>
> But out of these barbarians there fell from their boots, from their beards, from their helmets, from horseshoes, like sparkling little stones, luminous words that remained here, resplendent... their language. So we lost a great deal and we received a great deal... They carried away the gold and they left us the gold... They carried away everything and they left us everything... They left us their words.

1. THE FOUR VOYAGES OF CHRISTOPHER COLUMBUS (1492-1504)

It was in the context of the Portuguese expansion towards the Indies that Christopher Columbus, a member of the Genoese trading community in Portugal, had conceived the notion of finding a sea route directly westwards across the Atlantic to the mainland of Asia. This was not in itself an absurd idea at the time: it had been accepted in antiquity that the world was round, so it was possible, at least

---

in theory, to sail west to Cathay, thereby avoiding the long journey round the continent of Africa. The intervening ocean, however, was an unknown quantity, whose immensity deterred sailors from attempting a westward crossing to the fabled regions on the other side of the world.

A seafarer from his youth, Columbus had married into an important Genoese family long established in Madeira: his wife's grandfather had worked with Prince Henry the Navigator, the moving spirit behind the Portuguese explorations of the ocean, and her father had distinguished himself in Portugal's African ventures. Columbus had taken part in at least one expedition to the great *feitoria* at São Jorge da Mina on the Gold Coast of West Africa, where he had seen at first hand the workings of the Portuguese trading system of slaving and barter. He realized that a westward sea passage to the Indies would bring huge commercial rewards, not to mention glory and fame. Furthermore, such a link would facilitate Portugal's strategic and religious aims: it would allow Christians to make contact with the kingdom of Prester John in the East, so enlisting a powerful new ally and outflanking the Muslim enemy; it would also open the way to the conversion of many millions of pagan souls in preparation for the establishment of the universal monarchy that would precede the Second Coming of Christ Himself.

The question that had to be decided was the width of the ocean. Columbus was well acquainted with the theories of ancient and medieval cosmographers, and he knew that the distance separating western Europe from Asia was a subject of some controversy, stemming from the discrepancy between Ptolemy's estimate of the dimensions of the combined land mass of Europe and Asia, and that of Marco Polo. Columbus's contemporary, the great Florentine scholar Paolo Toscanelli, supported Marco Polo's more optimistic estimate, and he encouraged the Genoese mariner to believe that the width of the ocean was much less than was accepted by established opinion. Columbus, moreover, made other miscalculations of his own, which reduced his estimate of the ocean's width even further—to a mere 2,400 nautical miles from the Canary Islands to Japan, thus placing Japan where the West Indies actually are. If, as was likely, there were undiscovered islands along the way, then a western sea route was very much a practical proposition; it only remained to persuade the king of Portugal to give his backing to this new enterprise of the Indies.

John II of Portugal, however, was not well disposed towards the project Columbus put to him in 1485: its scientific basis was rightly questioned by his own experts, and, in any case, the Portuguese state had already invested too much in the search for a route to the Indies round Africa. The possibility of such a route seemed highly promising at about this time: in 1484 the explorer Diogo Cão had discovered the mouth of the Congo and was in the process of extending the limits of exploration well beyond, planting a marker as far as 21° 47' south; and in 1488 Bartholomew Dias would at last round the Cape of Good Hope, paving the way for Vasco da Gama's epoch-making passage to India in 1497–8.

In 1485, therefore, Columbus's plan appeared to the Portuguese Crown to be a far-fetched and wasteful diversion from the much more certain prospect of reaching the Indies round Africa. Columbus approached other European princes, including the rulers of Castile, but none was yet willing to embark on such an adventure. By 1492, however, Ferdinand and Isabella, and especially the latter, having obtained the historic surrender of Muslim Granada, were prepared to risk backing Columbus. The Genoese mariner was granted a licence to undertake an enterprise of discovery; the *Capitulaciones de Santa Fe* were extraordinarily generous, bestowing upon Columbus the hereditary titles of Admiral of the Ocean Sea, Viceroy of the Indies and Governor of all the lands he might discover on his voyage, as well as the right to a one-tenth share of all the riches yielded up by these discoveries. Ferdinand and Isabella also advanced him a loan, and commanded the little sea ports around Cadiz to help equip and provision the expedition. If Columbus were successful, the Crown would acquire sovereignty over new territories overseas and Castile might conceivably outdo Portugal in establishing a direct sea link with Asia and in controlling thereby the lucrative commerce with the great kingdoms of the East.

On 3 August 1492 Columbus set sail from the south-western Andalusian port of Palos. He had three ships—a Galician *nao*, the *Santa María* (100 tons), and two locally built Portuguese-style caravels, the *Pinta* (60 tons) and the *Niña* (50 tons). They were manned by a total of eighty-seven men—mostly tough, experienced sailors from the small ports of the region; the most notable were members of the prominent seafaring Pinzon, Niño and Quintero families, without whose help and experience Columbus would not have been able to carry out his project. On this expedition too was the great Biscayan mariner Juan de la Cosa, master and owner of the *Santa María*, who would gain fame in subsequent years as an explorer and map-maker.

Forced to stop for nearly a month in the Canaries for repairs, the expedition started out on its voyage of exploration proper on 9 September. After a fruitless month at sea, with his men growing restive and fortified only by his determination, Columbus began to notice favourable signs—flocks of birds passing overhead, branches floating by, and then a strange light flickering on the horizon in the dead of night. Finally, two hours after midnight on 12 October, the lookout on the *Pinta* sighted land - white cliffs lit up by the moon. When dawn broke, the vessels found a small bay and Columbus made the shore; he fell to his knees and thanked the Lord for the mercy of having finally reached land. An ocean had indeed been crossed, but this was not Japan; it was rather a small island in the Bahamas, which Columbus chose to call San Salvador, in honour of his Holy Saviour.

On seeing the three alien vessels, the inhabitants of the island swam out to visit them. The Admiral, as he was now called, noted their appearance: they went about completely naked, some had their bodies painted, their weapons were very primitive, and yet they seemed docile enough, and all too eager to exchange their possessions for trinkets proffered by the Spaniards. Still, this was not what he was looking for: he wanted to reach Japan, and these people were too barbarous to be the subjects of a powerful king. Columbus was a man of rather fixed expectations—he had gambled his life and honour on reaching the Orient, and he now stubbornly sought out evidence that would confirm his preconceptions. Moreover, used as he was to the commercial enterprises of the Italians and the Portuguese, he was keen to assess the economic potential of his discovery. Finding little on San Salvador—though the possibility that the natives might be used for the slave trade did cross his mind—he cruised around other islands in the Bahamas, continually struck by the beauty of the scenery, until he heard of larger islands to the south where gold was to be found. He then arrived on the north coast of 'Colba' (later Hispanicized as Cuba), which he hoped might be Japan; however, there was very little gold, though he observed that the natives relaxed by puffing at a large, burning stick of rolled leaves, which they called *tobacos*, a habit the Spaniards would eventually pick up and introduce throughout Europe.

On the eastern end of the island he learned of the aggressive, man-eating Caribs from the gentler Arawak tribes which he had so far encountered, and so he sailed on eastwards. When he came to another large island which he thought resembled Spain, he called it *La Isla Española* (Hispaniola—the island which today comprises Haiti and the Dominican Republic). Here the natives wore plenty of gold ornaments and were very welcoming—the naked women offered themselves freely to the strangers. On the north-western coast Columbus came across an important native chieftain, Guacanagari,

who, to his great relief, showed some of the attributes of kingship–for this was taken as evidence that they were drawing closer to civilization and, therefore, to Japan or China. When the natives talked of a place called Cibao, Columbus thought they were referring to Cipangu, the name by which he knew Japan.

On Christmas Day the *Santa María*, ran on to a coral reef and had to be abandoned. But Columbus took this disaster as a sign from God that he should the first Spanish colony there, and with the help of Guacanagari's men the settlement of Navidad (the Nativity) was built using the timbers of the wrecked ship. A group of twenty-one volunteers was left behind and Columbus, confident now that he had reached the Indies, set off on 4 January aboard the Niña on the return voyage to Spain.

Atrocious weather caused the *Niña* to put in first at the Azores and later at Lisbon as well. Nevertheless, John II received the Admiral with courtesy and allowed him to continue his journey to Spain. On 20 April 1493 he arrived before Ferdinand and Isabella at the royal court in Barcelona accompanied by a retinue which included six natives bearing parrots in cages. Columbus presented himself in triumph as the discoverer of new lands in the Indies, lands which bore gold and could be profitably used for trading by Spain.

The Catholic Monarchs could now look forward to overtaking Portugal in the contest to establish direct trade links with the Indies (the Portuguese would not reach India until 1498). The requisite legitimacy for their enterprise was obtained from Pope Alexander VI, a Spanish Borgia, who issued a series of bulls granting Castile dominion over all lands that might be discovered in the Western Hemisphere. In order to avoid conflict with Portugal, the bulls sought to allocate to each of the rival Iberian powers a section of the undiscovered portion of the globe. A line of demarcation was drawn in 1493 at a longitude 100 leagues west of the Azores and Cape Verde Islands, but at Portugal's request, and with the diplomatic concurrence of Spain, this line was moved a further 270 leagues westwards by the Treaty of Tordesillas in 1494, thereby unwittingly delivering to Portugal the as yet unknown territory that was to become Brazil.

Even before this diplomatic compromise had been agreed, Columbus had set off from Cadiz on 25 September 1493 with a large expedition of seventeen ships and some 1,500 men (there were no women on board), With the intention of founding a permanent colony on the islands he had discovered. In Hispaniola he found that the natives had destroyed the settlement of Navidad and killed the Spaniards in revenge for their rapacious behaviour. It was an ominous development, which revealed the nature of the men's expectations. These were hard-bitten adventurers, whose basic motives were not so different from Columbus's own, though far more crudely conceived. At considerable personal risk they had come out to these lands to find the kind of wealth and status largely denied to them in their mother country. It was patently not in their interest to settle quietly to a peasant's life tilling the soil or trading peaceably with the natives; there were, after all, great reserves of indigenous manpower that could be put to work to make the Europeans rich enough to live like lords when they got back home to Spain.

Upset by the destruction of Navidad, Columbus sailed eastwards looking for a new site to found a Portuguese-style trading station or *feitoria* like those on the African coast. A colony, which he called Isabela after the queen, was built in a rather ill-chosen place, and from there the Admiral sent expeditions into the Cibao to locate the source of the natives' gold. He then embarked on a reconnaissance which took him to Cuba once more and round Jamaica, returning to Isabela in September 1494 only to find more problems of indiscipline among the Spaniards—a faction of Catalans had rebelled against his brother Diego, whom he had left in charge. Facing a growing tension between, on the one hand, his vocation as an explorer and trader (recognized in his proud title, Admiral of the Ocean Sea) and, on the other, his role as governor of the new Spanish colony (Viceroy of the Indies, as his other great title had it), Columbus tried to satisfy the ambitions of unruly Spaniards who wanted quick rewards from colonization: he authorized more brutal expeditions into the interior to search for gold and made a *repartimiento* (distribution) of captive Indians to work for the Spaniards. He also considered starting a traffic in slaves to improve the economic prospects of his trading colony, and sent off a shipload of about 500 Indians to Spain (some 200 died of cold during the crossing and most of the rest expired shortly after they were put on the market in the Peninsula). The Indian tribes of Hispaniola rose in revolt and marched on Isabela, but they were easily put down by the Spaniards' guns and savage dogs.

In March 1496 Columbus went back to Spain to defend himself against slanders put about by disgruntled colonists who had returned from Hispaniola. His enterprise of the Indies was becoming discredited at court: there seemed little evidence of rich deposits of gold, no contact had been made with the rulers of either Japan or China, and Hispaniola was apparently seething with discontent; furthermore, the pious Queen Isabella was unhappy with the treatment of the Indians, whom she had expressly forbidden to be taken as slaves. Nevertheless, he was relieved to find that the Catholic Monarchs, despite their reservations, still had confidence in him—possibly because they were concerned about the intentions of the Portuguese, who were known to be preparing a fleet of exploration under Vasco da Gama in the hope of finally reaching India.

It took Columbus about eighteen months to put together a new expedition, which was financed this time by the royal treasury under the supervision of the archdeacon of Seville, Juan Rodríguez de Fonseca, an ambitious official who would accumulate over the next two decades immense influence over the direction of the enterprise of the Indies. Columbus set sail in May 1498 and reached the island of Trinidad in July; he then explored the coast of Venezuela, surmising from the strength of the fresh-water currents in the Gulf of Pana and in the delta of the Orinoco that it must form part of a large continent, a *tierra firme*. But obsessed as he was with his quest for the Orient, he did not realize the implications of his discovery of this great land mass, even though he referred to it metaphorically as an 'other world'. It would be another Italian explorer, Amerigo Vespucci, sailing on a Spanish ship along sea routes opened up by Columbus, who would formulate the powerful idea that a continent unconnected with Asia had been discovered: he was the first to call it a *mundus novus*, a 'new world'. Columbus, for his part, never quite lost his medieval cast of mind; he remained ever the apocalyptic visionary, intrigued by the marvels that were being revealed to him, speculating, for instance, that the Orinoco delta might be the four-headed river that, according to Scripture, irrigates the Earthly Paradise.

On reaching Hispaniola, however, the Admiral found the Spaniards in a state of civil war. The town of Santo Domingo, established in his absence by his brother Bartholomew, had become as ungovernable as the Isabela settlement. Although Columbus tried to achieve a compromise between the warring factions, he and his brothers were resented as foreigners, and his failure to bring the situation under control further eroded his authority. Finally, in August 1500 a royal official, Francisco de Bobadilla, arrived with orders from the Crown to investigate the trouble. The Columbus brothers were arrested and Christopher was sent back to Spain in chains.

This high-handed treatment was, of course, a terrible humiliation for the Admiral, but circumstances dictated a revision of Columbus's original enterprise of the Indies. The political problems of Hispaniola had become so intractable because the island could not be turned into a trading station such as Columbus had envisaged. Gold was not obtainable through barter as in the Portuguese *feitorias* on the African coasts; it had to be directly mined, and this required a far more complex operation, including permanent settlement and the organization of a labour supply, an operation which called for the intervention of the state in order to set up an effective apparatus of government. And so Columbus's personal monopoly of the enterprise, as set out in the *Capitulaciones de Santa Fe*, was broken. In February 1502 the Catholic Monarchs of Castile sent out an experienced administrator, Nicolas de Ovando, as the first royal governor of what would become known as the Spanish Indies.

But Columbus was still intent on finding a westward passage to Asia, and he was authorized to make a fourth voyage of exploration across the Atlantic, setting out in May 1502 on an expedition which was to last until November 1504. This voyage greatly extended Spain's knowledge of the newly discovered lands in the Western Hemisphere, for, in trying to find a passage that would lead him to the mainland of Asia, Columbus traced the coastline of Central America along Honduras, Nicaragua, Costa Rica and Panama. When he returned to Spain, he petitioned the Crown for the restoration of some of his privileges, and succeeded, at least, in securing the eventual appointment of his son Diego as governor of Hispaniola with due recognition accorded to the hereditary titles of viceroy and admiral. Christopher Columbus died on 20 May 1506, convinced to the last that he had found the western sea route to the Orient and that the lands he had discovered were islands and peninsulas in Asia.

2. THE CONQUEST OF THE MAINLAND (CORTÉS)

For over twenty years after Columbus's first crossing of the Atlantic, the Spaniards discovered little of consequence other than Hispaniola and Cuba. What lay beyond these islands was still a matter for conjecture: voyages of exploration had gradually traced the Caribbean coastline of mainland America but the extent of this Tierra Firme, as it became known, was yet to be revealed. As the native populations declined on the islands, Spaniards took to raiding Tierra Firme for slaves, and from slave-raiding thoughts turned to more ambitious expeditions of conquest and settlement to compensate for the waning attractions of the Caribbean.

In 1513 an expedition under Pedrarias Dávila set out from Spain with royal permission to conquer the isthmian region of Central America. On arrival, Dávila came upon another Spaniard, Vasco Núñez de Balboa, the leader of a group of survivors of an abortive mission to Tierra Firme in 1509, who had already created the settlement of Darién in this inhospitable tropical region. By 1513 Balboa had crossed the isthmus and raised the royal standard over the waters of the Pacific Ocean to claim them for the Catholic Monarchs of Castile. What is more, Balboa had heard rumours of a golden kingdom called Birú which appeared to live up to everything a Spanish conquistador could hope for in the Indies. Pedrarias Dávila soon quarrelled with Balboa and had him executed; he then went on to probe the isthmus for gold and slaves, but failed to turn up any loot which significantly improved upon what had been found on the islands. In 1519 he founded the city of Panama and from there he continued his explorations further afield in search of the fabulous kingdom of Birú.

In these restless times there were many other Spaniards who had dreams of conquest and plunder. Between 1517 and 1518 Diego Velázquez, the conqueror of Cuba, had sent out two expeditions to reconnoitre the coasts of the mainland around the areas we now know as the Yucatán peninsula and the Gulf of Mexico. These had brought back evidence of a rich civilization in the interior, so Velázquez set about equipping an expedition with the purpose of setting up a base as a preliminary to further exploration and eventual conquest. Following normal procedure, Velázquez applied to Spain for the requisite authorization from the Crown, but before the royal assent could reach Cuba the commander appointed to lead the expedition stole a march on Velázquez and set sail without permission from the port of Santiago. This upstart was Hernán Cortés, a 33-year-old hidalgo from Medellín in the province of Extremadura who had distinguished himself as a soldier and administrator on Hispaniola and Cuba since he arrived in the Caribbean at the age of nineteen. The expedition he led was modest: in his ships he carried some 600 men, 16 horses, 14 cannon and 13 muskets; yet with these resources he proposed to confront whatever might lie beyond the wall of mountains on the mainland that barred ready access to the riches or the Indies.

From Cuba, Cortés made the short crossing to the island of Cozumel off Yucatán, where he came across a Maya-speaking Spanish castaway called Jerónimo de Aguilar. Further up the coast in Tabasco he was given a woman called Malintzin – Doña Marina to the Spaniards—who spoke Nahuatl as well as the Maya tongue, and who was to serve Cortés faithfully thereafter as interpreter and mistress. With the services of these two speakers of indigenous languages, Cortés was in an excellent position to assess the nature of the opposition he faced and to devise an informed strategy for his campaign of conquest. Indeed, the quality of Cortés's strategic thinking was to prove crucial to his success, for very soon he came under observation by agents of the emperor Montezuma, following reports of the arrival of strange men with white faces who had been borne upon winged towers across the sea.

On Good Friday, April 1519, Cortés founded Veracruz, the 'City of the True Cross', at a place on the coast of the Gulf of Mexico which fell within the jurisdiction of the Aztec emperor. By so doing, he hoped to win some legitimacy for his enterprise, given that he had departed Cuba without royal permission and in defiance of Velázquez's authority. A few days later the first emissaries from Montezuma arrived bearing ritual gifts and advising the Spaniards to turn back. Cortés, however, would do no such thing; instead, he sent all the gold he had so far gathered back to Spain in the hope of appeasing the emperor Charles V and pre-empting any decision to disqualify him from enjoying the fruits of the conquest he was planning. Then he scuttled all his ships. There could now be no turning back: ahead lay the Aztec capital Tenochtitlán, and there was nothing for it but to march on the city and somehow take it.

As the Spaniards advanced towards the seat of Aztec power, Cortés learned of the political divisions within Montezuma's empire, and of the extent to which the Aztecs were resented by subject peoples and by other kingdoms. He determined to exploit these antagonisms while concealing from the Aztecs his true intentions. At Cempoala he was able to enlist the support of the Totonacs, and subsequently, after a ferocious battle, the Spaniards persuaded the Tlaxcalans, who were historic enemies of the Aztecs, to join them in their campaign to topple Montezuma. When they arrived in the kingdom of the Cholulans, the Spaniards made an initial show of friendship to these willing vassals of the Aztecs, but Cortés uncovered what appeared to be a plot to kill him and decided to carry out an exemplary massacre of nobles and priests assembled for a religious festival in the city. According to native sources, such equivocal tactics sowed confusion and dismay among the Aztecs, giving the invaders a psychological edge over the Indians.

Montezuma, for his part, would appear to have decided early on upon a similar strategy of perplexing the Spaniards, by combining ritual diplomacy with unspecified threats and covert attacks. However, it remains unclear what his real intentions could have been in allowing the Spaniards to advance so far into the heart of his realms. Speculation has focused on the apparent weakness of his character and on his alleged belief that Cortés was the god Quetzalcoatl come to reclaim his kingdom, but these suppositions must be treated with caution: Montezuma was not a hereditary monarch; he had been chosen by an aggressive, imperialist people and must therefore have been a man of outstanding qualities of leadership, one who would have been little disposed to give away a whole empire in the belief that a poorly equipped stranger was a visiting god. Rather, it is far more likely that Montezuma simply misread Cortés, amongst other reasons because the ends of war and politics in Middle America were quite different from those of Renaissance Europe. Where Europeans fought to kill, occupy and plunder, the Indians regarded battle as a ritual of dominance and submission, in which it was preferable to take prisoners alive in order to have them ceremoniously sacrificed to their bloodthirsty gods. Because the Spanish invasion ended in disaster for the Aztecs, Montezuma's tactical errors may well have been retrospectively embroidered by Nahuatl poets and Spanish chroniclers into a haunting fable of foreboding and doom.

There is no question, however, but that Montezuma underestimated the depths of Cortés's cunning and resolve. After two days' march from Cholula, the Spaniards arrived within sight of the Aztec capital and advanced towards it despite repeated warnings by friend and foe that Montezuma had laid a trap and was planning to destroy them. As they approached, the majesty of the setting caused great wonderment. Bernal Díaz, a soldier in Cortés's small army, later wrote:

> When we saw all those cities and villages built in the water, and other great towns on dry land, and that straight and level causeway leading to Mexico, we were astounded. These great towns and *cues* [temples] and buildings rising from the water, all made of stone, seemed like an enchanted vision from the tale of Amadís, Indeed, some of our soldiers asked whether it was not all a dream.*

When they reached the main causeway into the lake-bound city, the lord of Texcoco came out to

---

* Bernal Diaz, *The Conquest of New Spain* (Penguin Books: Harmondsworth, 1963). p. 214

greet the Spaniards and invite them to an audience with Montezuma. Even though he realized that he might well be walking into a trap, Cortés led his men into Tenochtitlán, the most densely populated metropolis in the New World. In the event, he was well received by Montezuma, who accommodated Cortés and his force of some 400 men in a complex of large buildings within the city. For about a week the Spaniards lived in constant fear of being set upon and killed despite the overt courtesies that were being shown to them by the emperor and his household. But with his commanders becoming increasingly agitated about the real intentions of Montezuma and his ministers, Cortés finally decided to seize the emperor and hold him hostage in the Spanish quarters, on the pretext that the emperor had treacherously ordered an attack on the Spanish garrison at Veracruz in which a Spanish commander had been killed. In effect, Cortés was attempting a *coup d'état*; with such a small force, it was plainly impossible for him to make a frontal assault on Aztec power. By capturing Montezuma, the trapped Spaniards could play for time and try to manipulate imperial authority to their own advantage. The fate of Mexico would therefore hinge on the outcome of a battle of wits between two men.

However, at a critical stage in the Spanish *coup d'état*, news arrived that Pánfilo de Narváez had landed at Veracruz with a large force of Spaniards from Cuba, with orders from the governor Velázquez to punish Cortés for his initial insubordination. Cortés decided that only he could deal with this untimely threat to his whole enterprise, and so he set off with the greater part of his force to confront Narváez, leaving one of his commanders, Pedro de Alvarado, in charge of guarding Montezuma. Alvarado was faced with a difficult and volatile situation: since the imperial office was elective and not hereditary, the emperor's authority was in danger of becoming discredited the longer he remained a captive. For their coup to succeed, the Spaniards needed to follow up their seizure of Montezuma with further decisive action in order to secure their position. But the arrival of Narváez had removed Cortés at precisely the wrong moment, leaving the depleted Spanish force in Tenochtitlán at the mercy of Montezuma's aggressive nephews. Alvarado became alarmed when he heard rumours of a plot by the Aztec nobility to attack the Spaniards; he therefore led a pre-emptive assault on an assembly of Indian priests and nobles attending a religious ceremony. The resulting massacre outraged the Aztecs, who rose in rebellion and laid siege to Alvarado in the Spanish quarters.

Meanwhile, Cortés had managed to persuade the bulk of Narváez's army to support his conquest of the Aztec empire rather than make war on fellow Spaniards. But on his return to Tenochtitlán he found the Spaniards at bay and the Aztecs in a belligerent mood. He also lost patience with the captive Montezuma, whom he suspected of having secretly contacted Narváez with an offer to help him against Cortés in return for his release. Montezuma's authority had, in any case, all but evaporated, since he had effectively been replaced as emperor by Cuitlahuac, one of his brothers. He died shortly after Cortés's return, allegedly from wounds received when he was hit by stones thrown by his own people as he went out to appeal for calm before an angry multitude besieging the Spanish quarters.

Montezuma's death left Cortés's strategy in ruins; provisions were running very low and there were many Spaniards dead or wounded. The Spanish commander therefore chose to withdraw from Tenochtitlán. On 30 June 1520 the Spaniards fought their way out of the city, sustaining very heavy casualties and losing in their retreat much of the gold and jewellery they had amassed. The *noche triste*, this 'sorrowful night' of defeat, marked the nadir of Spanish fortunes in Mexico: Cortés's *coup d'état* had failed disastrously and his remaining forces limped back to Tlaxcala to recover.

Having exhausted the ruses of psychological warfare, Cortés's only option was a full-scale assault on Tenochtitlán. For six months the Spanish leader planned his campaign at Tlaxcala; he summoned reinforcements from the Caribbean, recruited thousands of Indian soldiers, and had brigantines built in sections to be hauled over the sierras and reassembled for use on Lake Texcoco. The Spaniards also had a hidden ally they could have known nothing about; this was the smallpox virus, which had been brought over from Cuba to the mainland by one of Narváez's soldiers and was now spreading among the Indians, who had no immunities against this Old World disease. The new Aztec emperor, Cuitlahuac, was an early victim and he was succeeded by Cuauhtemoc, a ruler who could no longer entertain any illusions about Spanish intentions in Mexico and who was therefore prepared to defend his city and empire to the last man against the European invaders.

In December 1520 Cortés marched into the Valley of Mexico and spent a further three months preparing for war. Finally, in April, the Spanish offensive began: Cortés laid siege to Tenochtitlán, using his brigantines to patrol the lake so as to stop food supplies getting to the city. Still, the first direct assaults proved a failure and costly in lives, even though the Spaniards nearly succeeded in taking the central temple. It became clear that fighting in the maze of narrow streets cancelled out the advantage that horses and guns gave the heavily outnumbered Spanish forces. Cortés saw that if he was to take Tenochtitlán at all, he must raze it to the ground; and so, for some four gruelling months of bitter fighting the Spaniards and their Indian allies pulled down, building by building, the city Cortés was to describe as the most beautiful in the world. On 13 August, when barely a quarter of Tenochtitlán was left standing, the emperor Cuauhtemoc, who had led the heroic resistance of the Aztecs, was captured and forced to surrender. Anxious to reward his exhausted troops in the manner they expected, Cortés had Cuauhtemoc tortured in an attempt to discover the whereabouts of the treasure the Spaniards had lost during the *noche triste*.

After his victory Cortés devoted himself to rebuilding Tenochtitlán and unifying the former dominions of the Aztecs under Spanish rule. In this he succeeded brilliantly, becoming a revered figure for the Indian masses and acquiring the charismatic authority of a ruler in his own right. Charles V rewarded him with great estates, the right to receive tribute from thousands of Indians and the noble title of Marquis of the Valley of Oaxaca. Yet the extent of Cortés's personal power in New Spain, as he called the territories he had conquered, was to arouse the envy of rivals and the suspicion of the Crown itself, anxious as it was to curb the political ambitions of the conquistadors in these rich and distant lands. In 1527 Cortés was relieved of the governorship of New Spain and an *audiencia* (a judicial council of royal officials) took over the administration of the kingdom. Cortés saw fit to return to Spain on two occasions to defend himself against detractors at court, and, in fact, died there in 1547. After Cortés the government of New Spain degenerated under the rule of Nurío de Guzmán, president of the first *audiencia*, into a brutish exploitation of the Indians. In 1530 Guzmán was removed and a second *audiencia* restored some measure of order to the turbulent colony. Royal authority was at last firmly established when New Spain was created a viceroyalty in 1535 and placed in the charge of Antonio de Mendoza, one of the greatest administrators of the Spanish empire.

Hernán Cortés's splendid victory accelerated the tempo of Spanish expansion in America and raised the ceiling of individual ambition; it was as if the many Spanish captains in the Indies were in a race with one another to conquer a second Mexico. Cortés himself lost little time in embarking on further explorations, ranging northwards along the Pacific coast to a wild region he called California, after a mythical land of warrior women featured in *Las sergas de Esplandián* ('The Exploits of *Esplandián*'), a best-selling romance of chivalry of the period, and southwards to the kingdoms of the Maya and thence into Honduras.

In 1524 two of Cortés's captains led expeditions into Central America. Cristobal de Olid went to Honduras but tried to lay claim to the territory for himself, angering Cortés by making a deal with his old enemy Velazquez, the governor of Cuba. Cortés set off to punish Olid and found himself on a terrible march through swamps and jungles. As it turned out, Olid had been murdered by the time Cortés arrived in Honduras. In fact, the expedition proved to be entirely futile—no new kingdoms of gold were found and Cortés stained his reputation by ordering the death of the captive Aztec emperor, Cuauhtemoc, on suspicion of stirring the Indian soldiers on the expedition to mutiny. Central America was to disappoint the hopes of its first conquerors. Cortés's other captain, Pedro de Alvarado, spent the next ten years in the conquest of Guatemala and El Salvador without coming across anything to rival the riches of the Aztec empire. Pushing down into Nicaragua, he encountered other Spanish expeditions sent up from the isthmus by the rapacious governor of Panama, Pedrarias Dávila.

3. THE CONQUEST OF PERU (PIZARRO)

Since killing Balboa, Pedrarias Dávila had found nothing to compare with the fruits of Cortés's conquest, despite his brutal scouring of the southern parts of Central America, a region once optimistically known as Castilla del Oro—Golden Castile. However, news of the Spanish success in Mexico had convinced him that he should concentrate on Nicaragua, where the prospects seemed better than in the south, which had so far yielded not much more than fanciful reports of a land of gold called Birú or Peru. Even so, two veterans of the Indies, Francisco Pizarro and Diego de Almagro, obtained permission from Dávila to search for Peru. A first attempt in 1524 proved discouraging, but a second expedition in 1527 reached the city of Tumbes (north–west Peru), and brought back items of gold, and silver, and other evidence of an advanced civilization. On the strength of these findings, Pizarro went to Spain in 1528 to obtain a capitulación or licence from the Crown entitling him to conquer and settle Peru independently of Pedrarias Dávila. When he returned to Panama, Pizarro brought with him a large number of fellow Extremadurans, including his four half-brothers. His partner Almagro had been recruiting men in Panama in preparation for the conquest, and another partner, the priest Hernando de Luque, was responsible for raising capital for the venture from wealthy investors.

Francisco Pizarro and Diego de Almagro were established figures in the colony of Panama, owning profitable estates and rights to Indian tribute, but they were also hardened conquistadors with an extraordinary appetite for adventure: when they set off to conquer Peru, they were both in their fifties, an advanced age for the time. Pizarro had first arrived in the Indies in 1502 and had taken part in several expeditions of conquest. From Hispaniola he had gone to the mainland with Diego de Ojeda in 1509; then he had crossed the isthmus under Núñez de Balboa on the expedition which discovered the Pacific Ocean in 1513; some years later he went over to Pedrarias Dávila and conspired in Balboa's arrest, after which he received land and Indians from the new governor of Panama. Unlike Hernán Cortés. Pizarro was no gentleman: a former swineherd, he was born out of wedlock and remained uneducated and quite possibly illiterate. Almagro was no better: he was a foundling from Castile who had come to the Indies as a fugitive from justice and had managed to climb his way up to a position of lordship over Indians on the isthmus—such were the opportunities for advancement in the treacherous world of Panamanian politics under Pedrarias Dávila.

Although they had been partners in other ventures, the *capitulación* of conquest that Pizarro brought back from Spain disappointed Almagro; he resented the fact that Pizarro had been granted the title of Governor and Captain-General of Peru, while he had only been promised the much less lucrative governorship of the city of Tumbes. Another potential source of friction was Pizarro's reliance upon his half-brothers and friends from Extremadura, who formed a clique within the expeditionary force. Almagro's resentment subsided, but circumstances would later cause it to flare up into open hostility.

In December 1530 Pizarro set sail from Panama with the main expeditionary force, consisting of about 180 men and 27 horses; Almagro was to follow once he had recruited more Spaniards. On reaching the coast of Ecuador, Pizarro landed his troops and set off for Tumbes, a long march that was plagued by set-backs, disease and Indian attacks. When finally they reached Tumbes, the Spaniards learned that the great empire of the Incas, which they hoped to conquer, was in complete turmoil, having been torn apart by a dynastic war of succession caused by the death of the emperor Huayna Capac from smallpox (the mysterious disease had swept down from Mexico and was now ravaging the population of the central Andes).

The succession was being disputed by Huayna Capac's son. Huascar, and his half-brother, Atuhualpa, who had raised a rebellion in the northern provinces near Ecuador. At the time of Pizarro's arrival Atuhualpa had emerged as the victor and was making his way south to the sacred city of Cuzco, the centre of the Inca world, where his troops were holding Huascar prisoner. Pizarro learned that Atuhualpa was at the time encamped not far from Cajamarca, a city which had been abandoned by most of its inhabitants during the civil war.

Freshly reinforced from Panama, Pizarro decided to seek out Atuhualpa and, as Cortés had done with Montezuma, to take the Inca hostage. As had occurred in Mexico, the Indians kept the Spaniards under surveillance as they made their way to Cajamarca, but, again for reasons which are not clear, the native emperor forbore to destroy an invasion force numbering a mere 60 horsemen and some 100 foot-soldiers. In November 1530, nearly two years after he had left Panama, Pizarro reached Cajamarca and installed himself in the city. He then sent a party of Spaniards to invite Atuhualpa to a meeting. The Spanish emissaries sought to impress the Inca with a display of horsemanship, a ploy which appeared to succeed since the horse was completely alien to the Indians. Atuhualpa agreed to come to Cajamarca the following day, but, in the event, appeared in the evening, having been informed by his spies that the Spaniards unsaddled their horses at night and were therefore more vulnerable to attack.

As the sun declined on the evening of Saturday 16 November 1532, Atuhualpa entered the empty square of Cajamarca on a magnificent litter borne by 80 nobles and escorted by 6,000 men; thousands of warriors in full battle order had been drawn up on a plain outside the city awaiting further orders. For his part, Pizarro had hidden his hundred-odd men in the vacant buildings surrounding the square, where they had been waiting for hours in terrified apprehension. Atuhualpa was perplexed by the absence of the Spaniards and took it as a sign of fear at the strength of his army. But then the priest Vicente de Valverde appeared in the square accompanied by only a native interpreter, and commenced to recite the Requirement, a formal request that the heathen submit to the authority of the Pope and the king of Spain and permit the teaching of the Christian religion. Rejection of the Requirement was considered sufficient grounds for declaring a 'just war' on behalf of the Spanish Crown. Atuhualpa, who had never before set eyes on a book, took Valverde's breviary and examined it with curiosity before tossing it to the ground. Valverde then turned away and cried out to the concealed Spaniards that the Inca had repudiated the word of God. Upon an agreed signal Pizarro's men launched their attack: cannon and guns opened fire on the crowded square, horsemen charged out of the buildings and Pizarro tried to drag Atuhualpa from his litter—which he managed to do only after the Inca's bearers had all been cut down by the Spaniards while fiercely resisting the assault on their emperor. The Spanish horsemen and soldiers chased the panic-stricken Indians out of the city, and then turned on the Inca army waiting on the plain outside Cajamarca; between 6,000 and 7,000 Indians lost their lives, and many more were wounded.

Francisco Pizarro had pulled off an astonishing *coup de main*: in one evening he had seized control of an empire, for the rule of the Inca emperor, whose authority was believed to be divine, was absolute and unquestioned. Like Montezuma before him, Atuhualpa had utterly misjudged the Spaniards; he had found it impossible to conceive that so puny a force could presume to attack an empire which he himself had only just won after a bloody civil war. Out of curiosity he had allowed them to reach Cajamarca, and he later admitted that his intention had been to capture Pizarro and kill or enslave his men. What had spared the Spaniards this fate was their ruthlessness in catching the Inca by surprise.

With Atuhualpa as hostage, events began to move in Pizarro's favour. The Inca was still unaware of the ultimate intentions of the Spaniards: he thought it scarcely conceivable that they would actually want to rule his empire; more likely they were bandits who could be bought off with gold and later destroyed while trying to escape. Atuhualpa therefore ordered his generals not to attack the Spaniards, and instead offered them a huge ransom in pure gold, which Pizarro eagerly accepted with a solemn promise to release Atuhualpa once it had been collected. Atuhualpa also took care to consolidate his political position: he ordered the troops occupying Cuzco to execute his brother Huascar so as to prevent his defeated rival for the throne from taking advantage of his own captivity. For eight months the Spaniards waited with Atuhualpa for the ransom to arrive from Cuzco and other places. Word had been sent back to Panama for reinforcements; yet the dangers of waiting were ob-

vious: the Spaniards were easy prey for Atuhualpa's victorious armies. In Cuzco there were 30,000 troops under the command of Quisquis; in Jauja, halfway between Cuzco and Cajamarca, there was an army of 35,000 under Chalcuchima; and in the north there was another powerful army under Rumiñavi guarding Quito—any one of these generals might decide to move against the tiny Spanish force holding the emperor. In the circumstances the Spaniards' only recourse was guile. Hernando Pizarro, on his return through Jauja from a foray in search of gold, persuaded Chalcuchima to pay a visit to his captive emperor; at Cajamarca this powerful Inca general was taken prisoner, and yet another blow was delivered to the structure of imperial power.

A further setback for Atuhualpa was the arrival of Diego de Almagro in April 1533 at the head of a company of 150 conquistadors, all of them eager for booty. Finding himself still a captive after all the gold he had promised had been collected and melted down, Atuhualpa must have realized that only military force could rescue him. In fact, the Spaniards were in a quandary over what they should do with the emperor now that they had received their ransom. Rumours reached Pizarro that Rumiñavi's army was advancing from Quito, so he sent out a party of horsemen under Hernando de Soto to verify this information. However, even before De Soto had returned, Almagro and his followers were pressing Pizarro to kill Atuhualpa forthwith. Pizarro finally yielded, since he feared that the Inca might escape or be the cause of a general rebellion if he were taken with them on the long march to Cuzco. And so, the defenceless Atuhualpa was garrotted. It was a cruel and illegal act, regretted by many Spaniards in Peru, who believed the emperor should have been sent into exile instead, and it was subsequently criticized by the Spanish monarch himself, who was anxious to preserve Spain's moral and religious right to rule in the New World.

With Atuhualpa out of the way, the Spaniards prepared to march on Cuzco, the centre of the empire. Their forces were still very small, but circumstances had provided them with the opportunity to divide and conquer. The war of succession had exacerbated the political and tribal divisions in the empire, and Pizarro was able to play off one side against the other. His murder of Atuhualpa was welcomed by Huascar's branch of the Inca royal family, who began to collaborate with the Spaniards in the hope of regaining the throne they had lost to the usurper from Quito. Pizarro naturally seized this chance to present himself to the tribes loyal to Huascar as the restorer of the legitimate Inca line. He had one of Huascar's brothers, Tupac Huallpa, proclaimed emperor so that when the Spaniards arrived in Cuzco they would be seen as liberators come to expel the Quitan army of occupation commanded by Atuhualpa's general Quisquis.

The march from Cajamarca to Cuzco proved difficult: for the first time since their arrival in Peru the Spaniards had to engage Indian armies in open battle. Pizarro's political strategy collapsed when the puppet emperor Tupac Huallpa fell ill and died. Suspecting the captured Quitan general Chalcuchima of having poisoned Tupac Huallpa, Pizarro had him burnt alive for treason. Eventually, another brother of Huascar, the twenty-year-old Manco, was selected as the new puppet ruler. Finally, after a series of battles along the way, the Spaniards decisively defeated Quisquis's army in a bloody engagement in the mountains above Cuzco. On 15 November Pizarro led his men into the royal city of the Incas, where the Spanish conquerors were able to indulge their lust for gold by looting its abundant treasures.

Although the heartlands of the Inca empire had now fallen to Pizarro, the conquest was by no means complete. There remained the northern provinces of Quito (modern Ecuador), where Rumiñavi's army was based and towards which Quisquis's defeated troops were retreating. To the south the territories which today are Bolivia and Chile had yet to be penetrated. More important still, there were certain issues which needed to be clarified before Spanish power could be securely established in Peru. First, Manco Inca was still under the impression that Pizarro was an adventurer and not a conqueror; he nursed the ambition to rule over a restored empire once the Spaniards could be induced to depart. Secondly, Almagro and his men were growing resentful of the dominance of the Pizarro brothers, since they had not been given a share of Atuhualpa's golden ransom and their hunger for the rewards of conquest had yet to be properly satisfied. These unresolved matters would provoke further bloody wars and delay the pacification of Peru for some three decades.

The conquest of the northern provinces of Quito was undertaken by one of Pizarro's lieutenants, Sebastián de Benalcázar. This expedition, however, had to contend with a rival invasion led by one of the conquerors of Mexico, Pedro de Alvarado, who had proceeded unannounced from Guatemala in search of more riches to plunder. The two armies of conquistadors were poised to do battle with each other, but Alvarado finally agreed to be paid off in gold by Diego de Almagro, who had come up to reinforce Benalcázar. The campaign that followed was particularly hard and bloody; yet by the end of 1534 Benalcázar and Almagro had wrested the provinces

of Quito from Atuhualpa's surviving generals and the military power of the Inca empire was comprehensively destroyed.

Meanwhile, Francisco Pizarro, now styling himself Governor of Peru, had been busy consolidating the Spanish presence in the central provinces. A Spanish municipality was established in Cuzco itself, but Cuzco was too far inland and too high up in the Andes to be of use to the Spaniards as a capital. Instead, Pizarro chose to build a new capital city near the coast, close to the mouth of the River Rimac. It was officially founded on 6 January 1535 and called the 'City of the Kings' to commemorate the Epiphany, the feast-day of the Three Kings, though it soon became known as Lima, a corruption of Rimac, the river by which it stood. Pizarro had chosen well, for in the conflict that was brewing with his partner Almagro, Lima would give him the advantage of being supplied directly by sea from Panama.

The bone of contention between Pizarro and Almagro was to be the city of Cuzco. In early 1535 the partners had received an order from Charles V granting Pizarro jurisdiction over the northern territories of the Inca empire, while Almagro was to govern those of the south. Yet the royal decree did not make clear who should get the rich prize of Cuzco, which lay at the centre of the empire. The uncertainty produced tension between supporters of Pizarro and Almagro in the city itself; the quarrel was temporarily defused by Pizarro, who persuaded Almagro to lead an expedition of conquest into lands which are now part of Bolivia and Chile; these provinces were unquestionably under Almagro's jurisdiction and promised further riches. Accordingly, Almagro set off on a campaign which lasted two years and turned out to be a complete disaster. Despite inflicting great cruelty on the Indians and enduring horrible privations in crossing the freezing Andes and the torrid wastes of the Atacama desert, Almagro's expedition found little of value. On their return, empty-handed and forlorn, but possessed of a solidarity forged during that brutal episode, Almagro's 'men of Chile' would covet Cuzco more intensely than before, and they were now confirmed enemies of the Pizarro brothers.

While Almagro and his men were away, Gonzalo and Juan Pizarro were left in charge of Cuzco, but, in truth, their stewardship had proved a fiasco which was to put the entire Spanish conquest of the Inca empire in jeopardy. Few restraints had been placed on the greed of the numerous Spanish bounty-hunters who flocked to the holy city. As a result of so many abuses and outrages committed against the Indians, it became obvious to the puppet ruler, Manco Inca, that the rapacious Spaniards had no intention of quitting Peru. Already heavily censured by the Inca elders for his submissiveness, Manco decided in the autumn of 1535 to cease collaborating with the foreigners and to call for a rebellion to drive them out of his realms. By the spring of 1536 Manco had raised a formidable army and was laying siege to Cuzco, where there were only 190 Spaniards—though they were now led by the capable Hernando Pizarro, who had taken over from his irresponsible younger brothers. Another Inca army was besieging Lima, and there Francisco Pizarro, believing all would be lost, appealed for help to the Spaniards of Panama. As supplies and reinforcements came from all over the Spanish Indies, the siege of Lima was soon broken, but Cuzco remained in peril for nearly a year. The city was finally relieved when Almagro's 'men of Chile' returned from their expedition in April 1537 and forced Manco Inca to withdraw. Almagro then entered the exhausted city and arrested the Pizarro brothers before setting off for Lima to confront Francisco. The erstwhile partners failed to resolve their differences, and Peru, which had fallen to the Spaniards as a result of an internecine conflict among the Incas, was plunged into another civil war—this time between the Spanish conquerors themselves, who were unable to agree over the spoils of victory.

The war did not last long, though the bitterness of its legacy was extremely damaging to Spanish interests in Peru. After a number of skirmishes, Hernando Pizarro succeeded in reaching Cuzco, where he inflicted a heavy defeat on the Almagristas at the battle of Las Salinas on 26 April 1538. Diego de Almagro himself was taken prisoner, made to stand trial and, to the horror of many Spaniards, put to death by strangling. The Pizarros were now masters of Peru, but their hold on the conquered empire was precarious. They had to reckon, in the first instance, with a large faction of vengeful Almagristas now led by their murdered leader's half-caste son. Then there was the rebel Manco Inca, who was still at large raising Indian revolts which had to be put down with much bloodshed, thereby delaying the pacification of the country. To add to the turmoil, a stream of Spanish ruffians poured into Peru in search of Inca gold, only to turn into drifting malcontents when their hopes were disappointed. Finally, the Pizarros had to contend with the distaste felt by the Spanish monarch for the way in which Peru had been won on behalf of the Crown. Atuhualpa's death had caused enough disquiet, but now Almagro's execution provoked anger at the imperial court: when Hernando Pizarro came to Spain in 1539 bearing gifts of gold for the emperor, he was imprisoned and held in confinement for the next twenty-two years. For Francisco,

the repercussions of Almagro's murder were to be fatal: on 26 June 1541 twenty Almagristas broke into his palace in Lima and hacked him to death. The assassins then proclaimed the young Diego de Almagro governor of Peru.

Once again, Spanish Peru slipped into civil war, but this time the Crown intervened directly to restore order. A royal official, Cristobal Vaca de Castro, was sent out, and with an army of Pizarro supporters marched against the Almagristas, defeating them at the battle of Chupas on 16 September 1542. Even then the turmoil was not over: within two years the Spanish settlers in Peru rebelled against the viceroy, Blasco Nunez Vela, over his ham-fisted efforts to implement a new royal code regulating the relations between Spaniards and Indians. It was Gonzalo Pizarro who headed the rebellion, and he effectively became the ruler of Peru after Nuñez Vela was killed in battle in 1546.

With the death of the viceroy, the surviving Pizarro brothers and their many followers among the Spanish settlers saw an opportunity to declare their independence from Spain by having Gonzalo proclaim himself king of Peru. In order to prevent this, in 1547 a royal army entered the country under the command of Pedro de la Gasca; he suspended the new code to placate the settlers, and then on 9 April 1548 engaged and defeated the Pizarristas at the battle of Sacsahuana outside Cuzco. With the execution of Gonzalo for treason, the power of the Pizarros was at last broken; royal authority was vigorously asserted without direct challenge by a succession of able viceroys in the course of the 1550s and 1560s, more than twenty years after Francisco Pizarro and his band of warriors had first irrupted into the Inca empire.

There remained, however, one last major obstacle to the pacification of Peru in the survival of the Indian resistance initiated by Manco Inca, who had led major uprisings in 1536-7 and 1538-9. Deep in the virtually impenetrable jungles covering the mountains around the Vilcabamba valley midway between Cuzco and Lima, Manco had set up an independent neo-Inca state, in which the ancestral religion and laws were revived; from here he continued to launch attacks and foment revolts against the Spaniards until 1545, when he was killed by treacherous Almagrista fugitives, to whom he had given refuge from the Pizarro brothers. His successor, Titu Cusi, was careful to maintain relations, albeit fairly strained at times, with the Spaniards—even to the extent of accepting baptism in 1568 and permitting Augustinian friars to enter Vilcabamba to preach Christianity to his subjects. But this attempt to establish a *modus vivendi* was condemned to failure: the Spaniards could not accept the existence of a neo-Inca statelet in the heart of their realms. It was the viceroy, Francisco de Toledo, who perceived the need to break Inca power altogether if Spain was ever to secure its authority over the Indians of the central Andes. At the same time, the Incas abandoned their policy of accommodation when Titu Cusi died in 1571 from a strange illness. The Indians believed that he had been poisoned by a member of the small circle of Spaniards at the Inca's court, and, in retaliation, the new Inca, Tupac Amaru, repudiated Christianity and had a Spanish missionary put to death by torture. Subsequent efforts by the Spanish authorities to re-establish diplomatic relations were cut short by the murder of a Spanish emissary to Vilcabamba. These outrages gave Viceroy Toledo a pretext to order the destruction of the neo-Inca state; in 1572 the jungle enclave was wiped out by Spanish forces and the last free Inca ruler, Tupac Amaru, was executed. However, the memory of Vilcabamba lived on in the submerged folk-culture of the Indians of the central Andes, and Tupac Amaru became a powerful symbol of independence; so much so that in the 1780s an Indian chieftain took the name Tupac Amaru and led a massive uprising against the whites of Peru.

Still, resistance had not been the only Inca response to the Spanish Conquest. The rebel Manco himself began his political life as a collaborator, a policy that his half-brother, Paullu, continued to pursue after Manco had decided to rebel. Convinced that the Spanish presence was a *fait accompli*, Paullu rejected Manco's exhortations to join what he regarded as futile rebellion and decided instead to transfer his allegiance to the Spanish Crown. Considering the abrupt shifts of power that took place in the aftermath of the conquest, Paullu turned out to be immensely gifted in the arts of political survival, happily serving as puppet Inca under whichever set of Spaniards happened to be in charge of Peru, from Francisco Pizarro through Almagristas and Pizarristas to the first viceroys. Much of the Inca royal family and nobility followed Paullu's example, accepting the sovereignty of the king of Spain and receiving pensions and estates from the Crown as rewards for their loyalty.

4. OTHER EXPLORATIONS AND CONQUESTS

The conquest of Peru had proved a long, bloody and treacherous affair, in which many of the leading con-

quistadors lost their lives. But just as the conquest of Mexico had inspired further penetration of the American continent, so did the news of Atuhualpa's ransom spur other Spanish captains to set out in search of yet more kingdoms of gold. In the 1530s and 1540s the pace of exploration and conquest quickened once again. Interest centred initially on the areas north of the Inca empire—namely, modern Ecuador, Colombia and Venezuela. One of Pizarro's captains. Sebastián de Benalcázar, followed up his conquest of the provinces of Quito in 1534 with an excursion into the territory of the Chibcha Indians, where he founded the Spanish settlements of Popayán (1536) and Cali (1537). As he approached Bogotá, the capital of the most powerful Chibcha kingdom, he encountered two other Spanish expeditions, both of which had penetrated the hinterland of Tierra Firme from different points on the Caribbean coast—one was led by Gonzalo Jiménez de Quesada, who had already conquered the Chibcha kingdom of Tunja, the other by Nikolaus Federmann, a German subject of Charles V. Drawn to the upland savannahs of Bogotá by rumours of gold and emeralds —deposits of gold had been found in 1533 by Pedro de Heredia's expedition to western Colombia—the three rival conquistadors decided to avoid an armed confrontation and abide by the arbitration of the Crown. Eventually, Benalcázar was appointed governor of this new frontier territory and the other two commanders withdrew.

But rumours persisted—rumours which Jiménez de Quesada among others evidently believed—that beyond the Andes, in the mysterious interior of the continent, there lay a land so rich in gold that its king covered himself in the precious dust once a year to bathe in a sacred lake. Though nothing ever came of it, the legend of the Man of Gold, El Dorado, whetted the appetite of Spanish adventurers and, together with other tales of fabulous riches, gave an impetus to daring feats of exploration, which, if they did little else, opened up some very difficult regions of the Americas to the Spaniards. For instance, in 1541 Gonzalo Pizarro, then governor of Quito, crossed the Andes eastwards in search of El Dorado and wandered blindly through the rain forests around the tributaries of the Amazon. Desperate for food, he sent out a forage party under Francisco de Orellana, but, though Pizarro eventually returned to Quito, Orellana lost his way and floated down the entire length of the Amazon—a distance of some 2,000 miles—and then sailed to the island of Hispaniola.

The great river-system found a European name as a result of attacks on Orellana by female warriors, whom he therefore called Amazons.

In Mexico and the Caribbean Spaniards were seduced by equally fruitless chimeras of wealth and glory, which called forth equally amazing feats of heroic endeavour. The North American counterpart of El Dorado was the legend of the Seven Cities of Cíbola, whose buildings were said to be encrusted with gold and turquoise. This legend grew out of reports of another great Indian empire situated in the far north–west of Mexico; these reports had been brought back by Alvar Núñez Cabeza de Vaca, one of a handful of survivors of an ill-starred expedition of 400 men which had set out under Pánfilo de Narváez to conquer Florida in 1528 and had been ravaged by disease and Indian attacks. For eight years Cabeza de Vaca had journeyed over sea, swamp and desert from Florida to the Gulf of California, crossing the lands of many savage Indian tribes until he finally reached Mexico City in 1536. Four years later he decided to try his luck again on another epic journey of exploration, which took him through the rain forests of the Brazilian interior, and eventually to Paraguay, where he became for a while governor of Asunción.

The quest for the Seven Cities of Cíbola was undertaken in 1540, when the Spanish viceroy in Mexico sent an expedition of 300 Spaniards and several hundred Indians under Francisco Vazquez de Coronado into what is now New Mexico and Arizona. Finding nothing of interest there, Coronado pressed on eastwards, discovered the Grand Canyon and then crossed the Río Grande into Texas. Hearing tales from the Indians about Quivira, yet another kingdom of gold, he embarked on a second quest, which took him as far north as Oklahoma and Kansas. He returned to Mexico having failed to find what he was looking for, though he had extended Spanish claims over immense territories in the northern part of the Americas.

Another of the great explorers of North America was Hernando de Soto, who had distinguished himself with Pizarro in the subjugation of Peru. Hoping to make a conquest of his own, he led a large expedition of some 600 men to Florida in 1539—the third major Spanish attempt in twenty-five years to exploit that territory. Once again, De Soto found nothing worth conquering; he wandered through Georgia, Alabama and Louisiana, discovering the Mississippi along the way, but died of a fever in 1541. All of these great tracts of land in the northern part of the continent proved barren so far as the Spaniards were concerned—they lacked obvious sources of gold, and the bellicose nomads who lived there were too recalcitrant to settle to agricultural labour. Such areas were to remain dangerous frontier zones, formally incorporated into the Spanish empire, but sparsely populated until the middle of the nineteenth century, when they were taken over by Anglo-Saxon settlers migrating from the Atlantic seaboard.

In South America, too, vast expanses were neglected. The whole area to the east of the Andean chain—the mass of the continent, in fact—was explored and settled only very slowly because, unlike in Peru, the difficulties of climate and geography were not compensated for by economic resources attractive to sixteenth-century Europeans. The huge interior of Brazil, an area of rain forests and sun-baked savannahs, technically Spanish by the Treaty of Tordesillas but later occupied by the Portuguese, remained virgin territory until late in the twentieth century. The pampas of Argentina and the chilly wastes of Patagonia, like the prairies and deserts of North America, were largely shunned by Spanish settlers until the 1870s.

Attempts to settle the fertile land around the river-systems of the Paraguay and the Paraná were unsuccessful until the late sixteenth century. In the early years the great estuary of the River Plate was of interest only inasmuch as it appeared to promise a south-western passage to Asia. Juan Díaz de Solís began explorations in 1516, but fell victim to cannibals. Magellan tried again in 1520 before turning southwards and finding the strait which now bears his name. It was the Venetian explorer Sebastian Cabot, then in the service of Spain, who called the estuary the Río de la Plata, the River of Silver, in the mistaken belief that silver was to be found on its shores. Not until 1535 was any effort made to settle the area of the River Plate; an expedition led by Pedro de Mendoza arrived from Spain and founded the city of Santa María de los Buenos Aires, which, however, was destroyed by Indians in 1541. Mendoza's men moved on up-river to Paraguay, where they founded Asunción, the first permanent Spanish colony east of the Andes and the only one for another two decades.

In fact, by the middle of the 1540s the momentum of the Spanish conquest had begun to slacken: not only were tales of El Dorado and the Seven Cities of Cíbola turning out to be mirages, but several campaigns, initiated with the usual high hopes between 1527 and 1540, had become grim, bloody struggles against Indian peoples who refused to be `pacified' by Spain. The balance sheet of conquest was becoming distinctly unfavourable to the Spanish: costs in men and materials outweighed returns in either treasure or native labour supply.

The conquest of the Yucatán peninsula was an especially unrewarding business. It was started by

Francisco de Montejo in 1527, but by the 1540s the Maya Indians were still unpacified, as late as 1542 they staged a massive insurrection, which had to be put down with appalling violence. Despite evidence of luxurious civilizations in the past, the Yucatán yielded few riches to its Spanish conquerors and it was to remain a marginal area of New Spain. The west and north-west of Mexico were conquered over a long period from 1529 to 1575. In a notoriously vicious campaign, Nuño de Guzmán carved out the kingdom of New Galicia (comprising the modern Mexican states of Michoacán, Jalisco, Nayarit and Sinaloa), but little in the way of gold was found, and in 1541 the Indians of Jalisco rose in a bloody rebellion known as the Mixtón War, which nearly succeeded in overwhelming the Spaniards. Spanish dominion was extended further into the north-west by Francisco de Ibarra, who created Nueva Vizcaya in brutal campaigns which lasted from 1562 until 1575. For the most part, these territories remained underpopulated borderlands, continually raided by Indian tribes from the barbarous north, and eventually given over to large-scale ranching.

In South America the conquest of Chile followed a pattern similar to that of the Yucatán peninsula and the Mexican north–west. In January 1540 Pedro de Valdivia set off from Cuzco with authority from Francisco Pizarro to conquer and settle the southern extremities of the Inca empire, which Diego de Almagro had abandoned after his disastrous Chilean campaign of 1535. It took Valdivia's expedition a whole year to cross the Andes and traverse the Atacama desert. On 12 February 1541 Valdivia founded the city of Santiago, but within six months it was destroyed by Araucanian Indians, one of the most bellicose peoples encountered by the Spaniards; for over two years Valdivia held out on the island of Santa Lucía until he received reinforcements from Peru. After Santiago was refounded, the Spaniards pushed southwards, establishing the towns of Concepción in 1550, Valdivia in 1552, and other settlements; they were unable to get any further than the Bío-bío River, which became the frontier with the Araucanians, at whose hands Pedro de Valdivia himself died in 1553. The Spaniards came to have great respect for the martial qualities of the Araucanian Indians, qualities which were famously praised in the most accomplished of the Spanish verse epics of the Renaissance, *La Araucana* by Alonso de Ercilla, a veteran of the Chile campaign.

From Chile the Spaniards crossed into what is now Argentina, founding in the 1560s on the eastern foothills of the Andes the towns of Mendoza and San Juan, which became extensions of the Chilean col-ony. Other towns of the Argentine interior, such as Tucumán and Córdoba, were founded in the 1560s and 1570s by expeditions from Peru. These trans-Andean settlements, as well as those in central Chile, remained outposts of empire, all of them dependent on the Peruvian economy. In fact, for most of the colonial era what is now modern Argentina did not exist as a distinct entity. The city of Buenos Aires, abandoned by the Spanish in 1541, was refounded permanently in 1580 by an expedition from Paraguay. It was to languish until the late eighteenth century as a seaport of little consequence subsisting on an illicit trade in African slaves and Peruvian silver with Portuguese merchants from Brazil.

The process of conquest, on the wane since the 1540s, can be said to have reached its end by the middle of the 1570s. In the half-century that had elapsed since Cortés landed at Veracruz, Spain had explored and dominated an area many times its own size. It is remarkable that such a feat was carried out not by regular armies, but by small groups of adventurers acting against two great empires and a host of Indian tribes in harsh, dangerous and often unpredictable circumstances. What special advantages did the Spaniards possess?

In the first place, they could call upon superior military technology: they had armour, guns and ships. But in many instances the conquistadors were poorly equipped—Cortés had 13 guns and about 15 cannon when he arrived in Mexico—and difficult terrain often nullified this technical superiority. A more versatile resource was the horse, which gave the Europeans physical and tactical advantages in combat. But again Cortés had a mere 16 horses, and Pizarro 27; in neither case could cavalry have constituted a critical factor in the defeat of native rulers capable of fielding armies of thousands.

A more significant Spanish advantage lay in politics and military strategy. The Spaniards were not invíncible: battles were lost and many. Indian peoples proved impossible to defeat—at least for long periods of time. But the conquistadors skilfully exploited native rivalries and internal conflicts to win allies and weaken the established powers. And here Spanish success was facilitated by the viruses of the Old World, which swept into America with devastating effects—great epidemics depleted native resources and caused acute demoralization. There was no comparable traffic in the other direction—even syphilis may not have arrived in Europe from the Indies, as was once believed.

Demographic loss aggravated the psychological imbalance that existed between Indian and Spaniard. Though the Spaniards may have been amazed by their discovery of a New World, they knew exactly what they wanted from it, namely gold and power. What is more, in seeking to acquire these goods, the conquistadors firmly believed they were furthering the designs of Heaven. By contrast, the American Indians did not know what to expect from the intruders. By the time the Aztec and Inca leaders had organized their resistance, it was too late—the structure of imperial authority had been undermined and irreparable divisions had appeared among the native peoples. As a result there could be no concerted effort to repulse the European invaders, whose power and motives were in any case still quite impenetrable to most Indian peoples. However, those few who did have the chance to grasp the nature of the European onslaught were able to survive undefeated—in some cases until well into the nineteenth century, as did the Araucanians. These Indians developed an effective resistance by adopting some of their enemy's superior methods—learning to ride horses and handle guns, for instance. Had the Aztecs or the Incas been given a similar opportunity to respond, the Spanish Conquest might not have succeeded at all. In the final analysis the conquerors enjoyed the advantage of surprise: they were self-righteously on the offensive, whereas most of the indigenous peoples of America, having been caught unawares, fell back on inadequate defences.

And yet, even though there is no mystery about the victory of the conquistadors, the Indians explained their defeat in metaphysical terms. The Spanish friar Bernardino de Sahagún collated oral information related to him by the Aztecs concerning portents and prophecies of doom said to have anticipated the arrival of the Spaniards. From Sahagún's record comes, too, the haunting tale of the psychological prostration of Montezuma before Cortés, due allegedly to his belief that the invader was the god Quetzalcoatl come to resume his divine kingship. In Peru, Spanish chroniclers reported similar myths about the god Viracocha, who had once departed across the Pacific promising to return.

This mythologizing of the Conquest, however, is not devoid of truth; it captures in poetic terms the disorientation of people whose historic seclusion was suddenly pierced by beings from an alien sphere, beings whose intrusion into a familiar and circumscribed environment must indeed have made them appear as visitors 'from behind the sky'.

D. Three Centuries of Black Slavery in Spanish America

Hugh Thomas in his landmark book *The Slave Trade* reports that between 1492 and 1870, approximately eleven million black slaves were transported from Africa to the Americas, including the United States (before the Civil War). While many readers might connect black slavery with the antebellum cotton fields of the United States, in Spanish America one of the most important plants that required intensive labour was sugar cane—a cash crop that the Moors first brought to Spain and which later the Spanish transported to the New World. Black slaves could work much more efficiently in the plantations, mines, and fisheries of Spanish American than the indigenous peoples, who were not accustomed to European commercial endeavours.

Blacks initially arrived with the Spaniards in the 16th century as freemen and servants; a few were slaves brought from Spain. King Ferdinand (the Catholic Monarch) authorized the first shipment of black slaves from Africa to Spain's new territories for work in the gold mines in 1518. Abolition of slavery generally occurred in Spanish America before the end of the U.S. Civil War (1865); for example, in Mexico in 1829 and Peru in 1854. In Cuba, however, slavery as an institution lasted until 1886.

One interesting figure and a contemporary of Hernán Cortés is Juan Garrido, a black conquistador who had commanded of his own troops during the *Conquista*. He was the first person to plant wheat in the new world. Like many of the conquistadores, he died poor and unrecognized for his services to Spain.

1. THE AFRICAN EXPERIENCE IN LATIN AMERICA: RESISTANCE AND ACCOMMODATION

Darién J. Davis

The African diaspora had a major demographic and cultural impact on all areas of Latin America, from Mexico to the Bahamas to Chile and Brazil. Although it is unusual today to observe African features among the populations of many Latin American nations, it should not be assumed that the genetic contribution was slight. In some parts of colonial Latin America, Africans outnumbered Europeans by a margin of 15 to 1. Almost one half of the populations of colonial Buenos Aires, Lima, and Mexico City reflected varying degrees of African ancestry.

European familiarity and experience with Africa occurred long before contact with the New World in 1492. Many Africans had been involuntarily settled in the Iberian peninsula prior to the conquest of the Western Hemisphere. In 1455, Pope Nicolas V gave the Portuguese the right to reduce to slavery the inhabitants of the southern coast of Africa who resisted the introduction of Christianity, thus in theory becoming the enemies of Christ. As a consequence, the Iberians began a modest slave trade on the western coast of Africa. The Portuguese set up factories, or trading posts, to deal with local middlemen and tribal chiefs. Africans contributed to the diversity of Iberian cities such as Seville and Lisbon, which were already inhabited by Jews, Arabs, and Christians. Small communities of Afro-Iberians thus emerged.

The slave market in Seville, while still relatively small, became one of the most active in Europe. Many called the city the "New Babylon." Northern and sub-Saharan Africans comprised more than 50 percent of the inhabitants of several of Seville's neighborhoods. The African populations became so socially and politically important that in 1475 the Crown appointed Juan de Valladolid, its royal servant and mayoral, to represent Seville's Afro-Iberian community. Churches and charities catered to its spiritual and material needs.

African slavery met a steady but limited demand in Europe. Neither Spain nor Portugal could absorb profitably a large number of slaves into its peninsular economy. European-African relations thus did not revolve around the institution of slavery. Indeed; the Portuguese recognized the independent sovereign existence of many African rulers and sought to establish political and cultural alliances with them. The institution of slavery, although long established both in Europe and Africa, continued to occupy a relatively minor position in both regions.

"Introduction: The African Experience in Latin America—Resistance and Accommodation," by Darién J. Davis as appeared in *Slavery and Beyond: The African Impact on Latin America and the Caribbean*, pp. xi-xxv. © 1995 by Scholarly Resources, Inc. Reprinted by permission of Rowman & Littlefield Publishing Group.

At the same time, the flora, the fauna, and the many complex societies of sub-Saharan, or black, Africa fascinated European explorers. Characterized by distinct ethnic groupings with varying religions, customs, and practices, West Africa's inhabitants included the Ashanti, the Yoruba, the Ibo, and the Dahomey, all of whom subsequently affected culture in the Western Hemisphere. Tribes from the Muslim area of North Africa, such as the Hausa, the Amalinke, and the Mandingo, in addition to tribes from the central Congo region, such as the Bantu, also influenced culture in the New World.[1]

The role of Africans in the New World varied both in time and place. The initial period of conquest relied upon Africans residing on the peninsula to supplement the limited number of Europeans in their effort to reduce the native population of the New World to the altered economic and political order. Indigenous groups recognized them as part of the conquering party. Miguel León Portilla, the prominent Mexican historian, reported that Aztecs referred to the Afro-Iberians who arrived with the Spaniards in Mexico as "soiled gods."[2] The Spanish respected and rewarded their contribution. Thus, Juan Valiente, a fugitive slave who had fought alongside the conquistadors in Chile, received an encomienda in the 1550s for his bravery. Other men of African ancestry, such as Juan Beltrán and Juan Fernández, also took part in the conquest of Chile.

Juan Garrido, known simply as "Handsome John." participated in the conquest of Mexico. Both Manuel Orozco y Berra and Bernal Díaz del Castillo noted his arrival with the conquistadors.[3] Garrido, who lived in Castile and considered himself a devout Christian, went to Santo Domingo. After participating in several exploratory trips to other islands, he traveled to New Spain with one of the first groups of conquistadors. While he did not receive the same rewards or honors as those of other Spanish conquistadors, he nevertheless, in 1525, became a respected *vecino* (citizen). Peter Gerhard examines Juan Garrido's life in Mexico and provides an assessment of the extent of African participation in the conquest and development of Latin America.

Following the conquest, the new overlords began the task of constructing colonial economies and societies. At the same time, cultural disruption, exploitation of the indigenous populations, and epidemic diseases caused a drastic decline in the native American populations; resulting in a severe shortage of labor and retarding the rate of European development and exploitation of the newly conquered territories. In some areas, such as Brazil, it became evident that the native populations could not be transformed into efficient laborers to meet the needs of the Portuguese-controlled economy. Consequently, Europeans turned to African slavery, in some areas as a supplement to scarce indigenous labor and in other areas as the main source of workers. Henceforth, European-African relations centered on slavery and the slave trade, a reality that endured for over three hundred years.

The institution of slavery adapted to the needs of the particular region, the demographic reality, and the nature of the work being performed. A variety of tasks, from pearl fishing, mining, and carpentry to sharecropping and domestic chores, depended on African labor. Slavery in Mexico, Argentina, and Chile differed substantially from the plantation economies of the Caribbean and Brazil. Urban slave labor also differed from plantation life, which had its own set of laws. In both urban and rural areas, it is important to be aware of the distinction between laws and actual practices. Enforcement of the laws of manumission and marriage as well as the general treatment of slaves depended on regional and local considerations rather than on abstract laws or theoretical codes of conduct. Verena Martínez Alier, author of several works that focus on slavery in Cuba, has pointed out, for example, that although there were rigid laws that prohibited interracial marriage, widespread cohabitation and other sexual arrangements occurred.[4]

Slaves were not passive victims of the system. They struggled to improve their well-being in personal ways, including sexual alliances and the establishment of ties of loyalty that enabled them to mitigate the impersonal

---

1. Philip D. Curtin, in Atlantic Slave Trade: A Census (Madison: University of Wisconsin Press, 1969), identified the eight major regions in West Africa: Gambia and Senegal; Sierra Leone; the Ivory Coast and Liberia; the Gold Coast—modern-day Ghana; Togo and Dahomey; the Bight of Biafra; Angola; and Southern Africa.

2. Miguel León Portilla, *Broken Spears: The Aztec Account of the Conquest of Mexico* (Boston: Beacon Press, 1992), 34.

3. Francisco de Icaza, ed., *Diccionario autobiográfico de conquistadores y pobladores de Nueva España* (Madrid, 1923), 1: entry no. 169. See Hubert Howe Bancroft, History of Mexico, 6 vols. (San Francisco, 1883–1886), 2:423n. Some scholars report that Cortés's expedition included four hundred Spaniards and three hundred blacks. In *La corona española y los foráneos en los pueblos de indios de América* (Stockholm, 1970), Magnus Mürner argues that many more blacks participated.

4. Verena Martínez Alier, *Marriage, Class, and Colour in Nineteenth-Century Cuba: A Study of Racial Attitudes and Sexual Values in a Slave Society* (Ann Arbor: University of Michigan Press, 1989), 12.

cruelty of slavery. The African's survival depended on his or her ability to resist or manipulate, collectively and individually, a common institutional structure. Many slaves resisted their European oppressors through suicide, escape, sabotage, and the defiance of the laws of social conduct and religion. Others sought to preserve their own culture while accommodating themselves to the new social and cultural order.

The strength of African culture, despite the oppressive impact of slavery, is demonstrated by the re-creation of African societies in the areas of the New World that remained beyond the control of the Europeans. The most famous Afro-Creole settlement was the Republic of Palmares (1630–1682), established by runaway slaves in a remote region of Portuguese America. At least twenty thousand people lived within its boundaries, governed by West African customs (particularly Bantu) and cultural elements drawn from the Portuguese slave society from which they had fled. Other Afro-Creole settlements ranged from the small encampment of runaways to the *palenques* in Spanish America, the *quilombos* in Portuguese America, and the maroons in Jamaica and Guyana. A lesser known example of adaptation, not only to an independent existence but also to a hostile environment, was the re-creation of African societies on the coast of Ecuador.

Miscegenation, or the commingling of the races, inevitably accompanied the development of the New World. Contact among Europeans, aborigines, and Africans created a mixed people—Afro-Creoles—and facilitated a distinct New World culture through *mestizaje*, or the combining of elements of distinct cultures. Extensive miscegenation between the native populations and Africans in some regions forced the Spanish to create a legal category for them: the *zambos*. The Portuguese called them *cafuzos*. In colonial Mexico the Spanish felt so threatened by intermarriage between natives and Africans that they declared it illegal.

Portuguese and Spanish authorities often promoted miscegenation as a population policy in underpopulated regions. This policy stressed the importance of assimilating the African into the broader mestizo, or racially mixed, society. As a result, a psychologically important caste system emerged, based on color, in which blacks occupied the lowest rung and which collided with a developing class system based on economic considerations. As a result, miscegenation engendered a "flexibility" in which race as well as an individual's socioeconomic position determined social status.

Most Latin American societies had become decidely mestizo or mulatto by the end of the nine-

teenth century. Mestizos formed the majority in areas with high concentrations of indigenous communities, such as the Andes, Central America, and Mexico. In regions with small native populations, including newly formed Spanish cities, mulattoes became a dominant force. In these regions many mulattoes and mestizos achieved middle-class status and served as a buffer between the lower oppressed classes of blacks and natives and those who identified themselves as upper-class whites, many of whom were mestizos or mulattoes. However, class could not be strictly defined along racial lines. Dark mulattoes, *morenos*, and *pardos* and people of a wide hue of colors crossed class and social boundaries.[5]

Demographic data for the nineteenth century attest to the importance of miscegenation and the proliferation of the mixed population. Their contribution to major Latin American institutions such as the military needs to be examined. In cities such as Buenos Aires, Caracas, and Lima, mulattoes constituted a high percentage of those men who enlisted into the military, one of the few institutions that afforded Afro-Creoles some mobility within the broader society. Afro-Creoles played a significant role in the national struggles for independence throughout the nineteenth century. They fought valiantly on behalf of their emerging nations, side by side with their Creole counterparts.

Ideological leanings and political agendas influenced Latin American writers' and historians' views on miscegenation. In the nineteenth century, liberal elites preferred to focus on development issues rather than on race relations or racial origins. Most did not question the premise of inferior and superior races but hoped that miscegenation would eliminate the issue. They opposed slavery for economic reasons and believed that European immigration would promote progress and alleviate racial problems. The Brazilian notion of *branqueamento*, the whitening process, and becoming more European appeared to be the way to overcome the negative legacy of slavery. Thus, liberals such as Joaquim Nabuco advocated an end to slavery in Brazil because, among other factors, it repelled potential European immigration. Moreover, without slavery, Nabuco believed that his country could have been another Canada or

---

5. The origin of the mulatto class dates back to the colonial years, and mulattoes were often referred to as free people of color. Many slaves who bought their freedom or who gained it through manumission formed part of this class. Marriage and concubinage offered other forms through which one's child could ascend the socioeconomic ladder.

Australia. Nabuco's arguments are reflected in the writings of a wide range of Latin American commentators, who ignored the contribution of the native American and the African to the building of their societies. Their desire to modernize and attract investment reinforced the prejudice toward the nonwhite sectors of the region

In the 1920s nationalist writers recognized the contribution of previously ignored racial sectors to the formation of national identity. Latin Americans began to project positive racial images, celebrating the *mestizaje* of native, European, and African traits. In this era the Mexican José Vasconcelos noted that miscegenation had created what he called a "cosmic race."[6] Similar theories arose in the 1920s and 1930s throughout Latin America. Writers such as the Brazilian Gilberto Freyre and the Cuban Elías Entralgo wrote about miscegenation between Europeans and Africans in an approving manner. These views, in part, reflected the twentieth-century nationalists' attempt to see their Latin American identity and development in positive terms.[7]

Despite their lack of political and economic power, Afro-Creoles nonetheless have influenced many aspects of regional and local society. While music and food are the most obvious examples to the casual observer, Afro-Creoles have exerted a strong force on the social values and attitudes often conveyed through religious beliefs and practices. The Cuban Fernando Ortiz was one of the first Latin Americans to explain African transculturation, or the transfer of cultural values and rituals from Africa to the New World. Yoruba slaves from Angola brought with them to Brazil a philosophy and concept of the cosmos that provided the religious basis of *shangó; umbanda*, and *candomblé*.

In Africa the Yoruba people used anthropomorphic images to interpret and organize their world, a practice continued in the Americas and facilitated by Catholicism's organization of the saints in a pantheon similar to that in the Yoruba religion. While forced to acknowledge European saints and follow the Roman Catholic liturgical calendar, they associated African deities with Catholic saints. Santería, derived from Yoruba practices, provides another example of religious flexibility that preserved core beliefs while accommodating Catholic practices. Different Santería deities can be associated with various Catholic saints in the Caribbean, depending on the region. Many Yoruba customs and expressions that no longer exist in Africa persist in Cuba; Cuban Santería employs eighteenth-century Yoruba terms and prayers, for example.

Afro-Creole religions constitute powerful sources of inner strength, enabling believers to reaffirm their African identity. Priests and priestesses play an important role in Afro-Creole society, as religion and spiritual notions touch every aspect of daily life. The Dahomey, like the Yoruba, believed in a supreme god who governed a divine pantheon. Each divinity allowed men and women to serve as consorts, thereby providing believers with an active spiritual life in close association with powerful deities. Dahomey religious philosophy is clearly seen in voodoo. In the Fon language of Dahomey and Togo, vodun refers to a spirit or deity; and while the uninformed associate vodun or voodoo with sorcery and witchcraft, voodoo is a sophisticated, complex, and thriving religion.

Scholars frequently study the African aspect of Latin American religions in the context of syncretism—the fusion of two religions or faiths in the creation of a new religion—with the dominant European religion, Catholicism. In many cases, however, what is erroneously called syncretism is simply a loose association of Catholic saints with African deities. Many Latin Americans, for example, associate Yemanja, the Yoruba goddess of the sea, with Our Lady of Glory, Our Lady of Conception, or Our Lady of Carmen, depending on the region. Nonetheless, Yemanja retains all of the human characteristics afforded to her by the Yoruba and little or none of the European traits of the Virgin Mary. Luc de Heusch (Chapter 6) investigates African religious practices, concluding that Catholicism has very little influence in voodoo. His study of Haitian voodoo suggests the need for a reevaluation of the syncretic process.

Music also has provided an important channel for the cultural and social values essential to the survival of a sense of community. For Afro-Creoles, music reestablished and recreated the ancestral bond with Africa. It provided, as did religion, a mechanism by which people of African descent could reaffirm and celebrate their identity. Africa is the home of a wealth of musical instruments—xylophones, flutes, harps,

---

6. José Vasconcelos, *La raza cósmica: Misión de la raza Ibero-Americana* (México: Aguilar S.A. de Ediciones, 1961).

7. See Gilberto Freyre's Brazilian classic *The Masters and the Slaves* (1933) (reprinted ed., 1986 [Berkeley: University of California Press]), in which he developed his theory of Lustropicalism, crediting Portugal's racial tolerance as critical to its colonization efforts. Elías Entral go proposed his ideas about mestizaje and miscegenation in *La liberación étnica cubana* (Havana, 1953).

bells, horns, and drums—which produce complex musical sounds. Drumming, in particular, is a highly sophisticated activity in Africa; almost every ethnic group has its own type of drum, and different drums are used for different purposes. Some are sacred and used only in religious ceremonies, while others accompany various instruments in rhythmic ensembles. Africans brought to the Americas their unique blend of rhythms and musical practices, which they adapted to the new environment.

The musical experience, like other social experiences, reflects a distinct pattern of interaction. African music entered Latin American society at the lowest social levels and, therefore, was not accepted by the elites in its pure form. However, musicians adjusted to make it palatable to the upper classes. In the case of the Argentine tango, the Brazilian samba, or the Dominican merengue, the musical form was appropriated by mainstream society and celebrated as a national symbol.

Even though African rhythms have influenced all aspects of popular Latin American music, the contemporary term "black music," or, alternatively, "Afro-Latin music," refers to those forms in which the drumming is dominant. Many Colombians regard black music as sensual and exotic, yet for Afro-Colombians on the Caribbean coast this music reaffirms their identity in a country that has, in the past, refused to recognize them in official census reports. West Indian migration to Central and South America in the nineteenth and twentieth centuries has increased Afro-Creole cultural influences within the wider Caribbean basin. Panama is now the creative center for Jamaican-born reggae music in Spanish.[8]

Although Africans were cocreators of a new culture, they had come to the Americas as workers. After the abolition of slavery, Afro-Creole labor never ceased to have important economic consequences for the region. A competitive social order developed, but this did not ensure Afro-Creole participation in the modernization, given the debasing effects of slavery, pauperism, and isolation. The growing pool of unemployed workers provided a cheap labor supply and drove down real wages, and the rapid expansion and industrialization that began at the turn of the century were assured at a low cost.

Foreign investment in Latin America increased with the construction of railroads and utilities and the purchase of land by multinational agricultural corporations such as the United Fruit Company. Demographics within the region also began to shift as workers migrated to centers of industrialization or to the large multinational plantations across national barriers. International investors looked for transportation routes that would facilitate exchange throughout the region. Consequently, the most miraculous and economically important project, the Panama Canal, was under way.

The Panama Canal provided a new commercial passage through the Americas. Construction did not begin until the United States had arranged the independence of Panama from Colombia. The 1903 Panama Canal Treaty, often referred to as the Isthmian Canal Convention, gave the United States permission to construct the canal and rights to govern the Canal Zone as if it were its territory. Because of the magnitude and urgency of the project, a massive number of workers would be needed in a relatively short time. The United States turned to the West Indies to find the ideal workers: English-speakers accustomed to the temperate climate who could be trained easily and who could be relocated cheaply. Thus began a migratory pattern that would change demographics on the isthmus.

West Indian migration to Central and South America has increased cultural connections within the wider Caribbean basin. Well-known Afro-Creoles, such as the Costa Rican writer Quincy Duncan and Jamaican-born Marcus Garvey, have West Indian roots. Garvey, like many West Indians, traveled to the isthmus to work on the expanding banana plantation. Just as European migration changed the face of countries such as Uruguay and Argentina by the early twentieth century, so too did West Indian migration change Central America. Today, the Caribbean coast of Central America shows marked Afro-Creole influences. The West Indian population at first settled in the Canal Zone areas such as Colon City, but by the 1930s this migration had changed the demographics of Panama City.

In Puerto Rico, the Afro-Puerto Rican socialist José Luis González traces the formation of the nation by emphasizing the contribution of the Afro-Creoles and their relationship to subsequent immigrants to the island. Africans formed the base of Puerto Rican nationhood, according to Gonzalez, because they developed a unique sense of patriotism and attachment to the island due to their condition of bondage. González provides a provocative point

---

8. West Indies is the general term applied to the islands of the Caribbean basin because Columbus was intent on sailing west to find the "Indies of the East." Used without political implications, the term is synonymous with the Caribbean or Antilles. The term is especially used by the English-speaking Caribbean.

of departure for a discussion on the nature of race relations and national identity in Latin America.

Twentieth-century cultural rejuvenation and racial and ethnic pride represent another dimension of modern race relations. The writings of intellectuals such as the Cuban Nicolás Guillén, the Martinican Aimé Césaire, and the Brazilian Abdias do Nascimento have been instrumental in raising black consciousness. Cultural movements such as Negritude, Negrismo, and Rastafarianism have bound Afro-Creoles together. The period following World War I saw the rise of popular Afro-Creole social movements that challenged the status quo. Their emergence was due to a combination of international and national factors. Since then, black consciousness movements have emerged in virtually every region of the Americas. Chapter 10 provides examples from the French-speaking Caribbean, the English-speaking Caribbean, and Brazil.

One of the most celebrated exponents of Negritude in the Francophone Caribbean is the poet and politician from Martinique, Aimé Césaire. As cofounder of the Negritude movement, he provides a poignant indictment of European colonization. In the English-speaking Caribbean the philosophy of the Jamaican-born Marcus Garvey became very influential. As a precursor to the Negritude movement. Garvey began the Universal Negro Improvement Association in 1922. Previously, he had worked on a banana plantation owned by the United Fruit Company on the Caribbean coast of Costa Rica, where he founded the newspaper *La Nacionale*. From Costa Rica he traveled to Panama, Guatemala, Nicaragua, and several of the South American republics before settling in Harlem Garvey emphasized the solidarity of Afro-Creoles throughout the Americas, a theme that other social and cultural movements from the 1930s to today continue to stress.

The Rastafarians followed Garvey when he said, "Look to Africa where our new king will be crowned." In 1930, Ras Tafari was crowned King Haile Selassie of Ethiopia. Rastafarians claim the divinity of Haile Selassie and advocate a spiritual return to Africa. Leonard Barrett discusses their history, customs, and beliefs.

The Afro-Brazilian activist Abdias do Nascimento followed in the tradition of Garvey and Césaire. Nascimento was one of the founders of the Teatro Experimental do Negro (T.E.N.), which became the major consciousness-raising organization of the 1940s and 1950s. Although the agenda and programs of T.E.N. emerged out of the uniquely Brazilian milieu, Nascimento saw a connection with other types of cultural activity throughout the diaspora. Not always supported by their male counterparts,

women forged their own agenda within and outside of organized movements. The participation of artists, activists, and popular-class women in the transformation of the socio-political process in Brazil remains only partially explored.

As a result of the increased participation of Afro-Creole men and women in social, cultural, and political activity, governments in Latin America have begun to understand what the United States has long appreciated: Afro-Creoles are a powerful interest group. Nevertheless, in all Latin American societies, people of darker pigmentation occupy the lowest rung of the economic ladder and are often ignored by official government statistics, including national census reports. Consequently, the actual size of the Afro-Creole population in the hemisphere and its influence are misrepresented. Jack W. Hopkins's statistics on Latin America's population represent one of the more accurate compilations for the 1980s.

Rodolfo Monge Oviedo's statistics on the Afro-Creole populations in Latin America underscore the difficulty in obtaining reliable figures. Ethnic or racial classification may change depending on the perceptions of the person collecting the data. Moreover, individual nations, as well as regions within countries, may use different categories to classify people of African descent. Indeed; many nations do not include ethnicity or race in their census reports. All of these factors make it difficult to determine the exact number of Afro-Creoles in Latin America. By checking information from the *Britannica Yearbook* against other published sources, Monge Oviedo has provided two figures for Afro-Creoles from thirty-six countries: a maximum and a minimum. Based on data for 1992, the minimum (*Min.*) represents the smallest number recorded for Afro-Creoles in the indicated countries, while the maximum (*Max.*) denotes the largest.

The complexity of the African dimension is also difficult to grasp. Few works offer scholars and students of Latin America a comprehensive framework in which to study and analyze the legacy of Africans and Afro-Creoles to the region's history. Franklin Knight was one of the first scholars in the United States to examine the African experience in broad socio-economic terms.[9] Richard Jackson's work on the contribution of people of African descent to Latin American literature is also valuable.[10] Recent research in anthropology, ethnohistory, and social

---

9. Franklin Knight, *The African Dimension of Latin America* (New York: Macmillan, 1974).

10. Richard Jackson, *Black Literature and Humanism in Latin America* (Athens: University of Georgia Press, 1988).

history have unveiled new ways of approaching old documents that allow us to understand more fully the African presence in the region. Nevertheless, slavery and its bitter aftermath remain the focus of the majority of works that examine the African experience in Latin America. Scholars and students continue to debate differing interpretations of the institution and its lingering influence. Following in the footsteps of two of the forerunners of research on slavery and race relations—Frank Tannenbaum and Stanley Elkins[11]—historians, ethnographers, and sociologists have studied the similarities and differences between slavery in the United States and that in Latin America. Tannenbaum maintained that slavery in Latin America was more benign than it was in the United States because, in the former, the slave was recognized as a human being. Elkins agreed, arguing that slavery in the United States reflected a rampant capitalism, while in Latin America the presence of the Church and laws of manumission countered the tendency to reduce slaves to the status of a commodity. Manuel Moreno Fraginals later recognized the presence of many other factors in determining the nature of slavery but nevertheless argued that it was primarily an economic institution. Consequently, Latin Americans eventually abolished slavery because of the incompatibility of slave labor and technology.[12]

Florestan Fernandes is among the few scholars who have looked at the relationship between race and economic opportunity in Latin America. He examined the plight of blacks in the urban areas of São Paulo during the period of rapid modernization between World War I and World War II. As the new competitive economic order emerged, it did not eradicate to any significant extent the traditional social system. Participation in the modernization process required material and psychological skills as well as technological elements that neither the black nor the mulatto possessed, given their debasement by slavery, pauperism, and isolation.[13]

Despite their merits, such comparisons overlook the fact that the African experience is not a static one that can be defined easily by economic, political, or social paradigms. The dynamic African presence touched all aspects of society, as it continues to do today. Afro-Creoles, as active participants in the development of societies in the Americas, work within the social system yet also struggle to modify their negative circumstances and to safeguard their well-being.

Brazil and the countries that make up the Caribbean basin, including the islands and the littoral countries of South America from Colombia to the Guianas, show a different pattern of development from other regions. Based on a plantation economy and with a relatively small indigenous population, this region relied heavily on slave labor as did the southern United States. While most countries had abolished slavery by 1860, Cuba and Brazil held on to the institution until the late 1880s. Because of the duration of the system and the number of slaves introduced—exceeding the number that arrived in the United States—the African presence is most strongly felt in these two countries. It is also dominant in the English-and French-speaking Caribbean, where the ratio of African to European was very high.

In recognition of their historical and social relationship, both Brazil and Cuba have attempted to forge diplomatic, cultural, and political ties with nations in Africa. Cuba's willingness to become actively involved in Africa during the Cold War stemmed, in part, from this perceived relationship. Armando Entralgo and David González López (Chapter 12) give an overview of the Cuban policy in Africa from 1960 to 1990.

Africa has played an essential part in the creation of Latin American societies. Nevertheless, much remains to be done if we are to understand fully that contribution.

2. A BLACK CONQUISTADOR IN MEXICO

Peter Gerhard

The Iberian experience in America passed through two stages: exploration and conquest in the 50 years after Columbus's voyage; and colonization over the next 250 years, in which Spaniards and Portuguese began the transfer of their culture and institutions to the New World. This chapter looks at the role of Africans during the era of

11. Frank Tannenbaum, *Slave and Citizen: The Negro in the Americas* (New York: Vintage Books, 1946), 112; and Stanley Elkins, *Slavery: A Problem in American Institutional and Intellectual Life* (Chicago: University of Chicago Press, 1959).
12. Manuel Moreno Fraginals, *El ingenio* (Havana: Editorial de las Ciencias Sociales, 1978), 30–32.
13. Florestan Fernandes, *The Negro in Brazilian Society*, trans. Jacqueline D. Skiles (New York: Columbia University Press, 1969), 132–34.

exploration. From the beginning the encounter brought together the peoples of three worlds—Europe, Africa, and America. The earliest Spanish expeditions included freed blacks from the vibrant black communities in the Iberian peninsula, especially from Seville, the "New Babylon," and prominent conquistadors traveled with retinues that included numerous black slaves. Although their presence during the era is evident, little is known about these individuals of African descent.

Peter Gerhard, an independent scholar well known for A Guide to the Historical Geography of New Spain (1972), pieced together the following sketch of Juan Garrido, one of the conquistadors who accompanied Hernán Cortés in the conquest of Mexico. Gerhard reported that Garrido was one of a substantial number of Africans in New Spain during these years. Cortés's expedition to Baja California, for example, reportedly consisted of four hundred. Spaniards and three hundred blacks. Gerhard's sketch of Garrido's career offers a direction for further research on African participation in the first fifty years after the encounter between these different worlds. Above all, his essay suggests the outlines of race relations before the demands for plantation slave labor dominated Spanish-African interaction.

While the role played by the people of equatorial Africa in the colonization of Latin America is relatively well known, it is for the most part an impersonal history that emerges from the contemporary documents: the establishment of a Negro slave trade as a result of the demand for labor to replace a devastated native population; the employment of these black slaves in the more arduous tasks throughout the colonies; and, in most areas, their gradual assimilation through miscegenation with natives (and to a far lesser extent with Europeans). Information about individual blacks is usually confined to a brief statement of age, physical characteristics, and degree of acculturation at the moment of sale or the taking of estate inventories; less frequently, the place of origin of a slave is indicated. Only rarely do we hear about a Negro slave who achieved distinction in some way. Two examples that come to mind are Juan Valiente, the conquistador of Chile,[1] and Yanga, the famed maroon leader in Veracruz.[2]

Although most blacks who came to America in early years were slaves, records of the Casa de Contratación show that a good many black freedmen from Seville and elsewhere found passage on westward-bound ships.[3] Some of them settled in the Caribbean region, and others followed the tide of conquest to Mexico and Peru, identifying themselves no doubt as Catholic subjects of a Spanish king, with much the same privileges and ambitions as white Spaniards. "Benito el Negro" and "Juan el Negro" (the latter's real name seems to have been Juan de Villanueva) were encomenderos in the province of Pánuco and thus they should not have been slaves, but we cannot be sure of their origin.[4] Spaniards might call anyone with a very dark skin "negro," and indeed the fact that Villanueva was from Granada makes it seem likely that he was a morisco. On the other hand there is record of an African who apparently crossed the Atlantic as a freeman, participated in the siege of Tenochtitlán and in subsequent conquests and explorations, tried his hand as an entrepreneur (with both Negro and Indian slaves of his own) in the early search for gold, and took his place as a citizen in the Spanish quarter of Mexico City. His name was Juan Garrido, and he was still alive in the late 1540s when he wrote or dictated a short résumé of his services to the Crown:

> Juan Garrido, black in color ... says that he, of his own free will, became a Christian in Lisbon, [then] was in Castile for seven years, and crossed to Santo Domingo where he remained an equal length of time. From there he visited other islands, and then went to San Juan de Puerto Rico, where he spent much time, after which he came to New Spain. He was present at the taking of the city of Mexico and in other conquests, and later [went] to the island with the marquis. He was the first to plant and harvest wheat in this land, the source of all that there now is, and he brought many vegetable seeds to New Spain. He is married and has three children, and is very poor with nothing to maintain himself.[5]

---

1. Peter Boyd-Bowman, "Negro Slaves in Early Colonial Mexico," The Americas. 26 (Oct. 1969), 150–151. Robert Brent Toplin, Slavery and Race Relations in Latin America (Westport, Conn., 1974), 16.

2. `Gonzalo Aguirre Beltrán, El señorío de Cuauhtochco—luchas agrarias en México durante el virreinato (México, 1940).

3. Ruth Pike. "Sevillian Society in the Sixteenth Century: Slaves and Freedmen," Hispanic American Historical Review, 47 (Aug. 1967), 358.

4. Papeles de Nueva España publicados de orden y con fondos del gobierno mexicano por Francisco del Paso y Troncoso, director en misión del Museo Nacional, 7 vols. (Madrid, 1905–1906), I, nos. 566, 572–573. Francisco de Icaza, ed., Diccionario autobiográfico de conquistadores y pobladores de Nueva España, 2.vols.(Madrid, 1923). no. 1165.

5. Icaza, Diccionario no. 169

The early chronology of this statement is vague, but working backward from the fall of Tenochtitlán (1521), one can assume that Garrido arrived in America about 1510. It is perhaps more than a coincidence that a Spaniard called Pedro Garrido landed in Santo Domingo with his family and entourage in 1510, and later accompanied Cortés to Mexico.[6] Slaves were often given the surnames of their masters, and while we do not know whether Juan Garrido was ever a slave it seems most probable that he was at least a protégé of a Spaniard at one time. However, this is pure conjecture, and we might also consider the possibility that the subject of this essay was named for his physical appearance (Juan Garrido can be roughly translated as "Handsome John"). In fact, the matter of how and when Garrido got to Mexico, and what part he played in the conquest, are something of a mystery. The *Diccionario Porrúa*, perhaps relying on an inconclusive passage in Bernal Díaz, says that he arrived with Juan Núñez Sedeño, who accompanied Cortés's 1519 expedition in his own ship with a large retinue that included "un negro"; Manuel Orozco y Berra has him crossing a year later with the army of Pánfilo de Narváez.[7] Magnus Mörner, after claiming that "many" hispanicized and Spanish-speaking blacks took part in the conquest, leaves us without any details,[8] nor does one find any mention of Garrido by name in the various contemporary accounts of the siege and surrender of Tenochtitlán (indeed the same might be said of many Spaniards who were there). His name appears for the first time in the proceedings of Mexico City's cabildo on March 8, 1524, when that body granted a piece of land for the establishment of a smithy on the Tacuba causeway "going out of this city, just past

the chapel [*hermita*] of Juan Garrido."[9] Lucas Alamán identifies this as the church subsequently rebuilt and dedicated to San Hipólito de los Mártires, occupying the site where so many of Cortés's men died as they fled from Tenochtitlán on the Noche Triste.[10] It may have been the brief statement in Alamán that gave rise to a somewhat embellished and much-repeated version, of which the following is an example:

> *San Hipólito* ... Historically and sentimentally this is one of the most interesting churches in the city. In front of the spot where it now stands there existed in the year 1520 the second line of defenses on the causeway (now the street occupied by the horse railway to Tacuba) that connected the Aztec city with the main-land westward. At this point was the greatest slaughter of the Spaniards during the retreat of the memorable Noche Triste (July 1, 1520). After the final conquest of the city, one of the survivors of that dismisal night. Juan Garrido, having freshly in mind its bloody horrors, built of adobe at this place a little commemorative chapel.[11]

Terry's guide [to Mexico], drawing on the story as told by Orozco y Berra, identifies Garrido as "one of the Conquistadores [who] undertook to recover the bodies of his slaughtered countrymen and to erect a chapel wherein they could be buried with religious rites."[12]

While his role in the Tenochtitlan episode remains obscure, Garrido took part in at least one of the expeditions sent out by Cortés after the conquest of the Triple Alliance to secure control and investigate the economic potential of outlying areas. According to a *relación geográfica* of 1580, "a Negro . . . who called himself Juan Garrido" accompanied Antonio de Caravajal and three other Spaniards to the hot country of Michoacán and the coast of Zacatula, most likely in 1523–1524. This little group was received hospitably by the Tarascans of Zirándaro, after which it proceeded

---

6. Peter Boyd-Bowman, Indice geobiográfico de cuarenta mil pobladores españoles de América en el siglo XVI, 2 vols. (Bogotá, 1964 and Mexico, 1968), 1. 15.

7. Diccionario Porrúa de historia, biografía y geografía de México, (México, 1964), 357, 597. Bernal Díaz del Castillo, Historia verdadera de la conquista de la Nueva España, ed. by Joaquírez Ramírez Cabañas, 2 vols. (México, 1960), I, 87, 92. Baltasar Dorantes de Carranza, Sumaria relación de las cosas de la Nueva España con noticia individual de los descendientes legítimos de los conquistadores y primeros pobladores españoles (México, 1902), 384. In an earlier version of his list of conquistadors, Orozco y Berra does not specify how Garrido reached Mexico: cf. Diccionario universal de historia y de geografia, 7 vols. (México, 1853–1855). II, 499.

8. Magnus Mürner, La corona española y los foráneos en los pueblos de indios de América (Stockholm, 1970), 94.

9. Actas de cabildo de la ciudad de México (hereafter cited as AC). Mar. 8. 1524 (since there are several published editions. I shall refer only to the date).

10. Lucas Alamán. Disertaciones sobre la historia de la república mejicana desde la época de la conquista que los españoles hicieron a fines del siglo XV y principios del XVI de las islas y continente americano hasta la independencia, 3 vols. (México, 1844–1849), II. 285–287.Cf. Francisco Cervantes de Salazar, Crónica de la Nueva España (Madrid, 1914), 494, where the chapel's builder is identified as Juan Tirado.

11.Thomas A. Janvier. The Mexican Guide, 4th ed. (New York. 1890), 206–207.

12. T. Philip Terry, Terry's Mexico—Handbook for Travellers (London, 1909): 335–337.

across the Sierra Madre del Sur "on a deserted trail through a cold rugged area with lions and tigers and snakes and other animals."[13] Zirándaro belonged to the Tarascan empire which in 1522 had accepted Spanish rule practically without resistance, while the more truculent Indians of the coast had recently surrendered to the army of Gonzalo de Sandoval, which may explain how a small force could emerge unscathed from such an expedition.[14] In fact, Caravajal's mission was to introduce Christianity to the natives (although there was no priest in his party) and to make a careful census of the communities visited, noting the mineral wealth and the tribute-paying capacity of each, for the guidance of Cortés in the first distribution of encomiendas. We do not know whether Garrido stayed with Caravajal throughout the visitation of Michoacán, which lasted about a year: in any event, we find him once again in Mexico City early in August 1524.[15]

It must have been before he went off with the Caravajal party that Garrido became the first wheat farmer on the American continent. The importance to the expatriate Spaniards both as a matter of taste and as a measure of social status, of having wheat bread rather than casava or maize tortillas, can hardly be overstressed.[16] According to the conquistador Andrés de Tapia. "after Mexico was taken, and while [Cortés] was in Coyoacán, they brought him a small amount of rice, and in it were three grains of wheat; he ordered a free Negro [un negro horro] to plant them."[17] The Negro referred to by Tapia is identified in a parallel account by the seventeenth-century chronicler Gil González Dávila as "Juan Garrido, a servant [criado] of Hernando Cortés."[18] Both sources agree that the tiny crop harvested by Garrido at this time was the first in New Spain, and that all wheat subsequently grown came from its seed.

The conquistador community moved from Coyoacán to the rebuilt Mexico City at the beginning of 1524. If, as we surmise, Garrido was still occupied in the reconnaissance of Michoacán when this move took place, it was perhaps a year or so earlier that the pious black conquistador built his hermitage, next to which he lived and had a garden plot or huerta (undoubtedly a chinampa) where he could continue his horticultural experiments.[19] We can be sure that foremost among such activities was the cultivation of grapevines and the manufacture of wine, a product not only greatly desired by the Spanish laity but also desperately needed by the clergy for the celebration of mass. Before long, Cortés ordered all encomenderos to have wheat and other useful European plants grown in their villages and by late 1525, wheat and grapes cultivated by Indians in the vicinity of Mexico City were no longer a curiosity.[20]

Juan Garrido's position in the close-knit conquistador society of Mexico-Tenochtitlán in those early years can only be imagined, but surely he must have been considered a rarity because of his color. There were as yet relatively few free blacks in the colony (indeed as far as we know Garrido was the only Negro vecino in Mexico City in the 1520s), and the social complications of mestizaje had really not begun. At first, as we have seen, Garrido made his home outside the city limits or traza on a piece of land perhaps formed as the waters of the lake receded (a dry spell set in shortly after the conquest), adjacent to both the Tacuba cause way and the aqueduct bringing fresh water from Chapultepec. His may well have been the first of a great many huertas in the old lake bed west of the city acquired and developed by Spaniards beginning in the mid-1520s.[21] However, nearly all the conquistadors forming the original body of citizens (vecinos) had solares or house lots within the traza, and there is a suggestion of stigma in the fact that Garrido initially settled outside the Spanish quarter, and was not officially received as a vecino until February 10, 1525. At that

13. Relaciones geográficas de la diócesis de Michoacán, 1579–1580, 2 vols. (Guadalajara, 1958), II. 40. J. Benedict Warren. La conquista de Michocán, 1521–1530 (Morelia, 1977). 88.

14. Donald D. Brand et al., Coalcomán and Motines del Oro: An Ex-distrito de Michoacán. Mexico (The Hague, 1960), 56–58.

15. AC, Aug. 12, 1524. Warren, La conquista de Michoacán, 87–89.

16. Pierre Chaunu, L'Amérique et les Amériques ([Paris], 1964), 86.

17. Joaquín Garcia Icazbalceta, ed., Colección de documentos para la historia de México. 2 vols. (México. 1858–1866), II, 592–593.

18. Gil González Dávila. Teatro eclesiástico de la primitiva iglesia de las Indias occidentales, vidas de sus arzobispos, obispos, y cosas memorables de sus sedes. 2 vols. (Madrid, 1649–1655). 1. 8.

19. AC. Mar. 15 and Sept. 30. 1524: Aug. 11. 1525. Angel Palerm. Obras hidráulicas prehispánicas en el sistema lacustre del valle de México (México, 1973). 154–157. Cf. Manuel Toussaint. Federico Gómez de Orozco, and Justino Fernández. Planos de la ciudad de México, siglos XVI y XVII (México, 1938). 96–97.

20. Hernán Cortés, Cartas y documentos, ed. by Mario Hernández Sánchez-Barba (México, 1963), 349. García Icazbalceta, Colección, I, 488.

21. AC, passim.'

time, he was assigned a house site within the *traza* on Calle de la Agua, although he retained his country property.[22] The move may have been merely a matter of convenience, after all, to make it easier for Garrido to carry out his duties as doorkeeper (*portero*) of the city's cabildo, a position that he seems to have held from 1524 to the end of 1526.[23] This was not a particularly lucrative post, the salary being a mere thirty gold pesos annually. However, for a few months Garrido was also made responsible for taking care of the Chapultepec aqueduct with a stipend of fifty pesos a year, and he may have acted simultaneously as town crier (*pregonero*), starting the still-honored tradition of "moonlighting."[24]

During the years 1526–1527, frequent changes in the Spanish power structure in Mexico brought about equally frequent reversals of personal fortune among the adherents and the enemies of Cortés, and thus it is quite conceivable that Juan Garrido lost his small sinecures as a result of this factional strife. Specifically, an unsuccessful effort on Cortés's part to "pack" the Mexico City cabildo at the beginning of 1527 coincided with the appointment of a new *portero-pregonero*.[25] Whatever the reason, Garrido decided to leave the city and seek his fortune in the gold fields, in the same region which he had visited with Caravajal years earlier. By the spring of 1528, he had acquired on credit a gang of slaves and mining equipment and was reported to be in the province of Zacatula, perhaps in the famous placers of the Motines area, the objective of many Spaniards and the grave of literally millions of Indians in those terrible years.[26] The gold rush was at its peak, but Garrido does not seem to have enjoyed much success as a miner. In October 1528, he was back in Mexico City and had still not paid a debt of twelve pesos, the value of "certain washing pans," when he incurred a new debt for some pigs that he had purchased.[27] The anti-Cortés faction was soon to be considerably reinforced by the president and judges of the first *audiencia*, and Garrido no doubt retired to his *chinampa* farm to await better times.

In 1530, Cortés returned to Mexico from Spain with a title (marquis), ample resources, and great ambition, but only a shadow of his former political power. New Spain was ruled by a hostile *audiencia*, Guatemala by the ungrateful Alvarado, and New Galicia by the marquis's greatest enemy, Nuño de Guzmán. Cortés, frustrated and bitter, sulked in his marquisate and surrounded himself with lawyers and malcontents. The king had wisely provided a remedy for this dangerous situation by giving him a commission to search the shores of the Pacific for new lands and riches.

By the early 1530s, the gold rush was almost finished, and while favored Spaniards in Mexico were living munificently on Indian tribute, and others were building fortunes in the newly discovered silver mines, there was a growing body of restless young men looking for adventure and profit. Many of them from 1532 to 1536 headed for the conquest of Peru, and indeed Cortés himself had prepared two ships to sail southward from Tehuantepec when he heard that another of his vessels had discovered an "island" in the north supposed to be rich in gold and pearls and the home of the legendary Amazons.[28] The island was in fact a peninsula, the southern tip of Lower California. Learning that Guzmán had seized the returning ship and its treasure, Cortés ordered his flotilla to the north and marched overland to join it, gathering recruits on the way.[29] By the time he reached Chametla, a port in Guzmán's territory opposite the newly discovered "island." the charismatic marquis was accompanied by a formidable retinue which apparently included Juan Garrido. A contemporary witness testified that Cortés's followers numbered four hundred Spaniards and three hundred Negroes;[30] most of the latter must have been slaves intended for work in the gold mines and oyster beds. Garrido was no doubt in a privileged category, and in fact it would seem that he had his own complement of Negro, and Indian slaves at this time.[31]

The Lower California expedition was Cortés's last great venture and it was a disaster, an heroic undertaking carried out against impossible odds. There were far too many people and horses to be transported across the stormy gulf (the fleet had to make several trips to take them all), and once on that desolate shore they had to be fed with provisions brought from great distances. The nearest

22. AC, Feb. 10 and Aug. 11, 1525

23. AC Aug. 12, 1524; Jan. 13, Feb. 28, June 2, and Dec. 15, 1525; Aug. 17 and Dec. 10, 1526.

24.AC, Aug. 26 and Dec. 29, 1524; Jan. 4, 1525; Jan. 4, 1527.

25. C. Harvey Gardiner, The Constant Captain. Gonzalo de Sandoval (Carbondale, III., 1961), 178–179.

26. Agustín Millares Carlo and José I. Mantecón, Indice y extractos de los protocolos del Archivo de Notarías de México, D.F., 2 vols. (México, 1945–1946), I, no. 1263. Brand et al., Coalcomán, 64.

27.Millares Carlo and Mantecón, Indice, I, nos. 1664, 1674.

28.Woodrow Borah, "Hernán Cortés y sus intereses marítimos en el Pacífico: El Perú y la Baja California," Estudios de Historia Novohispana, 4 (1971).

29. Cortés, Cartas, 524–527.

30. Hubert Howe Bancroft, History of Mexico, 6 vols. (San Francisco, 1883–1886), II, 423n; William H. Prescott, The Conquest of Mexico, 2 vols. (London, 1957), II. 352.

31. Millares Carlo and Mantecón, Indice, II, no. 1889.

mainland was controlled by Guzmán, and in any event it produced little surplus as the native population on the whole west coast of Mexico was at this very time being decimated by a fearful epidemic. Thus, the settlers were dependent on what they could find locally (mostly fish) and supplies from the highlands of central Mexico, which had to be carried to the coast and shipped out of ports as far south as Huatulco.[32] Even the marquis's vast revenues were not enough to keep the colony going. The remarkable fact is that some Spaniards remained in the vicinity of La Paz, in a desert and surrounded by extraordinarily primitive Indians, for more than a year and perhaps two, from May 1535 to late 1536 or early 1537. Cortés himself, however, returned to Mexico via Acapulco in the spring of 1536, accompanied by a few California Indians and some of the colonists, including Juan Garrido, who was in Mexico City by July of that year.[33]

We know very little indeed about the further career of this unusual black man. How he made a living after his return from California, the details of his marriage, what role (if any) he played in the aborted black slave uprising of 1537 and its grisly aftermath, may some day come to light. Twice in 1536, Garrido gave a power of attorney to the municipal *procurador de causas* in Mexico City in connection with some unspecified suit, perhaps a claim for unpaid back salaries as the cabildo doorkeeper which was finally settled in November 1538.[35] Garrido's *hoja de servicios* was part of a group of such documents prepared between 1547 and 1550, and since it bears the notation "es ya muerto," it would seem that he died sometime during those years.[36]

---

32. Woodrow Borah, Early Colonial Trade and Navigation between Mexico and Peru (Berkeley, 1954), 22–25.

33. Millares Carlo and Mantecón, Indice, II, no. 1828.

34. Cf. Edgar F. Love, "Negro Resistance to Spanish Rule in Colonial Mexico," Journal of Negro History, 52 (Apr. 1967), 96.

35. AC, Nov. 19, 1538. Millares Carlo and Mantecón, Indice, II, nos. 1828, 2090.

36. Icaza, Diccionario, no. 169. Epistolario de Nueva España. 1505–1818, recopilado por Francisco del Paso y Troncoso, 16 vols. (México, 1939–1942), V, 8–9. Perhaps Garrido died in the great plague that was raging in 1547. On the other hand, someone called Juan Garrido was alive in Cuernavaca in March 1552; cf. Millares Carlo and Mantecón. Indice, II, no. 2647.

E. Colonial Spanish America

The colonial period in Spanish America lasted nearly three centuries, from the time of Columbus, Cortés, and Pizarro in the 16th century to the wars of Spanish American independence at the beginning of the 19th century. During this long period, viceroys in Mexico, Peru, and other regions kept control of the vast lands of Spain with the assistance of the Spanish naval and land forces. Also present was the watchful eye of the Spanish Inquisition, an organ of the Catholic Church that had the powers similar to a secret police force. While Spain's soldiers put down rebellions and fought pirates, the Inquisition insured orthodoxy in both religious and political beliefs.

Perhaps the central figure of the Spanish colonial period was Sor (Sister) Juana Inés de la Cruz. Despite having two strikes against her in the hierarchical Colonial society—she was poor and of illegitimate birth—her intellect allowed her to move among the most powerful families and viceroys of 17th Century Mexico. Her defence of women and her criticism of the patriarchal culture of her time seem very modern to contemporary readers.

The name of California originates from the beginning of the Spanish colonial period during the time of the conquistadores. The most popular reading among the upper classes of the Renaissance in Spain were novels of chivalry, which painted the exploits of famous knights doing battle with their enemies, defending the honor and love of their ladies, and challenging the magic of hostile wizards. One such bestseller was the text *The Adventures of Esplandián* (*Las Sergas de Esplandián*), by the novelist Garci Rodríguez de Montalvo (1510). In that work, a magical land is described—California—a rich island inhabited only by black women, powerful warriors in their own right with no need of masculine protection. The Spanish thus allotted the western-most part of their territories in Mexico this fictional name (which today we see in California in the United States and Baja California in Mexico). Incidentally, the last novel of chivalry was undoubtedly *Don Quixote* by Miguel de Cervantes, a work which mocked this famous genre.

Also during this period arose the famous California missions, first under the leadership of the Francisco Father Junípero Serra (1713–1784). The twenty one famous missions built along California's El Camino Real (the "Royal Road") are visited by thousands of tourists each year today. These early outposts of European culture in California are a product of the Spanish colonial period in California, built from 1769–1823 (only the last northernmost mission, San Francisco Solano, was built under Mexico rule). The missions brought not only Christianity to the region but also livestock, fruits, grains, and commerce, and above all, the Spanish language. Father Serra gave his life to his mission work, having died of a snake bite at Mission Carmel, where he was buried.

1. SOR JUANA'S LIFE AND WORK

Juana Ramírez/Sor Juana Inés de la Cruz (1648/51–1695): A Life Without and Within

Sor Juana Inés de la Cruz, author of the *Respuesta a Sor Filotea de la Cruz* (as the *Answer* is titled in Spanish), is a major figure of Hispanic literature, but still little known to readers of other languages.[1] Her poetry, plays, and prose move within and reshape the themes and styles of Renaissance and Baroque Spain and its far-flung empire. Indeed, she is considered the last great author of Spain's Golden Age (Siglo de Oro), during which an extraordinary number of outstanding writers and artists were active.[2] The emergent, differentiated, and multicultural New Spain–Mexico's telling name during the colonial period–was fertile soil for Sor juana's imagination. In turn, her influence helped create a Mexican identity, contributing to the consciousness and sensibility of later scholars and writers.

Sor Juana's prodigious talent, furthered by intense efforts that began in early childhood, produced a serious intellectual while she was still in her teens. She taught herself the forms of classical rhetoric and the language of law, theology, and literature. At every turn, from her courtly and learned yet marginalized standpoint, she contradicted–or deconstructed–artistic,

---

1 Her name is pronounced HWA-na ee-NES day-la-KREWS.

2 The term "Siglo de Oro" is applied to a period extending roughly from the mid-sixteenth century through the last decades of the seventeenth century.

---

intellectual, and religious views that would refuse her and others like her the right to express themselves.

The stratagems Sor Juana found useful for artistic and intellectual survival were so subtle that, given the continuity and pervasiveness of patriarchal values up to the present, the magnitude of her reinterpretations has often been missed or distorted even in our time. Sor Juana's power reaches us today both in her revolutionary reversal of the gender identifications typical of her culture and in the beauty of her expression. With most aspects of the literary tradition of the Renaissance and Baroque at her command, she crafted exquisite poems. The ease with which she versified, the verve and versatility of her style, and the irony with which she applied her wit gave her an enormous literary mobility.

Similarly, her status as a rara avis (strange bird), while setting her apart from others of her sex and class in the public regard, made possible the physical and psychic space in which she thought and wrote. Respect for exceptionality was in part a reflection of the profound seventeenth-century interest in unusual natural phenomena that viewed artistic talent and intellectual drive in females as fascinating abnormalities. Sor Juana learned to exploit the fact that she was catalogued as a prodigy; she both defended and derided the hyperbolic terms of praise her exceptionality attracted (see the poem "¡Válgate Apolo por hombre!" [May Apollo help you, as you're a man!]). Known to this day as the "Tenth Muse,"[3] in her own time Sor Juana was also called the "Mexican Phoenix." Such epithets of exceptionality, though common enough, kept Sor Juana on a pedestal, provisionally protected yet isolated amid the ceremony and turbulence of Mexico City. Praised and envied, criticized and acclaimed, for twenty-six years she wrote for the court and for the church as one of the most celebrated writers in the Hispanic New World.

Early Years: Country and Court. Juana Ramírez y Asbaje was born – in 1648 or 1651 – in Nepantla, some two days' travel from Mexico City by mule and canal boat, on lands her grandfather leased from the church.[4] There, perhaps more than her contemporaries, Juana was exposed early in life to all levels of culture. She experienced music, art, and magic, native

and imported. She heard the liturgy in Latin, cultured conversation in Spanish, and colloquial communication, including Indian, African, and *ranchero* (rural) dialects. Juana's grandfather, Pedro Ramírez de Santillana, was a learned man, although his daughter Isabel Ramírez, Juana's mother, was not educated. His large library fed the young Juana's appetite for reading. By the time her elders wished to still her curiosity, she had become so knowledgeable that they could neither put a stop to her restless quest nor convince her it was inappropriate. From book learning she drew authority and legitimacy for differing in her studious propensities, views, and aims from other Catholics, women, and Mexicans. Society's stigmas against *marisabias* (Mary-sages [female know-it-alls]) could not destroy her intellectual bent. The charm of Juana's own account (given in the *Answer*) of how she could read soon after she learned to walk, how she took to rhyming as others take to their native tongue, and how she became competent in Latin shortly after taking up its study has in the imagination of readers outweighed her insistence that her prodigious learning reflected tenacious effort even more than a sharp memory.

Tenaciousness may have been one of her mother's legacies. Isabel Ramírez was a strong and smart woman. Illiteracy did not impede her from managing one of her father's two sizable farmsteads for more than thirty years. She had six children, three with Pedro Manuel de Asbaje, Juana Inés's father, and three with Diego Ruiz Lozano; to neither man, she stated in official documents, had she been married.

Before the age of fourteen, Juana wrote her first poem. Knowing that women were not allowed to attend the university in Mexico City (*Respueta/Answer*, par. 8) she made the best of an isolated, self-directed schooling: she devoured books initially in Panoayán, where the family farm was located, then at court in Mexico City, and finally in the voluminous library she amassed in the convent. A convent was the only place in her society where a woman could decently live alone and devote herself to learning. Her collection of books and manuscripts, by the time she gave it away for charity near the end of her life, was one of the largest in the New Spain of her era.

According to Diego Calleja, a Spanish Jesuit priest who wrote her earliest biography, the young Juana while at court submitted to a public examination of her already notorious intellectual gifts by forty of the most knowledgeable men of the realm.[5] She defended herself, reported

---

3 "Tenth Muse" was a common term for women poets, whom men could not conceive of as other than unearthly. Sappho herself was referred to thus, as were poets of the seventeenth century, including Anne Bradstreet of England and the Massachusetts Bay Colony.

4 Different sources give Juana's name in various combinations and orders of her mother's (maternal grandfather's) and father's last names: Juana Inés de Asbaje y Ramírez de Santillana.

5 Calleja's biography appears as the substantive part of the required permission for publication (the *nihil obstat*) of the third and final volume of her works – that is, the assurance that nothing in its pages went against church teachings.

Calleja, "like a royal galleon attacked by small canoes."[6] Sor Juana's poetry sometimes expresses mistrust and mockery of her many admirers and defenders for seeing her in their own image and for turning her into a circus rarity: "What would the mountebanks[7] not give, / to be able to seize me, / and carry me round like a monster, through / byroads and lonely places" (¡Qué dieran los saltimbancos, / a poder, por agarrarme / y llevarme, como Monstruo, por esos andurriales! OC 1:147:177–80).

Were she to be compared with anyone, her preference—implicit in the numerous parallels she draws in her poems—would be the learned and legendary St. Catherine of Alexandria, who had also been subjected to an examination and who had furnished ultimate proof that neither intelligence nor the soul were owned by one gender above the other. Some of Sor Juana's last compositions were songs of praise to the saint.

Entrance into the Convent.   Juana gave her age as sixteen when, after five years as lady-in-waiting at the viceregal court of New Spain, she entered the convent in 1668 to be able to pursue a reflective, literary life. Sor Juana Inés, as she became known, claimed that her parents were married and that her birthdate was November 12, 1651. The church establishment officially required legitimacy for nuns; youth supported her reputation as a rarity. A baptismal record for one "Inés, daughter of the church," however, dated December 2, 1648, is generally accepted as hers; it lists an aunt and uncle as godparents. This earlier date establishes her age as nineteen when she entered the cloister. Modern awareness of the revised birthdate hardly tempers the myth of young Juana's precocity; she can be considered no less "a marvel of intelligence."[8]

---

6. A few decades earlier the Catalonian Juliana Morel, another child prodigy, who would become a nun and translator of St. Augustine into French, had been examined publicly in Lyon and Avignon. Reports of other precocious European women indicate that Sor Juana's status may not have been as unique as claimed. Public examinations by "experts" also reflected the Baroque fascination with prodigiously learned (young) women and with the commingling or blurring of gender categories. It was a hagiographic topos as well: St. Catherine of Alexandria had undergone perhaps the most famous of such legendary tests (see the discussion of *villancicos* in Selected Poems, below).

7. *Saltimbanco* (or *saltabanco*) may be translated variously as mountebank, charlatan, trickster, puppeteer.

8. Doña Leonor, the supposedly autobiographical protagonist of Sor Juana's *Los empeños de una casa* (*The Trials of a Household*), says that she was known in this way ("celebrada por milagro de discreción") OC4. 37:292–93.

Sor Juana's confessor, Antonio Núñez de Miranda, was not one who would graciously admit defeat before her prowess. A powerful, intelligent, and extremely ascetic man, Núñez was also confessor to the viceroy and vicereine and to many other members of the nobility. For him, as for those vanquished by St. Catherine, gender determined duty as well as destiny; the use of reason was an exclusively masculine privilege. In a world where females were associated with the Devil and the flesh, intelligent and beautiful women especially were blamed for all manner of ills; to lessen the threat to men's uncontrollable passions, they should be sent to a nunnery to embrace holy plainness and ignorance. If Núñez considered the young Juana's position in the limelight at court dangerous and untenable, her continued study and writing after entering the convent, especially on worldly subjects, he judged nothing short of scandalous. Indeed, "[H]ad [I] known [she] was to write verses [I] would not have placed [her] in the convent but arranged [her] marriage," he was reported to have said.[9]

Núñez, not being a relative, had no legal right to dispose of her thus. At first Sor Juana bore the humiliation of his remarks, she tells us. But as she achieved recognition and patronage from a new viceregal governor and his wife, who were closely connected to the Spanish king, Sor Juana gained confidence in herself. Eventually, she responded angrily to Núñez and relieved him of his duties to her as confessor.

Now her ex-confessor, Núñez nevertheless continued to hold sway in Mexican society. Sor Juana's ultimate clerical superior in Mexico, Archbishop Francisco Aguiar y Seijas, was a legendary misogynist.[10] Her friend and admirer Manuel Fernández de Santa Cruz, the bishop of Puebla, donned the name "Sor Filotea" when he finally threw in his lot with those who demanded conformity. These three ecclesiastics wanted Sor Juana to stop thinking and writing with the latitude she had exercised. She was warned to be more like other women in the convents of Spanish America, who were supposed to serve as both subjects and agents of a regime undertaking massive imperialist endeavors. That is, nuns were to

---

9. Quoted by Sor Juana in a letter to Núñez. See Paz, *Sor Juana*, p. 500.

10. See Paz, *Sor Juana*, pp. 408–9. Paz cites a nineteenth-century history of the church in Mexico and a biography of the archbishop written by the latter's confessor; these are, respectively. Francisco Sosa. *El episcopado mexicano* (Mexico City: H. Iriarte y S. Hernández, 1877–1879); José de Lezamis, *Breve relación de la vida y muerte del Ilmo. y Revmo. Señor Doctor Don Francisco Aguiar y Seijas* (Mexico, 1699).

be subjects of the Spanish church and crown; to serve as agents of the church's mission to Christianize heathens; to guard orthodoxy; and to ensure social obeisance. Beyond their spiritual roles, nuns—*criollas*[11] like Sor Juana and even a few *mestizas*[12]—were also influential in economic, social, and educational spheres. They contributed to the arts, crafts, music, and cuisine of the larger community. They dealt in real estate, lent money, and employed servants and slaves, without whom most of their activities would have been impossible. Many nuns wrote. The very nature of a female community allowed them to develop voices that were separate from those of the priests and confessors who officially controlled their lives. Sor Juana, though, was most unlike other women in her intellectual ecumenism and religious rationality as well as her celebrity. She was envied and considered arrogant.

For centuries scholars refused to believe the reasons Sor Juana gave in the *Answer* for taking the veil. They speculated airily on some unfortunate love affair. Yet, early and extensive readings in Christianity, the experiences of many of the women in her family (including her own mother), and not least her consuming interest in satiating her intellectual appetite easily explain her "absolute unwillingness to enter into marriage" (*Answer*, par. 9). She first tried the strictly ruled and aristocratic Carmelite convent, but she became ill and had to leave. Within a few months, after recovering, she entered the more relaxed Hieronymite[13] convent of Santa Paula, where she found some of the tranquillity she desired for study—the real love of her life.

The cloistered Sor Juana spent the rest of her days (from 1668 until 1695), in quarters whose comfort and amplitude made them seem more salon than cell. Attended by several servants and for ten years by a mulatta slave her mother had given her,[14] Sor Juana entertained numerous visiting aristocrats, ecclesiastics, and scholars, conducted wide but now lost correspondence with many others, and held monastic office as mistress of novices and keeper of the convent's financial records. Although the

dates of her terms in office are unknown, news of that service survived along with such details as her extraordinary brilliance as a conversationalist. Several contemporaries claimed that listening to her surpassed reading her work. Much of her poetry was destined to be heard. State and church officials commissioned all manner of compositions for the observances of holy days, feast days, birthdays, and funerals. Sor Juana earned not only favor but a livelihood—for each nun had a "household" to support—by fulfilling such literary orders.

It is hard to imagine exactly what a day in the life of Sor Juana may have included. The daily patterns for all nuns were set by the rules of the order. Upon becoming brides of Christ they vowed chastity, poverty, and obedience; but just as in Rome, where luxury surrounded the higher echelons of church officialdom, austerity was the exception in religious houses established by royalty. Actual practice at the wealthy convent of Santa Paula was far from ascetic. Laxity, as it was called, characterized observance in most convents of Mexico and Peru. Nevertheless, the normal day was punctuated by prayer time: it began at midnight with matins; lauds followed at 5:00 or 6:00 A.M.; then came prime, terce, sext, and none, the "little hours" spaced during the day; vespers were said at approximately 6:00 P.M.; and finally compline at 9:00 or 10:00 at night. There would be recreation periods, a time, often, for needlework. Periodically, nuns would go on retreat to remove themselves from the hustle and bustle of normal monastic existence. Sor Juana, as she mentions in the *Answer*, would retreat from time to time, to study and write.

Regular intervals were set for community work, prayer, confession, and Communion. Many holy feast days interrupted routines, calling for special masses, meals, and festivities. Pomp and circumstance accompanied the taking of final vows. Music—singing and playing instruments—and theatrical performances provided inspiration, religious instruction, and entertainment at all such events. Sor Juana was probably among the most visited of the nuns at her cloister. In addition to family members she received dignitaries from around the world. She would often be called to the *locutorio* (grate) to meet her guests, among whom on occasion were representatives of the *cabildo* (city council) with writing commissions.

In unstructured moments, some nuns chatted and gossiped; others subjected themselves to penances. Capable and creative, Sor Juana took the advantageous circumstances of her life and an ability to "condense [*conmutar*] time," as she phrased it, and put them to

---

11. Native-born of Spanish ancestry.
12. Of mixed white (peninsular Spanish or *criollo*) and Native American ancestry.
13. Followers of St. Jerome.
14. The forty-nine professed nuns (those who had taken solemn vows) were supported by about a hundred and fifty other women, including some slaves. The nuns lived in independent, two-storied quarters, shared at times by younger relatives.

what she considered better use. Conservative elements within the church in Mexico preferred penances.

Conflict Intensifies.   Troubles, as we have seen, had started almost from the beginning of Sor Juana's time in the convent. For more than a decade after taking the veil, she kept still in the face of the reports that her confessor was voicing disapproval of her scholarly and literary activities, even when he claimed they constituted "a public scandal." She outdid herself in public visibility, however, when in 1680, after showing initial reticence, she accepted the responsibility of devising one of two architectural theatrical triumphal arches that were to welcome the new viceregal couple (the other was entrusted to her friend Carlos de Sigüenza y Góngora).[15] The ambitiously mythological artwork, inscriptions, narrative poems, and prose explanations of her "Allegorical Neptune" both established her reputation throughout contemporary society and, because of the extraordinarily public nature of the occasion, deepened the rift with Núñez.

At last, in 1681 or 1682, Sor Juana decided to take steps to ease her plight and relieve her pent-up animosity—the result, she said, of holding back her reactions to his animosity. She would exercise her right to engage a new confessor. The letter she wrote to Núñez, distancing herself from him, bristles with ironic and prideful sarcasm. "Not being unaware of the veneration and high esteem in which Y[our] R[everence] (and justly so) is held by all, so that all listen to you as if to a divine oracle and appreciate your words as if they were dictated by the Holy Ghost," she writes, "nor unaware that the greater your authority, the more my good name is injured," Sor Juana sees no alternative but to change confessors. "Am I perchance a heretic?" she asks, concluding with further rhetorical questions: "What obligation is there that my salvation be effected through Y.R.? Can it not be through another? Is God's mercy restricted and limited to one man, even though he be as wise, as learned, and as saintly as Y.R.?"[16] On her own path toward salvation, with a more sympathetic confessor, Sor Juana spent the next decade studying and writing her most enduring works. The viceregal couple continued to visit almost every day, on their way to or from vespers, until they returned to Spain in 1687.

Love Poems to Lovers of Poetry.   With patronage such as the viceroy and vicereine provided, Sor Juana was free to persevere in her manner of being a nun. This was not so unusual from the standpoint of a long, scholarly, and even at times worldly women's monastic tradition, but it was certainly uncommon in her place and time. No doubt the churchmen were further scandalized by her "unchaste" writings, by what her poems indicated about an imagined if not a lived experience. Only verses that transposed courtly love into a divine framework of religious ardor, and clearly mystical writing infused with eroticism, were deemed orthodox by the censors. Sor Juana's courtly yet personal poetry followed the Renaissance conventions of troubadour love lyrics and Petrarchan sonneteering to express deeply felt earthly friendship, kinship, and sexual attraction.

Little can be known directly about Sor Juana's intimate loves, though speculation abounds. Finding that she wrote with an acute understanding of lovers and their emotional travails, readers have been convinced that she knew whereof she spoke. Did she have suitors at court? Did she suffer first-hand the sort of abuse and loss some descry in her poems? Was she in love with a man or men? With a woman or women? Biographical documentation is lacking. Her poetry attests first that she knew well the expectations of literary practice on these topics, and second, that the deepest personal ties she expressed were those to two recognizable figures: Leonor Carreto and María Luisa Manrique de Lara y Gonzaga, two vicereines (wives of the viceroys) of New Spain.

The social distance between Sor Juana and these two noblewomen, whom she wrote of lovingly and also served, was not unlike that of the Provençal troubadours (men and women) and their lords and ladies. That very distance allowed her to be explicit in expressing her affection, providing a public barrier to the realization of such sentiments. These were widely perceived as relationships that could not be consummated. What other forms, besides the written, her expressions of feeling may have taken remains unknown. No one denies that Sor Juana displayed in her writing depths of emotion and erotic desire associated for us with intimate relationships.[17]

---

15. The ancient Roman religious tradition of constructing arches of wood and painted canvas, elaborately decorated with mythological themes, was revived during the Renaissance. See Sabat de Rivers, ed., *Inundación castálida*, pp. 63–71.

16. In Paz. *Sor Juana*, pp. 495–96, 500, 502. (trans. modified by Powell).

---

17. Ester Gimbernat de González (in "Speaking through the Voices of Love") discusses three love sonnets by Sor Juana (nos. 177, 178, and 183) addressed to women. While Gimbernat identifies the (conventionalized) speaker in all three as male, evidence internal to the poems supports this determination only in no. 178—the speaker's gender is not explicit in the other two.

Notably, her most ardent love poems were dedicated to the two vicereines mentioned above. Well-educated and sophisticated readers, it was they who most energetically encouraged her scholarly and literary pursuits. When the first of the two aristocrats, the vicereine Leonor Carreto, Marquise de Mancera, died in 1674, Sor Juana had been in the convent for six years. But for almost the same number of years immediately before her entrance in the convent, Juana had been in Leonor's service—a favorite companion at court. Sor Juana used the literary "Laura" as the marquise's name in poems:

> Death like yours, my Laura, since you have died,
> to feelings that still long for you in vain,
> to eyes you now deny even the sight
> of lovely light that in the past you gave.
>
> Death to my hapless lyre from which you drew
> these echoes that, lamenting, speak your name,
> and let these awkward characters be known
> as black tears shed by my grief-stricken pen.
>
> Let compassion move stern Death herself
> who (strictly accurate) brooked no excuse,
> and let Love lament his bitter fate;
>
> who boldly hoping at one time to woo you
> wanted to have eyes simply to see you,
> that now do nothing more nor less than mourn you.
>
> (OC 1.300–301, trans. Amanda Powell)

> Mueran contigo, Laura, pues moriste,
> los afectos que en vano te desean,
> los ojos a quien privas de que vean
> hermosa luz que un tiempo concediste.
>
> Muera mi lira infausta en que influíste
> ecos, que lamentables te vocean,
> y hasta estos rasgos mal formados sean
> lágrimas negras de mi pluma triste
>
> Muévase a compasión la misma Muerte
> que, precisa, no pudo perdonarte;
> y lamente el Amor su amarga suerte,
>
> pues si antes, ambicioso de gozarte,
> deseó tener ojos para verte,
> ya le sirvieran sólo de llorarte.

This elegiac sonnet gives rein to Sor Juana's grief, implying a literary as well as affectionate relationship. It is one of three sonnets that issued from her sorrow over the loss of the woman who, her first biographer, Calleja, claimed, "could not live an instant without her Juana Inés."

Similar terms were used to describe her next long relationship of devoted friendship. To Vicereine María Luisa Manrique de Lara y Gonzaga, Marquise de la Laguna, Countess de Paredes, who became "Phyllis" in the poems, Sor Juana wrote:

> … as air is drawn to what is hollow,
> and fire to feed on matter,
> as boulders tumble to the earth,
> and intentions to their goal;
>
> indeed, as every natural thing,
> —all united by the desire
> to endure, which ties them tight
> in bonds of closest love…
>
> But to what end do I go on?
> Just so, my Phyllis, do I love you;
> with your considerable worth,
> this is merely an endearment.
>
> Your being a woman, your being gone:
> neither hinders my love for you,
> for who knows better that our souls
> notice neither geography nor sex.
>
> (OC 1.56–57:97–112, trans. Amanda Powell)

> como a lo cóncavo el aire,
> como a la materia el fuego,
> como a su centro las peñas,
> como a su fin los intentos;
>
> bien como todas las cosas
> naturales, que el deseo
> de conservarse, las une
> amante en lazos estrechos…
>
> Pero ¿para qué es cansarse?
> Como a ti, Filis, te quiero;
> que en lo que mereces, éste
> es solo encarecimiento.
>
> Ser mujer, ni estar ausente,
> no es de amarte impedimento;
> pues sabes tú, que las almas
> distancia ignoran y sexo.

María Luisa, Marquise de la Laguna, was a frequent visitor at the convent during the seven years she spent in Mexico, and she was an avid supporter of Sor Juana. It was she who took Sor Juana's poems to Spain and arranged for her first book to be published. With the exceptionally successful appearance of *Castalian Inundation* in 1689, the poet's celebrity grew in educated circles throughout Spain and its colonies (including the Philippines).[18] To the chagrin

---

18. In Sor Juana's lifetime, three more editions (entitled simply *Poems*) followed in 1690, 1691, and 1692; by 1725, a total of nine had appeared. See Sabat de Rivers, ed., *Inundación castálida*, pp. 26–27, 72–73.

of many of her superiors, spurred by her own great gifts and by María Luisa's instrumental patronage, Sor Juana flourished as a literary figure of the Spanish-speaking world.

Gradually, however; other factors began to weigh more heavily than viceregal support and fame. As the seventeenth century reached its last decade, Sor Juana's situation and that of New Spain veered drastically. Economic, social, and political crises engulfed the realm. Nature itself seemed bent on intensifying the troubles. A solar eclipse spread fear among the population, crops not devastated by rain in the countryside were eaten by weevils, and floods inundated Mexico City. Speculation and hoarding worsened the scarcity of fruit, vegetables, maize, bread, firewood, and coal. Rising prices touched off spontaneous protests. The viceregal palace and municipal building were set on fire. Punitive responses triggered panic, further rioting, penitent religious processions, and executions. Sor Juana's most significant supporters had returned to Spain or had fallen out of favor. The pressures mounted perhaps in her own mind as well as from without. Her writing, on religious and mundane subjects alike, came under more direct fire.

The Bishop, the Answer, *and—Silence.*   If it was irreverent for a nun to write love poems, it was worse for her to meddle in theology. For Sor Juana's biography and for the study of her writing, the significance of the "Letter Worthy of Athena," this nun's one incursion into theological argumentation—the only one in prose, written down and printed, that is—resides as much in its having heightened the envy and antagonism of the ecclesiastic establishment as in its admirable reasoning and style.

Piqued by Antonio Vieira's claim to have improved on the arguments of the fathers and doctors of the church[19] (viz., Sts. Augustine, Thomas, and John Chrysostom) concerning Jesus Christ's highest favor to humanity, Sor Juana in 1690 had ventured to refute the famous preacher's "Maundy Thursday Sermon" (written forty years earlier!). The refutation was heard in a conversation with guests at the convent, among them Bishop Manuel Fernández de Santa Cruz, who was on a visit to Mexico City. At his behest, she wrote down her critical disquisition disputing Vieira's argument as to the highest example of Christ's love. Three times she mentions her trust that the text will be seen only by the bishop's eyes; she invites his correction

and claims that, not having had the time to polish it, she remits it to him *en embrión, como suele la osa parir sus informes cachorrillos* ("in an embryonic state, just as the bear gives birth to her unformed cubs," OC 4.434:904).

Her double-edged claims of humility did not obscure the virtuosity of her argumentation, or her skill at logic. Was the bishop conspiring to silence her when he requested a written copy? He had long been an admiring friend, but he was also an official of convent governance, known for inspiring nuns with fanatical piety. He, too, must have been distressed by this, in his eyes, arrogant and wayward daughter. For years Archbishop Aguiar y Seijas and Fr. Núñez had sought to command from Sor Juana behavior more befitting a nun. Now, they were poised for their chance. Wittingly or unwittingly, the bishop of Puebla joined forces with them.

With the viceroy and vicereine gone, ecclesiastics may have found it easier to instigate or fuel the storm of controversy that broke out over the "Letter Worthy of Athena," as the bishop of Puebla titled her critique when he delivered it to the press, appending a letter signed "Sor Filotea" as a preface. Ambivalent and ambiguous enough to have confused many generations of readers, the bishop's letter was for Sor Juana a purportedly friendly—and therefore wily and more painful—attack. It prompted her to explain and defend herself as she never had before—to write the *Answer to Sor Filotea de la Cruz,* the only avowedly self-descriptive piece of prose she produced. For her, the printed letter from the bishop of Puebla disguised as Sor Filotea, with its pretense of saintly guidance (St. Francis de Sales had used the same pseudonym to write to nuns), served as a public admonition and delivered a threat of persecution. It is reasonable to assume that the letter produced in Sor Juana a combination of anger, resentment, shock, hurt, contempt, and fear, and that these emotions precipitated a decision to silence herself that had already been forming within her. In any case, in the three months it took to write the unusual reply to "Sor Filotea," Sor Juana created a text we now consider essential to a full understanding and appreciation of her genius.

From Spain the former vicereine, María Luisa, followed the events that would ultimately lead the poet to silence herself in the face of discouragement and inquisitional mentalities. The aristocratic Spaniard did all she could to come to the rescue. When the manuscript of Sor Juana's theological critique was circulated in Spain, many people took the nun's side or at least defended her right to argue. In Mexico, where Vieira was greatly favored by the Jesuits, Sor Juana was refuted with virulence, although she also had a

---

19. Vieira (b. Lisbon, Portugal, 1608, d. Salvador, Brazil, 1697) was a prominent Jesuit, considered to be one of the great prose stylists of his day.

few defenders. In Spain, the former vicereine marshaled seven respected theologians to praise the *Crisis* [Critique], as Sor Juana's refutation of Vieira was now called. Disregarding the bishop of Puebla's hyperbolic title ("Letter Worthy of Athena"), the marquise had it reprinted along with defenses and numerous poems of praise for Sor Juana, "Phoenix of America." The laudatory pages comprised the initial third of the second volume of Sor Juana's *Obras* [Works], a book that the author herself had cooperated in preparing so that some of her finest writing would see print. Behind the "Knight of the Order of Santiago" to whom Juana Inés was asked to dedicate the volume stood the tireless efforts of the ex-vicereine, who expedited publication in Seville, where she and her husband had considerable influence. But the paeans to Sor Juana's talent and glory that prefaced this 1692 volume probably backfired, causing Sor Juana even more problems with her superiors in Mexico.

That same year, in 1692, Sor Juana sold her library and musical and scientific instruments, contributing the proceeds to charity. She wrote her last set of *villancicos* (carols), those to St. Catherine. Little more would come from her pen. Two years later, in 1694, she renewed her vows, signed a statement of self-condemnation, and turned to penance and self-sacrifice.

Was Sor Juana's retreat from writing, study, and society a religious conversion? Was she under compulsion? How much the pressure came from without, how much from within is rigorously debated by scholars. It is notable that, at the end, Sor Juana took the ascetic path Núñez had earlier prescribed. In fact, in 1693 he became her confessor once again. Sor Juana's life ended two months after his, in 1695, when she fell victim to an epidemic while caring for her sisters.[20] The last of her three volumes of work was not published until five years later, in Madrid, in the first year of the new century.

2. THE SPANISH INDIES

Spanish Decline and Imperial Development

The seventeenth century saw the emergence of a distinctive society in the Indies. Far from being an offshoot of the mother country, what resulted was a hybrid growth—a Hispanic society still, but one

---

20. The exact nature of the "plague" is not known.

---

whose roots were nourished by a different soil and on to whose parent stock had been grafted cuttings from other races and cultures.

The coming to maturity of this society was facilitated by the decline of the mother country. Spain's economic and military weakness led to a loosening of its hold over the dominions in the New World, allowing colonial society to develop according to its own internal dynamics. The most significant factor here was the expansion of the hybrid Hispanic sector at the expense of the Indian world. The process of Indian depopulation continued spasmodically until the middle decades of the century, but native communities were further debilitated by a quickening rate of Hispanicization of individual Indians. Another important factor was the arrival—beginning in the last years of the previous century—of large numbers of African slaves. This influx contributed enormously to the racial mixture, which was one of the most visible distinguishing features of Spanish American society. Above all, the relative impotence of Spain permitted the formation of powerful local oligarchies, which became the effective ruling classes in the many and diverse regions that made up the Spanish Indies. This was the age of the creole (*criollo*)—the Spaniard native to America. Even though the term 'creole' was not current at the time, it is widely used by modern historians because it serves to indicate the growing sense of separateness from their peninsular cousins felt by these American Spaniards in the course of the century.

Spain went into decline because of proliferating military commitments for which it could not pay. Mounting debts led to rapid inflation, compounded by the repeated devaluation of the currency by a financially desperate state. After 1621, when a twelve-year truce with the Dutch rebels expired, the continuing tribulations of war brought the Spanish monarchy close to disintegration. By 1640, attempts at economic and political reform had foundered, and separatist rebellions sapped Spain's strength from within: the Catalans were in revolt, while the Portuguese, who had been united dynastically with the throne of Castile since 1580, declared the Duke of Braganza sovereign of an independent kingdom.

To meet these challenges Spain needed the silver of the Indies more than ever. But rising fiscal pressure on the colonies in the form of imposts, forced loans and confiscations of bullion precipitated a crisis of confidence in the transatlantic trade: less silver was being sent to Spain by American merchants, and therefore fewer goods could be shipped back to

---

the Indies via Seville. Confidence was further eroded by the vulnerability of the Spanish treasure fleets to foreign marauders. The Dutch had now joined the English and the French in their attacks on Spanish maritime trade, adding another massive burden to the defence budget.

In 1615 a Dutch fleet penetrated for the first time into the Pacific Ocean—thought of until then as a 'Spanish lake'—with the result that large amounts of silver had to be retained in the Indies to finance the construction of coastal defences along the newly exposed western seaboard of Spanish America. From the 1620s the Dutch began to seize territory claimed by either Spain or Portugal, both kingdoms being at the time united under the same sovereign. In 1624, and then again in 1630, they took rich sugar-growing areas in the north-east of Brazil and forced Spain to mount costly expeditions to try and dislodge them. In 1634 the Dutch occupied Curacao and other Caribbean islands; English and French privateers did likewise, until the seas of the Antilles were dotted with bases used by foreigners to pounce on Spanish treasure ships or to run contraband goods into the Indies. The greatest single blow to the *carrera de Indias* was delivered in 1628, when an entire treasure fleet was seized in the Bay of Matanzas off the coast of Cuba by the Dutchman Piet Heyn. Business confidence in the transatlantic link collapsed entirely towards the end of the 1630s; in 1640 no treasure arrived in Seville.

The problems of the *carrera* were compounded by a steady fall in overall output from the American silver-mines. Peru was most seriously affected, after about 1603, but Mexican silver production also suffered a sharp down-turn from about 1635. This decline was caused by shortages of mercury from Huancavelica and technical problems in the production process. Starved of precious metals, Spain slumped into an economic crisis much more severe and protracted than the general depression which overcame Europe in the middle of the seventeenth century. But did the Indies as a whole also undergo a depression? It was once thought that the difficulties in the silver-mining industry, the drop in the supply of labour, high prices and the collapse of the *carrera* were all signs of a deep economic crisis in America. The evidence is still not conclusive, but it now appears that no disaster occurred: while economic activity did slow down in the seventeenth century, particularly in mining, other sectors such as agriculture, industry and trade, both interregional and transpacific, did flourish, at least in many parts of the Indies. What is more, the fall in cargoes registered as arriving in Seville suggests that greater amounts of silver were being kept back in the Indies, not just to pay for defence but for

investment in local enterprises. This was, after all, the great age of public construction and architectural embellishment in Spanish America—ports, fortifications, roads, churches, palaces and mansions were built in the main centres of Spanish settlement.

The slow-down in the official transatlantic trade, moreover, disguises the extent of contraband activity, impossible-by its nature to quantify, but likely to have grown considerably as Spanish American capitalists and European traders tried to circumvent the heavily taxed and cumbersome Sevillian monopoly through the newly established foreign entrepôts in the Caribbean. As John Lynch observed, `The crisis in the *carrera de Indias* occurred not because the American economies were collapsing but because they were developing and disengaging themselves from their primitive dependence on the mother country. This was the first emancipation of Spanish America.'*

The relative economic autonomy of the Indies was accompanied by the growth of the *de facto* power of numerous creole élites. The financial difficulties of the imperial state afforded countless opportunities for leading creole families to infiltrate the institutions of the colonial government and Church, or else bend the law to their own interests by showering favours on royal officials. During this period the landholdings of the most powerful creole families expanded to form vast *latifundia*. Great creole clans bought seats in their local *cabildos* and kept them in the family. The interlocking interests of government officials and local patricians produced monopolies in the regional economies: the best lands, the water supplies and irrigation systems, access to dwindling Indian manpower, licensed monopolies to provision towns with basic necessities—all fell into the hands of closed oligarchies.

The seventeenth century thus saw the efflorescence of a Spanish American ruling class, exercising its power in partial or tactical disregard of the law and with little sense of responsibility for other sectors of society. As for the Indians, and those living in tribal communities in particular, they were treated as *gente sin razón*, persons of deficient reason, uncouth and shiftless.

Even the Spanish state now abandoned the pretence of raising the Indians to civil equality with the Hispanic sector; officially, they were still to be protected, but only because their wretched condition was perceived to be irremediable:

> First rhetorically and later (in the 1640s) juridically, they became identified as *miserables*. people recognized in the Old Testament and defined by the

---

*Spain under the Habsburgs (2 vols., Blackwell: Oxford, 1969), vol. 2, p. 193.

Emperor Constantine's jurists as disadvantaged—widows, orphans, and the like—who deserved public compassion and protection.[*]

It was a far cry from the vision of Indian destiny under Spanish tutelage entertained by Las Casas, Vasco de Quiroga, or, indeed, Philip II himself.

The Economy

Land and Labour

The seventeenth century is conventionally associated with the development of the hacienda, the great landed estate, which was the most powerful economic unit in the countryside and the pre-eminent source of social status. The hacienda was a peculiarly Spanish American phenomenon, not because it differed qualitatively from Iberian land holdings but because it represented the attempt to embody an Iberian ideal of land tenure within the legal constraints imposed by the Crown in the Indies after the Conquest. This ideal, as defined by James Lockhart, `would have combined jurisdiction over vassals with vast possessions of land and stock'.[†] Moreover, `aside from his mansion and numerous servants, guests, and vassals, he [i.e., the great nobleman] must have land, cattle, and horses, and various agricultural enterprises from wheat farms to vegetable gardens'.[‡] But since the Crown had prevented the *encomenderos* from turning Indians into their vassals, Spanish American landowners had to try and realize that Iberian ideal of lordly self-sufficiency with the opportunities available to them in the New World.

The roots of the hacienda went back to the land grants of the Conquest. These holdings. known usually as *estancias*, varied in size, and in the immediate post-Conquest period they were mostly cultivated for subsistence, not for commercial purposes. The larger the *estancia* the more substantial its labour requirements, but since the main sources of labour were the Indian communities, the landowner had to find ways of procuring drafts of temporary labourers—to work his estates. Thus a pattern emerged whereby the estate would employ a small permanent staff of workers—known as *naborías* or *gañanes* in Mexico and *yanaconas* in Peru—and would then by a variety of means recruit temporary labourers, usually from surrounding Indian villages. This pattern did not alter

in the course of the colonial period. What did change was the size of the estates and the methods of recruiting temporary labour.

The evolution of the *estancia* into the hacienda was a continuous process, responding both to social values and economic rationale. Large estates were associated with nobility, and the acquisition of noble status was a prime motive of the conquistadors and early settlers. Thus the trend to form ever larger estates was inherent in the social dynamics of post-Conquest society. In economic terms the growth of the estate was linked to the expansion of the Hispanic population in the Indies. As demand grew for agricultural products, landowners steadily increased cultivation of special crops or products to meet specific market demands, without giving up their drive for self-sufficiency and diversification of activities. The coexistence in the one enterprise of both subsistence and commercial agriculture promoted the formation of large estates. Another factor making for growth was the urge to corner markets by driving out competition. This monopolistic tendency meant that the larger landowners were constantly seeking to absorb lands of smaller farmers.

Enrique Florescano has described the economic rationale of the large estates.[*] Agriculture was a risky enterprise subject to unpredictable climatic fluctuations which could ruin a farmer's harvest. It made sense therefore to diversify the range of products produced on an estate. Unpredictable climates also led to varying prices, and so the temptation was to minimize the risks by reducing competition and achieving a monopoly position in the market. A great, self-sufficient estate was therefore the best insurance against an otherwise volatile rural economy. The best land on the estate would be used to raise cash crops. Of the remainder, some would be used to grow staples for home consumption, some to be pasture for herds of cattle or other livestock; certain lands would lie fallow, and yet others might be rented out to tenants in exchange for labour or a share of their crops. The very large estates, as occurred with the big mining complexes, manufactured many of their basic necessities, such as farm tools, carts, soap, candles, leather and textiles, in order to shield themselves further from the market.

The evolution of the sixteenth-century *estancia* into the seventeenth-century hacienda was achieved through various forms of land acquisition. Royal grants of land after the Conquest were made on vacant plots, but landowners enlarged their holdings either by purchase or by encroachment into common

---

[*] Lyle N. McAlister, *Spain and Portugal in the New World, 1492–1700* (Oxford University Press: Oxford, 1984), p. 395.

[†] 'Encomienda and Hacienda: the Evolution of the Great Estate in the Spanish Indies', *Hispanic American Historical Review*, 49, 3 (1969), pp. 411–29 (p. 427).

[‡] ibid., p. 424.

---

[*] *Cambridge History of Latin America*, vol. 2, pp. 171–82.

lands, the royal domain or Indian territory. By the end of the sixteenth century the question of boundaries and titles had become so confused that the Crown tried to regularize the status quo by a device known as *composición de tierras*, which allowed landowners to acquire legal title to land in their possession by payment of a fee to the royal treasury. *Composiciones de tierras* were permitted on several other occasions, partly as a means of increasing royal revenues.

Since the acquisition of land was a piecemeal process, the hacienda that eventually emerged was rarely a vast, continuous tract of territory. Rather, it comprised a number of scattered holdings of varying size, interlocking with the lands of other proprietors or of Indian communities. This was particularly the case in areas close to towns, where land concentration was greater and haciendas could expand only by absorbing smaller farms or Indian commons. In such areas there would be constant litigation over land titles and boundaries; Indian communities tended to be very jealous of property rights and were often extremely litigious, as might be expected given the pressures on their communities from Hispanic landowners. So it was not the case that the hacienda invariably swallowed up Indian land. In regions like Oaxaca, Yucatán, Chiapas and Guatemala, the Indian communities were almost entirely successful in resisting the usurpation of their lands throughout the colonial period.

Haciendas were not easy to hold on to beyond one or two generations. *Hacendados* were frequently in financial trouble, burdened as they were with the obligation to keep their numerous progeny and entourage in the high style expected of the *gran señor* —for that was the point of owning a hacienda in the first place. Social prestige also demanded that large sums of money be donated to the Church—a widespread practice among *hacendados*. With profit margins. generally low, great landowners were often mortgaged to the hilt, and a poor harvest or a long drought could well spell financial disaster for them. Moreover, Hispanic laws of inheritance, which required the division of an estate among all legitimate offspring, often led to the breakup of a hacienda into properties that were too small to be financially viable, and these in turn might have to be sold off to other, rising landowners. Only a minority of the very grandest *hacendados* managed to obtain from the king the privilege of a *mayorazgo*, a legal entail which allowed them to pass on their estates undivided to the first-born son in the family. Families with *mayerazgos* constituted the most select élite in the Indies.

Prey to such financial insecurities, *hacendados* took to politicking in the hope of consolidating their position: they curried favour with royal officials, bought seats on *cabildos*, placed relatives in government posts, and formed cartels with other producers to corner a market or drive up prices. Such were the internal pressures that created the oligarchic regimes which dominated much of the countryside. Still, the hacienda was not the sole form of landholding; in virtually all regions there existed many smaller *estancias* and ranches owned by Hispanics, mestizos and mulattos; a few of these might in due course expand into larger estates, or else they might be the residues of a dispersed hacienda. Land tenure in the Indies was in a constant state of flux–fragmenting or consolidating as some landowners rose in the world and others came down.

The basic pattern of rural holding in the Indies, then, was an estate employing a small contingent of permanent workers but relying otherwise on temporary labour drawn from the Indian villages. The methods by which temporary labour was procured from the Indian pueblos changed over time. Until the 1560s the *encomienda* was the principal means of getting Indians to work Spanish estates. The Crown granted the right to an *encomendero* to receive labour services as a form of tribute from a fixed number of Indians for specified periods of time. However, when labour service as an element of *encomienda* tribute was abolished, it was replaced by the system of *repartimiento*, whereby Crown officials were responsible for rationing and distributing Indian labour among Hispanic landowners for limited periods. Wage scales and working conditions were stipulated by the authorities but rarely adhered to in practice. The *repartimiento* system, however, started to break down in the early seventeenth century, when continuing Indian depopulation made labour so scarce in some areas that it became increasingly difficult for the state to identify the real labour needs of the economy. Landowners took to bypassing state-directed labour drafts by hiring temporary Indian workers on their own account for slightly better wages than would be offered under the *repartimiento*.

Over time, the haciendas tended to increase the proportion of permanent to temporary workers. In some cases these workers were attached to an estate through debt-peonage - the extension of credit to a worker by a landowner on the understanding that it would be paid off through labour. However, debt-peonage appears not to have been as widespread as was once believed. The more common situation was for a *hacendado* to attract peasants from nearby Indian villages to work on his estates on a temporary basis; gradually, some of these Indians would choose to reside on the hacienda as permanent employees, enjoying higher wages and more material security than the temporary workers;

the *hacendado* would then seek to retain his workers by establishing paternalistic relations of patronage and loyalty, through devices such as *padrinaje* (godparenthood) and *compadrazgo* (shared godparenthood). These informal labour arrangements were more prevalent in regions where there was a high density of Spaniards, such as central and north-central Mexico.

In parts of Central America and in the highlands of Peru and Upper Peru, the *repartimiento* survived until the late colonial period and even beyond, for there were many fewer Spaniards to Indians, and the competition for labour among landowners was therefore not so intense. Another reason for the survival of the *repartimiento* in Peru, where it was known by its Quechua name *mita*, was that it formed the basis on which labour was recruited for the silver-mines. A state-directed rotary system of labour drafts for the mines and public works had existed in Inca times and was also well-rooted in Andean tribal traditions. In Mexico a form of rotary labour draft called the *coatequitl* had existed in the pre-Conquest period, but because. the silver-mines of northern Mexico were outside the areas of traditional Indian settlement, free wage labour appeared in the mines by the end of the sixteenth century. By the 1630s Mexican haciendas in the central regions were also abandoning the *repartimiento* system.

The Church

In the Indies, as in Spain, the Church participated in the economy as the major corporate owner of land, real estate and capital after the Crown, and as the chief provider of educational and welfare services. Its enormous revenues consisted of tithes paid by the entire population, white and nonwhite, rents from its considerable properties, and voluntary donations from the faithful. These donations were usually bequests of money or property by a lay person, endowments from rich benefactors and dowries for daughters entering a religious order. Each diocese and religious house received such gifts from its parishioners or supporters, and degrees of wealth would vary widely between them. Naturally, these enormous capital assets were put to use in the economy; they were not `unproductive', even though they were not invested with a view to maximum profitability; huge sums were lavished on the construction of churches and convents, and on the *ornato del culto*, religious art and ornamentation, which were often sumptuous.

Church capital entered the secular economy through two principal channels. Like the merchant community, the Church acted as a major financial institution, providing laymen with credit and investment capital. Loans mostly took the form of mortgages on property over a long term and at low rates of interest. Alternatively, a diocese or religious house might receive bequests of haciendas, mines or plantations, and these could be leased out or managed directly by the clergy. Religious orders, which were often in charge of Indian communities, might employ these Indians to work their properties; in other cases ecclesiastical estates would receive their share of *repartimiento* workers or employ wage labour. Such enterprises tended to be managed very efficiently and were perhaps among the most vigorous and profitable in the colonies. The accumulation of Church land was considerable because it was held in mortmain and, unlike secular holdings, could not be alienated by individuals.

The other major economic function of the Church was as a provider of education, health care and poor relief to the general population. A great part of its income and manpower was employed in these activities. Religious orders such as the Jesuits. and the Dominicans would use profits from their haciendas to finance their schools, seminaries and colleges. A large number of orders, male and female, worked on this basis, running educational and training establishments which were fee-paying for the wealthy but free for the poor. Others operated hospitals, hospices for the mentally ill and the dying, poor houses, orphanages, shelters for homeless girls, and suchlike.

Society

The division of the Indies into two juridically distinct `republics' of Spaniards and Indians remained a basic feature of social organization throughout the colonial period. However, this bipartite social pattern became progressively more complicated as a result of two factors. First, there was a constant and even accelerating drift by Indians towards Spanish urban areas, and, conversely, growing Hispanic influence in the Indian communities. Secondly, there occurred an increasing intermixture of the races, to which the influx of large numbers of African slaves to many parts of the empire contributed. Even so, the institutional division remained between a Hispanic society and a clearly separate Indian sector comprising many and diverse communities—a distinction which has in practice persisted to this day.

The Republic of the Spaniards

The Hispanic society that emerged in the Indies was shaped by the circumstances of the Conquest. The distribution of rewards after an expedition of conquest created a rudimentary social hierarchy, which was expressed in the physical layout of the towns that the conquistadors were required to found. The result was the creation of a seigneurial society led by a natural aristocracy composed of those Spaniards who had received the biggest land grants and the greatest *encomiendas*. Throughout the colonial period, possession of land was to be the single most important criterion of social eminence: the larger the estate the higher the social status. The evolution of the hacienda in the seventeenth century and beyond owed its fundamental stimulus to this aspiration of all Hispanics in the Indies to achieve the noble status implicit in being a large landowner.

Nevertheless, the concept of nobility was inherently unstable because there were very few fixed symbols of status, other than wealth, that could differentiate the aristocrat from the commoner. The Crown, which was the true source of nobility, had refused to concede the traditional privileges of an aristocracy to the natural ruling class of the Indies. This accounted for the undercurrents of resentment and grievance against the mother country that existed among the creoles and which surfaced from time to time throughout the colonial period. The *encomenderos* had failed in their bid to convert the vanquished Indians into their vassals and lost the right to receive Indian tribute in the form of labour; they were not even permitted to keep as a hereditary privilege the limited rights to Indian tribute that were conceded in *encomienda*. They were also denied both a voice in the governing of the state and right of access to the higher echelons of Crown service. Unlike the gentry in the Peninsula they could not distinguish themselves from the lower orders by their exemption from direct taxation. In Spain commoners paid a head tax called the *pecho*, while noblemen from hidalgos upwards were exempt from it. In America there was no such distinction, for all Spaniards and creoles were free of any head tax; it was the Indians alone who paid direct tribute to the Crown. Finally, the Crown accorded American notables very few titular honours. Other than the earliest discoverers and conquerors. such as Columbus, Cortés and Pizarro, few creoles were awarded titles. In the seventeenth century some of the most eminent creole families were ennobled, others were admitted into one of the four military orders of chivalry, but such honours were granted very sparingly by the Crown. By the very nature of its foundation, Spanish American society was seigneurial and status-ridden, yet it lacked the means effectively to institutionalize differences in social status.

The creole élites had to fall back on less well-defined symbols of status–landed wealth, racial purity and reputation. The standing conferred by landownership can be appreciated by the fact that merchants and mine-owners, once they became sufficiently wealthy, would invariably purchase a hacienda in order to acquire social prestige. This applied also to officials in Crown service. Yet, as we have seen, haciendas were not financially secure enterprises, and so whatever nobility a landed estate conferred could be lost through financial ruin.

A white skin was an indispensable qualification for nobility, for any taint of Indian or African blood would just as surely diminish a creole's status as suspicion of Jewish ancestry compromised the nobility of a peninsular Spaniard's lineage. Medieval Spanish concepts of 'purity of blood' were thus transferred to the Indies, but given new meaning in a markedly different racial environment: whiteness distinguished those who belonged to the race of the conquerors from the conquered or the enslaved. Hence the obsessive interest shown by American Spaniards in classifying and ranking the various permutations of race (see below). But even racial purity was an unreliable guide to social eminence, for by the late seventeenth century miscegenation had become so widespread that very few families of *hacendados* were totally free of mixed blood. Since whiteness was no longer a sufficient criterion of superiority, it had to be supplemented, or the lack of it compensated for, by other symbols of social quality–the most powerful of which was the pedigree or reputation of a family.

The surest source of reputation was *mando*, the power to command subordinates and bestow favours on clients: it was the closest a socially eminent creole could come to the condition of the European aristocrat who had rights of jurisdiction over vassals. *Mando* was necessarily more diffuse and could be exercised in different spheres. Thus, the higher clergy, the great mine-owners and the very wealthy transatlantic merchants possessed *mando* and could belong to the upper class. The hacienda, in a sense, was an accessory of *mando*, not its source; it was the theatre in which a man of authority, whatever the origins of his wealth, could represent to others the extent of this authority in the number of his dependants, clients, retainers, servants and workers. Because it lacked the true stamp of royal approval, nobility in the Indies was highly gestural and charismatic–a matter of striking the right attitudes through lavish acts of generosity, disinterested hospitality, conspicuous consumption or displays of gallantry and honour. Thus the `non-economic' behaviour of the creole upper class–taking out a large mortgage for no other purpose than to endow a chapel, say–was no arbitrary indulgence, but a social performance whose object was to advertise social rank.

The quest for nobility had to be undertaken also in the field of politics, and was yet another incentive for oligarchic practices: the unlicensed grandees of colonial society sought to maintain their reputation by forging alliances through marriage with other distinguished families; they would also secure for their kinsmen positions of prominence in society by purchasing a seat in the *cabildo*, endowing a chaplaincy for them, obtaining a position in the royal bureaucracy, and so on. Once established, a great family or clan was a social entity which was capable in itself of conferring high status on its individual members, but the family as a whole had to maintain its standing from one generation to the next. Pedigree came to play a part in defining aristocratic status, though its quality was always more evanescent in America than in Europe.

At the apex of the social pyramid in any Hispanic region were clusters of interrelated creole families enjoying undisputed patrician status. Immediately below them was a varied class of families which had not attained the same prominence either because they lacked pedigree or sufficient wealth, or because they were simply not engaged in the right sort of trade. The professions, particularly the law and the Church (medicine was not held in high regard), were fitting occupations for the younger sons of noble families and had high status in so far as they were practised by patricians and were associated with patrician interests. Important positions in the royal bureaucracy also conferred status, and the top administrators, judges and treasury officials, many of whom were *peninsulares*, would be members of the upper class.

In the towns the middle classes of white society comprised self-employed artisans, craftsmen, petty officials, clerks and shopkeepers; these people would be quite as anxious as the upper classes to preserve their status in society – artisans, for instance, would seek to exclude rivals from below, who were often non-whites, by forming guilds and corporations. In the countryside, the middle classes comprised the major-domos of large haciendas and the owners of middle-sized estates and ranches.

At the bottom of the social pyramid were to be found the common run of Hispanics without trade or property, poor whites whose only distinction within the lower orders was the colour of their skin, for around them swarmed the masses of urbanized Indians, free blacks and mixed-bloods who lived in the republic of the Spaniards without being juridically members of it.

The Republic of the Indians

The republic of the Indians came into being as a separate polity within the realms of the Spanish Crown, and it possessed its own laws and institutions. The intention of the Crown was to protect the Indians from exploitation by the Spanish settlers, and to allow them to retain their culture in so far as this did not conflict with Catholicism. Thus Spaniards and creoles were forbidden to reside within the Indian communities, and Indians equally were confined to their lands. But the 'protection' of the Indians through segregation was undermined by the fact that they had to offer tribute in kind to Hispanics and work periodically in the Hispanic sector, where they tended to be harshly treated and exposed to European cultural influences. As epidemics ravaged the Indian villages in the sixteenth century, the burdens of the tribute and labour service forced many individual Indians to flee their tribal lands and seek work in the Hispanic settlements or on Hispanic estates. They joined, in effect, that class of detribalized Indian known as *naborías* in Mexico and *yanaconas* in Peru; these Indians were not members of either republic, but formed part of a mixed population of undefined status.

Conquest, disease and tribute put such stress on the Indian villages in many regions that by the 1560s the Crown decided on a policy of resettlement and concentration in new rationally planned communities. The programmes of *congregación* and *reducción* were disruptive in themselves, and many Indians had to be resettled by force. However, by the turn of the century, the new settlements were providing the basis for the reintegration of Indian community life. These communities had been remodelled by the Spanish state—and to this extent they were culturally hybrid—but they none the less retained much of the traditional structure of Indian society. Many communities were reorganized within the boundaries of tribal lands. Where resettlement took place outside tribal territory, new community lands were designated by the Crown. The traditional Hispanic pattern of provincial jurisdiction, consisting of *cabecera* (head town) and *sujetos* (subordinate villages), was reproduced, but the authority of dynastic ethnic chieftains continued to be exercised in the Indian *cabildo*, which became a sort of council of tribal elders. Thus the Indian world was constantly assimilating and adapting Hispanic influences for its own ends:

> Elements which were originally introduced from the outside became integrated inside Indian patterns of thought and behaviour to form stable associations of traits, all of which the Indian community identified with, not questioning which was indigenous, which Spanish, which a combination. On examination, nearly everything usually turns out to be the latter: Indian at the root and altered in some way at the surface, like the provincial units themselves.[*]

The Indian corporate world was still rooted in the kinship group called the *calpulli* in Mexico and the *ayllu* in Peru. Land tenure remained predominantly communal; agricultural work was performed on a reciprocal basis between groups of kin; and rotary labour systems were employed for the larger enterprises undertaken by the community. These were the abiding strengths of Indian life; yet elements of Spanish culture–clothing, artefacts, tools, farming methods, crops and animals–might filter through into the communities and be duly absorbed to suit Indian needs. This was particularly the case with the reception of the new religion and its practices.

Once it had been imposed, Catholicism performed a central role in strengthening and maintaining communal bonds. Church services, processions and festivals became focal events in the life of the native pueblos. Communities adopted particular saints or aspects of the Virgin as their patron, and used this very Catholic practice to reinforce their tribal identity and territoriality. Ritual dances and pageants, originating in pagan cults, acquired a Christian gloss while continuing to articulate tribal myths. The Hispanic medieval tradition of forming *cofradías* (religious brotherhoods) under the special protection of a saint was adopted enthusiastically by the Indians and became a prime means of expressing social solidarity. Church and municipality were closely knit together through the *cajas de comunidad* (community funds), which were used to finance religious festivals and to pay for the decoration of the community's church, a source of enormous pride. The Hispanic practice of *compadrazgo* (social bonding through godparenthood) became widespread among the Indians in the seventeenth century.

Indian communities, therefore, were profoundly conservative, demonstrating an extraordinary ability to incorporate alien influences and to make them underscore collective identities. But also they turned these influences to positive advantage in their relations with the outside world, using them to assert their independence. In the seventeenth century they actively defended their interests against Hispanics or rival Indian tribes, and learned to use techniques of lobbying and petitioning the Crown which–were fundamental to the political life of the Hispanic world. They were, moreover, notorious for their relentless litigation over property rights; in the 1600s special courts, *juzgados de indios*, were created to hear civil and criminal cases involving disputes between Indians or between Indians and non-Indians. When such methods failed, the communities would often riot to wring a particular concession from the Crown or overturn a ruling or have an official removed; this was a familiar political technique in the Hispanic world, which was also employed by other ethnic communities- creole, mestizo and black-and to which the authorities would respond according to circumstances, but as often as not by appeasing rather than repressing such collective displays of outrage.

Indeed, in parts of the Indies, such as in the *zona indígena* of southern Mexico, in Yucatán, and in Guatemala Indian communities and Spanish settlements existed as parallel structures largely independent of one another. In the region of Oaxaca, as William B. Taylor has shown, the Indian corporate presence was dominant and assertive.[*] Indian communities and individuals controlled about two-thirds of the agricultural land during the last century of Spanish rule, and the Indians chose to grow traditional crops-maize, beans and maguey-even though they were quite capable of producing an abundant variety of European foodstuffs.

In the long term, however, the overall trend was towards a more fundamental Hispanicization. Within the communities themselves, traditional features underwent change. For instance, the reciprocal bonds which tied ethnic lords to their commoners came under strain. The *caciques* were allowed privileges by the Spaniards, such as bearing arms, owning horses and wearing Spanish dress. They also collaborated with the Spaniards in organizing the tribute labour of the common Indians, and some used this as an opportunity to exploit Indian labour for their personal gain, amassing private land and property beyond that which was customary in traditional communities. Yet, at the same time, the hereditary *caciques* began to lose their hold over the *cabildos*, which were gradually filled by Indian commoners and even by nontribal outsiders, including mestizos who happened to have settled within the territory of a community. Hereditary and dynastic authority was being superseded by a more elective kind of municipal government. Further social levelling occurred when, as a result of widespread depopulation, *caciques* were required to pay tribute themselves in order to make up the community's quota.

Interaction between the Indian world and the Hispanic increased in the seventeenth century. Indians were constantly being drawn into the Hispanic economy by the settlers' demand for labour

---

* James Lockhart and Stuart B. Schwartz. *Early Latin America*, p. 175.

* *Landlord and Peasant in Colonial Oaxaca* (Stanford University Press: Stanford, 1972).

and goods. There were natives who hired themselves out as temporary labourers in Spanish towns or estates. Others migrated from villages to settle permanently or for long periods in Spanish areas, where they were free from tribute and exploitation by *caciques* and *corregidores*. Communities located near Hispanic towns raised crops for sale in their markets. Entry into the market economy, with the consequent use of money, very slowly wrought changes in native attitudes to land tenure and production, with a shift occurring from reciprocal and communal arrangements to a more individualistic conception of property. Conversely, there was a movement from the Hispanic areas into the Indian corporate world. Creoles and mestizos from the lower classes took up residence illegally in Indian territory and brought alien values into the communities when they employed Indian workers or established social ties with *caciques* through marriage or *compadrazgo*.

These informal contacts accelerated the rate of cultural change within Indian communities. However, James Lockhart and Stuart Schwartz have identified a pattern of acculturation which occurred at different rates in the various parts of the Indies. In the central areas of Mexico, there was a period of some fifty to eighty years, from about 1570 until roughly 1650, which they call a 'plateau of consolidation', when the communities had adjusted to the new Hispanic structures and flourished in a hybrid cultural situation, with their traditional social mechanisms operating effectively through Hispanic institutions.* This was a time when Indians from the pueblos built churches and decorated them with frescoes and carvings; they also participated in the Catholic liturgy in their communities, performing, and even at times composing, the rich sacred music introduced by Spanish priests. By the middle of the seventeenth century, the underlying rate of Hispanicization had reached a critical point, after which a majority of Indians could, as individuals, satisfy their aspirations more effectively in the Spanish sector proper than within their communities. From that point, the Indian communities of central Mexico can be said to have been steadily relegated to the margins of Indian life.

Lockhart and Schwartz trace this phenomenon in the interaction of Nahuatl with Spanish. Until the 1650s or thereabouts the native language borrowed only nouns from Spanish, but then verbs, prepositions, conjunctions and idioms were used, suggesting a rapid increase in bilingualism as more and more Indians learned to deal with the Hispanic sector in a whole range of areas. In other regions where the inter-

action was not so intense or where it had not started so early, the process of acculturation would have occurred later.*

The Patriarchal Order of Society

The social world of the Spanish Indies was patriarchal and hierarchical. The ideal was to live like a lord, owning vast estates and holding sway over other men. Such an ideal took its pattern from the Iberian family unit, in which the paterfamilias exercised a benevolent but unquestioned authority over his wife, children, dependants, servants, slaves and an extensive clan of relatives and clients. The rule of the patriarch was exercised through patronage rather than outright force: favours were extended in exchange for respect and loyalty; special protection in a harsh world was the reward for obedience from social inferiors; who were often bound to the family by ties of *padrinaje* and *compadrinaje*.

These values permeated political and economic behaviour. In politics, they led inevitably to oligarchy, for patriarchal clans sought to maintain their influence by infiltrating powerful institutions and conducting public affairs with the methods that ruled family business—namely, the exchange of favours between patrons and clients. Economic practice, too, was oligarchic, tending to the exclusion of equal competition as favours were used to dominate markets, to create cartels, of producers which kept prices high, to win monopoly rights from the state, and so on. In short, the great clans tried to capture and control markets in order to turn ordinary consumers into passive clients who would have to pay high prices for goods as a sort of tribute to the patriarchal power of the producer. On the other hand, high profits and rents were spent by the great families in economically `unproductive' ways—in acts of public generosity through donations to the Church, Crown and community, and in sustaining a luxurious style of life which would enhance the prestige and power of the patriarch and his kin.

Monarchy set the seal on this patriarchal order of society. The king was the father of the people, the personal source of justice and law, ruling also by virtue of his ability to grant favours in return for loyalty and obedience. His subjects had no inherent rights; instead, they directed petitions to the monarch for the concession of some grace or reward. Above the king stood only God, the Supreme Father, and

---

*   *Early Latin America*, pp. 165–7.
*   *Early Latin America*, pp. 165–8.

indeed, the social world was nothing but the material reflection of the spiritual hierarchy instituted by the Creator Himself. Because religion provided the ultimate rationale for political authority, the Catholic monarchy was a powerful force for unity: it acted as an overarching structure which held together the myriad, interlocking networks of reciprocal ties radiating outwards and upwards from the authority of the father in the humblest family unit.

3. SAINTS ALONG THE HIGHWAY

WHERE'S THE OLD MISSION?" visitors to California sometimes ask when arriving at a city or town with a "San" or "Santa" name. But there were only twenty-one Franciscan missions scattered along a seven-hundred-mile route between San Diego Bay and the region north of San Francisco Bay, within a hundred miles of the coast. The dozens of settlements whose saintly names commemorate missionaries, leaders, martyrs, and miracle workers in Catholic hagiology usually acquired their titles from geographical features or Indian rancherias in the area that were named long before a modern town was established.

A mission was a most particular institution. It was founded to minister to the local Indians: to attract them, to Christianize them, and to teach them the rudimentary skills of Western civilization. In the process, the neophytes were to assist the Spaniards in making their California colony productive—in agriculture, animal husbandry, and other basic industries—so that it could be nearly self-sustaining. Its padres were friar-missionaries, not secular priests who devoted their efforts to serving a parish of regular Christians. They had different interests, training, and duties. And they had chosen the kind of life they led in the New World. Almost all early padres had been born in Spain.

A town bearing a saint's name does not guarantee the presence of a mission within its boundaries. Nor does a mission necessarily have a "San" or "Santa" starting off its name. Two California missions—La Purisima Concepcion and Nuestra Señora de la Soledad—are exceptions. (The first, though, adds *de María Santísima*—of Holiest Mary.)

Furthermore, there are various Sans and Santas in California place-names that scarcely qualify as bona fide Hispanic-style saints. There was nobody named San Ardo. The name was originally San Bernardo, but when this caused confusion with the post office

at San Bernardino, the residents obligingly clipped it. San Marino is a transported name; the town's founder used the title of his family's manor in Maryland, which in turn had borrowed its name from the tiny European principality. San Ramon, San Anselmo, and San Quentin got their "Sans" attached later, after being named for Indians who at baptism assumed Christian names of saints. (The Americans also managed to misspell Quintín!) Then there's the transsexual, trans-cultural Santa Claus, a burg along Highway 101 south of Santa Barbara that tries to keep Christmas going all year round by erecting large plaster statues of the Germanic version of the Asia Minor bishop, Saint Nicolas, the patron saint of children, and by selling tourist wares and date milkshakes. More peculiar still are such post office names as San Lawrence Terrace, San Augustine, and Santa Western.

Another source for occasional confusion is the city of San Jose and Mission San Jose. The city began as California's first official pueblo, close to the already established Mission Santa Clara. Saint Joseph, always a favorite saint, as well as the patron saint of the California colonization, was given his own mission later on, some fifteen miles to the northeast. In the city of San Jose, located within the Santa Clara Valley and Santa Clara County, at the heart of Computerland's "Silicon Valley," one visits *Mission* Santa Clara. Misión San Jose de Guadalupe is located in Alameda County.

Since explorers on both land and sea took priests or friars along with them on expeditions to serve as chaplains, tenders of the sick, and diarists, an essential part of their baggage was a calendar book that listed feast days: dates of births, deaths, or other significant events in saints' lives or afterlives and church history itself. Any geographical feature or human settlement that seemed to require naming might be awarded a "San" or "Santa" according to the approximate date of discovery or the name maker's predilection for a particular saint.

The abundance of these Sans and Santas make California look like a land inhabited by people saintlier than the rest of Christendom. There are probably more commemorative holy names here per square map-quadrangle than anywhere else in the world. But ours is not an especially religious age, and the saints go marching across the landscape as unnoticed and as anonymously as the rest of our place-names, Hispanic or otherwise.

California has not yet produced her very own saint, but there is still time for that. Canonization

"Saints Along the Highway," from *California's Spanish Place-Names* by Barbara and Rudy Marinacci, Presidio Press, 1980, pp. 67-72, 74.

into sainthood is a long and complicated procedure. Several padres who devoted their lives to the California missions may someday achieve this highest honor that the Catholic Church can confer upon a mortal.

Ever since the 1930s Father Junipero Serra has been a candidate for sainthood. Martyrdom is the most direct route, but even though Serra fully expected it during his California trials, he died of natural causes. If he ultimately satisfies the Church's requirements—strong evidence of good works done in his lifetime and convincing proofs of miracles achieved afterwards by his spiritual intercession—we may someday have a San Junipero. Then the zealous little padre who rode mules or walked on a painfully ulcerated leg up and down El Camino Real, founding and then inspecting his missions, will be elevated higher in humanity's eyes than his namesake peak in the Santa Lucia Range that he passed through on his frequent missionary *jornadas*.

On becoming a friar, Serra took the Christian name of Junipero, a sturdy follower of St. Francis, who said he wished he had "a whole forest of such junipers." Serra was a hard worker who constantly practiced humility. His burning devotion to the cause of saving the Indian heathens warmed him as he lay in his cell on a narrow cot that had planks instead of a mattress—often blanketless because he had given away his only covering to some shivering *indio*. (Serra's cell is still on view at Mission Carmel.)

Men with such extreme dedication combined with organizational abilities and physical fortitude were what the Spanish colony in California needed, whether as military commanders, civilian leaders, or missionaries. Since the early settlements depended increasingly on the sustenance provided by the missions and on the padres' efforts to pacify and train the Indians within each area, it is almost certain that the California colonization itself would have failed, despite Jose de Galvez's careful preparations, if the missionary aspect of the venture had been less successful.

Father Serra was no saint as far as the comandante-governors were concerned. He was ever a nagging thorn in their sides. He demanded permission for more and more missions and would rarely listen to their reasoning. If they had no soldiers to spare as guards for these new missions he wanted, he was prepared, he said, to get along without them. The soldados de cuera misbehaved anyway and stirred up trouble with the Indians, teasing and tormenting them and abusing their women. The soldiers were indolent, rude, bestial, drunken, he said, and they set bad examples of Christian behavior. The comandan-

tes did not deal with them strictly, as Portola and then Anza had done....

Nevertheless, the missions and missionaries were required to have soldier-*guards*, an *escolta*: a half dozen at least, with a corporal in charge. The soldiers made servants out of the neophytes; many became too lazy to put on their own boots. But when the Indians ran away from the mission life, often taking horses and cattle with them, or when wild tribes raided, the soldiers proved useful in punishing them and in providing protection. On their parts, the padres fed them and heard confessions and gave them Communion. And when the vineyards began to yield their Mission grapes, to produce the essential sacramental wines, the soldiers began to get *vino* and aguardiente (brandy) with their meals.

The half century of Spanish dominion in California, from 1769 to 1822, when Mexico took over the often burdensome territory, is essentially the story of the mission chain stretched out to the right and the left of El Camino Real, established and maintained by the gray-frocked Franciscan Order. (The friars changed to brown robes at the end of the nineteenth century, by the Pope's ruling.) Almost all were set in prime locations that had good water sources, farmlands and pasturage, pleasant surroundings, and a population of Indians. Local Indian groups were often given new names based on the missions nearby, whether or not they trafficked there. Thus there were Diegueños, Gabrieleños, Barbareños, Luiseños, Juaneños.

Some missions were located at the ocean, alongside harbors. Others, farther inland, occupied fertile valleys and had routes that led to the sea and to the closest presidio and pueblo. It is no wonder that many of them remained central to California's development. Some of our largest cities and most prosperous or fastest-growing towns began as mission settlements.

There were other important Spanish settlements, secular ones—the four presidios and the three pueblos—making a total of twenty-eight official colonizing units established by order of the Spanish crown through the viceroy of New Spain. The padres themselves did not choose the names for the missions in the beginning. These and the names and locations of presidios and pueblos were decided by the administrators, acting through the *gobernador* of the Californias, both Baja and Alta.

Most of these early settlements bore the name of a saint. At three sites, eventually, both a presidio and a mission shared the same name: San Diego, San Francisco, Santa Barbara. Of the three pueblos, one honored a saint (San Jose), and one the Virgin Mary (Nuestra Señora la Reina de los Angeles).

Two places—the Monterey Presidio and the pueblo called Villa de Branciforte—commemorated viceroys of New Spain. All told, twenty-six out of the twenty-eight place-names were religious in intent. Of the twenty-three that commemorate particular saints, three were nonmortals—the Archangels San Gabriel, San Miguel, San Rafael. There were two kings—San Luis Rey de Francia and San Fernando Rey de España; a bishop— San Luis Obispo; three missionaries—San Francisco de Asis, San Francisco Solano, and San Diego de Alcala; two scholarly theologians—San Antonio de Padua and San Buenaventura; two reformers—San Carlos Borromeo and San Juan Capistrano; two relatives of Jesus—San Juan Bautista and San Jose; three women—Santa Barbara and Santa Ines (martyred Roman maidens) and Santa Clara (founder of a religious order).

Like stepping-stones, these outposts of civilization were placed sometimes singly, at other times in small groups—whenever the California governor granted permission along with a squad of soldiers. There was a certain pattern to the placements: attempts were made to "fill in" gaps between established settlements. However, the process was not necessarily harmonious. Church and state, as institutions and as individuals, almost perpetually feuded in California, though the tenure of Serra's successor, Fermin Francisco de Lasuen, was comparatively calm and productive, partly because the California colony was no longer precarious but also because Lasuen's diplomatic skills served the Franciscan mission system well. (Between them, Fathers Serra and Lasuen founded eighteen missions: nine apiece.)

F. Independence

The American Revolution of 1776 and the French Revolution of 1789, along with Napoleon's invasion and occupation of Spain 1808–1814, were important factors in fostering the independence movements throughout Spanish America at the beginning of the 19th century. However, in addition to these international struggles for freedom, the *criollos*, or the sons and daughters of the Spaniards, born in the colonies, had much to complain about. Despite being the most important class of the hierarchical Spanish colonial society, they were denied positions of leadership in government and the Church (Spaniards sent from the mother country having priority). In addition, the *criollos* yearned to trade freely with all countries, including the new United States.

So it was not unexpected that great patriots such as Father Miguel Hidalgo in Mexico, Simón Bolívar en Venezuela, and José de San Martín in Argentina along with thousands of followers would take up arms against Spain. The struggle was not easy, but by 1821 all of the continental Spanish colonies, from Mexico in the north to Argentina, Peru, and Chile in the south, had won their independence. Thus, the only remnants of Spanish colonial power remaining in the Americas were Cuba and Puerto Rico. The Dominican Republic gained full independence from Haiti in 1844. Cuba became independent shortly after the Spanish American War of 1898, while Puerto Rico, after the same conflict, became part of the United States.

1. SPANISH AMERICA: THE ROAD TO INDEPENDENCE

The First Phase (1810–14)

In the period 1810–14 the winning of some form of autonomy for the Indies within an imperial framework under a restored Bourbon monarchy seemed feasible, and it was a political solution that commanded the support of the majority of creole opinion. The beleaguered Regency Council at Cadiz had declared the equality of all the realms of the empire and summoned delegates to a constituent assembly. In 1812 a liberal constitution was proclaimed: a effectively provided for the establishment in Spain of a limited monarchy in which royal power would be accountable to elected Cortes and individual rights would be guaranteed. The 1812 constitution of Cadiz thus became the rallying symbol of Spanish American as much as peninsular liberals, for it promised the creoles what they had always aspired to—a greater voice in their own government, while retaining the monarchy as a source of legitimate authority.

However, the liberalism of the Cadiz government had its limits when it came to dealing with the empire. The government at Cadiz rejected a proposal from American delegates for a kind of commonwealth of autonomous constitutional kingdoms under one monarch—a liberal reincarnation, as it were, of the Habsburg theory of empire. The creoles wanted the right to trade with foreigners, proportional representation at the Cortes, and equal access to all government posts. However, the liberal Cortes in Cadiz was not prepared to concede any of this, for even the Spanish liberals could not contemplate surrendering political control over the Indies. Such control, after all, afforded the Spanish state huge revenues from taxes, duties, forced loans and Indian tribute, as well as guaranteed profits from the transatlantic trade monopoly for Spanish exporters and the merchants of Cadiz (many of whom were, not surprisingly, supporters of the liberals in the Cortes). The reality was that the economic dependence of Spain on its American colonies made stubborn imperialists out of political liberals.

Still, the Cadiz constitution enshrined rights to free elections and to a free press, which in principle gave the creoles the chance to express their grievances openly and to participate more directly in the political life of their regions. In the Indies, however, the viceroys, who were used to the ways of an absolute monarchy, tried to ignore the freedoms conceded by Cadiz, or, where that proved impossible, they sought to manipulate elections to the American *cabildos*. By 1814 the imperialism of the Cadiz Cortes, no less than the intransigence of royal officials, seemed to impede a negotiated solution to the imperial crisis, and this alienated many creoles. But so long as metropolitan authority was divided between liberal parliamentarians in Cadiz and conservative administrators in the colonies, the political situation would remain fluid.

While the search for a political solution had been going on, groups of creole radicals throughout the Indies had since 1810 taken to arms in order to win full independence from Spain. Though still small in numbers, they could only stand to benefit from the frustration of the majority with the inflexibility of the imperial government. The rebellions they led differed in character and extent from one region to another, and their effect on the creole majorities in their respective areas was likewise varied.

The Rebellion in Mexico

The rebellion in favour of independence in Mexico differed from all the other risings in that it came from outside the creole élite. It was sparked off by a creole priest, Miguel Hidalgo, who had been the rector of the prestigious college of San Nicolás in Valladolid (now Morelia), but had fallen foul of the royal authorities because of his interest in the ideas of the Enlightenment and his personal life (he lived openly with the mother of his two daughters). Hidalgo had been removed by his bishop to the small parish of Dolores near Querétaro, where he worked among Indians and mestizos. In 1810 he joined a conspiracy of wealthy creoles to set up a revolutionary junta. When the plot was uncovered, Hidalgo hurriedly called for a general uprising against the Spanish. This was the famous *Grito de Dolores* of 16 September (now celebrated as Independence Day in Mexico). The *Grito* was a cry for independence in the name of Ferdinand VII and the Virgin of Guadalupe. Hidalgo's aims were sweeping but unfocused: abolition of the Indian tribute, the return of Indian lands and death to all Spaniards.

The reaction of the peasantry was explosive, for the rich agricultural region of the Bajío had been suffering from drought and famine for the last two years, and the peasants were desperate. A mass of Indians and mestizos rose up and began looting and killing the whites. Within a week the rebels had captured two towns and entered the provincial capital, Guanajuato, where they besieged the Alhóndiga— the fortified municipal granary in which terrified creoles and Spaniards had taken refuge. A bloody massacre occurred, followed by the pillage of the city. Three weeks later Valladolid, the provincial capital of Michoacán, had fallen, and the insurgents, their numbers having swelled to over 80,000, moved on Mexico City itself. Their advance, however, was checked by a costly encounter with royalist forces. The rebels decided to retreat, but on their way back to Querétaro they were engaged by another royalist army and suffered a devastating blow. They divided into two dwindling forces, one withdrawing to Valladolid and thence to Guadalajara under Hidalgo, the other to Guanajuato under Ignacio Allende. Though Hidalgo was able to recruit more peasants at Guadalajara, his forces were crushed by royalists in January 1811. He fled north, but was captured in March and shot, along with most of his commanders; their heads were displayed at the infamous Alhóndiga in Guanajuato for the next ten years.

Resistance was patchy for about a year, after which the rebels recovered some of their former strength under the leadership of José María Morelos, a mestizo priest from Michoacán, whose military skill and political intelligence gave the independence movement greater coherence than under Hidalgo. Morelos cast aside the profession of loyalty to Ferdinand VII and outlined a radical programme, which included land redistribution and the full integration of Indians and mestizos into society. Capturing the city of Oaxaca in the south-west, he proceeded to organize a congress at Chipalcingo in 1813, where independence was declared on 6 November. This alternative republican government and its small army was continually harried by royalist troops—Oaxaca was recaptured early in 1814—and failed to attract wide support among the creoles. Nevertheless, despite internal disputes which led to the removal of Morelos from the leadership, the insurgency persisted doggedly against heavy odds. The republican congress issued a constitution at Apatzingan in October 1814, but by this time Ferdinand had been released and the absolute monarchy was restored in Spain and its dominions. Morelos was captured in 1815 and executed.

The Rebellion in New Granada

Of the several revolutionary juntas that appeared in 1810 in the viceroyalty of New Granada, the one at Caracas moved soonest towards republicanism and the inevitable armed struggle. The creole élites acted with dispatch to safeguard their privileges once it appeared that Spain had fallen to Napoleon. For the whites of Venezuela were in a minority, surrounded by a mass of Blacks, Indians and half-caste *pardos*, whose advancement under the Spaniards they regarded as a threat to their social authority. A congress was duly elected in March 1811 on a franchise which excluded non-whites.

However, a more radical group, calling itself the Patriotic Society of Caracas, urged the declaration of an independent republic. The Patriotic Society was led by men such as Francisco de Miranda, who had returned to Venezuela in 1810, and Simón Bolívar, a member of one of the richest and most powerful families of the Venezuelan oligarchy of cacao planters. It was this social group that had most to gain from severing ties with Spain, seizing political power over the non-whites and opening up trade with Britain and the USA. On 5 July 1811 the congress declared independence and founded the first republic of Venezuela. Miranda was nominated supreme commander of the republican army.

The constitution provided for a federal structure, the legal equality of citizens of all races and the abolition of clerical and military privileges. Yet, in reality, it did little for the non-whites: the *pardos* were mostly excluded from voting by a property qualification, slavery was retained, and the *llaneros*, the free-ranging horsemen of the plains, were alienated by policies designed to bring the *llanos* (plains) under private ownership. When a small Spanish force arrived from Puerto Rico in March 1812 under the command of Domingo de Monteverde, the non-whites threw in their lot with the royalists and within a few months the republican army had surrendered to Monteverde. Its chief, Miranda, was deported to Spain and died in prison some years later.

Simón Bolívar, however, escaped to New Granada, where the provincial juntas were quarrelling amongst themselves over the terms of their association. A precarious federation—the United Provinces of New Granada—had been achieved under the leadership of Camilo Torres late in 1811; but the junta of the vice-regal capital, Bogotá, rejected the federal constitution and set itself up instead as the independent state of Cundinamarca, under the leadership of Antonio Nariño, a noted liberal dissident under the Bourbons. Other cities and provinces, such as Panama, Santa Marta and Pasto, remained loyal to the Regency Council in Cadiz. The extreme political fragmentation of the viceroyalty resulted in bouts of armed conflict between revolutionary creole factions.

Despite this disorder, Bolívar managed to enlist the help of the United Provinces of New Granada for a renewed campaign against the royalists of Venezuela. His political objective on this occasion was to exploit the refusal of the Cadiz liberals to make concessions on autonomy for the Indies. In 1813 Bolívar entered Venezuela and declared a 'war to the death' against the authority of Spain with the aim of forcing wavering creoles to choose between independence or submission to an unyielding colonialism. Fighting a *campaña admirable* he reached Caracas in August and declared a second republic, assuming the functions of a military dictator, since he had become disenchanted with democratic assemblies after observing the chaotic situation in New Granada. The Second Republic nevertheless collapsed within a few months: Bolívar had failed to win over the *pardos*, many of whom were recruited by a Spaniard, José Tomás Boves, into a guerrilla movement loyal to the king. At the battle of La Puerta on 15 June 1814 Bolívar's army was defeated by Boves's royalist guerrillas.

Returning to New Granada, Bolívar joined in the perennial squabbling between centralists and federalists until he became disillusioned with the unruliness of the revolutionaries and left for Jamaica in 1815. The independence movements in New Granada would, in any case, soon fall to a royalist counter-strike organized from Venezuela by Pablo Morillo, an extremely able Spanish general who had been sent out from Spain in the spring of 1815 to pacify the Indies with an army of 10,000 men. By 1816 both Venezuela and New Granada were back under royalist control.

The Rebellion in Río de la Plata

The other theatre of military conflict in South America was Río de la Plata, a territory which, like New Granada, had been raised to the status of a viceroyalty only in recent decades, and where political authority had not become firmly rooted in the new capital, Buenos Aires. On 25 May 1810 a junta proclaiming direct loyalty to Ferdinand VII seized power in Buenos Aires and very soon fell under the rhetorical sway of Jacobin radicals such as Mariano Moreno, a liberal journalist and the translator of Rousseau's *Social Contract*. The liberal junta opened the port of Buenos Aires to trade with all nations and proclaimed the equality of all citizens regardless of race. But, in fact, the junta expressed the interests of the *porteños*—the Buenos Aires élite—whose measures were directed against the Spanish import-export merchants and who were careful to exclude non-white sectors from government.

The radical hue of the Buenos Aires junta did little to recommend it to the oligarchies of the interior provinces, and a loyalist reaction in the old any of Córdoba, seat of an *audiencia* and a university, was suppressed by the *porteño* liberals and its leaders executed; they included Santiago Liniers, who had commanded the militia forces which had expelled the British from the River Plate in 1806–7. Provincial hostility was, however, mollified when delegates from the interior were at last included in the Buenos Aires junta; their conservatism moderated the Jacobin fervour of the *porteño* politicians, but creole government in the capital continued to be riven by factionalism as the absence of any one strong leader. In 1813 the junta called a national assembly of what it now designated as the United Provinces of Río de la Plata, although independence from Spain had not yet been declared.

There were, nevertheless, important provinces of the viceroyalty which refused to accept the authority of the revolutionaries in Buenos Aires, namely Paraguay, the Banda Oriental (modern Uruguay) and Upper Peru (now Bolivia)—the Andean province where the great silver-mines of Potosí were located and whose economy until 1776 had been oriented towards Lima. Buenos Aires sought to reduce these provinces by force of arms. An army led by Juan José Castelli took Potosí and combined with local rebels to wrest Upper Peru from the royalists, but within months had been defeated by an army from Peru. Another expedition led by Manuel Belgrano reconquered Potosí, but was again expelled by royalists. A third attempt to take Upper Peru was repulsed in 1815, and the silver-rich province had finally to be abandoned by Buenos Aires.

Paraguay too was lost to Buenos: Aires. A *porteño* army led by Manuel Belgrano was beaten back by loyalist militias in 1811. Shortly afterwards, a junta was set up in Asunción which eventually gave way to the dictatorship of José Gaspar Rodríguez de Francia, under whose eccentric, unwavering rule this province thenceforward pursued an independent course. The Banda Oriental across the River Paraná was to give Buenos Aires constant trouble both during the independence wars and long afterwards. José Gervasio Artigas, a local cattle-rancher, initiated the revolt against the royalists of Montevideo and called on Buenos Aires for assistance. Yet Artigas proved reluctant to submit to the authority of the *porteños*, and relations between the allies fluctuated during the war to liberate Montevideo. With the fall of the city in 1814, Artigas won control of the province and proceeded with a radical land policy of breaking up the large haciendas and distributing land to Indians, half-castes and small farmers. However, in 1816 he was overwhelmed by an invading army from Brazil.

Already by 1815 the leadership of Buenos Aires over the United Provinces of Río de la Plata was decidedly shaky. Large areas of the viceroyalty had eluded its authority altogether, while other inland provinces were proving fractious; the *porteño* élite itself remained divided, and the conservative majority was becoming increasingly irritated with the political radicalism of lawyers turned professional politicians. As the movement for independence began to falter, it was Buenos Aires's great distance from the metropolis that saved the liberal revolutionaries from immediate military punishment by Spain after the restoration of Ferdinand VII to the throne.

The Return of the King (1814–19)

With the defeat of Napoleon in the Iberian Peninsula in 1814, Ferdinand VII, newly restored to his throne, sought to rebuild the authority that had so suddenly collapsed six years earlier. His return to Spain had been celebrated by the common people as a national victory and, taking advantage of this immense popular devotion, Ferdinand reverted to absolute rule: the Cortes of Cadiz were dissolved, the 1812 constitution abrogated and the breach with the Church repaired, even to the extent of reinstating the Inquisition and the Jesuit order. Conventionally portrayed by liberal historians as a mulish autocrat blind to his own self-interest, Ferdinand, though a Bourbon, was attempting to recover the traditional monopoly of legitimacy enjoyed by the Habsburg monarchs, a legitimacy which had served to secure over two centuries of obedience from the Crown's subjects in the Indies. After all, the modernizing reforms of his immediate Bourbon forebears had done little but weaken the authority of the throne and damage its compact with the Church; the liberals of Cadiz had gone even further, recasting the whole basis of royal sovereignty by deriving it from the will of the people. And the result of these innovations had only been rebellion in America and the risk of losing the empire to some foreign power such as Great Britain.

The prospects of Spain's regaining the ground lost in the Indies were very good: Mexico was all but pacified; New Granada had been won back by 1815 and was in the capable hands of General Morillo; the junta of Buenos Aires had proved unable to extend its authority to the interior provinces, and a well-equipped Spanish army would make short work of the revolutionary forces, composed as they largely were of the creoles' reluctant peons and black slaves. Indeed, Spain would come very close to crushing altogether the creole bid for independence, and her rule could conceivably have lasted for the whole of the nineteenth century, if not longer. (Cuba, Puerto Rico and the Philippines did not become independent until 1898.) The tide had turned against the advocates of independence, and it would run strongly in favour of the Catholic monarchy until 1820.

After 1814 the creoles faced a very different political situation from when Napoleon had seized the Spanish Crown and had apparently conquered the entire Iberian Peninsula. With the legitimate king back on his throne, opposition to the colonial administration could no longer be construed other than as treason. It seemed possible, therefore, that the traditional colonial pact might be restored, whereby the creoles forsook formal self-government in exchange for the unity and stability which the Catholic monarchy afforded the diverse and racially fragmented societies of the New World. As in the period 1808–10, the majority of creoles had to choose between embracing the devil of absolutism, which they at least knew, and taking a stride into the unknown behind a small number of squabbling radicals.

The leaders of this radical minority were aware of the change in the political circumstances and of the need, in consequence, to make their programmes for independence palatable to the mass of conservative creoles. Even in Buenos Aires—once a hotbed of republicanism—creole leaders were actively seeking a monarchical solution to the independence struggle. Although an accommodation with Ferdinand VII seemed out of the question, given his aversion to constitutionalism, envoys of the Buenos Aires junta had been sent to Europe to look for a prince willing to sit on the throne of an independent kingdom in the River Plate. Influential figures such as Manuel Belgrano, formerly a Jacobin republican and a supporter of Mariano Moreno, now argued for a monarchy under a descendant of the Inca. José de San Martín, a professional soldier who had served in Spain and who was shortly to take command of an army of liberation, also favoured the creation of an independent Spanish American monarchy.

Even that unwavering republican, Simón Bolívar, saw fit to give his programme a very marked conservative slant. Dismayed by the anarchy he had witnessed in New Granada, he concluded that republicanism in South America could not follow the North American model, much less that of the French Revolution. He became more and more convinced that unqualified electoral democracy would lead to catastrophe in societies which he believed had been kept in a condition of political immaturity by what he saw as the 'Spanish tyranny'. Instead, the way forward must be a compromise between authority and democracy. In his Jamaica Letter of 6 September 1815 he revealed a pragmatism born of disillusion, observing that Spanish America should 'not adopt the best system of government, but the one that is most likely to succeed'.[*] Without abandoning his commitment to republicanism, Bolívar now found a model for Spanish American constitutions in the British monarchy, and he envisaged that Great Britain would be invited to become tutor and protector of the nations freed from the Spanish yoke.

These ideological readjustments were accompanied by changes in political and military strategies. Both Bolívar and San Martín saw the futility of direct confrontations with royalist armies. Instead, they would seek the advantage of surprise by seizing vulnerable territory and setting up an independent government, thus offering the creoles an alternative political destiny to the Catholic monarchy. By 1817 San Martín and Bolívar were each ready to undertake new campaigns in their respective theatres of war.

The Wars of Independence in South America

In the River Plate, San Martín put together an 'Army of the Andes', but instead of advancing on Upper Peru, where three previous campaigns had come to grief, he chose to cross into Chile and, having liberated it, to proceed by sea towards Lima, the centre of royalist power in South America. Traversing the Andes in February 1817, he engaged a royalist force at Chacabuco and went on to the capital, Santiago. There he installed a government under Bernardo O'Higgins, a Chilean commander in his army, and in February 1818 independence was formally declared. After the victory at Maipú in April the liberation of Chile was virtually complete, though loyalist troops would continue to resist for a good while longer.

The next task was to prepare for the assault on Peru. For this he received material and financial support from the O'Higgins regime; many Chileans volunteered to serve in the army of liberation and San Martín's small fleet of warships, under the command of the Scottish adventurer Lord Cochrane. was manned mostly by Chilean sailors. Yet San Martín's underlying position was weak. A crucial element in his strategy was the logistical support O'Higgins would provide from liberated Chile. But even before San Martín had set sail for Peru, O'Higgins had run into difficulties: he had assumed dictatorial powers to impose liberal reforms which alienated important sectors of the Chilean élite. He had also failed to destroy the remaining strongholds of loyalist resistance. With O'Higgins's political base visibly deteriorating (he would be driven from office in 1823), the outlook for San Martín, as he set out in August 1820 to take on the might of the Spanish empire, was highly uncertain.

In 1817 Simón Bolívar had returned to Venezuela, where he initiated a campaign in the west, taking the strategic town of Angostura which, being situated on the Orinoco, allowed him to receive assistance by sea as well as providing him with a route upriver into the central plains. By the end of the year he had made contact with José Antonio Páez, the redoubtable leader of the half-caste llaneros (plainsmen), who had been conducting a guerrilla war against the royalists. This time Bolívar was careful not to

---

[*] *Escritos del Libertador* (Caracas, 1964-), vol. 8, p. 241. Quoted in translation by John Lynch. *Simón Bolívar and the Age of Revolution* (University of London, Institute of Latin American Studies' Working Papers, no. 10: London, 1983), p. 15.

repeat the mistake that had cost his Second Republic so dear: he provided certain limited political incentives for the *pardos* and black slaves to fight on his side. The alliance with Páez was to prove vital for the campaign, for not only did widen the ethnic base of the revolution, but it also gave Bolívar access to the central plains, enabling him to circumvent the northern coastal areas and especially Caracas, where General Morillo and the bulk of the royalist forces were concentrated.

At Angostura, Bolívar called a national congress in February 1819 and outlined a constitution for the future republic. He proposed a strong executive president, who would be financially accountable to a legislature consisting, like the British parliament, of two chambers, one elected, the other a hereditary senate. Bolívar also recommended an independent judiciary, and, as a further check on the evils of unlimited democracy, a 'moral power' formed by an unelected body of notable citizens charged with the promotion of virtue in the conduct of public affairs. The congress, however, rejected both the hereditary senate and the moral power.

From the central plains of Venezuela, Bolívar went east towards New Granada, avoiding the royalists in the north, and planning to join with republicans under the command of Francisco de Paula Santander on the other side of the Andes. His objective was to spring an attack on Bogotá, the seat of the viceroyalty. After suffering terrible hardships during the march across the plains and the even more arduous ascent over the freezing heights of the Andes, Bolívar's men linked up with Santander's and the republican army inflicted a decisive defeat on royalist forces at Boyacá in August 1819. When Bolívar entered Bogotá a few days later, New Granada had to all intents and purposes fallen to the revolutionaries. In December the independence of all the provinces of the viceroyalty was declared and the Republic of Colombia was founded. The rebels had created the framework of an alternative state: they had taken the viceregal capital, and large areas of both New Granada and Venezuela had come under their control. But there remained Quito, Panama and the most populated regions of Venezuela, including Caracas; and the main royalist forces under Morillo had yet to be engaged.

For five years after the restoration of Ferdinand (1814–19) the balance of power in the struggle for independence was with the royalists. Nevertheless, the two main secessionist armies in South America had made important strategic gains—they had still to confront the full force of the imperial state, but

before this confrontation there would occur another wholly unexpected change in the political situation which would shift the balance of advantage decisively in their favour.

The Cadiz Mutiny of 1820

The next critical turning-point in the zigzag process of independence came not in the Indies but, once again, in the Peninsula. On 1 January 1820. an army of some 14,000 men, which had been assembled at Cadiz for the express purpose of reconquering the rebel territories of the River Plate, suddenly mutinied. Most garrisons in Spain joined the *pronunciamiento* (revolt) and Ferdinand VII, his army having turned against him, was forced to renounce absolutism and accept the Cadiz constitution of 1812.

Why did the army revolt? The immediate cause had less to do with liberal convictions than with discontent over pay and with plans to reduce the size of the armed forces. But the consequences were so momentous because the Cortes of Cadiz had provided in the 1812 constitution an alternative source of political legitimacy which opponents of the royal will could invoke regardless of whether or not they were actually liberal in ideology. In earlier times this alternative had simply not been available to rebels against the Crown. The truth was that after Napoleon's intervention in the Peninsula it had become impossible for the Spanish Crown to reconstruct its monopoly of legitimacy; the Catholic monarchy itself had been set adrift on the sea of politics, and this latest storm in Cadiz would lead to the end of its authority in America.

The Cadiz mutiny undermined the position of Spanish viceroys and field commanders in the Indies. The new liberal government in Spain ordered the colonial authorities to seek a truce with the insurgents as a preliminary to the negotiation of a settlement of the protracted colonial crisis. As the Spanish American revolutionaries realized, this amounted to capitulation by Spain; for it showed that the Catholic monarchy could not hope fully to regain its authority either in Spain or in America, and, with royal legitimacy so contested and curtailed, what benefits could Spanish liberals offer the colonies that the creoles could not achieve for themselves? There was certainly no reason to submit to a trade monopoly and a political administration run by liberal imperialists in the Peninsula.

In effect, the Cadiz revolt put paid to the one outstanding benefit for which the creoles had been willing to accept colonial restrictions, namely, the unifying, stabilizing authority of the absolute monarchy. Once that had gone, the colonial pact was a dead letter. After 1820 the majority of creoles would move away from their inveterate loyalty to the Crown towards acceptance of the inevitability of independence. There remained, of course, the daunting task of defeating the royalist armies on the field of battle, but the political and psychological war had already been won by the secessionists.

The Independence of Mexico

Nowhere did the sudden shift of political and psychological advantage brought about by the Cadiz mutiny have a more dramatic effect than in Mexico. From 1815 until 1820 the cause of independence still flickered in the resistance offered by a harried force of rebels in the south, led after the death of Morelos by a mestizo, Vicente Guerrero. In November 1820 the viceroy Apodaca sent Agustín de Iturbide, a trusted creole veteran of the campaigns against Hidalgo and Morelos, to deliver the final blow to the secessionists. But news of the Cadiz mutiny had changed Iturbide's attitude to the question of Mexico's ties with Spain: he made contact with the rebel leader Guerrero and forged an alliance with him against the Spanish government. Together they issued the Plan of Iguala on 24 February 1821, and this became the document which steered Mexico through a virtually bloodless transition to independence.

According to the Plan of Iguala, Mexico would become an independent monarchy, limited by the 1812 constitution of Cadiz, with either Ferdinand VII or one of his brothers as emperor; Catholicism would remain the only legitimate religion and the Church would retain its property and privileges; all subjects, including Indians, mestizos and the many Spaniards living in Mexico, would enjoy equality before the law. These were to be the three pillars of the new order—Independence, Religion and Union—and they would be defended by an *Ejército Trigarante*, an Army of the Three Guarantees, formed by a fusion of Iturbide's royalist troops with Guerrero's rebel forces. The Plan offered something—though not everything—to every major interest in Mexico, from Catholic traditionalist to liberal reformer; it even honoured Spain as the mother country, a sentiment that was still shared by most Mexicans. Iguala, in short, was a creative compromise which very soon gelled into a national consensus. Within six months it had received the support of all the principal garrisons in Mexico, and the new viceroy sent out from the Peninsula had to recognize that the country had effectively won its independence, a fact that was ratified by treaty on 24 August 1821. A month later, Iturbide entered Mexico City in triumph and was installed as president of the Regency of the Mexican Empire.

The Plan of Iguala succeeded because it reconciled two historic interests of the creole élites which had never before coincided in the one political settlement: it allowed for legitimate creole self-government, while providing for social authority based on a monarchical and religious framework. It is little wonder, then, that it attracted other regional élites. The new Mexican empire invited the captaincy-general of the Yucatán, as well as the Central American provinces which comprised the Kingdom of Guatemala (namely, Chiapas, Honduras, El Salvador, Nicaragua, Costa Rica and Guatemala itself), to join it under the terms of Iguala. All agreed, except for El Salvador, which was promptly compelled to do so by a Mexican army.

But Spain would seek to destroy the settlement of Iguala by its unwillingness to come to terms with political facts. The liberal government, in the Peninsula refused to recognize Mexican independence. Worse still, neither Ferdinand nor any Spanish prince could be induced to accept the Mexican Crown. This repudiation of a Mexican monarchy by the Bourbons removed the lynchpin of the Iguala Plan, for with a break in dynastic continuity the legitimacy of the Mexican Crown would be compromised beyond repair.

Iturbide, nevertheless, tried to save the institution of monarchy in Mexico. On the evening of 18 May 1822 a public demonstration led by soldiers from his own regiment proclaimed him Agustín I of Mexico; succumbing to popular pressure, congress accepted him as emperor. But Iturbide would prove unable to conjure up the sacred aura of royalty, which alone could command the allegiance of all his subjects. The creole aristocracy would not forgive him for being the son of a merchant, his brother officers regarded him as a political schemer, and Spaniards resident in Mexico still wanted a real prince of the blood. Finally, calls for a republic, which until then had mostly fallen on deaf ears, began to find a response in Mexico. As the consensus which had sustained the Plan of Iguala crumbled, the new creole emperor took arbitrary measures to shore up his authority, and in doing so stirred up even more hostility. In December 1822 an ambitious young colonel, Antonio López de Santa Anna, opportunistically proclaimed a republic and swiftly won the backing of several dissatisfied generals. The bulk of the army came out in support of the rebels and on 19 March 1823 Agustín I abdicated. He would be shot a year later when he returned to Mexico from his European exile on the mistaken assumption that he could regain his throne.

Thus, only two years after the declaration of independence on the basis of the Plan of Iguala, the principle of monarchy had been destroyed by a military *coup d'état*, the first of many in independent Mexico. A federal republic was declared with General Guadalupe Victoria as its first president. The Central American provinces, except Chiapas, seceded, and after a prolonged civil war, their federation broke up into five separate republics. For the next fifty years Mexico itself would be repeatedly torn apart by civil wars, and not the least of the many complicating factors in the labyrinthine affairs of the young Mexican republic was the stubborn survival of conservative hopes for the restoration of a Mexican monarchy, hopes that would not die until well past the middle of the century.

The Independence of South America

In South America, where the insurgencies had been far more substantial than in Mexico, the immediate effect of the Cadiz revolt was to cut the ground from under the feet of the commanders of royalist forces. Ordered by the new liberal government in Spain to offer the rebels a truce, the colonial authorities found that the morale of their troops began to disintegrate; many creole officers and soldiers in the royalist armies started to defect to the insurgents, and even peninsular officers were divided between liberals and absolutists.

The events of 1820 in Spain influenced the tactics employed by San Martín in his campaign to take Peru. Establishing a base north of the capital, he did not attack Lima straight away, calculating correctly that if he waited long enough, the political confusion in the royalist camp would deliver a substantial portion of Peruvian creole opinion to him. San Martín therefore entered into discussions with the colonial administration in order to reach a negotiated settlement. He argued for a solution similar to Iturbide's Plan of Iguala: he wanted to establish a wholly independent constitutional monarchy with a Spanish prince of the blood on the throne. These discussions did not get very far because the royalists were too divided; a military *coup d'état* deposed the viceroy, replacing him with the intransigent José de la Serna, who decided in July 1821 to withdraw from Lima and take to the highlands, where stronger defences could be organized against the secessionists.

In July, therefore, San Martín entered Lima and declared the independence of Peru. But soon he was in trouble: the deeply conservative Lima aristocracy disliked the discriminatory measures he took against peninsular Spaniards, as well as the levies he imposed on creoles to finance his army; and logistical support from Chile was becoming unreliable as the O'Higgins regime ran into difficulties. By 1822, after a year of tactical delay, a delay which was beginning to look like a lack of resolve in the face of the royalist armies entrenched in the sierra, San Martín left for Guayaquil to confer with Simón Bolívar.

For his part, Bolívar had played to the full the advantage given him by the Cadiz mutiny. The Spanish general Morillo, having received orders to seek a truce with the rebels, resigned his post soon after it was declared. Hostilities broke out again within a few months, and in June 1821 Bolívar defeated Morillo's successor at the battle of Carabobo. When Caracas fell some days later, the whole of Venezuela was finally liberated. At the Congress of Cúcuta, Bolívar was acclaimed president of Gran Colombia, a state comprising Venezuela, New Granada and Quito (still to be liberated), and with its capital at Bogotá. A constitution was approved which incorporated many of the Liberator's authoritarian and centralist prescriptions for a republic. Bolívar next turned south and accomplished the conquest of the province of Quito (modern Ecuador) jointly with his lieutenant Antonio José de Sucre.

Thus, when Bolívar arrived to confer with San Martín at Guayaquil on 27 July 1822, he came in triumph as the great Liberator, with a series of resounding military victories to his credit and as head of the vase new independent state of Colombia. By contrast, San Martín's campaign had been bogged down for the past two years in Peru, and his control of Chile was uncertain. Bolívar was clearly in a far superior position, and so, after their famous secret discussions, San Martín chose to withdraw from the fray and leave for Europe, never to return. Bolívar's political victory over San Martín at Guayaquil signified the demise of monarchism as an option for a post-independence settlement; the new states of South America would be given republican constitutions.

Arriving in Peru in September 1823, Bolívar began to prepare for the final offensive against the royalists. By the middle of 1824 he launched his campaign, winning an important battle at Junín, which opened to him the road to Lima, the ultimate prize. In December, while Bolívar was in Lima, Marshal Sucre defeated Viceroy De la Serna's army at the battle of Ayacucho. Spanish power in America had been decisively broken and the Indies were at last free.

G. The Mexican and Cuban Revolutions

Among the many revolutions and conflicts of Spanish America since the independence of the region, the Mexico Revolution of 1910–1920 and the Cuban Revolution of 1959 have perhaps been the most notable. Not only did they radically change their own societies, but many Mexicans and later many Cubans fled to the United States in order to begin a new life, escaping the turmoil of their homelands.

The Mexican Revolution was the first great revolution of the Twentieth Century, foreshadowing the Russian Revolution of 1917. When the corrupt Porfirio Diaz was forced out of office by the mild mannered Francisco Madero in 1910, the aging dictator warned that that "Madero has unleashed a tiger… Let us see if he can control it." Madero was indeed unable to bring stabilization to Mexico and the great revolutionary leaders of Pancho Villa in the north and Emiliano Zapata in the south, and many others, tried to bring their vision of Mexican society to reality. In the end, a modern Mexico was born, a Mexico that continues to evolve today. During the conflict, many Mexicans walked across the mostly unguarded U.S. Mexican border to begin a new life in the north.

Fascinated by the Mexican Revolution and its aftermath during the first half of the Twentieth Century was the muralist Diego Rivera and Frida Kahlo, perhaps the most famous married couple of this critical period in their country's history. For a insight on Frida's life and art, see the CD attached to the *Voices of Latino Culture*, entitled *Life, Rebellion, and Pain Told in Four Paintings of Frida Kahlo*.

Refugees from the Cuban revolution and its aftermath, now nearly 50 years later, arrive in the United States every day, having crossed the dangerous waters between Cuba and Florida. Like the Mexican Revolution, the Cuban Revolution was born in order to combat corruption—in this case the dictatorship of Fulgencio Batista, a onetime Army sergeant. Taking advantage of popular discontent was the revolutionary leader Fidel Castro, assisted ably by the Argentine Ernesto "Che" Guevarra. By January 1, 1959, Castro and his forces had swept down from the Sierra Madre Mountains into the government offices of Havana, to the applause of most Cubans. However, Castro soon decided to put in effect a strict socialist state allied with the Soviet Union. Many Cubans fled the island because of the confiscation of private property, the closing of churches, and the totalitarian rule of Castro's regime. Now, with the retirement of Fidel Castro and the accession of his brother Raul to the presidency of Cuba (2008), the future of the Cuban Revolution in uncertain.

1. THE MEXICAN REVOLUTION

The Porfiriato

Porfirio Díaz was born in 1830 to a low-income family from Oaxaca. He never finished his law studies and joined the army instead. He took the liberal side during the War of the Reform and fought the French in Puebla. Díaz rebellions against Juárez and Lerdo were against presidential reelection and, therefore, in the liberal vein of the constitution of 1857.

Mexico in 1876 was not very different from years past but for a few incipient signs of modernization that had begun to appear during the Restoration. There were still sizable economic problems in agriculture and mining; problems of transportation and lack of decent port facilities; banditry, epidemics, floods, lack of drainage, and a high mortality rate; and, to make matters even more difficult, there was no money.

During his first four years in office, Díaz began to tackle the national economy and placed stiff measures against contraband while creating consular posts along the United States border. Smugglers and bandits crossed the border from both sides, but the president would not permit United States troops to enter Mexico in search of them. Instead, he enlarged the Mexican border patrol. In 1877, after Díaz agreed to honor US $4 million in claims by United States citizens against Mexico, the United States government finally recognized the Díaz government. In 1880, at the end of his term and despite his followers' wishes, he left office. The next president, Manuel González, led the country through a continuation of the modernization program (telegraph lines began to operate, railroad construction was kept apace, and so on). In fulfilling his foreign debt obligations, González stopped paying government officials, a move that led to a harsh campaign against the president. But this time there were no attempts to oust him.

Meanwhile, during González' tenure, Díaz gathered a large following that brought him back to office in 1884. Mexican positivism, embodied in the slogan "order and progress," was the backbone of the modernization scheme supported by the intellectual followers of Barreda, known as *científicos*.

There were material signs of Díaz' determination: telephones, telegraph, underwater cables, public health improvements, public works, and construction of public buildings. The *científicos*, who were led by José Ives Limantour, served as advisers to Díaz and developed a plan for economic recovery that was to be carried out through the next 27 years of the Porfiriato and that was to include the revision of import duties and restrictions and administrative control over the performance of government officials. Such a healthy political and economic climate brought notice to the Mexican administration abroad, and foreign investors began to pump their capital into Mexico.

The Railroad, Mining, and Oil Industries

By 1890 there were almost 3,200 kilometers of railroad track in Mexico held by three companies: the Mexican Central Railroad Company, the Mexican National Railroad Company, and the Sonora Railroad Company. In 1894 the coast-to-coast Tehuantepec Railroad was completed, but it soon became obsolete after the opening of the Panama Canal in 1914. Mexican railroads had expanded from 640 kilometers of track in 1876 to a grand total of 24,000 kilometers of track by 1911. The advent of the train brought modernization to distant areas connected by the railroads.

Investment capital was lured by a new mining code in 1884 that did not enforce ownership of subsoil reserves by the government. (According to an old Iberian legal tradition, these reserves belonged to the state, while exploration rights could be granted to individuals.) Mining taxes were also revised to attract investors. Modern mining technology provoked a boom in the industry and produced large revenues for investors and for the country. Between 1877 and 1908 the production of gold rose 26 times in value, while silver more than tripled its revenues in 1877 alone. Fortunes were made overnight, and in some cases money from mining went into other productive sectors of the economy. There were increased investments, for example, in agriculture and cattle raising.

Foreign investments competed for oil exploration concessions. United States capital and technology founded the Mexican Petroleum Company to exploit oil found near Tampico and Tuxpan along the Gulf coast; British investments went into El águila Company, which started oil operations in the Isthmus of Tehuantepec and then moved to the states of Veracruz, San Luis Potosí, Tamaulipas, and Tabasco. The British concession was the most successful in the long run; it became the major company in the infant Mexican oil industry and would later transform Mexico into one of the major oil producers in the world.

In addition to these industries, Mexico maintained a certain level of growth in the manufacture of other products, such as cement, textiles, tobacco, bricks, and beer. Even the steel industry in Monterrey, the industrial center of Mexican development, continued to grow. All of this was made possible by overall improvements in the tariff system and in the infrastructure of ports, transportation, and long-distance communications. Mexican credit abroad was considered very sound, but the people saw the changes in a much deeper way—in terms of a restored national pride.

Modernization versus Inequalities

The modernization program was brought about at the expense of personal freedom. Díaz made certain that "order" was maintained at all costs for the sake of "progress." Force was used whenever necessary to neutralize opponents of the regime, and there was no freedom of the press. The army and the *rurales* were the forces of repression for the maintenance of the Porfirian peace. Mock elections were held at all levels of government, while Díaz appointed his loyal friends as political bosses. Despite all of the modernization, Mexico was still very rural, and class stratification was entrenched.

Land values increased tremendously with the advent of railroads. It was imperative to have clear title to the land; otherwise, counterclaims could be filed to dispute landownership. Thus, Indian communities lost much of their traditional holdings to the *hacendados*, who held the land and the workers captive through debt peonage for life. All went well for the wealthy, and a dictatorial regime kept the rest of society under control.

The most important development in Mexico during the 30 years of Díaz', "reign" was the growth of the middle sectors of society: white-collar workers, priests, artisans, and small businessmen. There was no class consciousness, but rather a tremendous identification with the models set by the upper class in language and mores and in the image presented by the middle classes. The differences between rich and poor were further aggravated. However, Porfirian Mexico was aware of the stigma that poverty brought to society. The normal practice was to hide the poor, even if by force. During the commemoration of the one-hundredth anniversary of independence in 1910, the Porfiriato had no qualms about barring the poor from Mexico City. It was a question of presenting a good image of the country to foreign dignitaries.

Mexican cultural and intellectual life during the Porfiriato was encouraged as long as the glories of the regime were depicted and its control was not challenged. In the arts and in architecture, only foreign styles were acceptable. Liberal intellectuals, however, continued to voice their opposition to such controls over intellectual expression.

The Revolution

The Porfiriato was marked by the constant violation of the principles of the constitution of 1857. Díaz had been responsible for all kinds of excesses by favoring foreign interests above those of the Mexican peasants and workers, allowing the clergy again to become openly influential in temporal matters, and giving the army a free hand to violate guaranteed civil liberties while opponents to the regime were either co-opted or sent to jail. The "order" that had been maintained for so long was abruptly disrupted in 1910.

Liberal writers and journalists challenged the regime throughout the Porfiriato, but their attacks had become more coordinated with the organization of liberal clubs and a liberal convention at San Luis Potosí in 1900 and 1901 that defended the principles of the constitution of 1857. For the next two years, liberal congresses were held, but the persecution of representatives led many liberals to seek asylum in the United States. The exiles (the Flores Magon brothers, Juan Sarábia, Antonio I. Villareal, Librado Rivera, and others) issued a liberal proclamation on July 1, 1906, from St. Louis, Missouri, that called for the overthrow of Díaz, and they started a publication, *Redención*, to set forth their ideas. The Mexican Revolution was born out of the liberal program, which later would be incorporated into the Constitution of 1917. The program presented in the proclamation of St. Louis introduced new concepts in education, labor relations, land distribution, and agricultural credit. These ideas reached the Mexican workers through issues of *Redención* smuggled across the border. In 1906 and 1907 strikes broke out among the Cananea (in Sonora) mining workers and the textile workers of Río Blanco (in Veracruz), both of which were brutally suppressed by force.

In 1908 an unexpected development brought back real hope to the Mexican people. In an interview with an American reporter, Díaz stated that he would not seek reelection in 1910, and liberals and intellectuals immediately started their political campaign. The most important document of the period was a book by Francisco I. Madero, *The Presidential Succession of 1910*, in which he emphasized universal suffrage and no reelection.

Madero was born in 1873 into a wealthy family in the state of Coahuila. After receiving an upper-class education in Paris and at Berkeley, California, he returned home to take care of the family's business enterprises. Exposure to the hacienda environment and to the workers' complaints made him aware of social inequalities, while Díaz' interventions in local politics broadened his understanding of the underlying political causes of the problems, convincing him that only a major change in the political structure of government could lead to solutions in other areas. Madero campaigned in 22 states and in April 1910 was nominated as the liberal candidate for the next presidential election. In June partly as a result of the mass repression and imprisonment of the anti-Díaz political opposition, Díaz won reelection. Madero, himself imprisoned, was released from jail and soon escaped to the United States.

Meanwhile, Díaz was busy preparing a joint celebration—the one-hundredth anniversary of Mexican independence and his eightieth birthday in September. Mexico City went through a full refurbishing—buildings were dedicated, monuments were unveiled, and champagne was consumed like water during the balls and celebrations attended by the entire diplomatic corps. The streets of the capital were cleared of refuse and undesirables in order to present foreigners with a certain picture of the society created by the Porfiriato. The facade was European, but the underlying problems were Mexican. The grievances of an entire nation would soon engulf Mexico in a violent struggle for land, liberty, and democracy.

The Military Phase

In October 1910 Madero drafted the revolutionary Plan of San Luis Potosí, which called for coordinated revolutionary action to begin on November 20. Copies of the plan were circulated, and the people who revolted were in agreement that Díaz was responsible for their suffering under foreign capitalists, *hacendados*, local political bosses, and rampant corruption. People from all walks of life joined the fighting forces against the dictatorship of Díaz. By January 1911 the revolutionary forces had won significant victories in the state of Chihuahua, and soon the revolution spread through Sonora, Coahuila, Sinaloa, Veracruz, Zacatecas, Puebla, Guerrero, and Morelos. The rebels had the advantage of moving in small units and of having the support of the people in the countryside, while the military depended on supply lines and coordination from the central government. In March 1911 a presidential decree suspended all civil liberties in the country, which allowed anyone concerned with maintaining the status quo to use force against the opposition.

Zapata and Villa

Emiliano Zapata was born in 1877 to a family of poor peasants from the state of Morelos. Zapata followed his parents' ways and worked the land that they had traditionally owned but that was taken away by rich *hacendados* who were protected by the government. Zapata became the spokesman for other peasants from Morelos in their attempts to recover their lands legally. However, he found the situation hopeless and dared to tell them to take up arms against the government that had allowed such abuses against peasants. In response to his rebellious attitude, Zapata was drafted for military service in 1908. Thanks to the interference of a rich *hacendado* who liked Zapata as a worker on the land, he was released from service. He then joined the antireelectionist forces in the southern front centered in Morelos.

Doroteo Arango was born in Durango on October 4, 1877. At age 16 he killed a man for abusing his younger sister, fled to the mountains and, to evade the law, changed his name to Francisco (Pancho) Villa. For the next 15 years Villa was a cattle rustler and a bandit, too wise and too fast for the *rurales* to catch, but sometimes he worked the land. During this period, the Plan of San Luis Potosí was issued, and Villa was persuaded to join the revolutionary forces of Madero. After Madero's victory, Villa remained in the leadership of an irregular army.

The Fall of Díaz

By the time the attack on Ciudad Juárez brought Villa and Madero together, Madero (who was exiled in Texas at the time) was head of a provisional government recognized by the revolutionary forces. Madero vacillated in ordering the attack, fearing intervention from United States forces stationed in El Paso. In the end the revolutionaries took the city on their own initiative. Vacillation had been met with disobedience and underscored the dissension between the political leadership and the military forces. The war was impeded by fighting among various revolutionary groups, but the widespread fighting had one very positive result: the resignation of Díaz, who realized that his long reign had ended by the will of the Mexican people. On May 25, 1911, the 80-year-old dictator presented his resignation to Congress. An interim government was appointed, and Madero triumphantly returned to Mexico City.

Among the people waiting to greet him was Zapata. He had come to claim the land for the peasants of Morelos, which was the only acceptable result of the overthrow of the Díaz regime. Instead, Madero ordered him to disband his troops, and, reluctantly, Zapata acceded to Madero's request. The interim government did not think Zapata was demobilizing fast enough, however, and sent federal troops to disarm the revolutionaries by force. Even though Madero was not responsible for this action, Zapata withdrew his support for him. Finally, new elections were held in October, and in November 1911 Madero assumed the presidency.

Madero's Government

The fall of Díaz raised popular expectations of the new government. Madero soon realized that to the liberals, the Revolution meant political change, but to the Revolutionary fighters it meant radical social and economic transformations that Madero would not be able to fulfill. Madero dealt with the labor and land tenure problems politically through the National Agrarian Commission and the Department of Labor. The only tangible change was that labor groups felt free to organize, and they founded the House of the World's Workers as a meeting place for labor discussions. They were also allowed to publish the newspaper *Luz*. Labor unrest continued, despite the government's attempts to control strikes. Madero's democratic administration was failing its staunchest supporters, and rebellions began to surface.

In November the Zapatista faction revolted under the principles of the Plan of Ayala that asked for restoration of village lands to their rightful owners. The armed revolt spread through the states of Morelos, Guerrero; Tlaxcala, Puebla, Mexico, and even into Mexico City. By 1912 the Zapatista forces had caused severe damage to communications (railroad and telegraph lines) and had won battles with the federal troops. Revolutionaries from several areas began to challenge the new government, and an offensive was launched in March 1912 by Pascual Orozco, who accused Madero of abandoning the principles of the Plan of San Luis Potosí. Orozco was defeated, however, by Victoriano Huerta, who was commander of the federal forces. Meanwhile, Felix Díaz (Porfirio's nephew) was assembling an army in Veracruz to march against Madero, but Madero was able to order his arrest and bring him to Mexico City.

Felix Díaz and other counterrevolutionaries plotted a military coup from inside prison and proceeded to take the National Palace on February 8, 1913. With the aid of loyal troops under Huerta, Madero initially resisted the Díaz forces, but the

Decena Trágica (Ten Tragic Days) followed, and street fighting and chaos overtook the city. On February 18 Huerta joined the coup against Madero and had both the president and Vice President José María Pino Suárez arrested.

Huerta's decision to change sides was made with the knowledge and assistance of United States ambassador Henry Lane Wilson in what became known as the Pact of the Embassy. Huerta extracted a resignation from both Madero and Pino Suárez and had himself appointed secretary of the interior, which made him the heir to the presidency, according to the provisions of the constitution of 1857. That same evening Huerta was sworn in as president. Huerta's indignities had not yet ended: on February 21 Madero and Pino Suárez were assassinated while being transferred to the penitentiary in Mexico City.

The Huerta Dictatorship

Huerta was a poor mestizo from Jalisco whose military career as part of the repressive forces during the Porfiriato was uneventful. Huerta's notoriety came in 1911, when he commanded the federal forces ordered to speed up the demobilization of Zapata's troops. Once in power, opposition to Huerta began to emerge. Venustiano Carranza in Coahuila, Pancho Villa in Chihuahua, and Álvaro Obregón in Sonora formed a front against the dictator under the Plan of Guadalupe, issued in March 1913. Zapata preferred to maintain his troops' independence from the northern coalition, which kept the federal forces fighting on two fronts. Huerta's response was to increase the size of the military by forced conscription. The federal forces terrorized the countryside and looted villages, while political assassinations became a trademark of his rule. The federal treasury was empty, and each faction began issuing its own currency. To top it all, Huerta's government had not been recognized by the United States, which considered him a usurper of the previously elected government. The next move by the White House was to channel aid indirectly to the northern coalition and later to resort to military intervention by early 1914.

Huerta was clearly losing on all fronts by early 1914, but one event precipitated his resignation. As a result of a single incident of trespassing on dock facilities by American sailors at Veracruz and their subsequent arrest, the commander of United States naval forces off Tampico demanded ceremonial salutes of the United States flag by Mexican personnel. When the American demands were not met, United States troops occupied Veracruz. Indignation brought about a series of reprisals against United States citizens and their flag throughout Mexico. Huerta resigned on July 8, 1914.

The Constitution of 1917

After the fall of Huerta, Carranza, chief of the northern coalition, invited all Revolutionary leaders to a military conference, at Aguascalientes to determine the future course of Mexico. A split developed almost immediately: on one side were Carranza, Obregón, and supporters of the plans of San Lius Potosí and Guadalupe; on the other side were Zapata, Villa, and the supporters of the Plan of Ayala. The convention chose Eulalio Gutiérrez, who had the support of the Villistas and the Zapatistas, as provisional president, while Carranza, with Obregón's support, established a dissident government in Veracruz. The country went through another period of civil war and anarchy in which four governments claimed to represent the will of the people: Carranza in Veracruz, Obregón in Mexico City (after Gutiérrez had left the city and established his headquarters in Nuevo León), Roque González Garza (supported by the Zapatistas), and Villa in (in Guanajuato), and later that year Carranza emerged as the victorious commander of the Revolutionary forces. His government was soon recognized by the United States.

United States support for Carranza prompted an aggressive reaction from Villa. After 1916 he frequently raided United States border towns and would then retreat to Mexico. General John J. "Blackjack" Pershing's troops crossed the border in pursuit of Villa several times during 1917. Despite Villa's "victories" over Pershing, the true victor was Carranza. To consolidate his power further and to institutionalize the Revolution, he called for a meeting at Querétaro, where the constitutionalists would draw up a new supreme law for Mexico. The preliminary sessions for the Constituent Congress were held in November 1916. The Congress of Querétaro met for the first time on December 1, 1916. Since then, the inauguration of all Mexican constitutional presidents has taken place on December 1.

Carranza presented his personal draft of a constitution to Congress. It was similar in many ways to the constitution of 1857. but it gave extensive powers to the executive. Congress split over the issue of Carranza's draft. On one side were the Carrancistas, and on the other were the radicals clamoring for broader social reforms. Leading the radical faction in Congress was Francisco Mujica, who proposed a series of provisions to curtail the power of the church.

He would ultimately be instrumental in drafting three important articles of the Constitution: Article 3. which secularized education and at the same time made it free and mandatory; Article 27, which established ownership of the land by Mexicans (not foreigners), restored the Indian lands, and provided for national ownership of all natural resources; and Article 123, which addressed the labor question by establishing eight-hour workdays, six-day work-weeks, equal pay for equal work, and the right to organize and to strike.

The Constitution of 1917, despite Carranza's opposition to its most progressive provisions, was a major advancement for the Mexican people. It was the fruit of the Revolution—an expression of popular will that guaranteed civil liberties and protection against foreign and domestic exploitation.

Carranza's Presidency

After formally accepting the Constitution of 1917, Carranza won the presidential election and was sworn into office on May 1. 1917. Conditions in Mexico were close to chaos once again: the economy had deteriorated further during the years of internal war, communications had been seriously disrupted, and shortages had led to rampant inflation. Land and labor remained the basic issues for the Mexican people, but Carranza chose to overlook the constitutional provisions dealing with these issues. Despite the president's apathy, public enthusiasm for the labor provisions of Article 123 led to the organization in 1918 of the Regional Confederation of Mexican Workers (Confederación Regional de Obreros Mexicanos—CROM), which would provide leadership to the labor movement in the years ahead. Meanwhile. Mexico was relieved that the United States was engaged overseas in World War I, its thoughts and its troops distant from any further intervention in Mexico.

The Revolution was still being fought in several parts of the country, but the fighting was particularly fierce in Morelos. The Zapatistas wanted more than a Magna Charta, for they had very specific grievances and would not accept half-measures or unfulfilled promises. In March 1919 Zapata sent a communication to Carranza in an open letter. According to Zapata, such a letter would make the president aware of the Zapatistas demands while having the whole population as a witness. Zapata further expected that Carranza. once confronted by his fellow countrymen, would be willing to offer them his help. Carranza's response was very different, however. Jesús M. Guajardo, a colonel in the federal army, was contracted to deceive Zapata by offering allegiance to the revolutionaries. Zapata's cautious acceptance of Guajardo's protests of loyalty led to their setting up a meeting on April 10, 1919, at the Hacienda de Chinameca, in Zapata's territory. As he entered the hacienda, Guajardo's men looked prepared to do him honors by firing a gun salute, but instead they fired point-blank at Zapata. The men involved in the plot against Zapata were honored by Carranza.

In 1920 Carranza was about to announce that his choice for the next presidential nominee was Obregón, when Adolfo de la Huerta and Plutarco Elías Calles rose in opposition. Under the Plan of Agua Prieta, they raised a constitutionalist army of northerners and marched on Mexico City. Carranza fled the capital and was assassinated in May while on the road to exile. Carranza left a legacy of being adamantly against major social changes, a stance that frustrated the expectations of the Mexican people after the constitutional victory of 1917.

Life During the War Years

The decade of 1910–20 made a tremendous impact on the lives of the Mexican people. War ravaged the country, fratricidal battles left children orphaned, and the people were hungry and homeless. Military operations inflicted destruction everywhere, to the point of instilling fear at the approach of any soldiers in the countryside. To the peasants, it did not matter which faction came their way, for all troops destroyed their crops, drafted their young, and violated their women. *Soldaderas* (female soldiers) accompanied their men on the battlefield, many fighting side by side with them. Foreigners everywhere were harassed, with or without justification, as the hatred against them that had grown during the Porfiriato was expressed violently.

The fighting reduced the importance of Mexican regionalism because it promoted migration of people throughout Mexico, either by involving them directly in war operations or by causing them to flee the battles in their homelands. The war became an avenue of social mobility, and people were promoted through the ranks on the basis of merit rather than on traditional nepotism and favoritism. The new Mexican began to be recognized for his heroic conduct in battle and for the defense of popular aspirations. The Revolution was already irreversible; it had reshaped the values of an entire society. In time, the ideals of Madero, Zapata, the Flores Magon brothers, and so many others would take their place within Mexican reality.

THE CONSTRUCTIVE PHASE

The Obregón Presidency

The four years of Obregón's presidency (1920–24) were dedicated to beginning the realization of the objectives of the Constitution of 1917. The military phase of the Revolution was over, and the new administration began to build the bases for the next stage of the Revolutionary process of reconstruction.

The country was still suffering the effects of both a long war at home and the post-World War I recession. International market prices were low for all Mexican products, with the exception of oil, which financed the implementation of the Constitution of 1917.

Obregón's choice for secretary of education was José Vasconcelos, who was dedicated to introducing structural changes into the Mexican educational system, as provided by Article 3 of the Constitution. Vasconcelos adapted the curricula of all schools to Mexican reality by teaching students basic skills in reading, writing, mathematics, history, and geography. He believed in integrating the Indian into Mexican society through education. He also believed in instructing through images, and for that purpose he commissioned works by Mexican muralists that would decorate public buildings while teaching the people about important events in Mexican history and the ideals of the Revolution. Schools and libraries were built by the thousands, and books were printed for distribution to these institutions. Despite the secularization of education prescribed by the Constitution, the government realized that it could not afford to close parochial schools, but to counteract the influence of the church it began to promote Protestant groups.

Obregón defended labor through CROM, even to the extent of subsidizing its conventions. The government's support of a national union contributed to its growing membership. But Obregón's sympathies for CROM did not extend to other smaller labor unions, such as the communist Federation of the Mexican Proletariat, because of their affiliations with foreign organizations like the Industrial Workers of the World.

Obregón's agrarian policies were not revolutionary at all. He realized that the Mexican economy could not afford to cut productivity with radical agrarian reform. However, by 1924 about 1,215,000 hectares of land had been distributed to nearly 600 Indian communities. Obregón was careful in handling Article 27 of the Constitution, which restricted landownership by foreigners, because of fear of intervention by the United States. Despite this, American oil companies launched a campaign against the Mexican

government, fearing a possible implementation of Article 27. A joint Mexican-United States commission agreed to meet at Bucarelli Street in Mexico City from May to August 1923, and under the terms of the commission agreements, known as the Bucarelli Agreements, Mexico would uphold the principle of "positive acts." On the one hand, it implied that if a foreign enterprise did not improve the land (in the case of oil, by placing oil drilling equipment), the company's holdings could be claimed after May 1, 1917. On the other hand, the United States would fulfill its part of the agreement by recognizing the Mexican government in 1923.

The political climate was changing, and there was general dissatisfaction over the Bucarelli Agreements. At about the same time, Villa was ambushed and assassinated after he had expressed an interest in returning to a more activist role in Mexican political life. Responsibility for Villa's death was not established, but people believed at the time that it was politically motivated. When the time came for the next presidential nomination, Obregón's choice fell upon his secretary of interior, Calles. A strong opposition rallied against the nomination, and landowners, clergy, military, and others rose in armed rebellion. However, Obregón's position remained secure because he had the support of CROM, the nationalists, and the United States. In the end, Obregón's government had disappointed the more radical Revolutionary factions, as well as certain interest groups, such as the military, wealthy landowners, and conservative Catholics, but it achieved what it had set out to do: to bring Mexico a certain degree of political stability.

Batista's Dictatorship

The elections of 1952 were centered on the elimination of corruption in Cuba's government, and three factions nominated candidates for the presidency. The Ortodoxos had a very good chance of carrying the electorate on a platform promising decency in government, accompanied by a campaign against corruption. However, they lost their hero in August 1951, when Chibás shot himself at the end of one of his broadcasts. The loss of Chibás created a vacuum in the opposition, but Professor Roberto Agramonte was nominated as the new Ortodoxo candidate. The Auténticos wanted a man above suspicion to run against the Ortodoxos. They chose Carlos Hevia, who had been provisional president in 1934, because he was an honest man, though lacking in charisma. The third candidate was Batista, who had been elected in absentia to the Senate in 1948 and had recently returned to Cuba.

The contest between Hevia and Agramonte was favorable to the Auténtico candidate, and Batista realized he had no chance of changing the odds. On March 10, 1952, three months before the elections, Batista took power in a bloodless coup d'état with the help of his military friends at Camp Columbia. He suppressed the electoral process and appointed himself provisional ruler. Within a couple of hours, President Prío and his cabinet went into exile. Twenty years of political development in Cuba had suddenly come to a halt, and it was quickly evident that the next phase would be dominated by a military dictatorship. In short order Batista's men occupied the most important military posts, and Batista justified his actions by accusing Prío of having planned to establish a dictatorship in Cuba. Because of Batista's past record with international interest, he quickly gained recognition for his government by non-communist nations throughout the world. Batista suspended the constitution, dissolved all political parties, and created the Council of State to replace the Cuban Congress. Political dissidents were not immediately harassed, however, and students continued to demonstrate.

Cubans inherently did not trust Batista, however, and they expected to see him piling up more wealth through gambling payoffs. In 1952 sugar production reached 7.2 million tons, and to prevent falling prices, Batista decided to cut production by 2 million tons a year. Public works and small enterprises were favored by the dictator's policies. Overall, his six years in government were characterized by prosperity in exchange for freedom. Resistance kept growing, however, and the dictatorship applied repression even more often and cruelly. By the end of Batista's term, repression had reached unprecedented levels.

Fidel Castro was the son of Spanish sugar planters from the province of Oriente. He studied under the Jesuits and, as a law student at the university, became an Ortodoxo and a follower of Chibás. He was very active in student politics, both at home and abroad, which quite often took violent forms. In 1947 he participated in a failed expedition to assassinate the Dominican dictator Rafael Leónidas Trujillo Molina. As a representative of Cuban students, he attended a preliminary conference for the organization of a Latin American students' union conducted under the auspices of Argentine president Juan Domingo Perón in Bogotá in 1948. While in Colombia, Castro allegedly participated in riots known as the "Bogotazo," which followed the assassination of presidential candidate Eliécer Gaitán. Castro graduated from law school in 1950 and was invited to run as an Ortodoxo candidate to the Chamber of Representatives in the elections of 1952, which were preempted by Batista. After the coup the campaign went on for a short time, during which the daring Castro circulated a petition to depose the Batista government on the grounds of its illegitimacy. The court ruled against his motion that revolutions, in contrast, create their own legitimacy. One of the judges, Manuel Urrutia Lléo, did not comply with the majority, and Castro would not forget his independent and revolutionary stance.

On July 26, 1953, Castro led a revolt in which 165 men attacked the Moncada army barracks near Santiago de Cuba. The attack was a failure, but it planted the seed of future revolutionary fervor. Castro was arrested and sentenced to 15 years in prison. At the end of the trial, on October 16, 1953, the 26-year-old revolutionary delivered a historic statement that ended with the phrase "*la historia me absolverá*" (history will absolve me).

The Moncada attack prompted Batista to proclaim a 90-day state of siege to prevent public protests. By early 1954 the economy was booming, everything seemed to be under control, and he decided to hold the scheduled presidential elections in November. Batista nominated himself as the candidate of his newly formed Progressive Action Party to run against his former opponent, Grau. Grau withdrew his candidacy before the elections, however, on the grounds that the elections were likely to be fixed. A high rate of abstention by the opposition gave Batista the opportunity to inaugurate himself as constitutional president on February 1955.

The Moncada incident would have soon been forgotten but for the repressive measures undertaken by Batista against its participants and other Cuban dissidents. Several groups, among them lawyers, priests, lay Catholics, and students, began to defend the victims of Batista's repression. In May, in response to these pressures and as a measure of his self-confidence, Batista declared a general amnesty that allowed the return of exiled members of the opposition and freed most political prisoners, including Castro and his followers from Moncada. On July 7 Castro left Cuba for exile in Mexico.

In spite of opposition organized and funded by Prío and voiced in the press, times were good. Lower sugar production kept prices from falling, and industrial growth and tourism increased both revenues and the country's reserves of foreign currency. The way in which Cuba checked population growth and inflation was an example to the rest of Latin America. However, corruption and nepotism, which enriched some groups while allowing the rest of the population to grow poorer, were important ingredients in the island's prosperity. Several segments of society opposed Batista: the poor, the neglected labor force (whom Batista had favored in the past), the communists, and the old political and intellectual opposition. To the latter Batista was a profit seeker who had halted the development of democratic institutions.

Meanwhile, in Mexico the 26th of July Movement (Movimiento 26 de Julio—M–26–7), named after the date of the Moncada attack, was organizing Cuban exiles. Military training, fundraising activities, study groups, and clandestine politics were growing in numbers and participants. Ernesto (Che) Guevara, an Argentine doctor, joined the group. The conspirators in Mexico began to contact the Cuban opposition back home and in mid-1956 they issued the Pact of Mexico and later in the year created the Revolutionary Student Directorate (Directorio Estudiantil Revolucionario—DER), whose activities included urban terrorism and sabotage against the government. M–26–7 outfitted an expedition from Mexico, and on board the yacht *Granma* (bought with funds provided by Prío), 81 men set sail for Cuba under Castro's leadership and landed in the province of Oriente on December 2, 1956. A combination of factors preordained their initial failure. Poor communications between the expeditionaries and the Cuban underground, bad weather, and government knowledge of their arrival prompted a counterattack by Batista's forces. The revolutionaries dispersed, but the vast majority were killed or captured. The two Castro brothers, Fidel and Raúl, Guevara, and a handful of others fled to the Sierra Maestra with the help of friendly peasants.

Fidel Castro and the Overthrow of Batista

Batista's regime began to crumble after the landing of the *Granma*. One factor that contributed to the steady decline of Batista's leadership capability was an interview given by Castro to *New York Times* reporter Herbert Matthews in February 1957, after two months of government claims that the revolutionary leader had been killed. After a five-year period of calm, urban terrorism once again became common. While Batista was being publicly criticized at home and abroad, Castro became a folk hero to the underprivileged masses of Latin America.

In the Sierra Maestra, the revolutionaries were training for their next attack. On March 13, 1957, the DER stormed into the Presidential Palace in a frustrated attempt to assassinate the president. Batista's forces increased their repression, and censorship became very rigid. But the guerrilla fighters were not losing any ground either, though they were surrounded by Batista's well-armed forces in Oriente.

If they could not advance outside the sierra, neither could Batista's men penetrate the island's western mountains. Supplies to the revolutionaries kept arriving, mainly from the United States. The *zafra* (sugarcane harvest) of early 1958 marked a period of great violence and police brutality. In April Castro called for a general strike, but it did not materialize because of opposition by the PSP-controlled CTC labor confederation.

Batista's apparent victory over the strikers was a boost to his regime, and he went ahead with plans for elections in November 1958. Batista's candidate, Andrés Rivero Agüero, was named victor over Grau, an Auténtico, and Carlos Márques Sterling, an Ortodoxo, in the fraudulent elections of November 3. United States support had already been withdrawn from the Cuban government in early 1958, when an arms shipment to Cuba had been cancelled. After the rigged elections, it became even more clear that Cuba was being denied a free democratic process. By the end of the year, the revolutionaries had burst out of the Sierra Maestra. With his army deserting in droves, Batista fled into exile on New Year's Day 1959. The following day Guevara took Havana with the help of 600 revolutionaries.

The breakdown of Cuba's authoritarian regime was prompted by a combination of factors, including its political illegitimacy, disrespect for the people's legitimate expectations, and indiscriminate use of repression against political dissidents. Batista's dictatorship had alienated the middle classes. Thus, by the end of the 1950s, the traditional popular forces had been neutralized, and there was no other political group capable of offering the necessary leadership to all Cubans. Coercion was the only path open to the dictatorship in dealing with the revolutionary forces of the opposition, who were able to embody popular aspirations and turn the revolution into a truly popular one. Clientelism had prevented the development of a democratic process in Cuba prior to 1959, and its breakdown created new hopes for change.

REVOLUTIONARY CUBA

The End of Prerevolutionary Institutions, 1959–60

The fall of Batista left a political vacuum in Cuba, even though the revolutionary elite represented by Castro and his followers acquired control of the decisionmaking process. Castro was committed to political democracy and social reforms as defended by José Martí. The first revolutionary government was a facade, with Urrutia in the presidency. Urrutia was the judge who had voted in favor of the revolutionaries in the wake of the aborted 1952 elections. On February 16, 1959, Castro became prime minister, but because of conflicts between himself and the president, Castro resigned his post on July 17. The conflict was related to Urrutia's anticommunism, but Castro was initially unable to dismiss him because Urrutia was a patriot and considered an honest man. Castro had provided the Cuban populace with enough reason for withdrawing support from the president, however, and the general clamor reached such proportions that Urrutia had to take refuge in the Venezuelan embassy. Osvaldo Dorticós Torrado, a distinguished lawyer and aristocrat from Cienfuegos who was Castro's choice to replace Urrutia, became president on July 18. A loyal friend of Castro, the brilliant Dorticós announced to a cheering crowd on July 26 that, pressed by popular demand, Castro had agreed to resume his post as prime minister.

The first stage of the Cuban Revolution was characterized by the liquidation of the old power groups (the military, political parties, labor unions, and agricultural and professional associations) and their replacement by new revolutionary bodies, such as the Rebel Army, the militia, and the Committees for the Defense of the Revolution (Comités de Defensa de la Revolucion—CDRs). Few political organizations established during the prerevolutionary days were allowed to continue to operate, except the M–26–7, the DER, and the PSP. But their effectiveness was limited by the revolutionary elite, who controlled all aspects of the decisionmaking process. In the early days the elite's decisions were legitimized by popular acclamation at mass rallies. The confiscation of sugar lands began in mid-1960, and the collectivization of the means of production was coupled with economic management by the revolutionary elite.

Early revolutionary policies were formulated in response to the expectations of the middle sectors of Cuban society, which had backed the struggle against Batista. These included land reform, improvement of salary and benefits to workers, diversification of agriculture—less dependence on sugar—industrialization, regulation of foreign enterprises, and administrative reform. Wealth and income were redistributed to the middle and lower sector of society. Services improved and were extended to the whole population through social services and lower utility rates, taxes, and rents. In May 1959 the Law of Agrarian Reform created the National Institute for Agrarian Reform (Instituto Nacional de Reforma Agraria—INRA) to assist rural workers. In order to eliminate the traditional *minifundium* (small landholding) and latifundium (large landholding). it

established a minimum size of agricultural properties at 27 hectares for individuals and placed upward limits of 400 hectares on holdings by agro-industries. The country was divided into 28 zones under the administration of INRA, which also had the responsibility of providing health and educational services to the population. By 1961 land reform policies had already redistributed over 1 million hectares of land, 167,000 sugar workers had joined cooperatives, and about 50,000 still worked for wages at private farms. That same year saw the creation of the National Association of Small Farmers (Asociación Nacional de Agricultores Pequeños—ANAP). The revolutionary government had kept its promises to the underprivileged masses that rallied behind the new regime, while antagonizing the traditional propertied classes.

Dependence upon a single crop was an obstacle to development, and it made the Cuban economy vulnerable to fluctuations in production and in sugar prices in the international markets (particularly in the United States). To diminish dependence on sugar, the revolutionaries felt that Cuba had to industrialize through import substitution. Industrial development, it was felt, would free Cuba from its internal dependence on sugar, create new jobs, reduce imports, and diversify exports. Agrarian reform gave the government the necessary power to restructure the agricultural sector, making sugar the most important item in the agenda. On July 5, 1960, however, the United States canceled Cuba's quota for sugar exports to the United States. Cuba then nationalized United States enterprises operating in the country, including 36 *centrales*, the Cuban Telegraph and Telephone Company, the Cuban Electric Company, and all oil refineries. Three hundred eighty–two other large enterprises, all Cuban, and most foreign banks were nationalized on October 13. Only the Canadian institutions received compensation from the revolutionary government. Finally, on October 17 the remaining United States banking institutions were nationalized. These steps enabled Cuba to quicken the pace of socialization of the means of production.

As time went on, the revolutionary process grew more radical. The CDRs became the right arm of the Revolution, reaching down into the neighborhoods in constant vigilance against possible enemies of the Revolution. Lacking a democratic electoral process, the Revolution became the sole political arbiter. Dissidents were scorned and linked to United States interests. The main opposition to the regime came from both the People's Revolutionary Movement and the Revolutionary Movement of

Redemption, whose objective was to destabilize the consolidation of the leftist government. There was also marked dissension within the M–26–7 and between Castroites, whose loyalty to Castro was unconditional, and the former communists, who felt closer to Guevara and Raúl Castro. The nonradical groups lost, while greater power was shared among the Castroites (also known as *fidelistas*), *guevaristas* (followers of Guevara), and *raulistas* (followers of Raúl Castro). Above all factions stood Fidel Castro, who relied upon his charisma to justify his actions through magnificent oratory.

Relations between Cuba and the United States during the first period of the Revolution went from mutual uncertainty all the way to the rupture of relations and military action. In 1959 the Cuban communists from the PSP began applying pressure on Moscow in order to secure Soviet assistance and protection. The Kremlin and the White House, however, were in a process of negotiation that had begun with a meeting between President Dwight D. Eisenhower and Premier Nikita Khrushehev in September 1959. At this time Moscow's engagement in Cuba would have hampered these bilateral efforts.

In February 1960, however, First Deputy Premier Anastas Mikoyan of the Soviet Union visited Havana and signed an agreement for credits of US$100 million for the purchase of industrial equipment and technical assistance. The Soviet Union also agreed to purchase almost 400,000 tons of sugar in 1960 and another 4 million tons by 1964. Diplomatic relations between the two countries were established on May 8, 1960, three days after the Soviets announced the shooting down of a United States U2 reconnaissance plane over its airspace. In March, following the Cuban-Soviet economic agreement, the United States had already decided to recruit, train, and outfit a Cuban exile force. This decision would lead to the fateful events of 1961.

Part III
Readings
from the United States

A. Latinos in the United States

As was said earlier, Latinos now make up more than 15.1% of the total population of the United States. But who *are* the Latinos? As was noted in the *Voices of Latino Culture*, a good working definition of *Latino* (or *Hispanic*, a term also used by many in the United States as well as the Census Bureau) is one who speaks Spanish or had an ancestor that spoke Spanish.

As it turns out, it might be more accurate to speak of the "Latino cultures" of the United States, for those who prefer to refer to themselves as "Latino" might be quick to add Mexican-American, Puerto Rican, Cuban-American, Guatemalan, Honduran, *salvadoreño*–all indicating the original country of the family. When Earl Shorris was writing his seminal text *Latinos: A Biography of the People*, a close friend, Margarita Avila, advised him to tell his readers that "we are not all alike."

In the accounts that follow, a brief history is given of the three most numerous Latino groups in the United States–Mexican-Americans, Puerto Ricans, and Cuban-Americans. Following these histories, a brief overview of other Latinos from Central and South America is given. Each of these communities has its own story, its own history, its unique experience living in the United States, and a unique experience of meeting and knowing *other* Latinos in the United States.

After a general survey of the history of Mexican-Americans, two additional readings are given: a panoramic view of the war in Texas (1835–1836), including the battle of the Alamo, and an account of the U.S.-Mexican War of 1846–1848. These conflicts resulted in the loss of over half the country of Mexico as a sacrifice to the United States' adherence to its dream of *manifest destiny*, events well remembered and mourned even today in Mexico. As a result of the Treaty of Guadalupe Hidalgo which ended the U.S.-Mexican War (1848), many Mexicans awoke the next morning in the new U.S.-conquered territories —California, Arizona, New Mexico, and parts of Colorado, Utah, Wyoming, and Nevada—and found themselves face to face with another culture.

Finalizing our section on Mexican-Americans are brief accounts of the Sleepy Lagoon murder case of 1942 and the Los Angeles Zoot Suit riots of 1943. This is the period of the *Pachuco* memorialized in the great play and film by Luis Valdez, *Zoot Suit*. Taking place during World War II, in which many Mexican-Americans were serving in the U.S. armed forces, the Sleepy Lagoon "show" trial and the sight of American servicemen beating up Zoot suitors on the streets of Los Angeles revealed the injustice that many Mexican-Americans were suffering.

One sympathetic observer—none other than First Lady Eleanor Roosevelt—wrote from Washington that the riots were indeed a sign of a minority being mistreated, saying that "the question goes deeper than just [Zoot] suits. It is a racial protest." Thus the emergence of the struggle for civil rights in the decade of the 1940s lays the foundation for the Chicano movement of the 1960s as well as the ultimate success of the charismatic farm-labor leader, César Chávez (1927–1993).

Puerto Rico is presently a U.S. commonwealth (in Spanish, it is called *Estado Libre Asociado*). All Puerto Ricans in the island of Puerto Rico and on the mainland United States are U.S. citizens. However, as a commonwealth, the island of Puerto Rico does not have representatives in the House of Representatives or the Senate. Recently, Puerto Ricans have voted on three separate proposals: (1) to remain a commonwealth, (2) to become a state, and (3) to declare independence. In 1993 and 1998, the proposal for statehood lost by small margins, with the status quo (commonwealth) winning; the vote for an independent state has never reached beyond 5%. Will Puerto Rico soon become the fifty-first state? Or will it remain a commonwealth for the near future?

Beginning this section on the histories of Latino communities in the United States are some comments by Roberto Suro. In his essay, Suro discusses some of the contemporary issues confronting Latinos living in the United States, such as the conflict of cultures, the stress of traditional families, ethnic and racial conflicts, and cultural stereotypes. In addition, television personality Jorge Ramos reflects on the impossibility of "A Day without a Mexican" in California.

In general, Latino communities face many of the same challenges of acceptance encountered by other immigrants to the United States, such as the Irish in the 1840s and the Italians at the turn of the century. One difference of Latino immigration is accurately pointed out in director Gregory Nava's film *Selena*. In a scene from that film, Edward James Olmos, in the role of Selena's father, Abraham, points south to Mexico and reminds his children that "Japanese-Americans, Italian-Americans, German-Americans, their homeland is on the other side of the ocean; ours is right next door, right over there." Thus the cultural roots of many Latino families are nourished by the proximity of their former countries and the presence and comfort of spoken Spanish.

1. THEY ARE HERE

On Imelda's fifteenth birthday, her parents were celebrating everything they had accomplished by coming north to make a new life in the United States. Two short people in brand-new clothes, they stood in the driveway of their home in Houston and greeted relatives, friends, and neighbors, among them a few people who had come from the same village in central Mexico and who would surely carry gossip of the party back home. A disc jockey with a portable stereo presided over the backyard as if it were a cabaret instead of a patch of grass behind an overcrowded bungalow where five people shared two bedrooms. A folding table sagged with platters of tacos and fajitas. An aluminum keg of beer sat in a wheelbarrow atop a bed of half-melted ice cubes. For Imelda's parents, the festivities that night served as a triumphant display of everything they had earned by working two jobs each. Like most of the other adults at the party, they had come north to labor in restaurants, factories warehouses, or construction sites by day and to clean offices at night. They had come to work and to raise children in the United States.

Imelda, who had been smuggled across the Rio Grande as a toddler, wore a frilly dress ordered by catalog from Guadalajara, as befits a proper Mexican celebrating her *quinceañera*, which is the traditional coming-out party for fifteen-year-old Latin girls. Her two younger sisters and a little brother, all U.S. citizens by birth, wore new white shirts from a discount store. Their hair had been combed down with sharp, straight parts and dabs of pomade.

When it came time for Imelda to dance her first dance, her father took her in his arms for one of the old-fashioned polkas that had been his favorite when a band played in the town square back home. By tradition, boys could begin courting her after that dance. Imelda's parents went to bed that night content they had raised their children according to proper Mexican custom.

The next morning at breakfast, Imelda announced that she was pregnant, that she was dropping out of school, and that she was moving in with her boyfriend, a Mexican-American who did not speak Spanish and who did not know his father. That night, she ate a meal purchased with food stamps and cooked on a hot plate by her boyfriend's mother. She remembers the dinner well. "That night, man, I felt like an American. I was free."

This is the promise and the peril of Latino immigration. Imelda's parents had traveled to Texas on a wave of expectations that carried them from the diminishing life of peasant farmers on a dusty *rancho* to quiet contentment as low-wage workers in an American city. These two industrious immigrants had produced a teenage welfare mother, who in turn was to have an American baby. In the United States, Imelda had learned the language and the ways. In the end, what she learned best was how to be poor in an American inner city.

Latino immigration delivers short-term gains and has long-term costs. For decades now, the United States has engaged in a form of deficit spending that can be measured in human lives. Through their hard work at low wages, Latinos have produced immediate benefits for their families, employers, and consumers, but American society has never defined a permanent place for these immigrants or their children and it has repeatedly put off considering their future. That future, however, is now arriving, and it will produce a reckoning. The United States will need new immigration policies to decide who gets into the country. More importantly, the nation will need new means of assuring political equality and freedom of economic opportunity. Soon Americans will learn once again that in an era of immigration, the newcomers not only demand change; they create change.

When I last met Imelda, she was just a few weeks short of her due date, but she didn't have anything very nice to say about her baby or her boyfriend. Growing up in Houston as the child of Mexican immigrants had filled her with resentment, especially toward her parents, and that was what she wanted to talk about.

"We'd get into a lot of yelling and stuff at home because my parents, they'd say, 'You're Mexican. Speak Spanish. Act like a Mexican girl,' and I'd say, 'I'm here now and I'm going to be like the other kids.' They didn't care."

Imelda is short and plump, with wide brown eyes and badly dyed yellow hair. She wore a denim shirt with the sleeves ripped off, and her expression was a studied pout. Getting pregnant was just one more way of expressing anger and disdain. She is a dimestore Madonna.

Imelda is also a child of the Latino migration. She is a product of that great movement of people from Latin America into the United States that is older than any borders but took on a startling new meaning when it gradually gained momentum after the 1960s and then turned into something huge in the 1980s. Latino immigrants were drawn north when America needed their services, and they built communities known as barrios in every major city. But then in the 1990s, as these newcomers began to define their permanent place here, the ground shifted on them. They and their children—many of them native-born Americans—found themselves struggling with an economy that offered few opportunities to people trying to get off the bottom. They also faced a populace sometimes disconcerted by the growing number of foreigners in its midst. Immigration is a transaction between the newcomers and the hosts. It will be decades before there is a final tally for this great wave of immigration, but the terms of the deal have now become apparent.

Imelda's story does not represent the best or the worst of the Latino migration, but it does suggest some of the challenges posed by the influx. Those challenges are defined first of all by demography. No other democracy has ever experienced an uninterrupted wave of migration that has lasted as long and that has involved as many people as the recent movement of Spanish-speaking people to the United States. Twelve million foreign-born Latinos live here. If immigration and birth rates remain at current levels, the total Hispanic population will grow at least three times faster than the population as a whole for several decades, and Latinos will become the nation's largest minority group, surpassing the size of the black population a few years after the turn of the century. Despite some differences among them, Latinos constitute a distinctive linguistic and cultural group, and no single group has ever dominated a prolonged wave of immigration the way Latinos have for thirty years. By contrast, Asians, the other large category of immigrants, come from nations as diverse as India and Korea, and although the Latino migration is hardly monolithic, the Asian influx represents a much greater variety of cultures, languages, and economic experiences. Moreover, not since the Irish potato famine migration of the 1840s has any single nationality accounted for such a large share of an immigrant wave as the Mexicans have in recent decades. The 6.7 million Mexican immigrants living in the United States in 1996 made up 27 percent of the entire foreign-born population, and They outnumbered the entire Asian immigrant population by more than 2 million people. Latinos are hardly the only immigrants coming to the United States in the 1990s, but they will define this era of immigration, and this country's response to them will shape its response to all immigrants.

Latinos, like most other immigrants, tend to cluster together. Their enclaves are the barrios, a Spanish word for neighborhoods that has become part of English usage because barrios have become such a common part of every American city. Most barrios, however, remain a place apart, where Latinos live separated from others by custom, language, and preference. They are surrounded by a city but are not part of it. Imelda lived in a barrio named Magnolia Park, after the trees that once grew along the banks of the bayou there. Like other barrios, Magnolia is populated primarily by poor and working-class Latinos, and many newly arrived immigrants start out there. Magnolia was first settled nearly a hundred years ago by Mexicans who fled revolution in their homeland and found jobs dredging the ship channel and port that allowed Houston to become a great city. Latinos continued to arrive off and on, especially when Houston was growing. Since the 1980s, when the great wave of new arrivals began pouring into Magnolia, it hasn't mattered whether the oil city was in boom or bust—Latinos always find jobs, even when they lack skills and education. Most of Magnolia is poor, but it is also a neighborhood where people go to work before dawn and work into the night.

Like other barrios, Magnolia serves as an efficient port of entry for Latino immigrants because it is an easy place to find cheap housing, learn about jobs, and keep connected to home. Some newcomers and their children pass through Magnolia and find a way out to more prosperous neighborhoods where they can leave the barrio life behind. But for millions like Imelda who came of age in the 1990s, the barrios have become a dead end of unfulfilled expectations.

"We could never get stuff like pizza at home," Imelda went on, "just Mexican foods. My mother would give me these silly dresses to wear to school. No jeans. No jewelry. No makeup. And they'd always say, 'Stick with the Mexican kids. Don't talk to the Anglos; they'll boss you. Don't run around with the Chicanos [Mexican-Americans]; they take drugs. And just don't go near the *morenos* [blacks] for any reason.'"

Imelda's parents live in a world circumscribed by the barrio. Except for the places where they work, the rest of the city, the rest of America, seems to them as remote as the downtown skyline visible off in the distance on clear days. After more than a dozen years, they speak all the English they need, which isn't much. What they know best is how to find and keep work.

Imelda learned English from the television that was her constant childhood companion. Outside, as Magnolia became a venue for gangs and drug sales, she learned to be streetwise and sassy. Growing up fast in Magnolia, Imelda learned how to want things but not how to get them.

Many families like Imelda's and many barrios like Magnolia are about to become protagonists in America's struggles with race and poverty. Latino immigrants defy basic assumptions about culture and class because they undermine the perspective that divides the nation into white and nonwhite, a perspective that is the oldest and most enduring element of America's social structure. Are Latinos white or nonwhite? There is only one correct answer, though it is often ignored: They are neither one nor the other. This is more than a matter of putting labels on people. Americans either belong to the white majority or to a nonwhite minority group. That status can determine access to social programs and political power. It decides the way people are seen and the way they see the world. White and nonwhite represent two drastically dissimilar outcomes. They constitute different ways of relating to the United States and of developing an American identity. Latinos break the mold, sometimes entering the white middle-class mainstream, often remaining as much a group apart as poor blacks.

Most European immigrants underwent a period of exclusion and poverty but eventually won acceptance to the white majority. This process of incorporation occurred across generations as the immigrants' economic contributions gained recognition and their American-born children grew up without foreign accents. Too many Latinos are poor, illegal, and dark-skinned for that path to serve as a useful model.

African-Americans traveled an even greater distance to achieve levels of material and political success unthinkable fifty years ago, but as a racial group, they remain juxtaposed to the white majority. Blacks have formally become part of the body politic, but they remain aggrieved plaintiffs. Latino immigrants lack both the historical standing and the just cause to win their place by way of struggle and petition. And these newcomers are not likely to forge an alliance with blacks, but instead, these two groups are already becoming rivals.

Neither the European ethnics nor the African-Americans were free to choose the means by which they became part of American society. Their place in this country is a product of history, and in each case it is a history of conflict. After centuries of slavery and segregation, it took the strife and idealism of the civil rights era to create a new place for African-

Americans within the national identity. The Irish, the Italians, and other European ethnics had been coming here for decades but did not win full acceptance until after the Great Depression and World War II reforged and broadened the American identity to include them. Now the Latinos stand at the gate, looking for a place in American society, and the conflict that will inevitably attend their arrival is just beginning to take shape.

Latinos are different from all other immigrants past and present because they come from close by and because many come illegally. No industrialized nation has ever faced such a vast migration across a land border with the virtual certainty that it will continue to challenge the government's ability to control that border for years to come. No immigrant group has carried the stigma of illegality that now attaches itself to many Latinos. Unlike most immigrants, Latinos arrive already deeply connected to the United States. Latinos come as relations, distant relations perhaps, but familiar and connected nonetheless. They seem to know us. We seem to know them, and almost as soon as they are in the house, they become part of our bedroom arguments. They are newcomers, and yet they find their culture imbedded in the landscape of cities that have always had Spanish names, such as Los Angeles and San Antonio, or that have become largely Spanish-speaking, such as Miami and New York. They do not consider themselves strangers here because they arrive to something familiar.

They come from many different nations, many different races, yet once here they are treated like a pack of blood brothers. In the United States, they live among folk who share their names but have forgotten their language, ethnic kinsmen who are Latinos by ancestry but U.S. citizens by generations of birthright. The newcomers and the natives may share little else, but for the most part they share neighborhoods, the Magnolias, where their fates become intertwined. Mexican-Americans and Puerto Ricans account for most of the native-born Latino population. They are the U.S.-made vessel into which the new immigration flows. They have been Americans long enough to have histories, and these are sad histories of exploitation and segregation abetted by public authorities. As a result, a unique designation was born. "Hispanics" became a minority group. This identity is an inescapable aspect of the Latino immigrant experience because newcomers are automatically counted as members of the group for purposes of public policy and because the discrimination that shaped that identity persists in some segments of the American public. However, it is an awkward fit for several reasons. The historical grievances that led to minority group designation for Latinos are significant, but compared to slavery or Jim Crow segregation they are neither as well known nor as horrible. As a result, many Americans simply do not accept the idea that Latinos have special standing, and not every native Latino embraces this history as an inescapable element of self-concept. Moreover, Latinos do not carry a single immutable marker, like skin color, that reinforces group identity. Minority group status can be an important element of a Latino's identity in the United States, but it is not such a clear and powerful element of American life that it automatically carries over to Latino immigrants.

"Hispanic" has always been a sweeping designation attached to people of diverse cultures and economic conditions, different races and nationalities, and the sweep has vastly increased by the arrival of immigrants who now make up about 40 percent of the group. The designation applies equally to a Mexican-American whose family has been in Texas since before the Alamo and a Mexican who just crossed the Rio Grande for the first time. Minority group status was meant to be as expansive as the discrimination it had to confront. But now for the first time, this concept is being stretched to embrace both a large native Latino population with a long undeniable history of discrimination and immigrants who are just starting out here. The same is occurring with some Asian groups, but the Latino phenomenon has a far greater impact because of the numbers involved. Latino immigrants are players in the old and unresolved dilemma of race in America, and because they do not fit any of the available roles, they are a force of change.

Like all other newcomers, Latino immigrants arrive as blank slates on which their future course has yet to be written. They are moving toward that future in many directions at once, not en masse as a single cohesive group. Some remain very Latino; others become very American. Their skin comes in many different colors and shades. Some are black, and some of them can pass very readily as white. Most Latinos arrive poor, but they bring new energy to the labor force even as they multiply the ranks of the chronically poor. Latino immigrants challenge the whole structure of social science, politics, and jurisprudence that categorizes people in terms of lifetime membership in racial or ethnic groups. The barrios do not fit into an urban landscape segregated between rich and poor, between the dependent and the taxed.

Latino immigrants come in large numbers. They come from nearby. They join fellow Latinos who are a native minority group. Many arrive poor, illegally, and with little education. Those are the major ingredients of a challenge unlike any other.

2. THE MEXICAN-AMERICAN EXPERIENCE

Introduction

Today Mexican Americans are the fastest growing ethnic group in American Society. In 1993 there were approximately 14 million Mexican Americans in the United States, which gave this country the largest population of Mexicans outside of Mexico and the fifth largest concentration of Latinos in the world. With an average immigration rate of 155,419 per year (since 1970) the flow of Mexican immigrants is the highest of any group. Since their fertility rate is also among the highest of any group, their numbers will certainly increase.

For example, between 1970 and 1980 the Mexican origin population experienced a 93 percent increase. From a population of 8.7 million in 1980, their population increased to 12.6 million by 1990. Over the decade this represents a growth rate of 44.8 percent, compared to a national growth rate of only 9.5 percent, over the same period. The population projections predict that the Mexican American population will exceed 17 million by the year 2000. Eight out of ten (79.3%) Mexican Americans live in either California (6,119,000 or 48.4%) or Texas (3,891,000 or 30.9%). Today (1993) one out of five (20.6%) of the residents of California are of Mexican origin and it is estimated that by the year 2000 they will represent three out of ten of the state's population.

Mexicans in the Southwest: 1821–1929

The year 1519 not only marked the arrival of Hernando Cortés in Mexico and the onset of the conquest of Native Americans, but also resulted in the extension of Spanish domination throughout the Southwest. Three hundred years later (1821), Mexico gained its independence from Spain.

When compared to the United States, Mexico was not a strong military force and public opinion in the United States was very supportive of expansionism, and the philosophy of Manifest Destiny supplied the needed justification for America's expansionist goals. In a few short years Texas became the focal point of America's expansionist ambitions.

In 1821 Mexico granted Stephen F. Austin permission to establish a permanent settlement in Texas. By the late 1830s there were 20,000 settlers in Texas. Before long the American and European settlers in Texas viewed the Mexicans as intruders. The Texas revolt (1835) concluded with the defeat of the Mexicans at the Battle of San Jacinto (1836). Texas became a republic (1836–1845) and gained admission into the Union in 1845. This resulted in the declaration of war with Mexico, in May of 1846 (Acuña, 1988:5–15).

The Treaty of Guadalupe Hidalgo (1848), ended the war between the United States and Mexico, and gave the United States (what is now), California, New Mexico, Nevada, and parts of Colorado, Arizona, and Utah. In return Mexico received $15 million and promised to recognize Texas as part of the United States. The treaty also granted all the rights of American citizenship to those Mexican nationals living in the American Southwest at the time (Sanders, 1950:2). As a result, 75,000 Mexican nationals were granted, (1) American citizenship, (2) the right to religious freedom, (3) all property rights, and (4) the right to maintain their culture and traditions (Moquin and Van Doren, 1971:241–249).

Unfortunately these treaty provisions were quickly forgotten, as Mexicans living in the Southwest were treated as a conquered and defeated people. In short order their constitutional rights were ignored, their land was taken, and they were relegated to the lowest level of social existence. But with the construction of railroads and the development of the cattle and agricultural industries in the Southwest, Mexicans were considered an ideal source of cheap labor. Mexicans living in Los Angeles and Santa Barbara were hired by cattle barons to maintain their herds and move their cattle to market (Pitt, 1971:244–276). And the demand for Mexican labor increased significantly following the completion of the transcontinental railroad (1869), since crops grown in California could now be transported to the lucrative Eastern markets (McWilliams, 1971:61, 63).

The combination of the development of a rail system and the expansion of agricultural production in the Southwest resulted in an ever increasing need for cheap, tractable labor. Consequently Mexicans were eagerly sought by the railroads and growers throughout the Southwest. By the mid-1880s Mexican laborers constituted 70 percent of the section crews and 90 percent of the extra gangs on the railroads (McWilliams, 1968:168). And by the turn of the century, the railroad companies were sending labor contractors into the interior of Mexico (Cardoso, 1980:58).

The development of the agricultural industry in the Southwest was supported by federal funds, as the Federal Reclamation Act (1902) provided funds for the construction of massive irrigation projects. Besides the thousands of Mexican laborers recruited for the construction of canals, dykes, and reservoirs, thousands of other Mexicans cleared the deserts and prepare the soil for cultivation (Fernandez, 1977:97; Gann and Duignan, 1986: 36–41).

The *Mejicanos* were not only attracted by the promises of labor recruiters, the availability of jobs, higher rates of pay, and the ease of transportation between the U.S. and Mexico, but they were also escaping a life of poverty in their homeland. After 1910 they were also escaping from the ravages of the Mexican Revolution (1910–1924), when almost half a million fled the violence and bloodshed. Between 1900 and 1929, over 715,000 Mexicans crossed the border into the United States.

In terms of the number of Mexicans living permanently in the United States, there were 42,435 in 1870, 68,399 in 1880, 77,853 in 1890, 103,393 in 1900, and 221,915 in 1910. By 1920 the Mexican origin population in the United States was almost half a million (486,418) (Dept. of Industrial Relations, 1930). At the turn of the century seven out of ten (68.7%) of all Mexicans lived in Texas and less than one out of ten (7.8%) lived in California. By 1920 only half (51.8%) lived in Texas and one out of five (18.2%) lived in California (Dept. of Industrial Relations, 1930). Three out of four (73.5%) of the Mexicans living in California in 1920 were concentrated in southern California (Dept. of Industrial Relations, 1930:49).

The Great Depression

According to the census there were 1.5 million Mexicans living in the United States in 1930. Although there were more Mexicans living in the United States at the time, that is given the census under count and the fact that thousands of Mexicans crossed the border without inspection until the Border Patrol was established in 1924 (Reisler, 1976:12–13). But with the failure of thousands of businesses and the loss of millions of jobs in the United States during the Great Depression, a very critical look was given to all Mexicans.

With an unemployment rate of 25 to 30 percent it was not long before Anglo Americans were willing to pick corps in the field. In addition, the dust bowl conditions in Arkansas, Oklahoma, and Texas attracted thousands of Anglo migrants to California. Before long farmers established a policy of hiring their own, rather than the *Mejicanos*, who they said should return to Mexico. In a short time Mexicans were perceived as the competition by white labor (Majka and Majka, 1982:105–108).

In response to the dire economic conditions during the Great Depression the government created a

Repatriation Program. The objective of this program was to encourage Mexicans, many of whom were American citizens, to return voluntarily to Mexico. As a result of this program half a million Mexicans and Mexican Americans, primarily from Texas and California, were deported (Meier and Rivera, 1972:164). The Repatriation Program sent a clear message, that is Mexican laborers could be called upon when needed and deported when they were no longer needed. In effect Mexico was considered a reservoir of surplus labor for the American economy (Guerin-Gonzales, 1994).

In 1931, as a cost saving measure, the city of Los Angeles instituted a Repatriation Program of its own. The mayor of Los Angeles estimated that the cost of $14.70 to ship one person by rail to Mexico City was less than a week's board and lodging offered by the city's social services department to the indigent. During the first three months of the program it is estimated that the city saved $350,000 (McWilliams, 1933). From 1931 to 1934, the city of Los Angeles ordered the deportation of more than 13,000 Mexicans. Most unfortunately, many of these deportees were children born in the United States (Hoffman, 1974).

The Bracero Program

When the United States entered the Second World War the labor shortage was critical, particularly since thousands of men were drafted into the military forces. Laborers were needed in the industrial plants, shipyards, bomber factories, automobile and truck assembly lines, weapons factors, and in agricultural production. And, as in the past, America looked south of the border in time of need. The expectation was that Mexico would supply a continuous source of cheap labor during the war.

To this end the Bracero Program was ratified and allowed for the importation of Mexican laborers. The objective of the program was to offset the shortage created by the draft and wartime industries. This bilateral agreement between the United States and Mexico was approved in July of 1942. During the first year of the program, more than 80,000 Mexican laborers harvested crops in the Southwest.

Although the Bracero Program was initially adopted as a temporary wartime emergency, Congress approved annual extensions of the program since American farmers became totally dependent on cheap Mexican labor (Cockcroft, 1986: 67–75). The postwar Bracero Program was given formal approval in 1951, with the passage of Public Law 78. When the program was finally abolished in December 1964, an estimated five million Mexicans had participated in this international labor exchange.

An unanticipated aspect of the Bracero Program was that it stimulated the flow of undocumented aliens into the United States. Since the program placed restrictions on where Braceros were allowed to work and stipulated their rate of pay, the advantage for the *campesinos* (Mexican farm workers) was that they could undercut the wages offered to the Braceros and they could work in non-agricultural jobs, from which Braceros were legally barred. In addition the *campesinos* could cut all the red tape, inconvenience, and personal expenses involved in registering for the Bracero Program. Likewise, farmers could eliminate the red tape and save the $25 bond and the $15 registration fee required for each Bracero, (Grebler, 1966:32).

Operation Wetback

The fact that the Bracero Program encouraged illegal entry into the United States is substantiated by the records of the Immigration and Naturalization Service (INS). During the first year of the Bracero Program, 8,000 undocumented Mexican aliens were apprehended by the INS. By 1951 half a million undocumented aliens were apprehended and deported. In 1954 the INS responded with Operation Wetback. This was an all out effort to return the wetbacks (the derisive term for undocumented aliens who swam the Rio Grande river) to Mexico. During the five year period of this program, an estimated 3.8 million *mojados* (wetbacks) were apprehended and deported (Garcia, 1980).

It is also important to point out that the Bracero Program caused irreparable harm to Mexican American farm workers. Since the Bracero Program guaranteed growers a continuous source of cheap labor they had no incentive or reason to pay local Mexican Americans a living wage. As a result Mexican Americans had to live under a substandard regional economy based on subsistence wages paid to Braceros and *mojados*. The *mojados* applied a continuous downward pressure on wages, so that Mexican Americans could only expect to receive Mexican wages for their labor. The presence of this large surplus labor force also forestalled unionization efforts in the agricultural industry, as growers could always hire *mojados* as scabs (Copp, 1971). As a result it took Caesar Chavez, and other dedicated labor organizers, many years to establish an agricultural union in the Southwest.

The Sleepy Lagoon Case

California history is not only interlaced with accounts of racial attacks against Asians, but it is also a chronicle of racial violence against hapless Mexicans. The racial hatred and hostility toward Mexicans was made abundantly clear during the repatriation movement, when thousands of Mexicans were sent back to Mexico. In the Summer of 1942, war time tensions were high and Mexican Americans served as a convenient lighting rod for pent-up racial tensions in the city of Los Angeles.

Sleepy Lagoon was the name of an old gravel pit where Mexican American youth congregated during the hot summer evenings. On the night of August 1, 1942 a young man was slain near the gravel pit. The next morning the newspapers sensationalized the story and portrayed the killing as gang related. The police followed suit and arrested 24 juveniles, all reputed members of the 38th Street gang, on suspicion of murder. Following a mass trail, seventeen teenagers were convicted and sent to prison for the murder of Jose Diaz (McWilliams, 1968:228–229).

The Sleepy Lagoon case was important because it highlights the relationship between racial prejudice, the racially biased motives of the police, and the conspiracy by the press to sway public opinion against Mexican Americans. What followed was a long period of police brutality, acts that were sanctioned and condoned by the press and the American public. During the War it was not uncommon for the police to set up road blocks, stop and search all vehicles with occupants who looked Mexican, and incarcerate them. Clearly this was a case of officially sanctioned harassment. During one of these police operations, 600 Mexicans were taken into custody and 175 were booked on a variety of charges (McWilliams, 1968:236).

The Zoot Suit Riots

The police actions in the barrios of Los Angeles culminated in the Zoot-Suit Riots. The zoot-suit, popularized by Mexican American youth, was known for its baggy trousers, long draped jacket, and wide-brimmed hat. The zoot-suiters (or *pachucos*) were known for their tattoos, duck-tail haircuts, and spoke in their patois (Dieppa, 1973). The zoot suiters belonged to *palomillas* (neighborhood clubs), but the newspapers portrayed the zoot-suit as a badge of crime and gang membership.

The Zoot-Suit riots began in Los Angeles during the Summer of 1943, as tensions increased between off duty sailors and the zoot-suiters. As a result of negative press and police actions, the sailors considered the *pachucos* fair game. On the evening of June third, about 200 sailors piled into taxi cabs and arrived in the barrio to teach the Mexicans a lesson. The sailors assaulted any Mexicans they could find and stripped them of their zoot-suits. The next day, the newspapers portrayed the sailors as heroes and the police ignored the whole incident

(McWilliams, 1943). These racial attacks continued for a whole week that is until the State Department placed Los Angeles off limits to all military personnel (Fogelson, 1969).

The negative image that emerged from these incidents not only reinforced a racial stereotype of Mexicans as prone to violence and as a social problem in the community, but it also set the stage for the development of harsh feelings in the barrio against Anglos. These incidents made it very difficult for Mexican Americans to receive equal treatment under the law, whether in the courts or on the streets (Morales, 1972:20–46).

The Post War Period

It is ironic that public opinion toward Mexican Americans was so negative during the great war, that is at a time when more than 400,000 Mexican Americans were serving their country in the military services. On the positive side, military service offered Mexican American youth an opportunity to travel, live among Anglo Americans, and experience life on a vastly different level. In addition the new skills and educational opportunities obtained in the military were transferred to civilian life. And as veterans many Mexican Americans were eligible for educational benefits, home mortgages, and preference in government jobs (Morin, 1963).

The war also opened up new opportunities for Mexican Americans in the civilian labor force, since jobs that had been closed to them were made available during the war. For the first time Mexican Americans were hired by automobile plants, shipyards, steel mills, aircraft assembly plants, and by the construction industry. The result was a general upgrading of the job skills in the barrio and an increase in their standard of living (Acuña, 1988:260–261).

To their dismay many veterans returned from the war to discover that in many ways America had not changed, since they encountered prejudice and racial hostility at every level. The most blatant cases of racism occurred when decorated veterans in uniform were refused service in restaurants, were segregated in theaters, buses, and trains, encountered signs that read "NO MEXICANS ALLOWED" at public swimming pools and parks, were denied lodging in hotels, and were harassed by the local police (McWilliams, 1968: 261–263).

In one incident a mortuary in Three Rivers, Texas refused to bury Felix Longoria, a Mexican American war hero, because the cemetery was an all-white cemetery. This blatant act of racism is historic since it planted the seed for organized political protest, as Mexican Americans stood up for their rights and transformed their frustration into political action.

Political Participation

The fact that Mexican Americans have a long history of political participation is often ignored. The popular stereotype would have us believe that Mexican Americans are not interested in politics, are apathetic, are ignorant of political issues, and are guided by traditionalism. However, a review of American political history reveals that Mexican Americans have a long history of political involvement.

At the turn of the century, the general attitude was that *Mejicanos* were simply here to serve as a source of cheap labor, and were therefore considered apolitical. That is, they were viewed as apolitical until their votes were needed to insure the election of a local Anglo *patron* (political boss). The most blatant examples of this Southwestern version of the Yankee political machine occurred in New Mexico (Valdes y Tapia, 1976:53–80).

When it was not to the benefit of Anglo politicians to vote their Mexicans in mass, the common practice was to deny them the vote. This was achieved in several ways. In Texas, Mexican Americans were required to pass a literacy test and had to pay a poll tax before casting a vote. They were also required to register to vote once a year, usually at a time and place when most of them were at work (Foley, 1978).

Even when they were successful in overcoming these barriers, Mexican Americans found their political power diluted by such duplicitous practices as gerrymandering and at-large elections. Gerrymandering insured that no barrio would ever have enough eligible voters in it to insure victory for any aspiring Mexican American politician. At-large elections made it difficult for any Mexican American who secured a majority of the votes in his/her district in the primary election, to be successful in the run-off election (De La Garza, 1974).

Consequently, these political maneuvers either served to neutralize the Mexican American vote, or insured that their votes would not count on election day. In response Mexican Americans formed their own political organizations, since the establishment was unresponsive to their needs.

Mexican American political history can be divided into four periods from:

1. the signing of the Treaty of Guadalupe Hidalgo to the turn of the century (1848–1909),
2. from the Mexican Revolution to the Second World War (1910–1940),
3. from the Second World War to the mid-sixties (1941–1964),
4. from the Chicano Movement to the present (1965–1996).

Each of these periods is noted for the development of a particular type of political organization. The first period is recognized for the development of *mutualistas*, that is mutual benefit associations. The migrant generation (1910–1940), are known for their founding of melting pot organizations. The G.I. Generation (1941–1965), promoted the ideals of democracy and fought against racism and discrimination while the Chicano generation, relied on the politics of nationalism.

One of the first expressions of Mexican American political activity took the form of mutual benefit societies. In effect, they provided the community with basic social services that were otherwise unavailable to Mexican Americans. The earliest *mutualistas* were founded in El Paso, Brownsville, Tucson, and Los Angeles (De Leon, 1982).

The first assimilationist organization was founded in San Antonio, in 1918 and was known as *La Orden de Los Hijos de America* (The Order of the Sons of America), or simply as OSA (Navarro, 1974:62). The OSA encouraged the complete Americanization of all Mexicans and limited its political activities to voter registration drives, citizenship classes, and struggled to get qualified Mexican Americans to serve on juries. Politically the organization considered itself nonpartisan.

Following a split with the OSA in 1928, a group of Mexican Americans founded the League of United Latin American Citizens (LULAC) in Corpus Christi, Texas in the spring of 1929 (Marquez, 1988:13). Like the OSA, LULAC also had a strong assimilationist orientation and drew its membership from the Mexican American middle class. LULAC is still active today and has offices across the country.

Following the Second World War, the G.I. Generation founded several political organizations (Camarillo, 1971). The best known of these were the Community. Service Organization (CSO), the American G.I. Forum, the Council of Mexican-American Affairs (CMAA), the Mexican American Political Association (MAPA), and the Political Association of Spanish Speaking Organizations (PASSO).

The Community Service Organization evolved as part of a city-wide effort by Mexican Americans to elect Edward Roybal to the Los Angeles city council in 1947. In the process, the CSO registered over 40,000 citizens, most of whom lived in the barrios of Los Angeles (Navarro, 1974). The G.I. Forum was founded by Dr. Hector Garcia, a physician and Army veteran, in 1948 following an act of discrimination in which a funeral home in Texas refused to bury a Mexican American veteran (Ramos, 1982:11–12, 17–26).

In 1953, the Council of Mexican American Affairs was founded in Los Angeles, with the stated goal of uniting all Mexican American organizations into one unified group. Three years later a more activist group was founded in California, the Mexican American Political Association. Their goal was to encourage and assist Mexican Americans who sought political office (Dvorin and Misner, 1966). The Political Association of Spanish Speaking Organizations was founded in Texas in the early 1960s, primarily as an outgrowth of the Viva Kennedy Movement. Its primary goal was to form a coalition of Mexican American political organizations throughout the Southwest.

The Chicano Movement evolved during the sixties and initiated the politics of confrontation. *El Movimiento* relied on group demonstrations, boycotts, strikes, sit-ins, and civil disobedience to achieve its goals. Members adopted the name Chicano, to show their allegiance to the new political activism. The term Chicano was used by the activists to denote their ethnicity, militancy, rejection of assimilation, and their goal of self-determination (Meier and Rivera, 1981:83).

The Mexican American Family

The origins of the Mexican American family can be traced to the Spanish conquest, when the Spanish infused their political system, their religion, and their military ambitions into Aztec society. From the beginning the Catholic missionaries not only set out to convert the heathens, but also to insure that they would marry in the church and follow all Catholic religious teachings (Gonzales, 1986).

Following Mexico's independence from Spain, the Mexican government relieved the Catholic church of much of its secular power, guaranteed freedom of religion, and allowed for divorce. Nonetheless, the family maintained many of the traditions acquired during the Spanish period. When Mexicans began to settle in the Southwest, they often migrated as families (Griswold del Castillo, 1984:10–24). By the turn of the century family migration was encouraged by Texas growers, as they realized that families working in the harvest were a more stable work force than single men. The farmers also discovered that women and children picked almost as much fruit and cotton as the men (Gonzales, 1985a; Taylor, 1930).

As Mexican families settled in the larger cities of the Southwest, they evolved into extended family units. Naturally, these larger families were able to share in the child care and household expenses. This also meant that the adults could work longer hours and even remain away from home when required, since other relatives were always available to tend to their children.

By the seventies, Mexican Americans were predominantly urban. Life in the city not only encouraged the maintenance of nuclear families, but also promoted, out of necessity, smaller families. Therefore, while Mexican American families are larger than the general population, their overall family size is gradually declining.

In general the role that women play in the family has changed rather dramatically in the nineties. As with most women, Mexican American women have been influenced by the Women's Movement and the Civil Rights Movement. As a result the Mexican American woman is no longer the subservient-submissive female of the mythical pass (Baca-Zinn, 1975). While it is true that Mexican American women have always played a central role in the family, today they have carried their role beyond the family. Today Chicanas are independent, are active in the labor force, and play a more significant role in the family. In part, the decline in fertility rates can be attributed to the ambitions of upwardly mobile women in the Mexican American family today.

Given the gradual increase in the levels of education and the occupational mobility that Mexican Americans are experiencing, it is anticipated that their basic socio-economic conditions will improve. Additionally, as economic well being improves, there will be an improvement in family life style.

Chapter Summary

When Mexico gained its independence from Spain in 1821 thousands of Mexicans were already settled throughout the American Southwest. While the signing of the Treaty of Guadalupe Hidalgo (1848) ended the war between Mexico and the United States, it also marked a new period in the social and economic history of the Mexican origin population in the Southwest.

During the latter part of the nineteenth century, and the early part of the twentieth century, Mexican laborers were encouraged to migrate north across the border to provide the labor needed for the construction of railroads, highways, and irrigation systems. They also formed the backbone of the labor force in the agricultural and mining industry in the Southwest.

With the onset of the Great Depression the welcome mat was no longer set out for Mexican laborers. As a result of the economic hard times and the scarcity of jobs, racial tensions ran high. One solution to the unemployment problem, was to send the Mexicans back to Mexico. Under their Repatriation Program thousands of Mexicans, many of whom were American citizens, were shipped back to Mexico on chartered trains.

Following the Second World War Mexican Americans took advantage of their veterans benefits and obtained higher education's and learned new skills. In their efforts to improve their social and economic conditions they organized themselves and became active participants in the political arena. During the Civil Rights Movement young Chicanos throughout the Southwest marched and protested in an effort to secure their rights and improve their opportunities for success in American society.

3. MANIFEST DESTINY, TEXAS, AND THE U.S. MEXICAN WAR

Manifest Destiny was a peculiarly Anglo American version of the concept of a chosen people. By the beginning of the nineteenth century North Americans began to believe that their country was destined by divine providence to settle and control the area from the Atlantic seaboard to the Pacific Ocean. Subsequently more extreme exponents of this concept were convinced that the Arctic Circle to the north and the Strait of Magellan in the south were the only logical limits to inevitable Yankee expansion. The country to suffer most in the nineteenth century as a result of Manifest Destiny was Mexico, since approximately half its territory, about one million square miles, lay between the American southwestern frontier and the Pacific Ocean.

After Spain acquired the Louisiana Territory in 1763 the security of adjacent Texas ceased to be of major concern to her. Troops were withdrawn from the Texas region, which in turn led to an increase in Indian harassment. As a result of this more aggressive hostility, many missions and small settlements were abandoned, leading to a decline in tejano population. By the end of the eighteenth century only six of twenty-seven Texas missions were still functioning, and the civilian population had declined to about 3,500.

When the United States purchased the Louisiana Territory from France in 1803 there was limited emigration of Spanish speakers from that area

into Texas. Despite government encouragement of settlement in Texas, its population continued to decline. This trend became even more pronounced after the 1810 revolution for independence broke out. By the end of the revolutionary decade the population had dropped to about 2,000 and the governor was pressing for settlers from central Mexico to populate his vast province. His request was made in vain. Unable to persuade Mexicans to move into this buffer area, the Mexican government encouraged foreign colonization. Unfortunately for Mexico, this attempted solution to the serious problem of underpopulation ultimately helped bring about the loss of Texas.

Meanwhile horse and cattle traders on the southwestern U.S. frontier and southern cotton farmers were becoming keenly interested in eastern Texas. As early as 1815 a few aggressive Americans, ignoring the boundary, had crossed the Sabine River and established themselves on farms around Nacogdoches near the Louisiana border. In 1821 the Spanish government gave to Moses Austin of Potosi, Missouri, an *empresario* land grant, under which he was to receive free land for bringing a specified number of settlers into Texas. Austin, a Catholic and former Spanish subject (Missouri was a part of Spanish Louisiana until 1800) who still held a Spanish passport, died before he could carry out his project to bring in 300 families from formerly Spanish Louisiana.

Two years later his son Stephen received a similar grant from the newly independent Mexican government and began to implement it. Thus an approved influx of Anglo American settlers began. Eventually some fifteen empresario grants were awarded to United States citizens and other foreigners, mostly by the state of Coahuila-Texas. Stephen Austin chose his immigrants with considerable care and was generally scrupulous in carrying out the terms of his agreement with the Mexican government. These terms required that all settlers be of good moral character, that they either be, or be willing to become, Catholics, and that they swear an oath of loyalty to Mexico. Most empresarios, however, failed either to respect or to complete the terms of their grants, while their settlers generally ignored Mexican regulations and institutions. In 1826 the Mexican government tried to compel one of the Americans, Haden Edwards, to abide by provisions of his empresario grant, particularly to recognize earlier titles within its limits. This caused a minor uprising known as the Fredonia Revolt, which broke out at Nacogdoches and was supported by many recently arrived Americans. However, Austin and his colonists refused to side with the Anglos in the uprising and helped Mexican authorities suppress it.

By the end of the 1820s there were in Texas about 25,000 North American immigrants, including black slaves, and about 4,000 Spanish-speaking Mexicans. Many of the Americans were illegal aliens who had migrated from the slaveholding South and had set themselves up as cotton growers. Increasingly they saw themselves as on the way to becoming subjects of a country that they were convinced was politically and morally inferior to their own. Contemptuous of Mexican culture, government officials, and laws, most resisted integration into Mexican society. Because of this attitude the Mexican government became concerned in the late 1820s about the rapidly increasing number of aliens in Texas and tried to stem the tide of migration from the United States.

Alarmed by efforts of the American minister to Mexico, Joel R. Poinsett, to purchase Texas, and encouraged by the British chargé d'affaires, Henry George Ward, President Guadalupe Victoria sent General Manuel Mier y Terán to study the Texas situation in detail. Mier y Terán was critical of both Mexican and Anglo settlers and eventually recommended that the government take vigorous measures in Texas before serious problems arose. In 1829 Mexico's second president, former revolutionary leader Vicente Guerrero, implemented Mier y Terán's recommendations and abolished slavery in Mexico by executive decree in order to make Texas less attractive to cotton planters from the American South. Threatened economically by this law, Texas landowners protested vigorously, and the decree was suspended in Texas, the only Mexican state in which slavery was still important. However, in the next year the Mexican Congress, also following Mier y Terán's advice, enacted legislation completely prohibiting importation of slaves and severely curtailing legal North American immigration into Texas. At the same time, to offset the already sizable Anglo population, the government began to strongly encourage European immigrants. Another law established customhouses and presidios along the Texas–United States frontier, and soldiers were dispatched to enforce Mexican laws, especially customs regulations, since the seven-year tax exemption on imports granted to American settlers was beginning to expire. In eastern Texas, where most of the U.S. immigrants had settled, the conflict of cultures began warming up.

Collection of customs duties quickly became the most abrasive issue between Anglo colonists and the government, leading to organized anti-customs actions. At San Antonio de Béxar, Stephen Austin led a movement to seek legal redress and was successful in obtaining some concessions. Other colonists took a more radical approach. Some activists launched guerrilla attacks on customhouses and presidios, and in 1832 fighting broke out in Texas between Mexican troops who supported centralism and those who favored federalism. That same year Texas held a convention to discuss relations with the central government. Seeking repeal of the 1830 legislation and separation of Texas from Coahuila, a second convention voted to send Austin to Mexico City to petition for these changes. Austin found little sympathy for the Texas viewpoint and was jailed after he sent a letter to the Texas colonists urging them to form an autonomous Mexican state government. Finally, after a year, he was released and returned to Texas. Further changes introduced by the centralist government added fuel to the fire. On November 7, 1835, the Texans declared conditional independence, adding their voices to those of other Mexican federalists demanding a return to the 1824 constitution as the price of resubmission to Mexico City.

In response to these events early in 1835, President Antonio López de Santa Anna sent to Texas 4,000 federal troops under his brother-in-law, General Martín Cos. After establishing his headquarters in San Antonio at a former Franciscan mission popularly called the Alamo, Cos was soundly defeated by a group of federalist rebels in late 1835 and forced to withdraw. President Santa Anna, who had suppressed a similar federalist revolt in Zacatecas the year before, assumed personal command of an army to force the Texans to submit to his authority. Recruiting, training, and organizing a conscript army as he marched north to Texas in 1836, he was determined to avenge Cos's defeat. Santa Anna's subsequent actions must be viewed in proper historical perspective. Directed by the Mexican Congress to suppress the seditious revolt in Texas, he rightfully considered Texas rebels to be traitors and set out to smother the flames of rebellion.

Meanwhile, a Texas convention of Anglos and tejano federalists declared by a two-to-one vote that it wanted reinstatement of the federalist constitution of 1824. It also appointed Sam Houston commander of all Texas forces. Political differences within the provisional Texas government led to a second convention at Washington-on-the-Brazos, during which fifty-nine delegates unanimously declared complete independence on March 2, 1836. A few days later they elected David Burnett provisional president and Lorenzo de Zavala, a prominent Yucatecan federalist and Texas land empresario, vice president. They reappointed Houston to head the army.

The first major encounter between the soldiers of the fledgling republic and the forces of Santa Anna took place in San Antonio at the Alamo. Here the Texans let themselves be caught by surprise even though they had been warned of the Mexican army's imminent approach by tejano scouts. After a ten-day siege 187 defenders led by William Travis and including tejanos under the leadership of Captain Juan Seguín, all fighting under a 1824 Mexican federalist flag, were wiped out. Seguín himself escaped the massacre because he was sent to seek help before the final Mexican assault began. A month later the Mexican army reinforced this Alamo victory by slaughtering 450 Texas rebels at Goliad. However, Santa Anna's victories were costly and short-lived. Hundreds of Mexican soldiers lost their lives in massive frontal attacks, and the army's ruthlessness generated fierce resistance on the part of the Texas rebels.

On April 21 an overconfident Santa Anna and his army were routed at San Jacinto by a Texas attack in which tejanos under Seguín played a key role. Santa Anna himself was taken prisoner and a counterslaughter took place. This Texan victory led to the so-called Treaty of Velasco, by which Santa Anna agreed to Texas independence in exchange for his freedom. Needless to say, the government in Mexico City repudiated Santa Anna's personal arrangement, but it was unable to force the Texans to resubmit to Mexican authority. By 1840 the Texans had succeeded in obtaining recognition of their independent republic from the United States, France, and Great Britain.

Having achieved de facto independence from Mexico, Texas pressed for annexation to the United States. However, annexation posed a problem for antislavery congressmen and the country, which was trying to maintain a balance between the admission of slave and free states. As the slavery issue grew more intense in the United States and the abolitionist movement gained support, Texans devoted less and less effort to annexation. Instead, attainment of economic and political stability by other means became their prime concern. To achieve national viability some Texans suggested expanding the republic to the Pacific, while others preferred merely to annex the Nuevo México area with its valuable Santa Fe trade.

In an effort to persuade nuevomexicanos to secede from Mexico and become part of the Texas Republic an expedition to Santa Fe was organized by Texas president Mirabeau Buonaparte Lamar. If the nuevomexicanos refused, the Texans were willing to settle for a share in the lucrative Santa Fe trade, as documents carried by the leaders of the expedition indicated. With twenty-one wagons loaded with $200,000 worth of trade goods some 300 Anglo and Spanish-speaking Texans, organized into five military companies under General Hugh McLeod, left Austin for Santa Fe in June 1841. On the way they encountered blistering heat, raging prairie fires, and hostile Indians; and they also lost their way, thereby adding to their 600-mile journey. The poorly managed and ill-fated expedition split into two groups, believing that this would speed up the journey. When the members finally reached Nuevo México they were suffering intensely from hunger, thirst, and exhaustion. Here the naive participants allowed themselves to be disarmed by a ruse and were taken prisoners by Governor Manuel Armijo without a shot being fired. At Santa Fe some of the Texans were executed and the remainder were sent on a grueling death march to prison in Mexico City. The survivors were eventually released only after strong American and British protests.

The failure to annex Nuevo México and to participate in the Santa Fe trade on the one hand and reports of the brutal treatment of prisoners on the other incensed public opinion and contributed to further antagonism between republican Texans and nuevomexicanos. The threat of further expeditions caused the Mexican government to tighten its control of the Santa Fe trade until war with the United States ended Mexico's authority.

Meanwhile, the United States and Mexico were moving rapidly toward a war which neither country wanted. In Texas conflicts between Anglos, especially recent arrivals, and tejanos coupled with border raids by both Mexicans and Texans intensified mutual antagonisms. Between 1836 and 1846 various serious but unsuccessful attempts by plundering Mexican armies to reconquer Texas kept the border in a constant state of tension. Because of perennial financial difficulties Mexico was unable to pay its acknowledged claims debts to the United States, and the latter's repeated efforts to buy part or all of the Southwest were viewed in Mexico with great alarm. In the early 1840s new American claims against Mexico arising from border difficulties and outrages against American citizens kept animosities at fever pitch and helped provide excuses for U.S. intervention.

The climax came in March 1845 when the United States, by a joint resolution of Congress, annexed

Texas, an action which Mexico had previously warned might lead to war since it had not recognized Texas secession and independence. The Mexican government immediately broke off diplomatic ties with the United States, and relations between the two countries became critical. In August, President James Polk sent John Slidell to Mexico with instructions to purchase Alta California and Nuevo México for as much as $25 million and to discuss settlement of the disputed Texas-Mexican boundary. However, Mexican officials were reluctant to discuss these matters with Slidell because of intense anti-American feeling. Finally, Slidell was forced to leave Mexico by a new, strongly anti-American administration, installed by a coup.

Failing in his attempt to acquire the territory by negotiation and purchase, Polk sent General Zachary Taylor to the Nueces River area in southeastern Texas in hopes that a military clash with Mexico might lead to war and bring about acquisition of the entire Southwest. Polk made this provocative move in response to a widespread arrogant American conviction that the country was manifestly destined to rule over all North America. Armed hostilities soon broke out between the two countries.

As a result of a clash between American and Mexican troops in the disputed triangle of land between the Nueces and the Rio Grande, the United States declared war on Mexico in May 1846. Both sides saw the conflict as not just a fight for territory but as a struggle between two "races," cultures, and religions. Ordered to carry the war into the heart of Mexico, General Taylor crossed the Rio Grande and occupied Matamoros. In September he moved west from there to capture Monterrey. Meanwhile, Santa Anna, who had been returned to the presidency, organized another army to turn back the American invasion. The following February at Buena Vista near Saltillo, Coahuila, a hard-fought, indecisive battle took place between Taylor's troops and soldiers under Santa Anna. The ill-equipped and fatigued Mexican recruits fought valiantly against the Americans. Santa Anna, unaware of Taylor's plan to withdraw to Monterrey because of overextended supply lines, disengaged his forces during the night and headed back to Mexico City as his army disintegrated. Both generals claimed victory.

Meanwhile, Nuevo México was initially taken by the United States without a fight. Anglo traders in Santa Fe and the profits of trade with the United States had convinced many nuevomexicano businessmen that the province would be better off as part of the United States than under the ineffectual and unstable government in Mexico City. After organiz-ing a large body of militia, Governor Manuel Armijo decided not to oppose the invading army of 1,500 Americans under Colonel Stephen Kearny. Instead, he suddenly disbanded his larger force and departed southward for Chihuahua. Armijo's change in plan was perhaps influenced by Kearny's assurances to nuevomexicanos that he came as protector rather than conqueror.

When Kearny entered Santa Fe in mid-August, acting governor Juan B. Vigil and some twenty leading nuevomexicanos greeted him and the American troops warmly and promised that all citizens would be loyal to the United States. In response to this friendly reception Colonel Kearny assured them that the United States government would respect the property and religious rights of all who showed peaceful intent. Then, while the townsmen and Kearny toasted each other with wine and brandy, the American flag was raised over the governor's palace. Two days later a group of Pueblo Indian leaders came to Santa Fe and declared their allegiance to the United States, stating that their traditions foretold that one day they would be redeemed from Spanish injustice and oppression by men from the east. The apparently easy transition to U.S. control was in some ways anticlimactic, but disquieting portents of resistance and rebellion were heard from time to time.

After completing the formalities of imposing military control in Nuevo México, Kearny ordered the drafting of a framework for the establishment of a new American government in the Southwest. Known as the Kearny Code, this instrument was based on American and Mexican law and included provisions for the appointment of government officials. Despite President Polk's orders to retain the existing nuevomexicano political power structure, Kearny, after discussions with officials, generally ignored leading Santa Fe and Taos families in organizing the new government. He appointed Charles Bent, a leader of the Santa Fe traders and the pro-American faction in Nuevo México, as acting governor. Equally at home in the two cultures, Bent was a well-educated landowner and merchant of Taos, married into a wealthy nuevomexicano family since 1835. He had held minor political offices. From the existing Spanish-speaking political structure, Kearny appointed Donaciano Vigil secretary of the territory and named Antonio J. Otero one of three territorial court judges. Other high officials were merchants and recent arrivals from Missouri. Most minor Mexican officeholders, after taking an oath of allegiance to the United States, were continued in office.

With Nuevo México presumably secure, the ambitious Kearny set out for California late in September

1846 to help complete the conquest of that province. Shortly after leaving Santa Fe he encountered the Taos-based scout Kit Carson, who informed him that California was already under Anglo control. Upon arriving in southern California, however, Kearny found californios in full revolt and his dragoons opposed by a small force under the local commander, Andrés Pico. In the battle of San Pascual east of San Diego, Kearny's troops were severely defeated by Pico's lancers and he himself was wounded. Kearny was forced to seek help from Commodore Robert Stockton, who had arrived earlier on the California coast as commander of the Pacific Squadron. With support from Stockton's forces Kearny finally reached the security of San Diego on December 12, 1846.

To understand more clearly the californio experience during the war between Mexico and the United States, it is necessary to review some of the history that led to hostilities in California. Prior to 1846 California underwent economic and sociopolitical experiences similar to those of Texas and Nuevo México. As in those areas, the process of economic detachment from the central government began with trade. Starting in the 1820s, sailing ships from England and the United States began to bring manufactured goods to California in exchange for hides, tallow, and furs. This trade also initiated a small influx of Anglo American immigrants. Those who came in the 1820s and 1830s, nearly all by sea, tended to become an integral part of California society. Many married into californio families, accepted Catholicism at least nominally, became Mexican citizens, and acquired land grants; a few even held public office. However, Anglos who began to arrive in the early 1840s by way of the Oregon Trail were of a different type. Many came with their families, had no intention of becoming Mexican citizens, and deliberately settled in areas remote from Mexican control, especially in the Sacramento Valley. Supported by a firm belief in Manifest Destiny, they came as a vanguard of North American expansionism.

Accelerated American immigration, coupled with californio dissatisfaction with Mexican centralist government, led to a rebellion which broke out in northern California just before the war between Mexico and the United States began. This uprising, centered in the Sacramento region and known as the Bear Flag Revolt because its banner depicted a bear, quickly became a part of the Mexican War. Initially spearheaded by a group of Anglo adventurers, the revolt established a basis for Anglo conquest of California. John Charles Frémont, a United States Army captain who was illegally in the province on a reconnaissance expedition for the government, quickly took command of the revolutionaries. When word came that Mexico and the United States were at war, the Bear Flag was replaced by the Stars and Stripes. The arrival of the Pacific Squadron, at first under the command of Commodore John Sloat and later under Robert Stockton, readily secured American control of the entire area without bloodshed. However, inept leadership of the occupation forces in Los Angeles brought tensions to a climax that led to a californio revolt in September 1846 and to the only serious fighting in California.

Commodore Stockton had quickly antagonized californios, both by initiating a large number of restrictive and tactless controls and by placing Captain Archibald Gillespie in command of southern California. Gillespie, insensitive to local feelings and cultural practices, issued further unnecessary and irksome regulations, which caused the southern californios to launch a successful attack against his forces. Eventually, however, through the combined efforts of Gillespie, Stockton, Kearny, and Frémont the southern California revolt was subdued. American control was reestablished through negotiation of the so-called Treaty of Cahuenga with the californios in January 1847. This agreement, independent of the government in Mexico City, terminated hostilities in California. Nevertheless, in the heated atmosphere rumors persisted that californios were plotting further resistance.

Meanwhile, far to the south in central Mexico, Santa Anna and another hastily organized army battled American general Winfield Scott, who had landed near Veracruz with 10,000 men. The war went badly for Mexico. She was severely divided by internal bickering, her leaders were deeply mistrustful of each other, and the majority of Mexicans were demoralized and unclear as to the objectives of the struggle with the United States. Some Mexican states even refused to provide troops to defend the country against the invaders. The majority of the troops were poorly motivated, ill-trained Indian conscripts.

Within six months Scott's forces advanced from Veracruz to Mexico City, reaching the Valley of Mexico by mid-August 1847. In the last days of the fighting, at Chapultepec Hill just outside the capital, one hundred young Mexican military cadets showed how well Mexican troops could fight when trained effectively and motivated by patriotism. However, the bravery of these "Niños Héroes" was in vain. They were unable to turn back the United States invasion, and on September 14 the North American army successfully occupied the Mexican capital. With the conquest of Mexico essentially completed, the only item remaining on James K. Polk's agenda was to write a treaty of peace.

Earlier in 1847 Polk had sent a personal representative, Nicholas Trist, to Mexico to negotiate a treaty which would secure his expansionist goals. However, because of personal antagonism between Trist and General Scott, the president ordered Trist's recall. Trist ignored the order and continued negotiations with the provisional Mexican government. Finally, on February 2, 1848, agreement was reached and a treaty was signed in the village of Guadalupe Hidalgo outside Mexico City.

Although Polk was irritated by Trist's insubordination, the treaty basically achieved the president's original territorial objectives, and he therefore submitted it to the Senate. Widespread support of Manifest Destiny had led to a strong demand that the United States take all of Mexico, with Democratic representatives leading the cry in hopes of regaining fading political popularity. The U.S. Senate quickly studied the proposed treaty and made some changes. Article IX, dealing with the political rights and eventual citizenship of the inhabitants of the territory to be transferred, was replaced with a similar but shorter article taken from the Louisiana Purchase treaty of 1803, and Article X, which the Senate felt would have raised problems of landownership in Texas, was completely excised. However, when the amended treaty was discussed with the Mexican representatives in May, assurances were given that titles to all kinds of personal and real properties existing in the ceded territories would be recognized and protected. Moreover, all civil, political, and religious guarantees specified in the original Article IX would be retained. These promises were put into writing after the amended treaty had already been ratified by the Mexican Congress at Querétaro on May 21, 1848, and are known as the Protocol of Querétaro. Four days later, with the exchange of ratifications, the treaty went into effect. The protocol itself was never ratified by either government and therefore technically had no validity in international law.

By the provisions of the Treaty of Guadalupe Hidalgo the United States acquired the territory that now forms the states of Arizona, California, Nevada, New Mexico, and Utah and half of Colorado, and received clear title to Texas with the Rio Grande boundary that the Texas government had previously claimed. Mexico lost about one million square miles and was paid $15 million in partial compensation. Although Mexico lost approximately 50 percent of her national territory, she lost less than 1 percent of her population. Nearly all 80,000 Mexican citizens living in the ceded territory ultimately became U.S. nationals. Relatively few kept their Mexican citizenship. In Nuevo México about 1,500 to 2,000 moved southwest across the new political border and another 2,000 remained but retained their citizenship. In Texas about 1,000 crossed the border, and several hundred californios went south to Baja California and Sonora. Although the Mexican government encouraged settlement in Mexico both at the end of the war and in the following decades and sent agents to arrange details for those who wished to leave the United States, few accepted the proffered help.

The chief provisions of the Treaty of Guadalupe Hidalgo that relate to Mexican Americans are those concerning citizenship and property. Mexicans living in the ceded area had a year in which to decide whether they wanted to retain Mexican citizenship or to become nationals of the United States. Those still living in the area at the end of the prescribed time who had not specifically declared their intentions to remain Mexican citizens were presumed to desire U.S. nationality. Article IX of the treaty guaranteed that these former Mexican citizens would ultimately become U.S. citizens and meanwhile would receive the protection of the United States government in the exercise of their civil and political rights. It also specifically provided that they would have the right to worship freely and that their property rights would be protected. It is interesting to note that no mention was made in the treaty concerning the political and civil rights of local Indians, the more acculturated of whom had been given citizenship under Mexican law but had continued to be treated as second-class citizens.

A second important provision dealt with real and personal property of the inhabitants, whether or not they continued to reside within the bounds of the area. It stipulated that full title to all property would be retained with rights of disposal and inheritance, and it guaranteed complete protection of these rights by the United States government. Item Two of the protocol which "supplemented" the treaty specified that valid Spanish and Mexican land grants would be recognized by the United States and that the United States would accept as legitimate all property titles recognized under Mexican law.

By the terms of this treaty the United States gained not only an immense new territory but also a sizable group of new nationals who would become citizens when Congress so determined. Although they were left in their same geographic and cultural setting, these new United States nationals were now exposed to unfamiliar legal, political, and social institutions. Guaranteed freedom of religion, they remained Catholic, but they were inundated by a flood of Anglo-Saxon Protestants, many of whom held Catholicism in contempt.

4. THE SLEEPY LAGOON MURDER CASE AND THE ZOOT SUIT RIOTS

One major wartime incident, the Sleepy Lagoon case, as it was called by the Los Angeles press, began early on August 2, 1942, when a young gang member, José Díaz, was found unconscious on a rural road in the outskirts of Los Angeles. He died without regaining consciousness, and the autopsy showed that death had resulted from a skull fracture. No weapon was found, nor was proof of murder established, but Díaz had, taken part in a gang clash the preceding evening at a nearby swimming hole. Twenty-three Mexican American youths and one Anglo who had participated in the fighting were arrested and charged with murder.

Two of the indicted youths requested separate trials and were subsequently released. The other twenty-two were tried together on sixty-six charges in the fall of 1942. The judge in the case, Charles W. Fricke of the Los Angeles Superior Court, made little secret of his bias against Mexicans, and the prosecution was allowed repeatedly to stereotype the defendants racially. The defense charged that throughout the long court proceedings the defendants were denied haircuts and change of clothing; soon they began to resemble the prosecution's stereotype of sordid Mexican hoodlums.

In January 1943, the jury, without any concrete evidence, found three youths guilty of first-degree murder, nine guilty of second-degree murder, and five guilty of assault. The other five were found not guilty. This verdict led to the creation of the Sleepy Lagoon Defense Committee, chaired by Carey McWilliams and spearheaded by youthful reformer Alice Greenfield. Organized to appeal the convictions, the committee was smeared with the charge of being a Communist front. Despite Redbaiting, the committee persisted in its efforts to secure justice for the convicted-seventeen: Benefits were held to raise funds for the appeal, and about $100,000 was collected to hire lawyers. In October 1944 the California District Court of Appeals unanimously reversed the lower court's convictions and dismissed all charges for lack of evidence. This incident later formed the basis for Luis Valdez's well-known play and film *Zoot Suit*.

The Sleepy Lagoon case had widespread negative repercussions. Until the convictions were dismissed two years after the trial, it remained a focal point for extensive anti-Mexican feeling in southern California. The Los Angeles press, including the L. A. *Times*, and the Hearst newspapers exploited the situation with sensationalist journalism emphasizing alleged mexicano criminal activity. This "crime wave" in the newspapers put strong public pressure on police departments, which responded with systematic roundups of Mexican American teenagers and other repressive measures. Police harassed Mexican American youth clubs and overpoliced barrios; there were extensive arrests based on race and the vaguest suspicion. Concerned with Latin American relations, Washington pressured the newspapers to stop labeling suspects as "Mexican." The press responded with code words like "pachuco" and "zoot suit" to suggest negative racial designations.

At the time of World War II, Los Angeles had a large second-generation Mexican American teenage population, children of the large immigrant wave of the 1920s. Some of these found a sense of belonging or status by joining barrio gangs whose male members often affected a distinctive "uniform" known as the zoot suit, consisting of a flat-crowned, broad-brimmed hat; lengthy draped coat; and high-waisted, baggy-legged trousers with tight-fitting pegged cuffs. Long duck-tailed, squared-off hair and a long, elaborate watch chain usually completed the outfit. Chicanos had adapted this dress from a widespread style associated with jitterbugging, a dance fad originating in the East.

In April and May 1943, a few months after the convictions in the sensationalized Sleepy Lagoon case, some minor incidents between zoot-suiters and Anglo military personnel took place in Los Angeles and Oakland. Typically these fracases developed from quarrels over girlfriends. It was ironic that while Anglos and Chicanos were fighting side by side in the armed forces, military personnel roamed the streets of Los Angeles seeking out and attacking zoot-suiters. Rapidly mounting tensions soon led to tumult in Los Angeles during the first days of June when serious clashes broke out between zoot-suited Mexican American youths and hundreds of restless Anglo sailors and soldiers. Streetcars and buses were stopped, and zoot-suiters were pulled off; theaters were entered, lights turned on, and zoot-suiters dragged out. Many were assaulted and had their clothes ripped off, their long hair cut. These vicious attacks quickly became virtually an undeclared war on all young Chicanos by roving bands of unrestrained servicemen. The conflict reached a peak on June 7, when fleets of taxis filled with sailors cruised the streets of Los Angeles seeking victims. To make matters worse, officials responded to these attacks by following the cabs at a distance and then arresting the victims.

In this emotion-laden situation the conservative Spanish-language newspaper *La Opinión* called for a cooling off and asked Mexican American youths to forgo their rights of self-defense in the face of these criminal attacks. However, retaliation by gangs of adolescent Mexican Americans was inevitable. Fists, rocks, clubs, and on occasion knives were the language of response. Meanwhile the Los Angeles English-language press fomented further trouble with sensation-mongering headlines, inflammatory stories, and strident editorials against the servicemen's victims.

What had begun as a series of street brawls quickly turned into a full-fledged race riot incited by the press and condoned or ignored by major law enforcement agencies. Rioting also broke out in Pasadena, Long Beach, and San Diego. This violence triggered similar racial attacks against Mexican Americans in Chicago, Detroit, and Philadelphia during the summer of 1943. Throughout the country there was strong reaction to these outrages, and *Time* magazine later called the Los Angeles violence "the ugliest brand of mob action since the coolie race riots of the 1870s."

Eventually, the Mexican ambassador in Washington, Francisco Nájera, requested that the State Department investigate the Los Angeles incidents. This pressure, along with reports that the riots were being used in Axis propaganda, caused the State Department to insist that military police take steps to bring servicemen under control. Consequently, overnight passes and leaves were canceled and strict controls were instituted. As a result, the assaults quickly tapered off and order was restored by mid-June. At the height of the trouble several thousand people were involved; a few were seriously injured, no one died. However, fear of racial disorder persisted during the rest of the summer, and some southwestern cities experienced street brawling in 1944 and 1945.

Several official committees that investigated the riots failed to find ethnic tensions as a major factor in southern California. City and county officials seemed more concerned about bad publicity than with ascertaining the causes of the rioting. The official version of the Los Angeles violence was that the soldiers and sailors had acted in self-defense and that there was no element of race prejudice involved. However, a citizens' committee appointed by Governor Earl Warren and headed by Catholic bishop Joseph McGucken of Los Angeles found that, while the causes were complex, the riots were principally the result of racial antagonism stimulated by inflammatory news reporting and discriminatory police practices. Because the press exploited the prejudicially used term "zoot suit," guilt was often determined by length of hair and cut of trousers rather than by evidence of wrongdoing. The matter reached such ridiculous proportions that on June 10 the Los Angeles City Council seriously debated an ordinance that would have made it a punishable offense to wear a zoot suit.

In the long run the Sleepy Lagoon affair and the zoot-suit rioting had a few positive, though limited, results. Greater attention was focused on conditions in the Los Angeles Mexican American community. Open grand jury hearings on the problems of Mexican Americans were held and produced—at least temporarily—some Anglo concern about society's treatment of Mexican Americans. For example, in 1944 a Los Angeles Commission on Human Relations was set up to develop programs designed to improve mutual understanding between Anglos and Mexican Americans. For the next two or three years considerable interest was shown in what was referred to as the "race question." Los Angeles also expanded its educational and recreational budget for heavily Chicano East Los Angeles, and various committees and programs were set up to improve communication between officials and the Mexican American community. Many meetings, institutes, workshops, and teachers' conferences were held on the problems of la raza. Another by-product was the Civic Unity Council, which came in part out of the zoot-suit committee headed by Carey McWilliams. This grew out of demands by liberals for an agency that would give ethnic minorities greater representation in civic matters. Unfortunately, the Civic Unity Council became increasingly conservative and ineffective and disappeared in 1948. However, politicians continued to pay lip service, at least, to the concept of fair treatment and-political representation for Mexican Americans. Among Chicanos the zoot-suit riots continue to have emotional relevance.

5. A DAY WITHOUT A MEXICAN

What would happen if all of a sudden all the Mexicans who lived in the United States disap-

"A Day Without a Mexican," pages 23–25, from *The Other Face of America: Chronicles of the Immigrants Shaping Our Future,* by Jorge Ramos. Copyright © 2002 by Jorge Ramos. Translation copyright © 2002 by Patricia J. Duncan. Reprinted by permission of HarperCollins Publishers.

peared? Yes, all of them, the more than 7 million Mexicans who were born in Mexico but live here in the United States.

A similar question crossed the mind of film director Sergio Arau, and through what he called a "false documentary," he tried to answer it. I saw several scenes from the movie and what stood out, with both humor and insight, was the enormous importance of the Latino population in the United States. Giving an original twist to one of the most overused sayings—"You never know what you have until you lose it"—Arau has managed to capture on film what many have thought and hinted at for years: If all the Mexicans disappeared for a day, the U.S. economy would be seriously hindered.

The movie focuses on what would happen if all the Mexicans in the state of California, where most Mexicans in the United States live, suddenly and inexplicably disappeared. Let's try and imagine this.

A day without a Mexican in California would mean losses in the millions in the orange, avocado, lettuce, and grape industries. Supermarkets would be without fruits and vegetables, and wine shops without those famous California whites and reds. (According to the 1990 census, slightly less than 15 percent of all Mexicans in the United States, legal and undocumented, work in agriculture.)

A day without a Mexican in California would mean a complete halt in the construction and garment industries among many others. (Approximately 35 percent of Mexicans in the United States work in these sectors.)

A day without a Mexican in California would show that hotels, restaurants, stores, markets, gas stations, and offices depend on those workers who cross the southern border of the United States. (More than half of Mexicans in the United States are employed in the service industry.)

A day without a Mexican in California would mean that thousands of English-speaking men and women would not be able to go to work because their nannies would not show up to take care of their children and babies.

A day without a Mexican in California would leave the television and radio stations with the largest audiences in the Los Angeles area—which transmit in Spanish, although few are aware of this—without viewers or listeners.

A day without a Mexican in California would give the false impression that the official language in the United States is English.

A day without a Mexican in California would mean canceled operations because doctors would

not arrive, unkept court appointments because lawyers would not show up, and unfulfilled commitments because of absent executives.

Contrary to the trite stereotype that all Mexicans in the United States are poorly educated and are gardeners and work in the fields, the 1990 census revealed that there were 3,869 immigrants, born in Mexico, who held doctorate degrees. That tears the stereotype to shreds. It is worth mentioning that Mexican labor, in U.S. fields and gardens, just as in the assembly plants on the border, is considered among the best and most efficient in the world.

This exercise of magical migration where we make more than 7 million Mexicans disappear just like that can be applied to other Hispanic groups in the United States with the same results. For example, what would become of Miami without the Cubans and Nicaraguans? Or New York without the Puerto Ricans and Domincans? Or New Orleans without the Hondurans? Or Los Angeles without the Salvadorans and Guatemalans? What would become of the U.S. Army without the 7.9 percent of its soldiers who call themselves "Latinos"? Unfortunately, the positive impact of the presence of the more than 30 million Hispanics in the United States is not always recognized and appreciated by the rest of the population, despite their enormous cultural, social, and economic contributions.

Nevertheless, there are people who do not want us here in the United States. I received a phone call from a young man who had heard about the subject of Arau's movie—*A Day without a Mexican*—and he had the arrogance to tell me that, deep down, nothing would make him happier than if all Mexicans were to disappear from the map. Naturally, I hung up on him before he had finished speaking, so he would see for himself just what would happen if all Mexicans in the United States disappeared for a day. I wouldn't be surprised if the dreams of former California governor Pete Wilson and the xenophobic conservative Pat Buchanan were just like the wishes of that impertinent man who called me.

The United States has still not accepted its multiethnic and multicultural makeup. It has still not realized—or simply does not want to recognize—that the children in our families are not all white any-more. The "little brown ones," as former President George Bush said of his grandchildren of Hispanic origin—his son Jeb is married to a Mexican, Columba—are increasing in number.

It is a shame that Arau's short film was turned down by the organizers of the main film festivals in the United States. *A Day without a Mexican* would reveal to many in the United States the country they are really living in, a country far from the black-and-white one they have instilled in their minds.

6. THE PUERTO RICAN EXPERIENCE

Introduction

In view of the availability of bargain flights between San Juan and New York City following the Second World War, the Puerto Rican population on the mainland has increased dramatically. In 1940 there were 70,000 Puerto Ricans living on the mainland, and by 1950 there were 300,000, a better than four-fold increase. By 1960 there were 855,000 Puerto Ricans living on the mainland and by 1970 there were 1.4 million. Their population reached 2,013,943 in 1980. In 1990 there were 2,330,000 Puerto Ricans living in the U.S. mainland. Today (1993) their mainland population is estimated at 2,727,754 (Hoffman, 1993:388).

For historic reasons, mainland Puerto Ricans are concentrated in New York City, and live primarily in East Harlem, the Bronx, and Brooklyn (Chenault, 1970; Sanchez, 1983). In 1990 half (45%) of the mainland Puerto Ricans were living in New York state. Altogether almost two thirds live in either New York or New Jersey. More recent settlement patterns reveal that they have settled in other areas, such as Chicago, Philadelphia, Los Angeles, Miami, San Francisco, and Boston.

Although many people refer to the Puerto Rican immigration to the United States, they are not really immigrants, but rather they are migrants to the mainland. But in a historical sense they were immigrants, since they, (1) entered an alien English speaking environment, (2) experienced social resistance to their entry, and (3) they have suffered from discrimination, segregation, and economic exploitation (Miranda, 1974). Much like the Mexicans and the Filipinos, Puerto Ricans also were also the victims of U.S. military conquest and historically have been treated as a conquered people.

The Conquest of Puerto Rico

The island of Puerto Rico was discovered by Columbus during his second voyage to the New World on November 19, 1493. When Columbus landed on the island it was inhabited by 50,000 Tainos Indians. Ponce De Leon founded the first settlement in Caparra in 1510 and quickly pressed the Indians into forced labor (Hauberg, 1974:13). De Leon forced the Tainos to work in the mines, in agriculture, and on cattle ranches established by the Spanish. The Indians were forcefully pressed into the labor intensive needs of commercial production and were subjected to the relentless indoctrination of the Spanish missionaries (Cruz-Monclova, 1958:20–56; Golding, 1973).

By 1530 most of Indians had died of a combination of smallpox and exhaustion, and their rapidly dwindling population was soon replaced by slave labor (Moscoso, 1980:22–23). By the mid-nineteenth century (1846) there were 51,000 slaves in Puerto Rico, out of a population of 440,000 (Cordasco, 1973:4). Most of the slaves were required to work on tobacco and sugar plantations. The island was beset with slave revolts and a host of social and health problems. The Spanish finally abolished slavery in 1873.

Following years of social unrest and political agitation Spain granted Puerto Rico its independence on November 25, 1897. Three months later the American battleship *U.S.S. Maine* was blown-up in Havana Harbor. On April 21, 1898, Congress declared war on Spain (Golding, 1973:94). American troops landed on the south coast of Puerto Rico on July 25. On October 18, 1898 the Spanish flag was lowered for the last time in Old San Juan and was replaced with the Stars and Stripes.

The Treaty of Paris, ending the war between the United States and Spain, was signed on April 11, 1899. As a result of the Treaty, Puerto Rico became a colony of the United States and served as a base for U.S. naval operations in the Caribbean. As in the Philippines, the President appointed a military governor in Puerto Rico to administer the government and manage internal affairs.

The American Influence

Following the military conquest of Puerto Rico the American way of life became the law of the land. The American governor of the island was advised by a two-chamber legislative body. All decisions of the Puerto Rican legislature required the approval of the U.S. governor and any actions of these representatives could be nullified by the U.S. Congress (Golding, 1973:109–110). Without any doubt the people of Puerto Rico realized that they were now a colony of the United States (Santiago-Valles, 1994).

From the onset English was designated the official language of government and commerce. In March of 1903, the U. S. government established the University of Puerto Rico. The idea was that the children of the elite families of the island would be educated to accept the American way of life and American values as their own. In response to a critical labor shortage in the United States during the First World War, Puerto Ricans were granted American citizenship under the provisions of the Jones Act (1917). But this also made all Puerto Rican men eligible for the draft.

On the positive side, the first thirty years of American domination of Puerto Rico brought about much needed improvements in education, health care, transportation, and the development of commerce. But these improvements in the infrastructure also meant that these healthy and literate Puerto Ricans would make better factory workers and farm laborers (Falcon, 1991:147–150).

With the development of manufacturing, the agricultural industry was transformed into an export industry with heavy capital investment in sugar and coffee production. The value of Puerto Rican exports in 1901 was only $8.5 million but increased to $103.5 million in 1928, with sugar exports representing about half the total (Christopulos, 1980:136).

Following years of internal political turmoil and external conflict with the United States, Puerto Rico became a Commonwealth in 1948, and elected its first governor, Luis Muñoz Marin (1948–1964). Puerto Rico's new political standing, know as *Estado Libre Asociado* (Associated Free State), meant that while Puerto Ricans are U.S. citizens and can elect their governor, they cannot vote in Presidential elections and do not have representatives in Congress. But they are subject to all federal laws and their judicial system derives from the U.S. legal system (Cripps, 1984; Fernandez, 1994). While Puerto Ricans pay local taxes, they do not pay federal income taxes. Of course all Puerto Ricans born on, or living in the mainland enjoy all the rights and duties of citizenship granted to all U.S. citizens.

Background to Migration

Though some Puerto Ricans migrated to the U.S. mainland shortly after their colonization, their numbers did not become significant until after 1930. By one account there were no more than 1,600 Puerto Ricans living in the mainland in 1910 (Chenault, 1970:53). A decade later their population increased to 12,000. In 1930 there were more than 53,000 Puerto Ricans on the mainland. By 1940 their population increased to more than 70,000.

As with thousands of other immigrants to America, the Puerto Ricans also had their reasons for leaving their homeland, but in addition to the common push-pull factors of poverty, unemployment, overpopulation, and the wage differential, there were also planned structural factors that prompted their migration (Davis, 1953; Senior, 1953). When the U.S. government colonized Puerto Rico, it instituted a policy of modernization (Lopez, 1980).

The most important of these new policies was the land closure movement, whereby American investors were allowed to purchase thousands of acres of land below market value, prepare it for commercial production (primarily in sugar and tobacco), and mechanized the production process (Mintz, 1960). As a result of this policy, thousands of farm workers were displaced and forced into a life of poverty. Out of desperation thousands of peasants moved to the urban centers, primarily to San Juan and Ponce, where most of them sank into a life of squalor and despair (LaRuffa, 1971). For many the only way to escape a life of poverty was to migrate to the mainland (Davis, 1953). Most of these displaced migrants found work in the garment industry of New York, and others followed the agricultural harvest in New Jersey (Falcon, 1991:150–154).

Puerto Rican migration can be viewed as having occurred in three distinct stages:

1. The Pioneer Migration (1900–1945): consisted primarily of landless peasants and unskilled laborers.
2. The Great Migration (1946–1964): primarily based in New York City and concentrated in blue collar jobs.
3. The Revolving Door Migration (1965-Present): based on the movement of families between Puerto Rico and the mainland.

The Pioneer Migration: 1900–1945

Like thousands of other immigrants, the first Puerto Rican migrants were drawn to the mainland by their search for new opportunities. While most were unskilled and poorly educated, many found jobs in the labor intensive industrial sectors of New York City (Sanchez, 1983). Others found work as farm laborers and followed the crops from the heartland of New Jersey to the humid orange groves of southern Florida (Maldonado-Denis, 1980: 83–88).

But the early movement of Puerto Ricans to the mainland was not significant, as their average flow was about 2,000 per year between 1909 and 1930. This minimal flow was further reduced to 900 a year during the Great Depression (Senior, 1965:39). By 1930 53,000 Puerto Ricans were dispersed across the

48 states. In 1939 there were 63,000 Puerto Ricans living in New York, and only 1,900 in California, 780 in New Jersey, and 607 in Pennsylvania (Senior, 1953:130). Those who lived in New York settled in East Harlem, between 96th and 130th streets (Alers, 1985; Sanchez, 1988; Sexton, 1965:6–7).

While most Puerto Rican migrants perceived their move to the mainland as an opportunity to improve their lives, some were disappointed by the life they found in the big city (Sanchez, 1988). In their homeland Puerto Ricans did not make sharp distinctions between racial groups, rather they related to people in terms of their social and economic position. But on the mainland Puerto Rican migrants were confronted with discrimination and residential segregation, based on their ethnicity and race (Morales, 1986: 45–58). For example, in Manhattan (during the 1920s) they discovered that light skinned Puerto Ricans were accepted in the working class neighborhoods on the west side and around the Navy yard in Brooklyn. But the dark skinned Puerto Ricans were only accepted in upper Manhattan, where they served as a buffer group between Black Harlem on the west and the Italians to the east (Morris, 1995; Rodriguez, 1980).

The Great Migration: 1946–1964

Following the Second World War the flow of Puerto Ricans to the mainland exceeded all previous records. Between 1946 and 1964 a total of 615,000 migrants arrived in the mainland, for an average annual flow of 34,000. The high point in the migration occurred in 1953, when 74,600 Puerto Rican migrants arrived.

Several factors serve to explain this very rapid rate of migration. An important factor was the introduction of commercial air service between San Juan and New York City, following the Second World War. Before the war, the journey could only be made by boat, which took five days and coast around $150. Following the war, Puerto Ricans could purchase an airline ticket for $64 and land in New York City seven hours later (Levine, 1987:95–98; Senior, 1953:131). This became the first mass airborne migration in history.

The push-pull factors in the Great Migration were similar to those affecting other immigrants, mainly to escape from poverty and to find work. In addition some viewed the Great Migration as an escape valve, as it relieved the pressure of population growth in Puerto Rico (Davis, 1953; Maldonado, 1976). The basic human resources and the capacity of the infrastructure of the Puerto Rican economy could no longer support the growing population of the island. If the children born to these migrants are considered, it is estimated that almost two million Puerto Ricans were displaced by the Great Migration (Hernandez, 1967:13–28). Without this escape value it is very likely that the people of Puerto Rico would have, at some point, resorted to open rebellion (Maldonado-Denis, 1980:47).

On the pull side of the equation, the Puerto Ricans that arrived during this period were better educated, had a variety of job experiences, and were more motivated, that is when compared to the general population of the island (Sandis, 1973). This dramatic flow of migrants supplied American capitalists with an ideal source of unskilled labor for their factories, assembly plants, and farms (Hernandez, 1968).

The introduction of television into Puerto Rico also encouraged many to migrate, as they wanted to partake of the American lifestyle. Returning migrants, most of whom made it a point to display their new found success, also did their part to stimulate the flow of migrants. Before long friends and relatives living in New York City did their part to encourage migration, as having family and friends ready to assist new arrivals went a long way in encouraging the Great Migration (Doyle, 1982; Macisco, 1968).

While some migrants (12,500) were farm workers in 1952, most were employed in the industrial or service sectors of the economy (Senior, 1953: 132). But like other immigrants in New York City, the Puerto Ricans were forced to take those jobs that were routinely rejected by most Americans (Sanchez-Korrol, 1994). In 1950, two-thirds of the Puerto Rican men in New York City were employed as operatives (37.4%) or as service workers (29.3%). Eighty percent of the Puerto Rican women worked in the garment industry (Fitzpatrick, 1971:61). The occupational distribution of the Puerto Ricans living in New York City did not change significantly until after 1960. Obviously, Puerto Rican migrants were relegated to the secondary labor market (Delgado, 1974).

The Revolving Door Migration: 1965–1996

In view of the continuous movement of Puerto Ricans between the island and the mainland, the most recent period of migration is referred to as the revolving door migration. For example, between 1965 and 1974 a total of 109,800 Puerto Ricans migrated to the mainland, for an average annual flow of almost 22,000. But during the same period a total of 92,600 returned to Puerto Rico, for an annual average flow of 18,500 (Boswell, 1985). Therefore the overall annual net increase in arrivals was only 3,500 (U.S. Civil Rights, 1976:19–21; Stockton, 1978).

The primary reason for the revolving door phenomena was the evolution of the trans-national family. This means that Puerto Rican families have members who live on the mainland and others who live in Puerto Rico (Lucca and Pachcco, 1992). As a result, parents, children, and extended family members are constantly traveling between the island and the mainland (Levine, 1987:98–102). This has resulted in the development of the trans-national family. Particularly as retired parents return to the homeland and as younger Puerto Ricans set firm roots in the mainland (Mascisco, 1968).

A new settlement pattern has evolved among the more recent migrants, as they are more likely to settle in urban areas outside of New York and New Jersey. In part this is an effort to avoid the hustle and bustle of urban life, but it also represents an effort to escape the racism, crime, and drug problems that are so often associated with life in the big city (Chenault, 1970). It would appear that these more recent Puerto Rican migrants believe that their smaller numbers and greater dispersion will make it easier for them to blend into the core of American society.

The Puerto Rican Family

As is true of all Latino families, the Puerto Rican family and culture was most profoundly affected by the Spanish conquest. Historically five factors have contributed to the form and structure of the Puerto Rican family today:

1. The influence of the Tainos Indians
2. The infusion of the Spanish culture
3. Their indoctrination to Catholicism
4. The impact of slave culture and society
5. The evolution of a *mestizo* Puerto Rican culture

Unfortunately, very little is known about the family life of the Tainos, but it is known that they were a peaceful group of settlers who arrived in Boriquen (Puerto Rico) in 1270 from Venezuela (Golding, 1973:20). But we do know that their society was based on domestic agricultural production and was ruled by a chief and guided by a medicine man. As such the Tainos family was patriarchial and patrilinial in structure and organization.

When the Spanish arrived Boriquen society was destroyed as most of the population died of various diseases and forced labor. As was true in Mexico, the Spanish missionaries destroyed all symbols of the indigenous religion and replaced their beliefs with the teachings of Catholicism. Furthermore, they organized the natives into productive villages, they paired couples and insisted on early marriages, they required early baptism, and they demanded unequivocal allegiance to the Spanish Crown.

The Spanish introduced slaves into Puerto Rico in the 1520s, in order to replace the rapidly dwindling Indian population. Within the first generation the Spanish sexually exploited Indian and slave women. This resulted in a very diverse racial mixture on the island. To this day, family members draw clear distinctions between their racial features and their social standing in the community. This genetic intrusion is often referred to as the great *mestizaje*, or racial blending of *Latino America* (Rogler, 1946).

Following their migration to the mainland, the Puerto Rican family underwent some important modifications in terms of primary relationships and family structure. These fundamental changes in the family occurred in response to, (1) the influence of American culture, (2) the labor needs of an urban-industrial society, and (3) the economic and social problems that have plagued the Puerto Rican community on the mainland. When reduced to its most basic form there are four family types among mainland Puerto Ricans today (Gonzales, 1992:219–241; Zambrana, 1995):

1. The Nuclear Family—characterized by a two generational structure of parents and their children. The independent nuclear family is becoming more common today, specifically in response to the needs of urban society. These families face a whole range of social problems, such as cramped apartments, the demanding schedule of urban life, urban crime, drug addiction, limited economic resources, and high unemployment rates. Within a short period of time this structural pattern has contributed to a loss of community cohesiveness and cultural identity among the more recent Puerto Rican migrants (Gurak, 1988:60–64).
2. The Extended Family—found among the long term migrants in the central city. The extended family consist of three generations, the parents, their children, and their grandchildren. The extended family structure has traditionally provided social, emotional, and economic support to its members. As such it evolved in response to the harsh and demanding conditions of life in the barrio. This family structure promotes traditional cultural values and demands family loyalty, family interdependence, and mutual support.
3. The Attenuated Nuclear Family—is sometimes referred to as a blended family structure. While the blended family is viewed as a new phenomena among middle class Anglo Americans, it has existed for years among Puerto Ricans living in urban America. The attenuated nuclear family consist of two or more altered nuclear families who share a common household. Following

divorce or separation a man who has children from a former marriage may marry a woman who also has children from a former marriage. This merging of nuclear families is further complicated by the introduction of step-children, that is children who are born to the husband and wife in the attenuated family. To the outsider these family relationships appear complicated.

4. The Female Headed Family—is becoming more common in the urban Puerto Rican community. Female headed families are supported by women who are, separated, divorced, abandoned, widowed, or have had children out of wedlock. The high proportion of female headed families in the Puerto Rican community can also be attributed to their high levels of premarital cohabitation and the general acceptance of informal unions (Landale and Fennelly, 1992; Landale and Forste, 1991). Today, almost half (44%) of Puerto Rican families are headed by women, with no man present in the household (Safa, 1995).

Chapter Summary

Hispanic is the term that is used by the U.S. Bureau of the Census to categorize the Spanish speaking population in the United States. But the preferred term for these groups is Latino. Puerto Ricans are the second largest Latino group in the United States today. The largest group of Latinos are the Mexican Americans and the third largest are the Cuban Americans.

According to the provisions of the Treaty of Paris, ending the Spanish American War, the island nation of Puerto Rico became a colony of the United States. American manufacturers took advantage of the natural resources of the island and the available pool of unskilled laborers to produce products with a high profit margin.

Partly as a result of their concentration in a large metropolitan area plagued by a host of social problems, Puerto Ricans have had to struggle against the high unemployment rates, the pain of poverty, dilapidated and overcrowded housing, inadequate schools, crime, and drug problems. But in spite of these obstacles, Puerto Ricans have managed to increase their overall standard of living, have experienced a certain level of social mobility, and have increased their level of education.

As a group Puerto Ricans have also been very effective in making their voice heard in the political arena, as they have created a very effective organi-

zational structure for political representation in New York City. Over the years they have elected representatives of their community to high positions in city government, the judiciary, and in state political offices. In November of 1970 Herman Badillo, an attorney from the Bronx, became the first Puerto Rican to win a seat in the U.S. Congress (Gonzales, 1991: 171–174). The Puerto Rican community's most recent political success came in November of 1992, with the election of Nydia Velazquez to a seat in Congress. Ms. Velazquez became the first Puerto Rican woman to be elected to a seat in Congress.

7. THE CUBAN-AMERICAN EXPERIENCE

Among Latinos, Cubans are the third largest group. Since the Revolution (1959) the number of Cubans living in the United States has increased dramatically and today Cubans represent the fifth largest flow of immigrants. When they first arrived most Cubans settled in south Florida and as a result half (50.7%) of all Cuban Americans still live in the Miami area today. Consequently, the state of Florida has the largest concentration of Cuban Americans (58.5%), followed by New Jersey (10.1%), New York (9.6%), and California (7.6%).

The census reported 803,226 Cubans living in the United States in 1980, which represents a growth rate of 47 percent over the previous decade. This is a much higher growth rate than the general population and can be attributed to the large number of political refugees that arrived during this period. In 1990 the Cuban American population reached the one million mark (1,069,000), representing a growth rate of 33.8 percent for the decade. This is considerably higher than the 9.5 percent growth rate for the nation as a whole during this period. Today (1993) there are approximately 1,120,000 Cubans in the United States.

Although Cuban Americans only represent a small proportion of the total number of Latinos in the United States (5.3%), it is their historical and political ties to Cuba and their concentration in south Florida that has drawn national attention to their cause. Furthermore, Cuban Americans are well known for their social and economic achievements.

When compared to other Latinos, Cubans are recognized for their higher levels of education, higher income, greater representation in professional and white collar positions, entrepreneurial skills and business success, high rates of naturalization, and active participation in local politics. In August of 1989, Ileana Ros-Lehtinen was elected to Congress and became the first Cuban American to win a seat in Congress. Representative Ros-Lehtinen can attribute her successful bid for Congress to the strong support provided by the Latino community in Miami (Gonzales 1991:149–151).

In short Cubans have followed the model of immigrant success in American society. But the degree of their success can only be appreciated against the backdrop of their history and their flight to freedom.

Cuba: An Historical Sketch

Cuba was ruled by the Spanish for four hundred years (1492–1898), as it was one of the first Spanish colonial possessions in the New World, and one of its last. Its name derives from the Indian name, Cubanacan. On his first voyage of discovery Columbus landed in Cuba to secure provisions for his ships. But the Spanish did not colonize the island until 1511, when they surveyed the island for the presence of natural resources. In 1515 they established the ports of Havana and Santiago (Suchlicki, 1975).

It is estimated that there were 100,000 Indians living on the island of Cuba when the conquistadors landed, but within thirty years there were only about 3,000 left alive (Boswell and Curtis, 1983:12). As in all areas of European settlement in the New World, the Indians in Cuba died as a result of war, forced labor, and diseases. During this initial period of settlement cattle husbandry and the production of tobacco and various food crops constituted the basis for the colonial economy. In an effort to replace the dwindling Indian labor the Spanish began importing slaves in 1517. With the full scale production of coffee and sugar cane in the mid-nineteenth century, the slave trade became an indispensable aspect of Cuba's economy. By 1846 there were 660,000 slaves in Cuba, 220,000 free Blacks and mulattos, and 565,000 whites (Blutstein, 1971:32).

In 1898, Spanish domination on the island came to an abrupt end when the United States defeated Spain in the Spanish American war. When the Treaty of Paris was signed in 1899 (ending the war) the United States not only gained the territories of Puerto Rico and the Philippines, but also took possession of Cuba. Between 1898 and 1902, U.S. military forces occupied and administered Cuba as a colonial possession. In 1902 Cuba gained its political independence from the United States and remained a quasi-democratic capitalist state until January of 1959.

During this quasi-democratic period (1902–1959) Cuba experienced the political corruption of one regime after another and became economically dependent on the United States. American inves-

tors were involved in every aspect of the economy. Within a few years American capitalists monopolized the sugar industry (which accounted for 80% of Cuba's exports), the tobacco industry, the mines, the railroads, and all public utilities. In total, the United States purchased 75 percent of Cuba's exports and provided 65 percent of their imports (Boswell and Curtis, 1983:18). Unfortunately, the United States' strangle hold on Cuba's economy was only possible because of the support of corrupt political leaders, who sold favors to American investors and left office as multi-millionaires. Perhaps the most corrupt of these was Fugencio Batista, who entered Cuban politics in 1933 and ruled with dictatorial power until his overthrow in 1959.

As a young attorney, Fidel Castro was one of the leaders of several popular opposition groups that opposed Batista's dictatorship. Following a bloody confrontation with Batista's troops in July of 1953 Castro was sentenced to 15 years in prison. In celebration of his re-election as president in 1955, Batista freed all political prisoners. His newly obtained freedom gave Castro the opportunity he needed to travel and gather support in Mexico and the United States. And in January of 1959 Fidel Castro assumed power in Cuba (Chaffee, 1989:6–12).

An Overview of Cuban Immigration

A close review of the immigration data reveals that the real immigration of Cubans to the United States did not start until 1959, when Castro came to power. Before the Revolution the flow of Cuban immigrants to the United States was insignificant. For example, the 1870 census only counted 5,000 Cubans in the United States. And due to the political instability in Cuba during the 1880s, a wave of political refugees moved to Key West, Tampa, and New York City. This was also the period when the Cuban cigar manufactures established themselves in south Florida, as the first Cuban cigar workers arrived in Tampa in 1886, aboard the side-wheeler *S.S. Hutchinson* (Mormino and Pozzetta, 1987:66).

By 1900 there were 11,000 Cubans in the United States, and this increased to 15,000 in 1910. In 1930, when Miami first became a center for Cuban settlement, their population in America was still only 35,500. On the eve of the Cuban Revolution (1958) their population was estimated at only 40,000, with the majority residing in south Florida (Bach, 1985:79).

As with other immigration experiences the segmentation of Cuban immigration is rather clear, as their influx responded to the changing political conditions in Cuba. For example, the first wave of so-called anticipatory refugees began late in 1958, when it was clear that Castro would assume power (Kunz, 1973:131–135). This period of immigration ended with the onset of the Cuban missile crisis in October of 1962. The next period of immigration is marked by high levels of political tension between the United States and Cuba.

From late 1965 until April of 1973, Fidel Castro reluctantly allowed his people to emigrate. It was during this period that the U.S. government organized the Cuban freedom flights, that brought more than 340,000 refugees to our shores. Unfortunately, Cold War tensions reduced the flow of refugees between May 1973 to April 1980. The most recent mass movement of Cuban refugees occurred during the summer of 1980, when more than 125,000 Marielitos arrived in south Florida (Hernandez, 1985).

It is estimated that more than 800,000 Cuban refugees arrived in the United States between 1959 and 1980. This represents about one-tenth of the island's population (Portes and Bach, 1985:84). However, according to the Immigration and Naturalization Service a total of 533,600 Cuban refugees arrived between 1961 and 1980. And between 1981 and 1989, an additional 148,600 Cuban refugees were admitted. Therefore the official government data reveals that a total of 682,200 Cuban refugees were admitted to the United States between 1961 and 1989 (U.S. Census, 1991). The point also should be made that these immigration figures do not include the 40,000 to 50,000 Cubans who settled in Puerto Rico, or the 61,000 to 126,000 who settled in Spain, Mexico, Canada, Venezuela, Costa Rica, and Peru (Boswell, 1985:101; Duany, 1992).

The first wave immigrants were mostly political elites who supported Batista, and as a result lost their freedom and investments to Castro's communist regime (Pedraza-Bailey, 1985a:18–23). Before long wealthy land-owners and businessmen joined the exodus. Castro's communist government expropriated all the farm land and all American owned factories and businesses were seized, (i.e., collectivised) by the Cuban government in July of 1960.

This first wave of Cuban refugees are popularly referred to as the Golden Exiles, as they were the social, political, and economic elites of Cuban society (Bach, 1987:113). Most were investors, businessmen, and professionals, whose businesses were adversely affected by Castro's economic policies. One study found that two-thirds (64%) of these refugees held white collar positions in Cuba (31% professional-managerial and 33% clerical-sales), compared to only one-fourth (23%) of the general Cuban population (Fagen, et al, 1968:115). For Cuba, the departure of the Golden Exiles represented an immediate brain drain.

The flow of refugees was greatly reduced as a result of the political fallout following the Cuban missile crisis. Most of the refugees from this period (1962–1965) were forced to rely on various clandestine methods to escape from Castro's Cuba. While others had to immigrate to another country first, usually Mexico or Spain, before obtaining a visa to come to the United States.

In December of 1965, the United States and Cuba signed an agreement allowing refugees to be airlifted to Miami. The two daily freedom flights, operated from December 1965 to April 1973, brought more than 340,000 refugees to the United States. Most of these refugees were from the working classes of Cuban society, although a few were small merchants and independent craftsmen (Pedraza-Bailey, 1985b:16). In May of 1973, for no apparent reason, Castro abruptly terminated the freedom flights to America. Consequently the flow of refugees was greatly reduced for the next seven years, that is through April 1980.

The last significant flow of Cuban refugees arrived during the Mariel boat lift (May to September 1980), which captured the nation's attention. During this five month period more than 125,000 refugees arrived in south Florida. The Marielitos were different from previous waves of Cuban refugees in several important respects, as most were men (85%), most were single (65.6%), most were blue collar workers (86.2%), and a disproportionate number were Black (40%) (compared to only 4% of U.S. Cubans). Though some Marielitos were detained in government camps, as they were suspected of being convicts or mental patients. (Portes and Bach, 1985:87), only a small proportion (16%) were actually released from Castro's prisons (Bach, et al, 1981; Bach, 1987:114–127). And of these, only four percent were hard-core criminals (Boswell, 1985:100).

Unfortunately riots in some U.S. government camps and malicious propaganda issued by the Cuban government—that described the Marielitos as social misfits, delinquents, and anti-socials—resulted in negative press coverage in the United States. In response, many Americans disapproved of the boat lift and some Cuban-Americans avoided the Marielitos (McCoy and Gonzalez, 1985:26–35).

The Cuban Community in Miami

Historically Cubans have had a natural attraction for south Florida, as some 40,000 lived in Miami before the revolution. Many pioneer refugees settled in Miami as they considered their stay temporary and they were only waiting for the inevitable overthrow of Castro's regime (Azieri, 1981:58–60). Furthermore, the dynamic density and cultural support system available to the recent arrivals in Miami naturally attracted other Cuban refugees.

Most Cuban refugees were attracted to south Florida by the availability of government assistance programs. Early in 1959 President Eisenhower allocated $1 million for refugee assistance, while the Kennedy administration provided millions more for education, job training, welfare benefits, and housing programs (Pedraza-Bailey, 1985a; 40–42).

In 1970, four out of ten Cuban Americans lived in Miami. Today it is estimated that six out of ten live in the Miami area. Two of the most important reasons for their concentration in Miami is the absence of a language barrier and the general availability of jobs. Little Havana is an area where Cubans can live and work in a totally Spanish speaking environment (Fradd, 1983). It is also a customary practice for Cuban businessmen to hire their compatriots, as the refugees offer their loyalty and the Cuban entrepreneurs guarantee them a job (Butler and Herring, 1991:80–83). Unfortunately these ethnic loyalties sometimes result in wage and labor abuses (Model, 1992:67–70; Wilson and Portes, 1980).

One reason for the success of those living in Little Havana is the financial and business support provided by Cuban Americans. Besides the high proportion of professionals in the first wave immigration, there were also many businessmen and investors. In 1967 there were less than a thousand (919) Cuban owned businesses in the Miami area, but by 1976 there were 8,000 (Portes and Bach, 1985:89). By 1990 there were more than 28,000 Cuban owned businesses in the greater Miami area (Portes and Rumbaut, 1990:20–21). In Dade County there are over 18,000 Cuban owned firms, most in construction, finance, textiles, leather, furniture, and cigar making. In addition sixteen Cuban Americans are presidents of banks, 250 are vice presidents, 3,500 are doctors, 500 are lawyers, and they own 500 supermarkets, 250 drug stores, and over 60 auto dealerships (Boswell, 1985:112).

Income, Occupation, and Education

When the socio-economic characteristics of Cuban Americans are compared to other Latinos, it is obvious that they are economically advanced. Briefly, there are three reasons why Cuban Americans have been so successful in American society, (1) the selective nature of their immigration, (2) the advantages they received from government assistance and training programs, and (3) their strong economic base in Miami.

The very fact that Cuban Americans are, as a group, an older population (38.7 years compared to 32.2 years U.S.) also means that their human capital is more highly developed. In effect they have more skills and experience upon which they can draw. Their higher market skills in part derive from the knowledge that they probably will never return to Cuba, hence they invest in education to increase their human potential (Borjas, 1982).

When compared to the annual income of other Latinos, Cubans had the highest average family income of $27,294 in 1987 (compared to $30,853 U.S.). But this level of income is only achieved by combining individual family members' incomes (Perez, 1985: 9–11). Nonetheless this still leaves an income gap of $3,559, when compared to all Americans. Almost half (46.2%) of the Cuban families earned less than $25,000 per year and 13.8 percent live below the poverty level (compared to 10.6% U.S.) (U.S. Census, 1988).

The rapid rate of economic success of Cuban Americans can be attributed to, (1) their higher positions in the labor force, (2) the higher proportion of women who are employed full-time (47.1% compared to 40.1% U.S.), and (3) more workers per family (18.6% had three or more workers per family, compared to 12.5% U.S.) (Perez, 1985). The fact that half the Cuban American women are employed outside the home is in sharp contrast to the role of women in pre-revolutionary Cuba, where only 9.8 percent of the women were employed outside the home (i.e. in 1958). From their perspective having a wife at home was considered an indication of a man's wealth and enhanced his social standing in the community (Keremitsis, 1989:102).

According to the 1990 census, one out of four (23.7%) of all Cuban Americans held professional or managerial positions and one out of three (33.5%) were in technical or sales positions. Therefore almost three out of five (57.2%) were working in white collar positions, and only four out of ten (42.8%) were working in blue collar jobs (U.S. Census, 1991).

In 1988, 23.7 percent of Cuban men were professionals and managers, and 27.8 percent were in technical sales and clerical positions. Overall half (51.5%) were employed in white collar positions, compared to 46.1 percent of the general population. But more Cuban American women (69.1%) were white collar workers, as compared to Cuban men (51.5%). However, most of these women holding white collar positions were relegated to low status, low paying, clerical-sales positions (44.7%). On the other hand, more Cuban American women (27.3%), than Cuban American men (23.7%), held professional-managerial positions (U.S. Census, 1988).

Four out of ten (39.7%) Cuban Americans were blue collar workers in 1988. Of these blue collar workers, 9.1 percent were in craft positions, 17.9 percent were operatives and laborers, and 11.8 percent were in service positions. Their representation in these positions is only slightly different from the general population. Within the blue collar category, both Cuban men (21.1%) and Cuban women (14.7%) were concentrated in the operative-labor positions, compared to 20.9 percent and 8.8 percent respectively in the general population (U.S. Census, 1988:).

Their higher levels of education and technical training can account for the higher representation of Cuban Americans in white collar positions. Among Latinos, Cubans have achieved the highest levels of education. Part of the reason for their success is the higher social status of the pioneer refugees who encouraged their children to take advantage of every educational opportunity. Furthermore, as refugees they were eager to take advantage of a college education. Therefore, they were highly motivated in their pursuit of a higher education (Portes, et al, 1982:6–7).

According to the 1990 census, almost two-thirds (63%) of all Cuban Americans were high school graduates and one out of five (19.8%) were college graduates. This compares to eight out of ten (78.4%) Anglo American high school graduates and one out of five (21.8%) Anglo American college graduates (U.S. Census, 1991). Their median years of education was 12.4, compared to 12.7 among all Americans, 12.0 among Puerto Ricans, and 10.8 among Mexican Americans (Schick and Schick, 1991:35). But as is still true among other Latinos, Cuban Americans still confront such problems as the language barrier, segregated schools, the racial tracking system, and insensitive teachers, counselors, and administrators.

The Cuban American Family

Like other Latinos, Cubans place great importance on family relationships. And in view of their refugee experience, Cuban Americans place an emphasis on the role of the family in their community. Over the years they have worked assiduously at family reunification refugee assistance programs (Richmond, 1980).

When compared to other Latino families, the Cuban family is the smallest. In 1988 the average Cuban family size was 3.16, compared to 3.17 in the general population, 3.79 among Latinos, and 4.06 among Mexican Americans (U.S. Census, 1988). This small family size obtained despite the fact that Cubans were more likely to have other relatives living in their households (9%), as compared to other Latinos (6%)

and Americans in general (4%). The smaller family size among Cuban Americans can be attributed to, (1) the older age of their population (38.7 years), (2) to their low fertility rate (16 per 1,000, compared to 17 U.S.) (Boswell, 1985:107), and (3) to their higher socio-economic positions. Their smaller family size is also related to the higher labor force participation rate among Cuban women (53.6%), which is the highest among Latinos. This is important since there is a direct relationship between the proportion of women in the labor force and lower fertility rates.

It is interesting to discover that while Cubans have the highest proportion of married couples (58.5%) and the lowest percentage of singles (24.8%) among Latino (57.1% and 32.1% respectively), they also have the highest divorce rate (9.1%) among Latinos (6.9% Latinos and 7.4% U.S.) (Schick and Schick, 1991:35). This is related to several factors, such as their immigration experience, refugee status, the greater number of women in the labor force (giving them greater independence), their lower fertility rate, and the greater acceptance of divorce in the Cuban-American community (Aguirre, 1981). However, Cuban men are not only more likely to remarry following divorce, but they also remarry sooner. In contrast, Cuban women are not as likely to remarry following divorce and are more likely to be the primary parent following divorce. As a result, three times as many single parent households were headed by Cuban women (16.1%), as compared to Cuban men (5.8%) (Schick and Schick, 1991:35). The proportion of female headed households in the Cuban American community is similar to the number found in the general population.

The higher divorce rate among Cuban Americans may be related to their higher rate of exogamy (outmarriage). This is true since divorce rates tend to be slightly higher among those who marry outside their group. One study found that among second generation (i.e. American born) Cuban women the rate of exogamy was 46 percent, compared to 33 percent for Puerto Rican women and 16 percent of Mexican American women (Jaffe, et al, 1980:63–68).

More recently, the 1990, census found that 14.6 percent of Cuban American men married a non-Latino wife, as compared to 14.9 percent of Cuban American women who married a non-Latino husband (about 1,000 more marriages). But the same proportion of Cuban American men and women (10.9%) married another Latino (U.S. Census, 1991). Therefore, Cuban American women have a slightly greater propensity to marry someone outside their ethnic group (primarily Anglo American men). Overall, this high rate of exogamy indicates a higher rate of acceptance of intermarriage between Cubans and non-Latinos.

Recently the Cuban American family has undergone some important changes, primarily in response to changing social and economic conditions. As with other immigrant groups, a common point of conflict within the family is the difference in values between traditional parents and their Americanized children. Even within the Cuban enclave, it is not unusual to find that children are torn between the demands and expectations of their parents, and those of the youth culture in American society.

Another important area of change, is the greater equality that exit today in the Cuban American family. While the first generation was strongly attached to the patriarchial orientation of the Latin culture, with its emphasis on machismo, the second generation is moving toward greater social equality and greater independence for women (Richmond, 1980:33–39). This in large part is due to the higher proportion of Cuban American women in the labor force and the higher levels of education achieved by Cuban Americans (Boswell, 1985:108–109).

Chapter Summary

Like Mexico and Puerto Rico, Cuba was also conquered by the Spanish and was transformed into a vast plantation system dependent on slave labor. As a result of disease and the harsh treatment they received at the hands of their Spanish landlords, the Indians on the island died off by the thousands.

Following the Spanish American War, and the signing of the Treaty of Paris (1899), the United States assumed political control of the island nation. But in 1902 the United States granted the Cuban people their independence. For the next fifty years Cuba was ruled by a series of corrupt political leaders who became wealthy at the expense of the people. In January of 1959 Fidel Castro assumed control of the government.

In order to insure total control of the government and economic structure of Cuban society, Fidel Castro ordered the expulsion of thousands of entrepreneurs, professionals, and scholars. For this reason the first wave of Cuban refugees are often referred to as the Golden Exiles. With the help of federal government programs the Gold Exiles established themselves in south Florida and quickly created a robust Cuban American community in Miami (Olson, 1995). Thousands of Cuban refugees have entered the United States since the arrival of the first refugees in the early 1960s. The most recent mass movement of Cuban refugees occurred in 1980, during the Mariel boat lift.

Today, Cuban Americans are very successful and have adapted to the needs and expectations of American society (Perez-Firmat, 1994). As a group Cuban Americans are not only recognized for their educational achievements, high standard of living, and occupational mobility, but also for their success in the political arena and in the market place. Today Cuban Americans living in south Florida are represented at every level of government. In addition some Cuban Americans have become nationally recognized leaders in business, politics, and in industry (Rieff, 1993).

8. CENTRAL AND SOUTH AMERICANS

Three push factors—overpopulation, economic hardship, and political turmoil—have triggered the significant increase in emigration from several Latin American countries. After Mexico, the largest contingents come from the Dominican Republic, Cuba, Colombia, and Ecuador; they have been joined in recent years by growing numbers of refugees from El Salvador, Nicaragua, and Peru. From 136,379 Central and South American immigrants in the 1950s, their numbers expanded to 359,284 in the 1960s and 430,381 in the 1970s and then leaped to 929,935 in the 1980s. Included in the 1980s total are undocumented aliens who applied for permanent residence under the amnesty provision in the Immigration and Reform Act of 1986. About 13 percent of the total applications were from Central America, led by El Salvador (143,070) and followed by Guatemala (52,544), Colombia (26,363), the Dominican Republic (18,273), and Nicaragua (16,012).

Occupations of Hispanic Workers Age 16 and Over, 1980 and 1993

Percentages in Each Occupational Category

	All Hispanics	Mexicans	Puerto Ricans	Cubans	Other Hispanics*
1980					
White-collar	35.0	31.0	35.3	NA	NA
Service	16.5	16.6	19.3	NA	NA
Agri/Forest	3.4	4.7	1.0	NA	NA
Blue-collar	45.2	47.7	44.5	NA	NA
1993					
White-collar	39.0	34.8	51.2	57.9	40.9
Service	19.9	19.1	19.9	12.9	23.8
Agri/Forest	5.8	8.0	1.2	2.2	2.3
Blue-collar	35.4	38.1	27.7	27.2	32.9

*Includes Central and South Americans and others of Hispanic origin.

Source: U.S. Bureau of Labor Statistics, *Employment and Earnings*, January issues, 1981, 1994.

About a half million Central Americans live in Los Angeles. Substantial numbers also reside in San Francisco, Houston, Washington, DC, New York, Chicago, New Orleans, and Miami. As the largest Central American group in the United States, Salvadorans usually constitute the majority of Central Americans in most cities, followed by Guatemalans. However, Nicaraguans predominate in Miami and Hondurans in New Orleans among Central Americans.

The Dominicans

More than 529,000 Dominican immigrants have left their Caribbean home-land for the United States since 1971, their numbers averaging about 41,000 annually—which makes the Dominican Republic the second-leading Spanish-speaking country to supply immigrants to the United States. Two of every three Dominicans live in New York State, for a total of 357,868, according to the 1990 census. Most live in New York City, particularly in Washington Heights in Manhattan and in the Bronx, where Dominicans will be a majority in the borough at about 52 percent in the year 2000. Other primary areas of residence are New Jersey (52,807), Florida (34,268), and Massachusetts (30,177).

Number of Western Hemisphere Immigrants from Leading Countries, 1971–1994

1.	Mexico	3,696,245
2.	Dominican Republic	580,225
3.	Cuba	456,997
4.	Jamaica	417,652
5.	Canada	414,490
6.	El Salvador	365,438
7.	Haiti	275,581
8.	Colombia	255,603
9.	Guyana	179,627
10.	Ecuador	137,019
11.	Peru	139,795
12.	Trinidad and Tobago	129,618

Source: U.S. Immigration and Naturalization Service, *Statistical Yearbook 1994,* U.S. Government Printing Office, Washington, DC, 1990, pp. 28–31.

Dominicans are more likely to live and interact within their own ethnic neighborhoods instead of integrating into mixed Hispanic neighborhoods. A common pattern is to coexist alongside Puerto Ricans, each ethnic group keeping mostly to itself. In the South Bronx, however, where Dominican immigration is primarily male and the Puerto Rican family is headed predominantly by women,

Dominican–Puerto Rican marriages and liaisons are becoming common.

Most of the Dominicans are dark-skinned people who have fled the poverty of their land. Because of lack of skills, they have a high unemployment rate. Many live in poor urban neighborhoods, suffering the deprivation and family disruption so common among those with low levels of education and job skills. Racial discrimination further compounds their problems, and some find work as migrant farm laborers, away from urban troubles.

The Salvadorans

Several push factors account for the large-scale Salvadoran emigration to the United States. Agricultural modernization and expansion by the landowning oligarchy displaced tens thousands of rural peasants. Relocating to such urban centers as San Salvador, many could not find work despite the growing industrialization. Conditions deteriorated when protests and demonstrations were met by government repression. Death squads composed of members of the ruling elite and the security and military forces targeted peasant leaders, union militants, and political activists. Revolutionary movements arose, and guerilla offensives in the 1980s caused escalating violence by the security and military forces as well as by the death squads. Attacks against civilian populations in rural areas occurred, including massacres of entire villages believed to be sympathetic to the guerillas.

Number of Central and South Americans Living in the United States, 1990

Central Americans	1,323,830
Costa Ricans	57,223
Cuatemalans	268,779
Hondurans	131,066
Nicaraguans	202,658
Panamanians	92,013
Salvadorans	565,081
Other Central Americans	7,010
South Americans	1,035,602
Argentineans	100,921
Bolivians	38,073
Chileans	68,799
Colombians	378,726
Ecuadorians	191,198
Paraguayans	6,662
Peruvians	175,035
Uruguayans	21,996
Venezuelans	47,997
Other South Americans	6,195

Source: U.S. Bureau of the Census.

As a stream of undocumented Salvadorans fled into the United States, immigration agents sought to apprehend and return them, denying them refugee status. The State Department ruled that although El Salvador might be a wartorn country, none of those leaving had been specifically singled out for persecution and thus did not really have a well-founded fear of persecution. Out of this conflict was born the sanctuary movement in the United States: Clergy defied the government, hiding Salvadoran refugees in churches and homes. The clergy and members of their congregations provided food, shelter, and clothing and secretly helped the refugees get to safe locations. It is these refugees who were the 143,070 Salvadoran applicants for amnesty and permanent residence in the United States.

Although the political situation has improved in El Salvador, most Salvadorans in the United States are remaining, putting down roots and enjoying the support system within their evolving ethnic communities. Through chain migration, other relatives and friends join them, continuing a steady migration flow that ranks El Salvador sixth among Western hemisphere countries providing immigrants to the United States.

Nicaraguans have entered the United States as immigrants, refugees, asylees, and undocumented aliens. A *refugee* is someone outside one's country unable or unwilling to return because of persecution or a well-founded fear of persecution. The definition of an *asylee* is the same as that of a refugee, except that the alien is physically in the United States or at a port of entry. After the communists came to power, over 46,000 middle-class refugees fled—between 1980 and 1990. As the Contras led a guerilla war against the new government, between 1988 and 1990, about 1,000 additional pre-approved refugees came each year. Yet others, about 79,000, streamed into Texas, filing asylum applications. Most of the new arrivals, unlike their predecessors, were poor, unskilled, and illiterate *campesinos* from the countryside. Some had lived for months in refugee camps in Honduras and in other Central American countries that pressed the United States to accept the refugees.

Just slightly over 11,000 asylum seekers were granted asylum by 1990. Five years later, 24,000 cases still had not been heard, and new rules denying work permits for the still-waiting applicants brought protests from those trying to meet expenses while their cases were pending.

Drawn by the Latin American population and the already established Nicaraguan communities in Miami and southern California, most refugees chose one of those two destinations. Miami–Dade County schools, for example, almost quadrupled their Nicaraguan student enrollment in 1988–1989. With no previous educational experience, most of the 13- to 15-year-olds could not read and had to be taught the basics of reading and arithmetic. Sweetwater, a western suburb of Miami, became almost completely Nicaraguan, earning the nick-name "Little Managua."

When the Sandinista regime came to an end in February 1990, the 11-year widespread exodus of refugees dropped considerably. Some Nicaraguans returned to their homeland, but most chose to stay in the United States. The 1990 census identified 202,658 Nicaraguans, of whom 79,056 were in Florida and 74,119 in California. Officials estimated the actual number of Nicaraguans in Dade County, both legal and illegal, at closer to 150,000. Other states with sizable population concentrations were New York (11,011), Texas (7,911), New Jersey (4,226), Maryland (4,019), and Virginia (3,471).

The Colombians

Colombia is the South American country supplying the most immigrants, more than 256,000 since 1971. Population pressures, better economic opportunities, and chain-migration networking have increased the annual immigration totals, which now average over 14,000 yearly. Of the 378,726 Colombians tallied in the 1990 census, 80 percent were foreign-born. Most of the remainder were children born to these first-generation Americans.

Colombians are mostly a light-tan-skinned people, making them less susceptible to racial discrimination than some Caribbean Hispanics. They are a mixture of educated professionals and low-skilled peasants seeking a better life. Living mostly in urban neighborhoods near other Hispanics, they too form their own social clubs and institutions, attempting to preserve their culture through ethnic folk-dance groups and holiday celebrations. In 1990 Colombian Americans were found mostly in New York (85,600), Florida (68,609), New Jersey (42,339), and California (32,024).

A minute percentage of Colombians is involved in the cocaine trade and the drug-war killings. The high profile of this small number of criminals unfortunately smears the rest, just as Italian Americans have suffered guilt by nationality stereotype because of the Mafia. In reality, almost all Colombian Americans are decent, law-abiding people who are working hard to make a life for themselves in their adopted country.